Wing Over Three Continents

Diary Of An Air Observer

1939 to 1945

Published by

Librario Publishing Ltd

ISBN: 1-904440-94-0
978-1-904440-94-0

Copies can be ordered via the Internet
www.librario.com

or from:

Brough House, Milton Brodie, Kinloss
Moray IV36 2UA
Tel /Fax No 00 44 (0)1343 850 617

Wing Over Three Continents

Diary Of An Air Observer

1939 to 1945

Edited and with Commentary
by Andrew Collins

Librario

Contents

		Page
Introduction		5
Acknowledgements		6
Dedication		7
Chapter 1.	I Realised I Ought To Go	9
Chapter 2.	Aircrew Training	35
Chapter 3.	Flying Training	57
Chapter 4.	Operational Training	81
Chapter 5.	Transit to War	107
Chapter 6.	Operational	129
Chapter 7.	To Aden and Back	179
Chapter 8.	Back to Work	209
Chapter 9.	Transport	237
Chapter 10.	Into Europe	273
Chapter 11.	India	301
Chapter 12.	Hospital Again	331
Chapter 13.	The Journey Home	365
Chapter 14.	Non-Effective, Sick	383
Chapter 15.	Grounded	409
Chapter 16.	Administrator	433
Index		445

Introduction

Diaries are written for all sorts of reasons. They are written by great men for posterity, with an eye to publication. They are written by great men, not for posterity, but for a wife or child, who may then judge their actions not through the eye of history but through the mind of the writer. These are generally composed with reference to world events as well as to the personal experience of the writer. But more usually diaries are written as a simple narrative of daily events, relating only those events that impinge directly on the writer's own life. It is just such a diary that forms the bulk of this book. However, even such a diary can be of considerable interest when the writer is himself involved in great events, and perhaps the greatest event of the twentieth century was the World War from 1939 to 1945. We are fortunate that Charles Collins kept not only a diary but had also developed the habit of keeping a log of events or situations that interested him. Here he would describe scenes and locations and record his general impressions and his views. Furthermore, he was an enthusiastic letter writer and his correspondence with his family was full of details and opinions. He asked his family to keep the letters he wrote during his time overseas in the war, and they are the source of much the material contained herein.

Because the bulk of his diaries was increasing, Charles summarised the contents of those up to the end of 1940, and it from those summaries that the initial entries are taken. His writing was generally awful, and he tended to use a personal shorthand for some frequently used words, so at times a certain amount of interpretation has had to be used, particularly with names of people and places.

What follows is a record of the life and thoughts of one ordinary man living through extraordinary times.

Acknowledgments

In preparing the commentary that goes with this diary I have received welcome help from a number of sources. Air Marshal Sir Richard Wakeford kindly gave me the benefit of his own wartime experience as a pilot in Coastal Command to explain some of the more obscure references and abbreviations in the diary. Charles's brother, Peter Collins, likewise assisted me with some of the references to family and friends from the wartime era. Bryan Rostron, Charles's Captain and pilot on 459 Squadron, willingly gave me permission to use extracts and information from his own memoirs published on the 454/459 Squadron website, and Tony Martin, also a pilot on 459 Squadron, kindly gave permission to use the picture on Page 219, showing him receiving the "Gambut Cup". Finally, my thanks go to my wife Jennifer who read the draft of the whole work and wielded a tactful red pen to help eradicate errors and to suggest improvements to style or clarity. Any errors that remain are entirely my own.

Andrew Collins
July 2007

Dedication

This work is dedicated to the late Charles Collins, whose story this is, and who wrote most of it himself.

About the Author

Andrew Collins is the only child of Charles Collins, the subject of this book. After leaving university in 1967 he joined the Royal Air Force, serving for thirty years as aircrew, mostly on maritime patrol aircraft. In 1998 he left the RAF and worked at British Aerospace on the Nimrod MRA 4 project until his retirement in 2005. He now lives in northern Scotland with his wife.

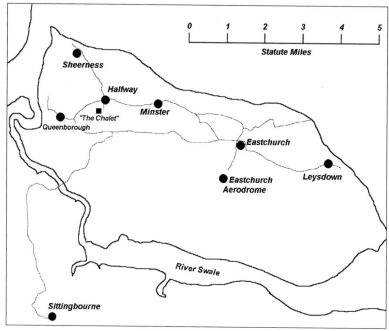

The Isle of Sheppey

Charles Collins was born in 1915 on the Isle of Sheppey in Kent at the mouth of the Rivers Medway and Thames, and for all his life he regarded it as "home". His Father lived all his life in "The Chalet" in Southdown Road in Halfway, and this was always the base to which Charles and his brother Peter returned throughout their wartime service.

CHAPTER 1

I Realised I Ought To Go

> And so 1939 drifted to a close. It meant I had to cancel
> my studies. But that is about all the difference it made.
> True I had more work in the office and ARP exercises.
> Huddersfield Harrier Rovers activities changed. But I
> continued hiking, theatre, tennis and badminton, a few
> dances and the usual Christmas festivities. But about
> now I realised that it would be a long war, and that I
> ought to go. I had nebulous ideas about joining the RAF
> to fly, but then did not think seriously of it.

With these words Charles Collins closed the summary of his
diary for 1939. Like so many men in their twenties, he had not
at first considered seriously that the war, now in its fourth
month, would affect him directly. Inconveniences there would
certainly be, but life would go on. On the first day of September
he had written:

> Hospital cleared. Germany invades Poland. I guessed
> war was on us now, but did not seem impressed, as I did
> not think it would last long or affect me.

At the end of the month the entry was:

> War continued slowly and with few events in its way. I
> had very little change in life. Rovers programme changed
> and work increased, but I still went walking and to

shows. I did not want to join as I wanted to make sure of keeping a job.

But now it was clear that it would not "all be over by Christmas".

Charles Collins pre-War

As the crisis in Europe deepened in 1938 and 1939, Charles was a Hospital Superintendent in St Luke's Hospital in Huddersfield. He had rather drifted into this role, and though he certainly took the work seriously, it was a job rather than a vocation. He was making steady progress through the ranks of Local Government, achieving the qualification of Associate of the Chartered College of Secretaries in August 1939, and was continuing his studies.

Whenever possible he would return home to the Isle of Sheppey in Kent where his father had retired from his job as a dock labourer and now concentrated on his small field, producing for the family an ample supply of vegetables and fruit. He also had a sizeable apiary with about 30 hives of bees from which he extracted clear clover honey. Charles's mother had died in 1936, and his father was devastated. The housekeeper, Mrs Wilburn, looked after his father and younger brother Peter and sister

Margaret, but Charles was away at work in the Midlands most of the time.

His major recreation was the Rover Scout group with whom he would often go hiking. When he could not walk with them, he would walk alone or with other friends. His pre-war diaries show that he covered hundreds of miles over the more rugged parts of the United Kingdom, so that as well as being physically very fit, he had developed a great self-reliance. Both of these qualities would stand him in good stead over the following years.

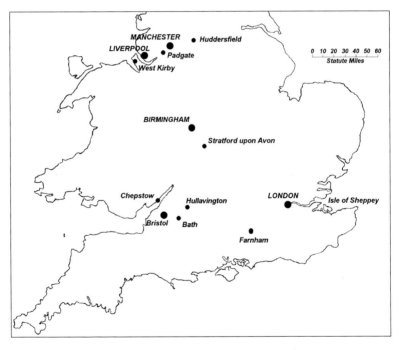

Charles's Travels – January 1940 to March 1941

1940

> 9/1/40 Arthur Turner "called up" and that was the start.
> Slowly they went, and slowly I realised I would want to
> go soon. All my diary appears to be about work.
> 8/2/40 Master asked committee for my exemption!

In December 1939 all those aged between 19 and 41 became
liable for conscription. However, application could be made for
exemption for those in 'essential' posts. It seems that the Hospital
Master considered Charles to be essential; clearly Charles thought
otherwise. Poland had quickly been overrun by Germany from
the west and by Russia from the east. France was threatened, and
a British Expeditionary Force was now in place awaiting the
inevitable German assault. Merchant shipping in the Atlantic was
under attack from German U-boats, and Russia was invading
Finland. The position of Britain did not look promising.

> 9/3/40 Registered for RAF Flying. More and more work
> and less time off.
> 6/5/40 Medical exam - A1
> 7/5/40 Started vigil at 10 pm. To Rovers on Tuesdays.
> 10/5/40 All holiday leave cancelled so no holiday with
> Peter! Rapidly losing all direction in life. Seems so
> purposeless now, with no aim possible.
> 25/5/40 Dunkirk starts.
> 14/6/40 Donald called up.
> 14/7/40 Jack Hepworth called up.
> 31/7/40 Arranged to meet Peter at Chepstow for weeks
> cycling in Wye Valley in September.
> 10/8/40 Calling-up papers, so no holiday.

Despite the urgent need for aircrew, a period of five

months elapsed between Charles registering for RAF service and his receiving his call-up papers. This apparent sloth in the bureaucracy of war was to raise comment in his diaries on many subsequent occasions.

14/8/40 Arrived Padgate and introduced to RAF queuing and billets!

Charles's service records show that his career started on 18 August 1940 at No. 3 Recruit Centre, RAF Padgate near Warrington. This early arrival therefore must have been for the purpose of initial registration and signing on.

15/8/40 Accepted as air observer. Medical A and B and signing on.
17/8/40 Went home to say "'bye" and to see Dil. I slept at 28 Alexandra Terrace – she on ARP duty.

"Dil" was Dilys Jones, one of many girlfriends who appear in the diaries. She, however, features more than most.

20/8/40 Back to St Luke's Hospital and Rovers and final packing and clearing.
22/8/40 Report to Padgate.
24/8/40 Issued with uniform which apparently did not meet with my approval.
26/8/40 Inoculations and Vaccinations. Getting used to RAF "organisation" now.

AC2 Collins C A 1064164

13

Taking things and finding they are not wanted and then taking them back etc.

The stay at RAF Padgate was brief indeed, for within a few days Charles's course was posted to RAF West Kirby on the Wirral peninsula.

> 28/8/40 Arrived at West Kirby and started square bashing course. I first noticed that I was spending well above 2/6 a day and so started to keep a record and keep it down to 2/- a day. Hard, but I found it could be done. Except that I existed and not lived. Pettiness narked me, as they stopped me using my electric razor. Pay parades. Blankets must be folded just so etc. FFI.s!

FFI is the Serviceman's jargon for "Free From Infection" – a euphemism for checks for venereal disease. 2/- per day was the basic pay for airmen undergoing training. It must have been a major contrast to the pay of a Hospital Superintendent, although it was in effect 'pocket money', for all food and accommodation was provided.

> Wonderful sunsets in this part of the country.
> 6/9/40 2nd inoculations. Lots of air raids.
> 9/9/40 All camp to parade at 6.00 p.m. and 8.00 p.m. nightly until the man who blew a raspberry at Warrant Officer owns up!

Charles kept a few pages from his original diary and included them in his summary. He must have found them particularly descriptive of the way of life at West Kirby!

> 19/9/40 Very full day. Up at 3.00 a.m. to get a tablet of

Codeine as I had a rotten cold. Lovely night with full moon in blue clear sky, well starred and white clouds. But at 6.00 a.m. it was raining really hard. In the morning, foot drill and rifle drill all time. In the afternoon PT and standing lecture and parade for pay. Magnificent sum of 50/-. So on my feet all day and I was rather tired. I had tea, a shave and went off over Mat Truett's property again. It was grand among the birch, heather, gorse, blackberries, corn flowers and harebells. Up on old red sandstone crags I could see Great Orme in Wales. There was an air raid on way back, but it did not affect sunset or moon rise. I called in at the NAAFI for chocolate and tooth-paste. At the hut I found Ron back from leave (his father had died suddenly) and he was pretty cut up so I spent time with him in the NAAFI and gave him a drink. Then back and shower as usual. To bed at 10.30 p.m. We had photos taken as group. Spent 3/4. All the lads were back and being happy in bar and with some rotten tales to tell, mainly about women.

20/9/40 Up as usual and we had a hectic three hours as it was a full kit inspection by the CO. All over by 10.15 a.m. After a break, PT and as it was cold we ran round the camp for two hours and then had a shower! In the afternoon the lecture should have been on be on *(unreadable)* again but it developed into general discussion. Then foot drill and equipment cleaning in the hut. Evening. Domestic night so we stayed in till 7.00 p.m. and I then went out with lads to a canteen in Frankby. Good cheap food and game of ping pong. Spent 8d. To bed at 10.30 p.m. Last night after turning in all sorts of row developed with scrapping, locking doors etc. It was jolly funny till Corporal Tasker came out and said we would have two days' fatigues which sobered them down. Then this morning the Messing Corporal threatened to put us on a charge for pinching butter. But we got out of both.

21/9/40 Up at 6.00 a.m. and had another injection in the morning till 10.00 a.m. The rest of time till noon was spent on foot and rifle drill. Group Captain came all round the wing and there were a lot more small alterations in kit layout. The afternoon was free. As it was fine most of them went out. I stayed in for a rest and nap, read and finished a letter to Joan. After tea, I had a shave and then off out for long walk with John to Meols, and all along coast. Plenty of coast defence and soldiers. We saw two boats with smoke blowing in opposite direction and two rainbows from common starting point on horizon. I was told of Chestnut soup and Marigold petals in soups. Meols and Moreton via cart tracks and a level crossing with a push bell for operation. From Moreton we went to Frankby canteen for food, getting ready for harvest festival. Back at 9.15 p.m. and to bed. Donaldson came back drunk, but was only talkative. He was glad he had given me some money to mind as he was now spent out. Bill came in late from dance at Meols. After lights out we had a very heavy raid and very close. Spent 8d.

The 'Battle of Britain' was drawing to a close at this time, and Enigma decodes had shown that Hitler had decided that Operation Sea Lion was to be postponed until the next year. Night raids, however, continued on strategic targets, such as nearby Liverpool, and there was little that the RAF could do to intercept these in 1940.

21/9/40 Up 6.30 a.m. and breakfast 7.30 a.m. Parade for church at 9.30 a.m. so I filled in the time by reading and yarning with the Corporal. After church I had time for bath in very dirty bath, and the water was not so hot. Geoff said his crew were going to Cardiff on Friday! I felt very hungry but did not get too big a dinner again. In the afternoon I had a good sleep and wrote letters and read. It turned to rain. I was on defence duty all day and had to lug a rifle about with me and could not get out so went for an early tea. Plenty of time for reading Lhasa, the Holy City. I wrote a long letter to Margaret. Only one air raid till 10.00 a.m.! Parade at 1.30 p.m., 6.00 p.m. and 9.15p.m. Donaldson fell and broke thumb and was taken to hospital. To bed at 10.00 p.m. Spent 6d.

23/9/40 My hut job was changed from stove to windows. In the morning we did a little foot drill and PT just to fill in time. In the afternoon we were definitely told we were passing out on Thursday officially! And then we had a lecture by a flying Squadron Leader on bomb effects on land. Had a bit of drill as a flight. Fine all day but in the evening it turned dull, and in any case I was tired so I spent the evening in marking all my kit. Heavy raid. Letters from Peter containing one from Nurse King and one from John Hawksworth. Spent 1/4. To bed at 10.00 p.m. I am noticing the difference between evening in billets and those in my flat at Huddersfield.

24/9/40 Up very early so a full kit parade at 8.00 a.m. and all the lads who had kits were mighty busy packing them to meet with approval. All I had was a gas cape to wear and I was not sorry. Warrant Officer McCann inspected us and was very meticulous and took a long time and left us standing ages. Did nothing much rest of time in the morning. In the afternoon we had another parade on the parade ground, and marching. Not too bad. Some of the lads in the hut were posted but not us. In the evening I went to West Kirby with John to send greetings telegram to Patey for his twenty first and to buy something for John, but could not do so. Alas we could not book a room for farewell to Corporal Tasker. We had a couple of drinks and back 8.30 p.m. Someone pinched my mug, so I had to buy another. In the afternoon we ran round camp for PT and had shower. Reading and to bed at 10.00 p.m. Spent 2/9 and 1/6.

That was the last of the original diary pages for 1940. The subsequent entries for that year were from Charles's summary of his diaries.

26/9/40 Passing out parade. Not a posting through – yet. I spent rest of my time in SHQ doing clerical work – some unfortunates got the heavy gang! But then I saw for first time how many it took to do so little work. It is a good thing the RAF has not to show a balance sheet.

2/10/40 Posted to Hullavington – for Ground Defence. Imagine my horror when I was issued with rifle, bayonet, webbing and ammunition.

Morning and evening "stand to"s on gun sites. Guards on dispersal sites, taking our bedding with us and doing two on four off, or three on three off for 24 hours. Main gate guard for 24 hours with two on four off. Oh how I loathed it and felt myself getting in a rut. One small consolation was a pub in Hullavington Village with good beer, cheese and bread and cider. But I had to keep to 2/- a day, so it was not very often visited.

5/10/40 to 10/10/40 On Crash Guard at Bathford near Bath. Did a lot of walking round country and round Bath. Back at Hullavington I soon learned the art of hitch hiking and spent most of my time off on tours around country. Also I went into Bristol fairly often for BBC symphony concerts.

I started a Rover group on camp and we met weekly and I met Poulton, who had come with me at Rover Moot.

I seemed to be sleeping alternate nights in uniform and then in blankets that do not appear to have been washed for ages! All I got was 30/- a fortnight and then people wondered why I was fed up.

What annoyed me was that here we were – mugs and no redress while in every daily paper they were asking for aircrew, in the cinemas on the radio, visiting schools and asking boys to volunteer and applying for men to remuster.

21 and 22/12/40 I got a weekend off to go to Margaret's wedding, hitch hiking both ways.

25/12/40 At Christmas there was little doing that interested me, and I was not on guard on 25th so offered to help serve etc. in cookhouse for Christmas dinner. I had plenty to eat (for a change) and so kept busy and did not have much time to think, which got me miserable here; it's deadly. And so ended an eventful year in a slough of despond.

In Europe there was little in the news of the war to raise spirits as 1940 drew to a close. In North Africa, however, Allied forces were meeting with much more success. The Italians had been successfully engaged at Sidi Birani and the town had been captured. By the middle of December they had been pushed out of Egypt completely.

1/1/41 Wednesday. Off on site as usual, and an easy day. In the afternoon I wrote letters, and in the evening I set off for Bath at 4.00 p.m. I got straight in and collected my photos and tried to buy a diary. I got back to Chippenham and caught a bus to camp before dark. Tried to ring Joan again. I heard that I was to be posted on Monday, and it seems genuine. Spent 1/4.

2/1/41 Thursday. Up early and found snow two inches deep. I had a bath. On E site. Then I heard I was going to Stratford with Jack Worsdale and not to Scarborough. It was perishing cold and only five of us were on, so we had to do two on three off day and night. Spent 5d.

3/1/41 Friday. Washed, shaved and cleaned buttons on site. I had an early dinner and then off to Chenil to see Miss Walsh at Manor House, a lovely old place, and had walk with her on the Downs in snow and wind. We got onto RAF property and a Cop took us to the Guard Room; we got clear though. In the late afternoon and evening I talked to Mr Walsh most of the time. After tea and supper I took a bus to Colne, but the train to Chippenham was half an hour late. So I missed the last bus and got lift with madman on a motorbike. And with an icy road! Spent 1/-.

4/1/41 Saturday. On C Site and no official news of posting. Up early, bath, and off on armadillo. Usual sort of day, cold and dry. In the afternoon we came back to camp. In the evening I went to phone Joan but sirens went, so I came back and wrote and read.

5/1/41 Sunday. Did some cleaning etc on C site. After lunch I set off immediately by going through MQ and 10 MU! I got a lift to Bristol and called on Miss Vickery. She had just got up (1.30 p.m.) as she had had no chance to sleep with heavy air raids, so while she was dressing I went and got some water as the supply was damaged. After another dinner we went for a lovely walk through Naise Castle Woods. We came back to tea and for a yarn and I set off at 7.30 p.m. After a long wait at Bristol I left at 9.40 p.m. and arrived at Chippenham in time to fight for the last bus.

6/1/41 Monday. Awoke early to find I was on Main Gate armed guard. Feeling real miserable about this rotten raw deal, I had a bath and reported sick with rheumatism, and was ordered massage three times a day. So I got out of that. I then just pottered about and read most of day.

7/1/41 Tuesday. Up late, to find more snow. Three massages and reading etc. The evening was in the billet with Lofty and Jack Worsdale.

8/1/41 Wednesday. Officially told of posting and spent all day getting clearance papers signed up. I finished by 4.30 p.m. and then wangled a 48 hr pass, though they would not accept it with Huddersfield as the destination and asked for my word that I would not go there. So I decided not to set off till tomorrow as it was now dark and I was not ready. In the evening I packed and did some writing, and then went to Hullavington for drinks with Jack Worsdale.

9/1/41 Thursday. Up early and getting ready. After breakfast, off with Jack Worsdale on a 48 hr. I got lifts to Reading and caught the 11.00 a.m. train to Farnham. Arrived at Auntie's by 1.00 p.m. for lunch. The afternoon and evening were spent lying by fire and yarning, and I really enjoyed it.

Charles's posting was to 9 Receiving Wing at Stratford-upon-Avon. Here he would start the training as RAF aircrew, with the emphasis on basic mathematical and practical skills, as well as continuing the normal military training. His Aunt Marie's home at New Moon Service Station near Farnham became a frequent refuge from the boredom of RAF training. He and his brother

Peter met there on occasions when their military service allowed them, and Aunt Marie became a sort of clearing house for exchange of information on their movements and arranging meetings in London or elsewhere.

10/1/41 Friday. Wash and shave etc and then for walk and drink with Grandpa. In the afternoon we went to Aldershot in car with Auntie and did some shopping. Still not able to get a diary. I caught the early train to Reading. The trains were not running late and I arrived at Chippenham at 7.00 p.m. There I had a drink with an RAF chap I had met and got back to camp at 8.00 p.m. I missed pay parade, so had to cash a cheque for £2-0-0. Then packing and writing letters.

11/1/41 Saturday. Up early. Bath and then leisurely packed and off in tender 11.30 a.m. Train 12.05 p.m. to Swindon, Didcot, Leamington and Stratford on Avon by 8.00 p.m. It was dark, and we began queuing outside hotels much as at Padgate. I got a poor impression, as I realised we had to do foot drill again. I eventually got settled in room with six others and had good clean up. Then writing, unpacking and settling in and to bed at 11.00 p.m.

12/1/41 Sunday. Up at 7.00 a.m. and to breakfast in the Shakespeare Hotel after long queue which seems to be usual here. We went on a short run, and had the rest of the day free. Jack and I had good look round town and a walk on river as the weather was grand, and then we had a drink in the evening. I moved to another room. To bed at 10.00 p.m. The beauty of town and hotels has been destroyed by the RAF being here. The electricity is DC so I could not use my electric razor.

13/1/41 Monday. Up early and changed room to a two bedder with Jack Worsdale. In the morning we dodged drill by lying low in our room upstairs. In the afternoon it was inoculations and blood test and the rest was free. The weather was still fine and we had another good look round. In the evening after supper we had a stroll on the river in moonlight then back to room and early bed.

14/1/41 Tuesday. Up early and we were lying low when we were grabbed for one hour drill. In the afternoon there was an equipment parade. I also had a haircut. I broke my one remaining pipe. The evening I spent in the room reading and writing.

The routine of the course continued, and the diary records the same series of daily events – drill (frequently avoided), PT, route marches and lectures on maths. Snow in the middle of the month gave the young recruits the chance to enjoy themselves on a borrowed sledge. Occasional evenings out at the Rose and Crown are recorded, but the more usual evening entertainment was a walk by the Avon, and he comments on the rise of the river as the thaw set in in late January. Towards the end of the month he is delighted at the prospect of a 48-hour pass.

29/1/41 Wednesday. Up early, rather tired. The morning was spent on special Hotel cleaning and Jack and I wandered all over roof. Then PT. The afternoon should have been Maths and Drill but Jack and I disappeared and went to Birmingham for the afternoon. We heard that we could all have 48 hours for the weekend! Hooray. The evening was mainly reading, cards and writing.

30/1/41 Thursday. The usual morning with drill and a route march. In the afternoon more drill and another route march. But when they called us out on parade for this somehow Jack and I did not hear and so lay low for the time. In the evening a bath, supper, a drink, and cleaning up for tomorrow's 48 hour pass. I had intended getting away at dinner time, but then found that we had to parade at 2.20 p.m. for equipment! Rotten RAF.

31/1/41 Friday. Up early and it was the usual drill in the morning. I had hoped to get away on 48 hrs at 11.00 a.m. but we had a kit parade at 2.30p.m. We got through early and set off intending to hitch as far as Sheffield, but I had a rotten job getting to Birmingham and did not arrive there till 4.30 p.m. There was rain and snow and I realised it was too late to get out on Darby Road before dark, so I had tea with Uncle Bert and caught 5.30 p.m. to Huddersfield. I missed the connection at Stockport which should have got us in to Huddersfield at 9.30 p.m, and so had to wait four hours. So arrived in Huddersfield at 1.00 a.m.

Dad married Mrs Wilburn.

This is one of the few direct references in the diaries to Mrs Wilburn – now Mrs Collins. Florrie Wilburn had been his father's housekeeper. All his later letters home started with "Dear Dad and Florrie", but the content is clearly aimed only at his father. However, his visits home were no less frequent and it seems that his step-mother was tolerated rather than liked. However, free time that was not spent at home on the Isle of Sheppey was usually spent back at St Luke's Hospital in Huddersfield, where he still had some of his kit packed away in his old flat. The Nurses and Sisters in particular always seemed well pleased to see him on his frequent visits.

1/2/41 Saturday. Walking up Pinefield I passed four Rovers just returning from the Nurses panto that I had just missed! I spent the night wandering round seeing night staff and at 7.00 a.m. called on Joan and stayed for breakfast. Back to St Luke's at 10.00 a.m. and saw the Master, (in bed sick), Miss T and all nurses etc. At 4.00 p.m. it was back to Lindly and in the evening told Joan not to care for me too much for many obvious reasons, but realised too late for she was apparently very fond of me. Returned to St Luke's at 11.00 p.m. and yarned with Mr Deacon, night staff and Mr Stokes till going to bed at 1.00 a.m. Then at 1.30 a.m. Nurses Fairy and Nevin dragged me out! They gave me a hundred fags and 3/9 Christmas gift from staff.

2/2/41 Sunday. Up 7.00 a.m. and I went to Nurses Home and then down to MPB and called on all Rovers and Mr Potter. Then to see the Master again, and dinner. At 1.00 p.m. to Lindly again and early tea. Joan saw me off on 5.20 p.m. train. I slept most of way on the slow train that arrived at Birmingham 10.06 p.m.! It was too late for the Stratford connection, so I went to Snow Hill for RTO *(Rail Transport Officer)* signature and looked round for buses, but there were none, and it was snowing hard so that I went to United Services Club for night and was up and away early in the morning. I met Jack at Birmingham and came back together.

3/2/41 Monday. Arrived Guard Room 8.00 a.m. and was just in time to get crossed off absentee list. (About a hundred were on a charge over leave). We got back to the Hotel very tired and got down to cleaning. On parade for half an hour drill in snow. In the afternoon we dodged the route march and played snooker and went to equipment to get part of webbing! Then a maths lecture. In the evening just writing. There is now another bloke in our room.

4/2/41 Tuesday. Up late and tired. In the morning a lecture and fast drill. I went to sleep in the lecture. In the afternoon PT (Rugger), and a route march, but the sun was out and it was not too bad. In the evening, reading and writing. I tried to get Joan on phone.

5/2/41 Wednesday. In the morning we had rotten drill and then went to the canteen instead of route march. In the afternoon we should have drilled with Riverside but stayed up at Avonside and had yarn with a chap who had been at ITW *(Initial Training Wing)*. In the evening I washed some clothes as they would not accept laundry.

6/2/41 Thursday. The usual morning. Two yarns in the Rest Room and one hour drill. In the afternoon, one hour of drill and one hour of route march and yet we get tired and grumble! I spent most of the day running round trying to make up a party of twenty to get special prices at Theatre for Ralph Lyons in Nap Hand. Did so and it was a jolly good show. We paid 1/3 for 6/- seats. Afterwards we called in to the pub for a drink. Back 10.00 p.m. and to bed.

7/2/41 Friday. Up very early, and the usual slack day. In the afternoon I got pay of £1 and did route march in lovely weather. I got caught by booby trap and swamped with water from a mug over a door. I did not go out to supper but stayed in and read and wrote.

8/2/41 Saturday. Up very early and in the morning we went Beagling. We started at a Colonel's house with a free glass of beer at noon and then had a grand run in shorts etc till the kill at 3.00 p.m. Back at 4.00 p.m. for a foot bath, change and tea. In the evening I did a lot of washing, socks and woollens and odds and ends. And I had a hot, real hot, bath. Too late for supper, so out for drink. To bed at 10.15 p.m, very tired after the day.

9/2/41 Sunday. Up late and had late breakfast. Then back and tidied up and Jack and I cut church parade and went to hitch hike to Birmingham. We got a car right in, and he agreed to pick us up at 6.00 p.m. and bring us back and invited us out to tea! Oh luck. Had a good time and saw Hawkins, Sister Siddey, Nurses Campbell, Cox, Miss Brewer, and Miss Smith. We left at 5.45 p.m. and were back at Stratford on Avon in time for supper.

10/2/41 Monday. I was not called till 7.15 a.m. and had a big rush to get breakfast and on parade by 9.30 a.m. All they did was pick men for Saturday's special parade and Jack and I dodged it. So while they rehearsed we scrounged. In the afternoon we went to watch the inter-hotel rugger match, which we won. It was a lovely sunny day after the rain yesterday. In the evening we went to tea and supper with Davies who we met in car yesterday, and got back just in time. Put in a pass for weekend 48 hour.

11/2/41 Tuesday. Up early and I got dragged in for parade rehearsal for Saturday. In the afternoon I was to have played rugger but the match was cancelled so I watched soccer then cleared off at 3.30 p.m. and got ready for the evening when Jack and I had put in for late pass for his twenty-first birthday. After tea we went to the Bird in the Hand, Henley-in-Arden, where we consumed whisky. Then we got a lift back to Stratford and went to the Rose and Crown. Back by 11.30 p.m. and to bed. Happy!

12/2/41 Wednesday. Usual morning, apart from feeling tired. Felt no ill effects although Jack had a bit of a head. I got roped in for parade rehearsal again. The afternoon was spent in reading and gas lecture. In the evening it was reading, as I had got two books from the town library, and writing. Supper at the Sugarloaf.

13/2/41 Thursday. Up as usual, and scrounged all day. I dodged parade in the morning and in the afternoon lay in the sun and watched rugger as our match was scratched. In the morning I had been told to put in for seven days leave instead of a 48 hour pass! So in the evening after a bath, I went to town and tried for two hours to phone Joan.

14/2/41 Friday. In the morning we paraded but I dropped out at 11.00 a.m. to try to pick up seven days leave. Could not get it till 12.00, when I got advanced pay and ration book. I hitch hiked to Birmingham, got to Sutton and picked up lorry to Sheffield! I arrived there at 5.00 p.m. and then went wrong. I should have caught 5.45 p.m. bus but decided to get out on road and try to hitch hike or pick up a bus. But I got on the Barnsley road and did not get onto Flouch road till late and got a lift to Flouch which got me there at 7.00 p.m. I walked for half an hour and picked up bus to Lockwood Bar. I finally arrived at St Luke's Hospital at 8.00 p.m. and rang Joan to come up. Then, washed and shaved, I created a stir by walking into the Staff Dance. I had ripping time till midnight. We took a taxi to Lindley, and back. After a yarn with Sister Corwan I got to bed at 1.00 a.m.

15/2/41 Saturday. Up 7.00 a.m. and had a stroll round before catching the 11.30 a.m. bus and Lindly to dinner with Joan. The afternoon was with Joan going to see Audrey via the town, and as she was sick we took flowers. We walked back, had tea in town and then went to see Tom Walls in A Canary Sings. Jolly good. We went back to Lindly for an hour and then I got into town and caught 11.30 p.m. train to Sheerness. It was a good trip to London, arriving at 8.00 a.m. I slept most of way.

16/2/41 Sunday. Slept pretty well in the train and I tried to get to Victoria to catch 8.55 a.m. but on the tubes I changed 4 times and was too late. I caught the 9.15 a.m. and arrived 12.30 a.m. Slow! Then walked round the field till dinner. After dinner Dad and I walked to Minster. In the evening I tried to ring Joan to tell her I could not meet her at Lut tomorrow for the show but I could not get through. We played Monopoly. To bed at 11.30.

17/2/41 Monday. After a good night I was up at 7.00 a.m. and saw Dad off. After breakfast I sent a telegram to Joan and then went along to see Margaret. Then with her to see Ella Lewis, Auntie Nellie, Mrs Reid, back to Margaret's and then back to the Chalet for dinner. I had to dash to catch the 2.07 p.m. train to London and had good journey. I spent the afternoon looking round at widespread damage and bought a pipe. After tea at the YMCA I was out again in evening to see night time effect. (Saw all shelterers taking bedding down to tubes). A raid started at 7.00 p.m. so I went back to Euston and caught 8.45 p.m. instead of the 11.55 p.m.

It is in the natures of diaries that they are a personal record, so it is hardly surprising that Charles's diaries make scant comment on the war itself. Air raids are mentioned only when they affect him directly, and apart from the brief entry in the summaries of May 1940 "Dunkirk starts" there is little to indicate the progress of hostilities. This is a suitable point to review the situation in which the country found itself while Charles's training made its slow progress.

German forces had effectively overrun Europe completely by May 1940, and Britain declared itself as standing alone against the Third Reich. In fact, of course, Britain was far from alone, and was really the protagonist in an alliance of several Commonwealth nations. In addition the United States had openly declared its support for the allied forces against the Axis powers. The Axis now consisted of Germany, Italy and Japan, this last having joined in September 1940. Two months later Hungary would also join the Axis. In the early summer of 1940 it seemed likely that German forces massing in Europe would invade Britain as soon as they had achieved mastery of the skies. It was against this background that the Battle of Britain was fought, and eventually won. Much has been written on the strategy of that battle, but to those in Britain at the time it was seen as a series of daily air raids. These raids changed to nightly raids after September 1940, with up to four hundred being reported as dead and seventeen hundred injured on 8 September alone. It was at about this time that the London underground became effectively a permanent air raid shelter. Nor were the raids confined to London alone. Coventry and Portsmouth were but two of the many centres of industry and population targeted by the Luftwaffe by night in late 1940 and early 1941.

Abroad the situation appeared brighter. Progress was being made against the Italian forces in Egypt and Libya in early 1941. Swordfish aircraft of the Royal Navy struck a punishing blow against the Italian fleet at Taranto. Support from the USA was becoming more positive, with the supply of up to three thousand aircraft per month agreed in July 1940, and progress being made towards the Lend Lease agreement.

The effects on everyday life at home were apparent in the introduction of rationing, with the weekly meat ration reduced from one and sixpence to one and twopence per head. Certain restrictions on movement were introduced, and the Home Guard was formed. By January 1941 Churchill could announce that a total of four million men were under arms, including Home Guard forces.

18/2/41 Tuesday. We had good run and good connections

at Crewe and Manchester. I slept most of the way. I got into Huddersfield at 6.00 a.m, so went to sleep in the waiting room. Then at 7.00 a.m. I went for a wash and brush up and shave and up to Lindly for breakfast. I spent the morning there as the weather was too bad to go out. In the afternoon I went up to St Luke's Hospital and went through my cases. All others were pleased to see me but I got the impression that Harry F not too pleased, maybe on account of food which seems to be worrying him. I had tea with Miss T and in the evening went to see the Sisters. I had a game of badminton with Dr Gibson etc, and then went to the Rovers. Arthur Turner was there on leave. I finished at midnight and spent night with Cyril.

19/2/41 Wednesday. Up 8.00 a.m, had breakfast and wandered up to Saint Luke's Hospital. I went to see the Master about sleeping and then yarned with Audrey about provisions. After a wander round I got a Doctor to look at my ear which had been bad, but he said it was only a cold. Then I went to town for dinner at the YMCA, then up to Lindley and stayed for tea. In the evening I took Joan and Audrey to a dance at The Princess. Nurses Baker and Thompson and Cyril, Arthur and Bill were also there, so we had a good time. I came back with Audrey and Joan in a taxi, then walked from town to the hospital, and found a bed with Ellis.

20/2/41 Thursday. Up 11.00 a.m. after a good rest! I had lunch with the Sisters in Nurses' home and a yarn. In the afternoon it was up to Lindley for games, and we spent the evening yarning by the fire. I caught the last bus back to Saint Luke's Hospital in the snow, then went round the wards and say cheerio to the night staff. To bed at 1.00 a.m. It snowed heavily on Tuesday,

Wednesday, Thursday and Friday all the time – about two foot six.

21/2/41 Friday. My last day. Up 7.00 a.m. and went round the wards and offices etc to bid goodbye and packing. The Master still seemed very cold and atmosphere in office anything but cordial. Then up to Lindly for dinner and had the afternoon with Joan for walk and snowballing. We had early tea and then down to catch 4.30 p.m. train with Joan. After changes at Stockport, Crewe and Stafford I arrived at Birmingham one hour late, and therefore missed Stratford connection. So I put up at United Services Club for night. Bed 11.00 p.m.

22/2/41 Saturday. I was called at 6.00 a.m. and made a quick dash to the station, caught early train and arrived in lovely sunshine just in time to argue myself off absentee list! I should have been on a digging party but got off as I had not washed or shaved etc. So I had football and that was all. In the afternoon I went to see London Symphony at Theatre with Moisowith; Beethoven Egmont, Debussy Petit Suite, Rachmaninoff Concerto No 2 C minor, and Tchaikowsky's Symphony No 4. Jolly good show. In the evening a bath, writing and tidying up. Jack W. was on leave. To bed early

23/2/41 Sunday. Up 7.15 a.m. and did all cleaning and tidying before going to breakfast. Then went church parade. Sun just coming through in the morning mist so walked slowly along far bank right out of town till sun got real strong then sat on log by river and read and wrote. After a while fellow came along with a dog and we got talking. Young PT teacher waiting for RAF calling up. Just wed, and invited me along to tea. After lunch/dinner changed and finished letters etc and along to their house for evening. Fine bright young couple and interesting. Back 9.30 p.m. Bed early.

The course continued for another week, with drill (frequently dodged) route marches and lessons on air raid precautions, aircraft recognition and the other basics of war. Some of the course members were given their postings, but Charles heard nothing officially until the end of the week, when he was given a posting that was cancelled just a few hours later. He was not pleased. By the end of the week those who were posted departed, and those who were left had the job of clearing out the vacated accommodation. After that, however, they were given five days' leave. Charles went to Dunfermline where he met up with his brother Peter and visited other friends and relations. Then he set off to return to Stratford-upon-Avon.

> 6/3/41 Thursday. Up 6.15 a.m, cleaned up and caught 7.45 a.m. to Edinburgh. Snowing hard, had one hour in Edinburgh and walked down Princes St near the Castle in snow. The King and Queen arrived! I changed at Carstairs to a through train to Carlisle and we then ran out of the snow. Arrived Crewe 5.00 p.m. so rang Joyce, missed the connection and met her after a wash and brush up, at 6.00 p.m. After tea and a yarn caught 7.00 p.m. train, changed at Stafford and arrived Birmingham with just time to get to Snow Hill to catch 9.40 p.m. arriving Stratford on Avon at 11.30 p.m. At Avonside told I had been posted to Cambridge on Saturday.
>
> 7/3/41 Friday. Up 6.00 a.m. Breakfast and ironed washing done a week ago. Then parade for CO's talk about ITW. In the afternoon pay parade and FFI, hair cut, bath and packing. Evening packing, writing and drink with Jack.

CHAPTER 2

Aircrew Training

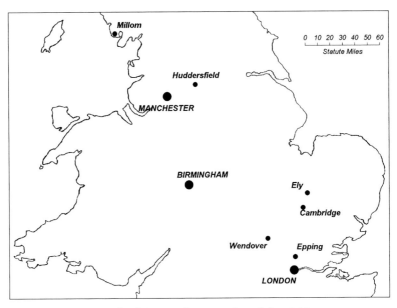

Charles's Travels – March to July 1941

The training that Charles had received thus far was primarily a general introduction to service matters, though at Avonside he had consolidated the basic educational standards that would be needed for aircrew training. He could now march, salute and generally behave in a military fashion. At No. 2 Initial Training Wing at Cambridge the emphasis would shift more towards his future role as aircrew. However, he was soon to find that the basics of the military existence were not to be overlooked.

9/3/41 Sunday. Up 7.00 a.m., washed and showered. In the morning FFI and dental parade – seven cavities. Lecture

35

on general routine. In the afternoon, Pay Accounts and then free. Adjourned to sitting room and wrote. Evening, out for drink and cleaned boots and buttons etc.

10/3/41 Monday. Up 6.00 a.m. Gargle and parade. Given the programme for the week. Morning, lecture, signals and drill. Afternoon, OC squadron and maths. Evening, shopping, writing, study. Mess orderly.

11/3/41 Tuesday. Up 6.00 a.m. and rushed to do mess orderly. Morning anti-gas, signals, maths. Afternoon should have been games, but I went for night vision test and could not see a darn thing! Then had rest of evening free, so writing and swotting.

12/3/41 Wednesday. Up a bit late and terrific rush. Usual sort of day. Law and admin, drill, recce of craft, maths (2), gas chamber, morse. Usual rush for meals and stayed in in evening writing up notes etc.

13/3/41 Thursday. Up very early and usual shower and rush. Morning, drill on low park and maths; did bit better. Afternoon inspection by CO – very red tapish. Then gas cartridge was let off behind us and we had to whip out masks at speed. Mine contained books as usual. Then anti gas lecture and morse at which I did not shine. Evening writing up notes and study. Bed early. I had choice between pilot and air observer; I chose A/Ob.

This was the point at which aircrew were streamed to be either pilots or air observers – a trade soon to be more accurately titled as navigator. Although Charles later considered re-mustering as a pilot when he was on his operational squadrons, he always maintained that the navigator was "the brains of the aircraft", and felt himself more at home in that role. His enlistment had been, in fact, as an air observer. For both roles the initial training was the same. They were to learn the principles of navigation, the basics of how flight instruments operated, and the required skills of sending and receiving Morse code, both by W/T and by Aldis lamp.

14/3/41 Friday. Up 6.00 a.m., shower etc. In the morning, inspection, anti-gas and pay parade (10/-). Afternoon, hygiene, morse, maths. It was a lovely hot day and the punts on river looked grand and inviting. Found a building dated 1624. Evening, on guard and got the 7.00 p.m. to 10.00 p.m. shift, so I was free to go to bed after usual clearing for the morning.

15/3/41 Saturday. Up as usual. Morning, parade and then hung around in rooms for inspections. Then maths, followed by CO's interview, but it was very cursory. He said I did not look like my photograph – owing to my moustache. The afternoon was free, so I went out shopping, then back and writing and swotting. Same in the evening.

16/3/41 Sunday. Up 7.00 a.m. and parade 9.00 a.m. for Church. Then free for the day. Spent the time writing and studying. Went for short stroll in the afternoon and evening. Bed early.

17/3/41 Monday. Up as usual. Morning, law, admin and morse. Then psychological test – keeping a spot in a square. I did not do too well, but took all morning on it. Missed clothing parade. Afternoon, film and maths. Evening, study and notes.

18/3/41 Tuesday. Usual morning. In the afternoon, played rugger for C flight. Lovely day and good game till half way through the second half, when I got kicked in eye, stud entering eye and corner and covering me with gore. Rushed to SSQ where an eye specialist operated on me, with three Docs and umpteen nurses etc watching. It was very uncomfortable, but he made a good job of it and saved my sight. Bed by 5.30 p.m. and got some sleep.

19/3/41 Wednesday. Eye bunged up, but felt better. Told I should lie in several days. Got small kit (some of it!) from St John's. In bed all day. Did bit of reading.

20/3/41 Thursday. Got up in afternoon. The dressing came off but I could not see through the eye. Read.

21/3/41 Friday. Got leave to go to the gas examination (got 90%) in the morning and to maths in afternoon. I was going to try to make up 24 hours for examining and so prevent being re-flighted.

This eye injury would haunt Charles for the rest of his life, but for the moment he was desperate to pass out of this course on time. To be 're-flighted' (transferred to a later course) could mean several weeks delay in getting to the next stage of training. He felt that he had done enough hanging around already.

22/3/41 Saturday. Morning, had again to go to maths and rest of day reading. Brought back some maths papers with me and a morse buzzer. Had a hair cut. Saw the CO.

23/3/41 Sunday. Much same day. Had service in morning. Stayed in for the afternoon. It snowed a bit.

24/3/41 Monday. Tried to get 4 hour pass for maths. But SMO said "No" and I would have to be re-flighted in any case. So I stayed in all day.

25/3/41 Tuesday. Eye fellow said he would take stitches out tomorrow. He gave the eye thorough examination in clinic and said I would have to be in a day or two yet and he was afraid of infection etc, and said it would water for some time too! So I did nothing all day, getting fed up.

Toying with idea of applying for sick leave, but I'll see how I stand with re-flighting. I want to stay up at St John's with the course.

26/3/41 Wednesday. Eye chappie did not come to remove stitches as he was too busy. Lazy day as usual. I was moved to another room in evening.

27/3/41 Morning, Sister took out stitches and I felt lots better for it. An old carbuncle coming up on my rear again but I decided to delay reporting it so as to get out. In the afternoon I went for run through agricultural country with Lady Stanley and to tea.

28/3/41 Friday. The eye specialist said I could go out tomorrow, and what is more told me I was to have seven days' leave. But the carbuncle is now large and painful. Usual day. Good hot bath in the morning.

29/3/41 Saturday. Did not get through sick parade till 11.30 a.m. Had to change and pack, get warrant, leave pass, stuff from store and adjutant, pay, ration card etc. Then caught the 3.30 p.m. train, changed at Ely, Peterborough and Leeds and arrived at Huddersfield at 10.00 p.m. and went direct to the YMCA for a bed.

30/2/41 Sunday. Up early, washed etc and then up to Lindly. Breakfast, then Joan and I went off for a walk as it was quite a good day. We walked out of the lane, down to the valley and up to the reservoir before coming back along the road from Aunt Sarah's. Good long walk and stayed in for the evening. Stayed the night at Lindly.

31/3/41 Monday. Up 9.30 a.m.! After a leisurely wash clean etc, up to Woodhouse Hall for the morning to see Sister Pachter and for dinner. Then to Saint Luke's Hospital. I did not see the Master but had tea with the Sisters. Then met Joan at 5.30 p.m. and had tea at the Fields', before going to see Berkley Square at the theatre. Back for supper and to bed 11.30 p.m. Joan was in a huff and without a goodnight kiss.

1/4/41 Tuesday. Up at 9.00 a.m. and breakfast then spent morning by fire writing and reading. After dinner set out to find Nurse Hill, now Mrs Hutton with a family. Spent an hour looking for her house in the rain but found it in time for tea and a yarn. It appears Donald was there on Sunday and Tom on Monday, so we missed each other by one day! Then up to Saint Luke's Hospital but the carbuncle was too painful and large to play badminton. So yarned with Ellis and down to see Miss Mallinson. Then with Blackburn for drink and down to Rovers. All there; yarn and snooker. Stayed the night at Potters and in night carbuncle burst. Rotten mess!

2/4/41 Wednesday. After carbuncle burst felt easier and had good sleep. Did not wake till 10.00 a.m.! Went up to Woodhouse Hall for day and got Sister Pachter to clean it up and dress it as it was still discharging and likely to for some days. She gave me spare dressings and I had a hot bath. Lot more comfortable but not really well. Spent the afternoon yarning. After tea for a walk with her along canal and then up to Lindly for evening. We wanted to go to a dance, but none on.

3/4/41 Thursday. Up 9.00 a.m. after first good night. Up to Saint Luke's in the morning and yarned with the Master and office staff. Dinner with Miss T and Sisters. Saw house staff and then to town. Called in PHO to see Miss Berry and PAR to see Raymond and Boothby. Then met Audrey and took her to tea at Field's and then we met Joan and went to Palace to see, inter alia, Tommy Handley and Elsie and Doris Walters. Walked back up with Audrey and we walked to Lindly for very pleasant evening. Joan actually played piano and sang a little. Weather still rotten. Joan and I say goodbye here.

4/4/41 Friday. Up late and spent the morning yarning and reading. In the afternoon out to see Miss Mallinson 3.00 p.m. for tea and evening till 7.30 p.m., then back to Saint Luke's for a party in Sisters' Room till 1.50 a.m., then over to see night nurses till 2.30 a.m., then to female annexe with Miss Mallinson till 5.00 a.m.! Slept on Doc's couch for remainder of night.

5/4/41 Saturday. Up late and after breakfast said farewells and afterwards caught 1.00 p.m. to Leeds, changing at Peterborough and March. Arrive camp 8.30 p.m. with all the usual bedding drawing etc. and straighten out things and bed early.

6/4/41 Sunday. Up 7.00 a.m. and had leisurely wash etc and off to sick parade where Eye Specialist was not, so I was only ordered bathe 3 times a day. Writing, reading etc. In the afternoon bathing eye, met Jack for feed and walk as it was fairly fine. Then a nap and off to concert at Guildhall. Back for cleaning and reading. Bed early. Eye had swollen up slightly in the night and by evening was quite painful.

7/4/41 Monday. Up early and shower etc. Eye much more swollen but oculist not at SSQ when I got there. In the morning aircraft recce and that was all. Afternoon, saw oculist who was pleased with eye but annoyed with swelling which he said was stye and was to have hot foments till came to head and put me on light duties. Back to St John's but could do nothing as not re-flighted. Had long sleep and one and a half hours in the bath in the afternoon. Then to SSQ, WVS and collect registered parcel from HQ from Joan.

8/4/41 Tuesday. When I went to treatment I reported sick

with bad foot with object of wearing shoes; got wearing shoes OK (for 3 days) but when SMO saw size of eye, said I had to be admitted and hot foments hourly for half an hour at a time! So I spent 50% of my time bathing it! Reading, writing and bed early. Eye discharging a little but not going down a lot. Waters a lot.

And so it went on for the rest of the week. Charles was stuck in Sick Quarters having his eye bathed, and becoming more frustrated at not getting on with the course.

14/4/41 Monday. Had to see both new SMO and Oculist before I could get discharged but got permission not to wear boots for 3 days. Back to college and put in I block to wait re-flighting. Afternoon, went to aircraft recce – epidiascope – and went to sleep. The others went to navigation so I stayed and wrote, read and arranged things and had hair cut. Evening reading and fixing radio in new cabinet. Bed early.

15/4/41 Tuesday. Up very early as I had to shave with safety razor. On Daily Routine Orders yesterday 2 men got 14 days for using electrical equipment without permission! To SSQ in the morning. Wrote letter in WVS then sunbathed till Jerryman came at 10.00 a.m.! Back and reading in room till dinner. Afternoon, badminton and some good games. Evening just sat in front of fire listening to TSF. And at 9.30 p.m. went out for a drink with Jack. Back 10.00 p.m. and early bed.

16/4/41 Wednesday. In the morning saw the eye chappie again and was told to report in two days. Stayed in all rest of the day reading. Evening writing and bed early. Shifted over to D block again with Jack etc.

17/4/41 Thursday. Up early and put on boots – whacking

great lot of iron-mongery in there – for first time, and reported sick as three days shoes had expired. But did not press desire to wear shoes and said feet were better so back to boots. Spent some time in WVS reading and back to St John's. Afternoon had inspection, then had to report to dental, but when got there, date postponed. So back and reading. At 8.30 p.m. Jack and I went out to pub and had plenty to drink. Back and smoking an Egyptian cigarette finished me off and had to run and be sick! Felt rotten.

18/4/41 Friday. Up early and to eye clinic after long walk round. Jerryman said OK now. Back to St John's and out to do PT. Had rough and ready rugger and put finger out of joint, so had to go special sick again. Very painful and swollen. It was strapped and then back to St John's reading for the evening. Re-flighting came through and I had to pack and go to Trinity College. Not expecting me and I only got rough shakedown. Letter from LAC Jack Hepworth. Bed early.

19/4/41 Saturday. Up at 6.00 a.m. and down to SSQ for dressing on finger. Very painful in night and swollen, but better in evening. Went for walk, had meal at WVS and to St John's. Wandered around Trinity. Afternoon I was going on river but it was raining so went to films. Not bad. Evening to St John's as no settee even at Trinity, and wrote and read. Back and bed early.

20/4/41 Sunday. Reported sick with finger. SMO said thought bone broken and to go for X-ray tomorrow. Rest of morning visiting, as now on flight and they had FFI etc. Afternoon I was going on river with Jack but he had gone out, so had nap at John's and then for stroll towards Granchester. Evening for stroll and to WVS for grub and read. Back early and cleaning etc. and bed.

21/4/41 Monday. Up early for inspection then to SSQ and on to Aldenbrooks for X-ray of finger and walk to WVS and back in time for maths. Afternoon morse and anti-gas. I went to canteen. Then to SSQ for X-ray plates, chipped bone! Back and rest till tea. Evening mucking about and writing. Bed early.

Charles now established himself on the new course. His injured finger was a nuisance, but did not hinder his progress, and he continued the daily round of lectures and drill for the rest of the month. His eye, however, continued to give trouble.

26/4/41 Saturday. Morning, morse, drill, maths and clothing parade, but tunic not ready. Afternoon, to have clean bandage on hand. Ran into oculist – Jerryman – who told me more about eye. I would have to have another board and if the eye still watered in six months I would have to have another op to put new duct in, as eye would not be healed enough till then!

And at the end of the month the entry was:

30/4/41 Wednesday. Up early. Morning, maths, morse, aldis lamp and gas, so to town and hair cut and collect ticket for tonight. Afternoon, to SSQ for exam by Wing Commander, Lieutenant Colonel and RN Commander – all specialists – and they agreed I should have immediate op on the eye to put in a duct. But I arranged to wait till end of course. Put in for another 48 hr pass for weekend. Evening to see the Beggars' Opera but had to leave not seeing last scene to get back by 10.30 p.m.

1/5/41 Thursday. Up early as mess orderly. Reported sick

and had splint off finger, but still stiff and painful. Had it wrapped in cotton wool for padding. Collected new tunic and slept in common room rest of the morning. Afternoon, maths. Went and saw CO and got 48 hr pass! Evening, Duty Cadet in orderly room (on phone) and stayed there all evening and slept there. Started lengthy letter to Gran. Bed 11.00 p.m.

2/5/41 Friday. Up early but had to wait about till relieved. Cleaned up. In the morning, morse then dental and had three fillings, then maths. Afternoon, given 48 hr pass and at 2.00 p.m. set off in grand weather. Lifts to Royston and then to Luton and Dunstable – out of way, but then got grand car to London. Caught 6.00 p.m. bus to home and arrived 8.30 p.m. Spent evening yarning and felt a lot better being home this time.

3/5/41 Saturday. Had a rotten night as was kept awake with heavy cold. Up 9.30 a.m. and then to Minster to see Margaret in hospital with abscess and look round the place. Afternoon, to see Aunt Nellie and Uncle. Then to Miss Jones and to tea with Eileen Hoad. Back at 10.00 p.m. and yarn with Dad. Bed midnight as clocks were put on another hour – i.e. 2 hours beyond Greenwich.

4/5/41 Sunday. Up 9.30 a.m. and to Minster again to see Margaret and the cemetery. One of the nurses was going to London in car in the afternoon so I cancelled my ticket and went with her at 2.30 p.m. and caught the bus. It turned out a lovely day – really hot and the orchards looked a treat. Damage in London. She dropped me at Finsbury Park and I went across to Epping Forest and called on Nurse King and went for a walk through forest – lovely. At 8.00 p.m. I started hitch hiking and at 10.00 p.m. got to Saffron Walden. By then it was getting dark and little traffic, so I got worried till the 10.45 p.m. bus brought me right in to arrive at 11.45 p.m. Happy day. Bed midnight.

In order to extract the maximum daylight from the working day, the Government introduced 'Double Summer Time', so that the clocks throughout the summer were two hours ahead of Greenwich mean time – thus, coincidentally, bringing the United Kingdom into line with the rest of Western Europe. The rather terse diary comment "Damage to London" reflects the fact that the capital was now in the throes of the Blitz. Nor was London the only target, and cities with ports and industrial centres had suffered badly from the almost nightly raids. Meanwhile, unknown to the British public, the 'Battle of the Beams' was being fought and won, with the German bombers' radio navigation beams (Knickebein, X-system and Y-system) being detected and more or less successfully countered. Elsewhere the war was not going well. In the Atlantic in March nearly half a million tons of Allied shipping had been sunk by U-boats. Rommel was advancing successfully in North Africa and the German army had advanced through Yugoslavia and into Greece. The United States had recently passed the 'Lend Lease' bill, allowing US military equipment to be leased to Britain. However, though undoubtedly sympathetic to the Allied cause, the US remained steadfastly neutral. No wonder Charles wanted to get training finished and on to active service.

Back at Cambridge, Charles swung back into the routine of the course.

5/5/41 Monday. Up late and feeling fit. In the morning epidiascope for aircraft recce, drill, maths. Afternoon, morse lecture, armaments, aircraft recce film and drill. Took dressing off finger, but still stiff and swollen. Evening stayed in for a bath. Did a maths paper. Writing and rang Joan to say I could not write for day or two. Bed 11.00 p.m. Weather rotten. Got six oz. St Bruno.

6/5/41 Tuesday. Up early and to SSQ with finger. Still stiff painful and swollen. Told I was to go to Ely! Back, but did nothing till the afternoon. Started Vickers 90 Gun, then aldis lamp followed by last maths period. Evening stayed in reading and writing as best I could. Been trying daily to get from Gable £1 I lent him three weeks ago!

7/5/41 Wednesday. First two periods maths exam and did not do too bad but finger mucked up graph and I made mistake on significant figures, but should get 75%. Then armament and morse. Afternoon, drill (when I sat on river bank), aircraft recce and hygiene, then free. Evening to TOC H and lounged away evening.

So the course went on. He bade farewell to the others on his original course, and a week later wrote:

13/5/41 Tuesday. Up early. In the morning it was OC squadron and so did private study. Then law and admin, then two drill periods so I went for a walk to wing orderly room for warrant etc, and to SSQ for reports and station for ticket. Back to dinner then straight away to Ely Hospital. Lot of waiting about. But surgeon X-rayed it and said it was OK and only wanted working! Back for tea, and evening signals – about 97$\frac{1}{2}$% – and bath. Still looking for Gable and £1!

14/5/41 Wednesday. Morning morse, armament, navigation. Afternoon drill, when I went for treatment and wrote letters and notes. Then hygiene and law and admin, which as usual was not very constructive. Then free period, when I studied. Evening was on fire picket but got someone to stand by and went to hear Sadler's

47

Wells Opera at theatre. The Wise Virgins, The Wanderer and The Wedding Bouquet. All very good.

A week later:

22/5/41 Thursday. Up early. Morning aldis and armament, navigation. Afternoon, aircraft recce and law and admin and interview by CO. Evening on guard at Magdalene. Got best shifts, i.e. 7–8, 11–1. Intended swotting but got into a discussion. Saw Gable but he wiggled out of it again.

23/5/41 Friday. Up 5.20 a.m. and back to Trinity to shave change etc. Morning morse, aircraft recce (not so good), navigation and a nap. Afternoon pay and interview with the Wing Commander. I think I favourably impressed him. He told me if I was re-mustered pilot and wanted air observer to go and see him. To SSQ as had to go to Ely again on Monday. Then study. Evening stayed in studying.

24/5/41 Saturday. Up late. Navigation, morse and to clothing parade but did not get hat for the cheese cutter. After dinner flight went to SSQ for inoculation, but got out of it myself. Spent rest of the afternoon swotting and writing. Evening bath and to YMCA to read papers etc. Back by 9.00 p.m., reading and bed early. Had group photo taken but did not bother to buy one.

25/5/41 Sunday. Up 7.00 a.m. To SSQ for treatment. Day dull and raining, so spent the morning studying. Afternoon, writing, nap and to aircraft recce room for half an hour. Evening stayed in writing and reading. Bed early. Mess orderly.

26/5/41 Monday. Up late. Morning to Jesus and SSQ for gen to go to Ely. Then to navigation. Afternoon to Ely Hosp. Seemed satisfied with my finger though still won't bend. Kept me waiting two and a half hours. Then I had to run for tram without seeing the cathedral. Evening extra navigation and writing.

27/5/41 Tuesday. Up early. OC squadron and Law. Two drill periods and went for treatment and wrote in YMCA. Also saw Jerryman who said I would have to have an operation on my eye before posting as I would not be passed OK for posting on aircrew duties till it was done, and certainly not overseas. Might not even after the operation. Afternoon morse, armament and navigation. Evening to pictures – Russian film. Bath and bed early.

28/5/41 Wednesday. Up early and told I was to report sick. I was there two hours and all he wanted was to see my finger! And I missed navigation, aldis and armaments. Afternoon filled in a census form and then had drill when individuals took the flight. Then MO lecture on altitude flying and PT which I dodged. Evening writing and studying. Lamond came round looking for me to go on guard, so I vanished to bath and dodged it! Bed very early.

29/5/41 Thursday. Up late and rush to get ready. Morning, morse buzzing test (100%) and armaments. Drill, so I went to SSQ and YMCA and read and wrote. Afternoon, navigation and went to sleep, law and free period. Evening I was guard commander. However, I did the first hour when someone was put on guard as punishment so I got off it and went to see Jack Hulberd and Cicely Courtnage in Under your Hat, a real laugh.

And so the course continued. Charles did well in the practical examinations, though not so well in admin and law. Arrangements were made for him to go to the RAF Hospital at Ely for a major operation on his injured eye. But first, with a few weeks to spare till the end of the course, they were sent on a week's leave. Charles went to Huddersfield again, and visited the Hospital staff and Joan.

11/6/41 Wednesday. Up early and after breakfast to Saint Luke's to change and see office etc. Changed and got into uniform again. Caught 12.30 p.m. to Stockport, Stalybridge and Crewe, arriving at 4.00 p.m. and, strange to relate, I saw Dr Rosehill on station, so went for a drink with him. Then met Joyce at 6.30 p.m. (Had been to RTO to get my pass stamped to certify that there was no train.) Went to tea in town and then to her home and for grand walk in country. Back to Crewe by 10.30 p.m. and waited in the station till the train came.

12/6/41 Thursday. Caught 1.13 a.m. Changed at Bletchley and arrived Cambridge 9.00 a.m. Nothing was said about being late. Telegram from Peter delivered here last Saturday to say he was called up! Too late for me to do anything about it. But C Flight back and on the car park so I got my kit out, had bath and hair cut. Afternoon, cricket, as after a rotten weekend the weather turned out fine. Evening, reading and to YMCA. Telegram from Joan asking me to ring so had to get up at 11.30 p.m. to take it but I could not get through.

13/6/41 Friday. In the morning the chaps were on drill but I to SSQ etc. Got some Bruno, then read. Afternoon spent all time trying to get away for hospital on Monday. Got warrant and 260 but not 48 pass from SSQ. So have till tomorrow when I shall have to fix the Sergeant. Spent evening packing up kit. Bath and bed early.

14/6/41 Saturday. Up early and finished packing. The Sergeant would not give me a pass till SSQ cleared me, so went to SSQ and got some forms, then got pass and back to SSQ where actual pass produced and ran for 9.00 a.m. train. Arrived London 10.45 a.m. and wandered around then caught 11.40 a.m. to Sheerness arriving at 1.40 p.m. Went to Miss Jones but she was home with pneumonia. Home and then along to Margaret's and found Peter there, so we all went along to Auntie Nellie's. Peter and I then home for tea and wander round field with Dad and tree climbing just like old times. Then to town for drink. Met Eileen and family and for final drink and then Peter and I walked home very merry, but Dad abed, so OK.

15/6/41 Sunday. Up 10.15 a.m. and felt OK. In the morning I looked at the bees with Dad. Afternoon to Margaret's with Peter and walked to Minster. Met Margaret and Henry and walked back via Mrs Reed's. Then home and looked at bees again. Split hive – one nucleus and one packed in travelling case to send away. Then for walk over hill and to Margaret's for an hour or so. Back 10.00 p.m. Bed early.

16/6/41 Monday. Up early and caught 7.30 a.m. with Peter to London. Watched Dockies going to work! Left Peter at Chatham. Arrived in London 9.30 a.m. Caught 10.00 a.m. train to Wendover – grand run and Wendover seems a jolly country town. Went straight to the Hospital. Got Hospital Blue – rotten fit and cut still. In the afternoon the consultant examined my eye with probes and syringes! Rotten. Spent most of time writing and jigsaw puzzle. Bed 9.30 p.m.

17/6/41 Tuesday. Up 6.30 a.m. and discovered no AC electricity, so shaved with a razor. Did ward job and spent rest of day lounging about. Not going to operate till Thursday.

18/6/41 Wednesday. Up early and rotten shave. Lazy day in sun. Told operation put off till Saturday! Group Captain Livingstone came round to see us and suggested a new operation. Read East Lyon. Bath.

19/6/41 Thursday. Usual day in sun, swotting meteorology and navigation. Evening for a stroll to Wendover.

20/6/41 Friday. Usual day. CO's inspection. Anaesthetist examined me. Evening went to town through the woods.

21/6/41 Saturday. 8.00 a.m. first shot. 9.00 a.m. taken to theatre for a sleep and given second shot and off I went. In theatre three hours and did not wake till 6.00 p.m. Very sick all evening. They found broken nose as well and no tear sac. Rotten night. Parcel from Margaret of green salad.

22/6/41 Sunday. Lyle did not remove dressing or look at it – did not want to disturb it. Just lay all day, could not read or write, although only one eye covered.

23/6/41 Monday. Had eye redressed – nine stitches. Afternoon up for a bath.

24/6/41 Tuesday. Usual sort of day. Dressing changed.

25/6/41 Wednesday. Usual day. Dressed, up for a bit.

26/6/41 Thursday. Stitches out and up all afternoon.

27/6/41 Friday. Up and to Library. Bandages off, shade on.

28/6/41 Saturday. Usual day.

29/6/41 Sunday. Morning church. Rest of day as usual sunbathing and reading. Shade off eye and dark glasses, but the eye started to water.

30/6/41 Monday. Washing up duty in the morning. Joan arrived in the afternoon for a week with her Mother. Met them at the station and then for a walk with Joan. Back 9.00 p.m. Pay. Bed.

And so it went on for weeks. Joan and her mother left after a week, and Charles had just to let the healing process take its course. He read, sunbathed and took walks into Wendover when he could.

13/7/41 Sunday. Better sort of day – i.e. had eye syringed which was not so good and then, what I found afterwards was the CMB *(Central Medical Board)*, though I thought it was just an exam. Spent the afternoon reading and sleeping and in evening I was told I was to parade tomorrow for discharge to light duties – i.e. no leave, which shook me. Weather thundery all day till evening, when turned out really fine.

14/7/41 Monday. Told to parade in the morning, but then told to wait till the afternoon. In the morning I had syringe again! Afternoon paraded but no leave! Had argument with Orderly Sergeant but got my own kit, so changed and went for walk in the afternoon to the War Memorial, but did not bother about a drink.

15/7/41 Tuesday. Left Hosp 9.10 a.m. after lots of chasing about and saying bye bye. Should have caught 9.15 a.m. train arriving at Cambridge 1.30 p.m. but no! Caught 10.15 a.m. after posting lots of my stuff on. Called to see Marion Young at Edgware but out at work so yarned with her Mother and then to town. Rang Gordon. Had dinner and nap in Services club. Met Gordon 5.00 p.m. in Streatham – to Victoria and met Peter and all to Streatham again. Had a real ripping night on tiles and the Locarno Dance Hall. Took Irish girl home and she wants me to write. Back to Gordon's flat 1.00 a.m. and bed.

16/7/41 Wednesday. Up 4.30 a.m. and rush off without a shave. Caught 5.30 a.m. and arrived at camp 8.15 a.m. Got in with nothing said. Went to SSQ with a bit of wangling got seven days leave. Back for a bath, shave and haircut and filled in forms. Then went to the CO. He called me in and offered me a posting or leave. So I took the posting as others seem to be left hanging about a lot, drilling, guarding etc. In the afternoon paraded fifteen of us for FFI. Waited one and half hours and came back without! I went to Accounts and collected £5 and did nothing for rest of the afternoon. Evening went to see La Traviata by Sadlers Wells Opera Company and late to bed.

17/7/41 Thursday. Up 6.00 a.m. and very busy doing nothing. All we did was FFI and slept or started packing. Afternoon to Equipment and got props* and third shirt, collars and socks and that was that! Bought new C de L pipe. Evening writing packing and Bath then to YMCA for big supper and read papers. Bath and bed early.

18/7/41 Friday. Same lazy day. Packed up all kit. Afternoon had pay £3 and sign for flying kit and that was all for the day. But they made a hopeless mess getting us off. In the morning I heard that there was an overseas posting in two weeks. But it was too late for me to get off this one! Am I mad! Left 6.15 p.m. via Bletchingley and got to Crewe at 11.30 p.m. and had three hours wait.

19/7/41 Saturday. At Crewe got in a coach of chaps from Torquay going through to Millom via Preston. Arrive at camp, way out along coast at dinner time!! Spent afternoon just standing about in camp as our huts were well out. After tea we were free. Went to Millom to have a look round and to NAAFI. Back to hut and unpacking and bed 11.00 p.m. Huts seem pretty comfortable but as yet no power and no hot water, so to camp for bath and

---

* "Props", or propellers, are a badge of rank. The two bladed prop indicates that Charles was promoted to Leading Aircraftman when he completed his course at ITW.

shave. Little red tape and easy hours, but Millom is rotten. Country seems good.

RAF Millom was a remote station on the Cumbrian coast about eight miles from Barrow-in-Furness as the crow flies, but about twenty miles by road. It was the home of No. 2 Air Observers' School. Charles was now about to start the real business of flying, and could feel that, eleven months after joining up, he was at last making real progress.

CHAPTER 3

Flying Training

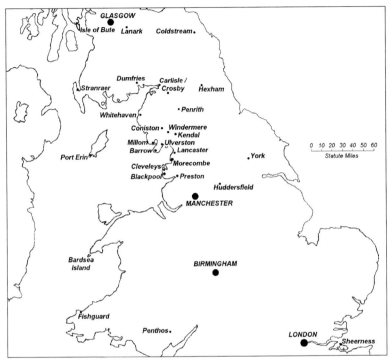

Charles's Travels – July to December 1941

20/7/41 Sunday. Did not wake till 9.30 a.m., so up 10.00 a.m. and spent the morning writing and tidying and sewing etc. Afternoon walked into Millom for some food and back another way to tea. Evening walked by road to Silecroft and had drink and yarn with local coast guard and back via golf links and coast. Bed 11.00 p.m. and left shave till tomorrow.

21/7/41 Monday. Started on mucking about; had classroom quizzes. Wing Commander's parade with gramophone. Photos, FFI, PT, Officer's lecture, Wing

Commander's lecture etc etc. Hell of a job in the morning getting washed and shaved and up to breakfast and waiting for it. Evening writing, NAAFI, repairs and eats. Bed 10.30 p.m.

22/7/41 Tuesday. Still no power, so shaving with razor and cold water. Got going today with DR, instruments, morse and airmanship. Evening out to send telegram to Joyce for twenty first and got pally with phone girl. Then NAAFI for supper. Wrote up notes. Rigged up intercom and bed. Got rotten cold.

23/7/41 Wednesday. Usual sort of day, but still no electricity. Still doing ITW work apart from instruments. Got very poor result in aldis. PT and showers jolly good. Evening I phoned Miss Wilkinson again but did not fix date. Then to Millom to see about trains to Blackpool. Put in for weekend pass. Back to supper then writing and studying. Bed early as had rotten cold.

24/7/41 Thursday. Navigation etc in the morning. Afternoon went for hour's spin in Anson. Quite good run down coast to Morecombe. Evening rang Barrow again and then supper in NAAFI and to concert. Did some sewing and study. Put through pass to Blackpool for weekend. Still no mail. Bed 10.30 p.m.

The Avro Anson had been in RAF service since the mid-1930s. It started life as a Maritime Patrol aircraft powered by two 295 hp Cheetah VI engines, and had a wing span of 56 ft 6 in. With a maximum speed of 163 knots, a cruising speed of 137 knots and a bomb load of two 100 lb bombs and eight 20 lb bombs, it was barely up to the task of taking on the German Navy. In an unfortunate incident where an Anson crew attacked a British submarine in error and scored hits, the only damage to the submarine consisted of broken light bulbs. The damage to the pride of RAF Coastal Command was perhaps more lasting! By 1941 most Coastal Command squadrons had been re-equipped with the Lockheed Hudson, a much more effective aircraft in the role. The Ansons, however, continued service as training aircraft for pilots, navigators and air gunners, a role to which they were much more suited.

> 25/7/41 Friday. DR *(Dead reckoning)* navigation and instruments etc all day. Pay parade and PT in the afternoon. Still no power! No letter from Joyce to say where staying at Blackpool so evening sent telegram (2/4)! Supper and then sewing repairs and prepare for quick getaway tomorrow.
>
> 26/7/41 Saturday. Usual morning. Afternoon collected 36 hour pass and to cricket. Wicket keeper and hurt finger. Got away at 4.00 p.m. Lift to Millom, return to Barrow and connected straight to Carnforth when paid return from Grange. At Carnforth got lift and an Army van to

The course photograph. Charles is seated on the extreme right of the picture. The snow on the ground indicates that it was taken late in the course, and the empty chair may be for Tom Bradbury, killed on 17 October 1941. Crosses above the heads of some of the course members indicate later deaths. Annotations on the back of the picture indicate that most were killed in action.

Lancaster then a car right through to Cleveleys and tram to Blackpool. Found Joyce out and left no message; went looking for her then back but not in so went to see if she would meet my train in. Back again at 10.30 p.m. but still not in and was I mad and mudded whole evening. So kip in Salvation Army place.

27/7/41 Sunday. Up 6.30 a.m. and off up to toilets for wash and brush up – 2d. Then along to South Shore and met Joyce. I of course had a long tale of woe and she very poor excuses. The fact that she knew I was arriving on the 9.20 p.m. and was not likely to know her address she seems to have dismissed as all she could say was that she did not think I would come. I learnt afterwards that Perce was there with them. Anyway, we went for a walk and sit on sands etc in the morning. Afternoon we met Perce, had a drink and lunch then Joyce and I went mad on funfair till tea when I had to leave to catch 7.00 p.m. train and she saw me off. But I feel after last night this will have to end. Tiring journey (only paying to Preston) back and arrive camp just on midnight when I did all my polishing.

28/7/41 Monday. Got up at quarter to six and did all bullshit for CO's parade and after breakfast found I was hut orderly and so had to come all way back and need not even have got up till 7.00 a.m.! 10.00 a.m. went down for two hours flying, but after we had drawn chutes etc the weather clouded and it was cancelled, so wasted the morning. Afternoon as usual. Evening stayed in writing and swotted and then out for drink. Bed 10.20 p.m.

29/7/41 Tuesday. All day on plotting and instruments etc with PT and shower. Evening writing, reading and nap and went to NAAFI for supper and out for drink.

30/7/41 Wednesday. Up early but in time nevertheless and did lots of really interesting plotting. At 3.00 p.m. we were told we were flying, and I had arranged to see Miss Wilkinson at Barrow. I was all togged up for it, so at 5.00 p.m. I dashed out to phone on bike and just caught her. And back and away – were going to Dumfries but over Kendal we got caught in really terrific storm and I thought we were finished. But we got to the coast and way down to Millom. Supper and to Hut. Bed late.

Such was the routine of the course. Even at the height of the British summer flying could be curtailed because of bad weather, but at least some progress was being made. At the weekends Charles liked to get away from the military environment and visit friends and relations. Now he had another girl friend – Olive. She seemed to share his love of the open spaces.

2/8/41 Saturday. Up 5.30 a.m. and rush around as were flying at 9.30 a.m. However, after all when we got as far as Whitehaven the cloud was so heavy and low that we came back. Navigation most of the day, and morse, PT etc till 5.30 p.m. Tea, change etc and caught 6.50 p.m. train to Barrow. Had wash and brush up and shave and met Olive, but could not find anywhere to sleep. So went to dance and I came back to camp to sleep.

3/8/41 Sunday. Up 8.00 a.m. and did all necessary and got into hiking kit and what a treat. Caught 9.50 a.m. train to Coniston and it was a lovely day. In the morning I walked all along lake side and had a nap. (Had dumped gas bag at hotel). Afternoon met train with Olive and Isabel and we went straight away climbing and God it was great. Visibility was fine and we had grand view. After tea and rest, down another way and just in time for a good drink and to train which got me back early and then bed 11.00 p.m.

Then back to the real world of lectures, PT and lessons. Soon he was flying again.

8/8/41 Friday. Morning started lectures and then told we were flying. Went out at 8.30 a.m. and did not get up till 11.30 a.m. Had good trip up to Scotland (Kelso) in an Anson. Back 2.00 p.m. for late dinner and to lectures. Evening pay and writing and reading etc. Bed early.

9/8/41 Saturday. Had to get up at 4.20 a.m. to fly at 6.00 a.m.! Had good trip and saw sun rise above clouds over Scotland. Back for breakfast and DR navigation. Noon collected tunic from tailor (made a good job of it) and Haircut. Afternoon flying again and should have gone over York, but pilot muffed it and ran off runway and nearly into other planes – shook me. So spent the afternoon writing, reading and morse as there were no other kites. Evening to town to see if bike arrived, but no. Shopping and sandwich for tomorrow. Back to supper and writing, reading etc. Bed 10.00 p.m.

10/8/41 Sunday. Had extra hour sleep as clocks put back. Got up at 8.30 a.m. and caught 9.50 a.m. train to Coniston. Clouds very low and dull. Walked up round Old man and into Dunnerdale. Down Dunnerdale and had lunch, then over tops again. Met another girl hiker and joined up down to Foxfield. She to Barrow and I on to Millom. Back 10.00 p.m. and still dark so straight to bed early.

11/8/41 Monday. Up early and reported sick with teeth to avoid Wing Commander's parade and had blighter filled. Most of day on bombing and then flying in evening but did not get far as was map reading again and cloud very low, so to NAAFI for supper and back to hut, but dark comes on early now and with no light little time to swot. So bed early.

12/8/41 Tuesday. Up early but parade scratched as rain. Morning on AMBT, Bombing and Bombing Test (theory). Afternoon just very easy, in fact I went off to sleep. Evening to Millom and collected bike and now it's fine to ride about instead of walk. To NAAFI and then back to bed.

13/8/41 Wednesday. Up a little later as I had a bike. Good mixture of DR, bombs and compass and meteorology. Also PT. Evening flying and in spite of bad weather completed cross country to Corlick and Stranraer. Then four of us to West County pub for dinner to celebrate Butcher's girl's birthday, and on to dance, but I only danced once. Bed midnight.

14/8/41 Thursday. Full parade again, then all day on bombs etc. Nothing too interesting. PT again. Evening reading etc and then NAAFI for supper. On way back got a puncture so spent evening mending it and clearing up. Bed early again as still no power.

15/8/41 Friday. In the morning I should have done first navigation exercise to York, Hexham and back but weather bad and cloud low, so went up to get a three drift wind and that was OK. Briefed again for evening but turned worse and was cancelled. Evening to Millom shopping and to station to get my ticket for tomorrow. Did bit of study and rest of time in NAAFI. Bed early.

The routine of the course continued. Charles went to Huddersfield for a weekend, studied, and flew when aircraft serviceability and the weather allowed it.

26/8/41 Tuesday. Up 5.00 a.m. and to Ops room at 6.00 a.m. and prepared 441 for long flight as I was first Nav. Then at last moment kite put unserviceable and so drifted back to get some more breakfast. Had signals and astro. In the afternoon DR and at 3.30 p.m. a flight to Penrith, Coldstream, Lanark, Stranraer, Port Erin, base. Fine trip but longest so far and did not get back till 7.00 p.m. Belated tea and to hut to sort things out and to NAAFI for supper. Electric lights on so I now have radio and electric razor. Bed late and tired.

27/8/41 Wednesday. At 9.30 a.m. had to take a Squadron Leader to Penthos. Navigation not too good, but pilot lousy. He did not keep course or know what a 60 / 120* was. Back 3.00 p.m. and idled. Evening study and NAAFI. Three planes did not come back from A flight. One we know is safe. Bed early.

28/8/41 Thursday. Very slack day. Afternoon should have been in AMBT and Spotlight but only did quarter of an hour in Spotlight all afternoon. Evening swotting and writing. All missing men came back including Hayman and Hanah this evening after a crash landing on the Isle of Bute. Bed early.

29/8/41 Friday. Up early and very easy morning and even went to sleep. Afternoon had bombing inter exam and it was lousy! Stayed in to do a plot but with little success. Rang, or tried to, Olive. Then to NAAFI and spot of study.

30/8/41 Saturday. Up late. Dashed off for flying. Three drift. Spot of bombing theory. Afternoon Spotlight trainer and turrets. Evening another plot and Millom for grub for tomorrow. NAAFI and swot.

* A 60 / 120 is an alteration of heading 60° either side of the required heading to allow the Navigator to find the drift on three different headings without delaying the aircraft's progress significantly. The Navigator can then calculate the wind at the aircraft's altitude.

31/8/41 Sunday. Up 7.45 a.m, dashed around, had breakfast and caught 9.45 a.m. to Coniston. Met Olive at Foxfield alone this time and together we set off up Old Man. Stopped for grub and co and so darned hot stayed from noon to 2.40 p.m.! Had good rest, sunbathed and bits of fun and frolic. Then on up to the Old Man and down to Torver, but alas no grub so had drinks while waiting for trains and so back by 10.00 p.m. and to bed.

Over the next two and a half weeks the weather deteriorated and many flights were cancelled or curtailed. At the weekends Charles went hill walking in the Lake District with Olive or to Huddersfield. But in the middle of the month the course was given four days' leave.

18/9/41 Thursday. Up early, all excitement but we had to have the usual day with exams! Pay parade and away 4.00 p.m. Caught 4.45 p.m. and arrived Preston 6.20 p.m. but too late for dinner we had ordered. So Bradbury, Flying Officer Batiah and I went out drinking. Took two lasses home and got 10.50 p.m. to London. Tom sick but we both slept all way.

19/9/41 Friday. Arrived London 5.05 a.m. but on way I had had my case and hat lifted. Reported it to Lost Property Office and caught 6.15 a.m. to Sheerness and home 9.20 a.m. Wash and brush up and to see Margaret. To Sheerness to buy hat, pyjamas etc which were pinched. Chalet for dinner stroll round field and along to Margaret. Auntie Nellie was out so I stayed and yarned till Peter arrived. After two hours and long pow wow through to see Dil, but she out so popped in for drink etc and at 10.10 p.m. to see Dil again - this time in. Peter went to sleep and we yarned. When he woke sick all over place and Dil and I had to clear it up. Got him away at 12.15 a.m. and taxi home and so put him to bed. I felt OK strangely.

20/9/41 Saturday. Up early and caught 8.30 a.m. to London with Peter. Spent the morning shopping etc. Soon met Gordon and had drink. Then for lunch. Rang Maureen but she was on duty and Marian, so we just had a threesome. Had few taxi rides and walk round Hyde Park. Booked in Tuscan Hotel and had tea. Then to Palace to see Chu Chin Chow in Stalls with Mr Jetson. Very good indeed. Took Marian (King) to East Ham and then back at midnight. Had big meal in Lyons Strand Brasserie and on to Tuscon Hotel at 1.00 a.m.

21/9/41 Sunday. Up 5.00 a.m. and breakfast and off to Victoria. Arrived Auntie Nellie's 11.45 a.m. Up to Chalet for dinner and spent the afternoon with Dad, but he was busy and it meant dashing about. After tea along to Margaret till 7.45 p.m. when I went down to Dil's and had a jolly nice tea. Left midnight.

22/9/41 Monday. Up early and after clean up along to Margaret's then with her to the station and caught 11.18 a.m. train to London. Went to Euston about my case and dumped luggage (apples) and after dinner to Streatham. Met Maureen and to town – saw Lady Hamilton. Tea and chat on Embankment till 9.00 p.m. when I went to meet Bradbury off train, but Oscar did not turn up. To Brasserie Universal and on to Euston. Had not too good a journey.

23/9/41 Tuesday. Arrived Millom 6.00 a.m., boarded a bus to camp and arrived just in time for Parade. We all felt pretty scruffy for the morning but did nothing much. Afternoon on range with pistols and VGO. Sergeant got shot in belly. Evening to Millom shopping, but could not get an attaché case. Then thoroughly overhauled bike and oiled it. Bed late.

Charles achieved just one flight before the end of the month. He picked up an ear infection which needed treatment, and despite the accident to the Sergeant on the range, the course did plenty of gunnery. He had some further correspondence with LMS Railway on the subject of his lost suitcase.

2/10/41 Thursday. Treatment - Lectures. Got 98% on compass exam pre-leave. Afternoon flying, high level bombing grouping 50 yds error. Evening study and NAAFI. Bed early.

3/10/41 Friday. Up early and Oscar and I on three hour trip to York, Scotland and Isle of Man. He was first nav. Afternoon meteorology. Evening just as I was changing for football, Oscar and I were sent for to take Wing Commander and Signals Officer for night Navigation trip as an experiment to see if possible. Strato-cumulus cloud at 2000 ft. Sedbergh, Carlisle, Dumfries, Isle of Man and back to base. But W/T went unserviceable at Dumfries so set course base. I was first Nav and did pretty well. Late supper and Bed 11.30 p.m. Missed pay parade.

4/10/41 Saturday. Up 5.30 a.m. for early bombing and dropped from 7000 ft. Back 10.15 a.m. and down for pay. Afternoon I was not on early detail so kept out of way down in classroom doing nothing and then dodged off early on bike and caught 4.45 p.m. train. Went right through to Huddersfield and arrived at midnight. Popped down to Annexe. Then night staff –

5/10/41 Sunday. – and day staff. Office, shave etc. Collected some civvies and camera and to Nurses home to see the Sisters and then breakfast with Sister Wilkie.

Saw Miss T and went to town with her. Did not see the Master. Met Audrey in town and for walk. Then to see Joan at noon and to Lunch. Back 4.00 p.m. with Joan to Leeds. 5.45 p.m. back to Millom arriving at midnight after good sleep in train.

6/10/41 Monday. Up late and for treatment. Lectures all day and meteorology exam. Evening played goalie for house and won 6 – 1 against workshops. Noon dashed into Millom and collected lost case – all OK except electric razor which had been pinched. Bed early.

The win was clearly a major event for the course – and the photograph shows Charles as goalkeeper in the team photograph, now sporting a fine moustache.

9/10/41 Thursday. Up early for bombing but after we had bombed up we were cancelled. So lectures all day. From noon had continuous downpour which had not stopped when I went to bed. Evening drying things out and writing.

The Football Team.
Charles is in the centre of the back row.

10/10/41 Friday. Up early for navigation trip. I was first nav but only up for one hour when turned back through bad weather. Afternoon a second navigation trip and got right round though as first nav I missed *(unreadable)* and arrived in Eire. Went along coast for long time but not challenged and then arrived back home OK. Back late. So study till late bed.

11/10/41 Saturday. Up late and should have been bombing. Weather not fit so did practically nothing all day. Evening went to book up at Grange for the weekend but all hotels full. So decided to spend the weekend in camp. Very disappointed. Went to Millom for radio but not ready yet. Spent evening polishing and tidying, yarning and sewing. Then reading till late.

12/10/41 Sunday. Such a grand morning that I got on my shorts etc and set off on my bike, struck all across some great country (very hilly) and arrived at Lake Windermere for a super lunch at the Swan, Newby Bridge. Then after rest back to camp along a different route. Spent evening writing and reading. Bed early tired and happy.

(On the modern roads that is 22 miles each way. It was probably further on roads in 1941!)

13/10/41 Monday. Bombing day, but weather bad and only got one low level trip and apart from that did nothing. Evening to Millom for radio but not ready yet. Swotting and bed late.

14/10/41 Tuesday. In the morning went to see MO about my ear, and he gave it a good hiding! Rest of day waiting for gunnery and as usual did not get up till 6.00 p.m. and then got stoppage. Late tea and stayed in classroom and NAAFI as on camp defences and had to stop in camp. So I did some reading till early bed.

15/10/41 Wednesday. Up early and shower. Down to dispersal for shave etc and back for breakfast and treatment. Morning AMBT and turrets. Afternoon gunnery. Noon Flying Officer Harvey saw me and said he had put my name forward for a commission subject to MO's approval for my eye! Evening studying all time.

16/10/41 Thursday. Up late and lectures all day. Morning eight of us were told we had to go for interview for commission. So dashed down to change and clean up etc. But I was on end of list owing to medical acceptance and did not get in in time, so it was postponed. Evening played football in goal, but let two impossible ones in. Then to hut and preparing 441 for trip tomorrow. Usual choring and reading. Bed late.

17/10/41 Friday. Up early for trip. First nav with Oscar. Peel, Fishguard, Bardsey Island, Great Ormes Head, Base. Jolly good trip over three hundred miles. Tons to do and plenty to see with various alterations of weather. Took three hours. One plane landed in Wales and one crashed near Fishguard and Tom Bradbury was drowned. Afternoon bit of plotting and W/T as weather too bad for more flying. Evening to Millom for radio but not ready yet. In hut yarning all evening. Bed late.

18/10/41 Saturday. Up early but did not go on parade. Weather lousy, had poured with rain all night. Put on best again but did not see the Wing Commander! Lectures and plotting all morning. At noon dashed off for train to Blackpool at 12.40 p.m. Left my case on Millom Station and arrived Blackpool 4.30 p.m. Phoned Millom Station and asked them to send it on but had not arrived by bed time. Went to see Tom's brother and told him the bad news, then back to Stuart Hotel and met Joan. Went to Tower dancing and looking around. Walked back and bed midnight.

19/10/41 Sunday. Had good night in double bed. Up 8.00 a.m., cold bath and after breakfast to Station with Joan for my case, but had not arrived. Therefore I could not shave etc! Icedrome was not open in the morning so we took a taxi up to Cleveleys and walked back in sea spray along prom. Dinner at 1.00 p.m. and then to Pleasure Beach and to the Icedrome. Had to join the club and become a member to get in! After tea back to Station for 4.50 p.m. train. Had lost my return half at the Hotel. Landlord gave me one to Manchester! My case had not turned up yet! Hotel only cost 13/2. Slow train did not arrive till 12.25 a.m. Had job getting bike out. Bed 1.00 a.m.

20/10/41 Monday. Hut orderly then flying. Down 2.00 p.m. and told I was to see the Wing Commander, so hastily washed and changed etc and to interview. Was one of eight who got through him. Evening to Millom for radio. Cost 5/9 and it's bit better but wants a valve. Back intending to swot but did little. Bed late.

21/10/41 Tuesday. Quiet day in lectures. Afternoon, had medical board for commission – OK. Evening preparing for trip tomorrow and swotting. Bed early.

22/10/41 Wednesday. Up early for navigation. York, Hexham. Landed at Crosby. Stranraer – Base. Afternoon, in classroom as no time for another trip. Heard from Olive who was sick again so as I am not going tomorrow. Spent evening swotting, writing and yarning.

23/10/41 Thursday. Bombing all day but only got 160 – 180 yds on high level application so did not pass. Evening to Millom but case had not turned up. Then swotting and bed late.

24/10/41 Friday. Bombing all day again. High level

application, but got passes by fluke today. Down late in evening and little time to do anything. Bed very late.

25/10/41 Saturday. Morning lectures etc. Afternoon did nothing constructive. Got away at 4.30 p.m. and so caught train, arriving at Huddersfield at midnight and to female Nurses' home for the night.

26/10/41 Sunday. 6.30 a.m. to see the night staff. Breakfast. To Nurses home and to see all day staff. Up to Joan for lunch and caught 4.00 p.m. bus to Leeds. And so train to Millom. Had slept and did not arrive Millom till 12.30 a.m.

Flying came in fits and starts. As autumn changed into winter, more flights were cancelled, and the course fell behind schedule. From the beginning of November they started working on Sundays as well as on Saturdays. However, at the weekends Charles generally saw Olive, sometimes going walking, but often, as the weather deteriorated, just socialising and going to the pictures.

15/11/41 Saturday. Up 8.00 a.m. Breakfast, wash and general tidy up and off to Barrow on 11.30 a.m. Booked up at Duke of Edinburgh hotel and had lunch there with Olive. Then 1.30 p.m. train to Morecombe. Had half an hour or so in Lancaster. In Morecombe we had a look around, tea and drink. Then to see On Approval with Diana Churchill and Barry Barnes. Another drink, chips and 10.40 p.m. train. Arrived Barrow 1.00 a.m. and to hotel and lovely bed.

16/11/41 Sunday. Had breakfast in bed and did not get up till 10.30 a.m. Good long bath and general clean up and lunch 12.30 p.m. Then read paper in lounge till 2.00 p.m. when I went out to meet Olive. But as the weather was so bad we went to Reggie's for the afternoon and stayed to tea and evening. Learnt that Olive could play piano and sing. Caught 10.45 p.m. train and got wet through walking back.

17/11/41 Monday. All of us overslept and did not get up till 7.15 a.m. Bags of panic. Had very easy day doing nothing. Evening phoned Olive and wrote letters and yarned. Now beginning to feel really matrimonially inclined with Olive.

18/11/41 Tuesday. Gunnery in the morning and fired 200 rounds and got 50 hits. Afternoon on turrets and easy till tea, then prepared flight plan for tomorrow and off to Barrow. Met Olive at 8.00 p.m. and for quiet drink and back on 9.20 p.m. train – broached subject of marriage after this war!! Bed 10.20 p.m. very tired.

19/11/41 Wednesday. Up early for flying. But did not complete original trip owing to bad weather and no W/T so went north. First nav. Did not fly in the afternoon. Eric Claridge and Bingham killed. Hit side of mountain. Evening rang Olive and yarned in hut till late.

20/11/41 Thursday. Up early as hut orderly. Morning bomb panel and turrets. Afternoon played football in goal. Evening just mucked about, phoned Olive and out for chips and drink. Bed 11.00 p.m. Been trying to decide whether to go to Huddersfield for the weekend as Phyllis had asked me to, or to see Olive. But Olive now says she has tickets for the dance at Barrow on Friday. However I still can't decide.

21/11/41 Friday. Up early. Morning turrets. Afternoon yarning in classroom. Wanted to go to Huddersfield but Olive had bought tickets for dance so caught 6.45 p.m. train, booked at Duke of Edinburgh, wash shave etc and to dance at town hall. Had jolly good time with Isabel and Billie. Bed 1.30 a.m.

22/11/41 Saturday. Slept in till 10.30 a.m. Breakfast in bed, bath etc and out to meet Oscar and Bill off train and to lunch with them. Then shopping and met Olive and Billie and for tea and yarn in Ritz. Stayed all afternoon and had hot tea and saw Olive to work at 5.00 p.m. and we four to movies. Met Olive at 8.00 p.m. and for a drink. Caught 9.20 p.m. train back. Bed 11.30 p.m.

23/11/41 Sunday. Up early and parade. Should have flown but weather unfit so mucked about all morning. Afternoon astro. Evening stayed in and read and wrote and yarned. Bed early.

24/11/41 Monday. Up very early for parade. Morning, left on our own. Afternoon, 200 yard range. Evening stayed in alone.

25/11/41 Tuesday. Morning flying on gunnery. Afternoon football in goal as usual. Evening astro sights and night bombing – one direct hit. Bed 11.30 p.m.

26/11/41 Wednesday. Morning in astro room with astro graph. Noon – turrets. Afternoon just filled in. Should have been on air firing but after waiting about did not get up. Evening should have been on extra turrets, but cut it and went to Barrow to see Olive. Back 10.00 p.m. and after usual clearing up. Bed 11.30 p.m.

27/11/41 Thursday. The big event was Exam results. Average 86.5%, position 17th. DR 82.7%, compass 95.9%, instruments 95%, maps and charts 91.7%, meteorology 75%, D/F W/T 60%, photo 87.5%, recce 92.5%, signals 96%, photo oral 100%, a/c Recce 95% – Not bad. Spent all day trying to get my 200 rounds off, but did not fire – only flew once. Got battle dress issue. Evening stayed in writing and yarning and cleaning. Bed early.

28/11/41 Friday. Morning finished off turrets – sighting Browning and pyrotechnics exams and tried to get 200 rounds in but no flying – so astro sights and yarn with Flying Officer Harvey. Learnt my commission had definitely got through. Afternoon got off 200 rounds air firing OK but down too late to catch 4.45 p.m. so arrived Barrow 7.40 p.m. Booked at Duke of Edinburgh and met Olive and Isabel and to Criterion. Then saw Isabel home and Olive and I walked home and discussed the pros and cons of marriage after war and why. Bed late.

29/11/41 Saturday. Up 8.30 a.m. and down to breakfast then back and bath and clean up and to writing room till lunch when I met Olive and we had it together. Then caught bus along coast road to Fisherman's and set off to walk to Ulverston but after two hours found ourselves back where we started, so walked to Bardsea and had great tea in Bardsea Arms in small sitting room to ourselves and Olive played piano – had ham and eggs inter alia. Caught 6.10 p.m. bus back and had drink with lads at Criterion and then to see Once a Crook. Caught late train back! Bed 1.00 a.m.

30/11/41 Sunday. Up early and way up for flying but cancelled so on astro. Flew in the afternoon but turned back on account of weather! So just played about dreaming, stayed in hut and did some packing.

1/12/41 Monday. Hut orderly so up later and missed bullshit parade. Morning in the DR trainer. Afternoon easy and astro. Evening reading and yarning and down to ring Olive and for chips. Had rotten cold in head.

2/12/41 Tuesday. Morning astro. Afternoon kit inspection. Evening swot on astro, rung Olive and yarned as usual. Bed late.

3/12/41 Wednesday. Astro exams all day and think I did

pretty well. Evening to Barrow again and to Criterion with Olive. Bed 11.30 p.m.

4/12/41 Thursday. Up early, but did practically nothing all day. Evening the course dinner at Broughton with twenty odd guests. Went out and back in station transport and had real rip snorting do. Almost everyone got tight and leapt about on tables etc and were sick as fun on way back and had to be put to bed. I was fortunate and did not have too much. Bed 1.00 a.m.

5/12/41 Friday. Up at 6.15 a.m. and had to go and call all the others! Again did nothing all day except football in the afternoon. Evening to Barrow. Did not intend staying night but felt too tired so booked at Imperial. Spent evening with Olive and Billie at Criterion and took Olive home and in air raid shelter where we went too near the danger point so had to maintain terrific self control. However all OK. Bed 11.40 p.m.

6/12/41 Saturday. Did not get up till 10.45 a.m. Bath (breakfast in bed) etc. Shopping before met Olive at 12.30a.m. To Arnadall with lads for grub and on to Ritz lectures. Olive on duty 5.00 p.m. to 8.00 p.m. so after tea took Billie to see Dorothy Lamour and then met Olive again and to Criterion for evening. Back in late afternoon.

7/12/41 Sunday. Up early and in the morning mucked about a lot from one thing to another. Afternoon flying! Weather over sea foul with snow, hail etc and had to fly up to 15,000 ft to get over it and no Oxygen. W/T froze and no winds but got back OK. Caught 7.30 p.m. train to Barrow with Olive and Isabel and to Reggie's for evening. Isabel and Reggie left early and left us. Same as Friday evening – nothing disastrous happened but I regretted it – it will spoil everything. Back on late train and bed 12.30 p.m.

8/12/41 Monday. Up early and full parade. Morning in the classroom with some lectures. Afternoon I was told by the Squadron Leader that my commission is official and some "gen". Then with whole course to Millom to see Target for Tonight. Tea at YMCA and back to camp and packing and sorting things out. Bed 11.00 p.m.

9/12/41 Tuesday. Lazy day again till afternoon when postings came through. Only alternatives are overseas Wellingtons – i.e. Bombers – or School of Recce. I chose overseas which also meant seventeen days leave as against seven days. But later in evening on thinking things out while packing decided to change it if possible and have Xmas leave. Prepared three parcels to send on by post and still have tons of stuff left. Yarning and bed 11.30 p.m.

10/12/41 Wednesday. Up for flying but kite unserviceable and afternoon flying cancelled for weather. So in classroom and I gave talk on bees. Evening dodged off to Barrow again for last time and to Criterion for quiet drink. Back and bit of packing and bed. Definitely changed posting with Oscar and am going to Squires Gate on recce course.

11/12/41 Thursday. Another day dodging about and handing in instruments. Evening took bike to station and sent it off. Then to West County Hotel and up to Olive who was staying the night for A4B's farewell dinner. With Harvey and wife, Brookes, Beattie and wives and Mrs Coates, Allen and Arnott. Had really good dinner and time after. Olive spending most of time on piano and me with the lads. I drank too much gin and was sick in Olive's room saying good night! Then had job getting bad sleep. Bed 2.30 a.m.

12/12/41 Friday. Up late. Morning passing out parade. Afternoon handed in uniform and change into civvies!

Then final packing and all off down to station to catch 11.45 a.m. train for last time. Rang Olive. Had dinner at Preston with Coates and Arnott and wives and on to London.

13/12/41 Saturday. Arrived 6.00 a.m. and went for turkish bath and some breakfast. Then to Moss Bros and got my uniform and met Margaret and Peter at Victoria and surprised them. Rest of the morning buying presents, booking hotel and shave, then down to Mitch's wedding for the afternoon. Back to town and at hotel too late to book a show, so Margaret, Peter and I saw Deanna Durbin film and had a meal at Strand Corner House. Bed 11.00 p.m.

14/12/41 Sunday. Breakfast in bed. Margaret said bye bye and went home by bus. Peter and I wandered about and caught 12.30 p.m. home. Spent the afternoon with Dad and evening with Dil. Peter left at 9.00 p.m. and Dil said that if I asked her again to marry her she would! I believe she meant it. Picked Peter up at the Goat and bed at 11.00 p.m.

Sheltered from the events of the war out on the Cumbrian coast, Charles had worked (and played) hard, and now proudly wore the brevet of an RAF air observer and the thin stripe of a Pilot Officer. Raids on British cities had continued, and London had suffered terrible damage in the Blitz. The RAF had carried the war to German cities too, and in August there had even been daylight raids on Cologne. Three hundred bombers had raided Germany in mid-October, but losses in Bomber Command were barely sustainable, with 35 bombers lost on one night alone in early November. Some of the pressure on Britain's cities had been relieved by the movement of German forces to the invasion of Russia in June 1941, and the spectacular advance of the

German armies almost to the gates of Moscow was halted only by the arrival of Russia's oldest ally, the winter. The ebb and flow of fortunes in North Africa saw Allied troops enter Benghazi once more in December. United States' neutrality had become more and more pro-Allied, but any ambiguity was finally ended by the Japanese assault on Pearl Harbour. America and the United Kingdom now formally declared war on Japan on 8 December, and three days later Germany and Italy declared war on the United States. The war was now truly global.

CHAPTER 4

Operational Training

Charles stayed at home with his father on the Isle of Sheppey for a few more days and then went with Peter to see his Aunt Marie at Farnham until the weekend.

On 18 December he made his way to Huddersfield once more, and there he stayed for Christmas. He took Joan out, saw old friends, and took part in St Luke's Hospital Christmas festivities, dressing up for a pantomime for the patients on Christmas Day. While there he received a

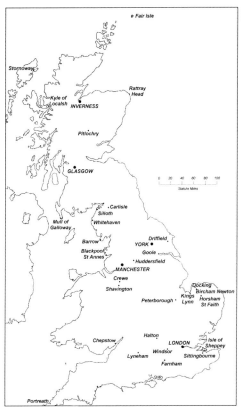

Charles's Travels – December 1941 to June 1942

telegram telling him to report to No. 3 School of General Reconnaissance at RAF Squires Gate, Blackpool on 27 December. Operational training was about to start.

27/12/41 Saturday. Caught 11.00 a.m. train to Blackpool. Slept all the way and arrived 1.30 p.m. Usual muck

81

about and then transport to St Anne's Hotel, our billet. Very comfortable and a contrast. Evening writing, then with Nev to Blackpool and drink and met three girls. Saw them home and took taxi to St Anne's. Bed midnight.

28/12/41 Sunday. Up 9.00 a.m. and met Joyce and 11.00 a.m. for coffee, back for lunch with Nev. After coffee, Nev back to the hotel and I and Joyce for walk etc. and dinner. Met Nev and Connie at Palatine in evening and had good drinking session. Back on last bus.

29/12/41 Monday. Up 7.00 a.m. and off to camp. Did nothing much in the morning except get books issues. Afternoon some introductory lectures. Collected seasons, but could not trace my kit bag. Evening stayed in hotel.

30/12/41 Tuesday. Up early and off to camp. Train very late as very foggy. In the morning signals, aldis, ship recce. Afternoon signals and finished early as Sergeants had to leave to move. Fixed up with Accounts Office for future marriage allowances if any etc. Identity cards altered. Collected outstanding mail. Evening stayed in writing and notes etc. Moved bedroom.

31/12/41 Wednesday. Up early and usual lectures all day. Had arranged a ripping party with Joyce, Tim and friends at her cousin's house – now empty. But alas I got on to Officer of Watch duty and just could not get off it. And so Nev went and told them bad news. While on duty sewed brevet and braid on battle dress and read. Bed early.

1/1/42 Thursday. Up at 6.30 a.m. and dashed for 6.41 a.m. train to St Anne's for wash etc and breakfast. Morning and afternoon usual lectures, ship recce, coding, aldis, DR etc. Spent evening in writing and reading. Bath and bed.

2/1/42 Friday. Up 7.00 a.m. Usual day of lectures. Kept late and caught late train to St Anne's, so had hell of a rush to get to Blackpool and meet train at 7.30 p.m. Was too late to go anyway, so first sat thinking and spent lots of money and got very pally and then had to dash for last train.

3/1/42 Saturday. Up as usual. Should have been flying but cancelled owing to weather, so did DR plot in the morning and got off after lunch. Met train (Joyce) at 3.00 p.m. and went to see George Formby as it rained hard. After tea went to dinner dance at Baronial Hall and had grand evening to finish on as she goes back tomorrow. Caught last train back and bed 11.20 p.m.

4/1/42. Sunday. Up at 7.00 a.m. as flying, but when we got there was cancelled. So did DR Plot. Back again for the afternoon and actually took off, but we were called back on account of bad weather and so wasted day. Wrote some letters and then to see Diana Durbin in Three Smart Girls. Back 10.00 p.m. and sat in lounge listening to Pirates of Penzance. Bed 11.15 p.m.

5/1/42 Monday. Up 7.00 a.m. and away for flying in the morning. Two planes were unserviceable and we got off late so back late and had a short lunch hour. Afternoon tactical floor*. Evening to see Diana Durbin in One Hundred Men and a Girl, and to Reggie Alan's for supper. Bed late.

Course flying was frequently interrupted by bad weather, as snow closed the airfield at Squires Gate for days on end. Olive came to visit, and expressed a wish that they should marry sooner rather than later. After she had departed, Joan came from

* The "Tactical Floor" is used even today to train those involved in maritime operations. Rows of tiered seats look down on a floor where training staff move model ships, submarines and aircraft, displaying a tactical problem to which students are expected to offer solutions.

Huddersfield with her mother for a week's visit to Blackpool, and was duly taken out. After a visit to Olive at Barrow towards the end of January, Charles confided to his diary that he was less than sure about the idea of early marriage. On February 2 the course came to an end with just two productive flights recorded in Charles's diary. All the others had been cancelled because of bad weather or aircraft unserviceability.

After four days' leave at Huddersfield and at Barrow seeing Olive, Charles arrived at No. 1 (Maritime) Operational Training Unit at RAF Silloth, 20 miles west of Carlisle.

3/2/42 Tuesday. Caught 3.20 p.m. train, changed at Whitehaven and arrived Carlisle 8.00 p.m. Had one hour wait for Silloth and met Bedwell on the train. Arrived Silloth 10.30 p.m. No-one knew anything about us and eventually we were sent out to Queens Hotel to sleep – real luxury.

4/2/42 Wednesday. Up 7.20 a.m. and at breakfast found the CO was staying here! Morning, late for first lecture and spent all day running round, but did nothing special. Had photo taken and lecture by RN Officer about submarines. Could not get any billets so had to stay at Queen's again. OK. Evening writing and then drinking in Officers' Mess lounge.

5/2/42 Thursday. Up early and to camp for breakfast. Morning exams on bombing and gunnery! Afternoon lectures mainly on what we had done – i.e. revision. Evening was billeted out went looking for the place. Walked right to Skinburness – two miles – and back and eventually found it not far from the camp. Proved a really comfortable place and they made me quite at home. Yarning in front room till late.

6/2/42 Friday. Up 6.30 a.m. and called the girls. Flying but did not get up as weather bad. So morning did nothing. Afternoon lectures on bombing etc. Got 77% yesterday. Evening stayed in billet. Very nice.

7/2/42 Saturday. Late up and then spent all day in crew room. Had one flip only and bump for thirty minutes with pilot on his first solo in a Hudson. Evening stayed in again. Bath and bed late. Letter from Mrs Acton re-Joan!

8/2/42 Sunday. Up early and away without waking others. In lectures all day and froze. Tomorrow's day off is cancelled for flying. So after dinner went for drink. Back early and bed with hot whisky.

9/2/42 Monday. Day off cancelled and up early for flying. Called girls and away, but weather not fit in the morning so had early lunch and up for four hours in the afternoon. Think I will crew up with one Sergeant Rostron. Evening home and reading and writing. Did some meteorology.

The decisions about forming a crew seem to have been left to individuals on the Operational Training Unit. Sergeant Bryan Rostron has written his own account of his RAF career, and in it he describes the process by which his crew was formed:

Chuck Collins joined me as navigator on February 9th and I was wondering what to do about the rest of my crew when Lee Barrett and Jimmy Craig approached me in the mess and asked if they could fly with me. I said I would be delighted and we first took to the air as a crew on 18th February by which time I has amassed the grand total of fourteen hours on Hudsons. Over the next few months I didn't think about it again, but, one night, when we were in the desert with 459 Squadron, sitting staring at the stars as the mess had run out of beer, I asked Jimmy why they had asked to be crewed up with me and his reply surprised me – apparently they had spent all their spare time at the end of the runway watching the trainee pilots landing and decided that I looked one of the safest – I was flattered!

10/2/42 Tuesday. Up early and early breakfast for flying. Did three hours in the morning. Afternoon we were sent for lectures on account of weather and then recalled as weather cleared. But by time I got there, the pilot was up on check so I disappeared at 4.00 p.m. and went to various places in camp, including library before going home. Back in to dinner and phoned Olive. Evening quietly indoors as had hell of a cold.

11/2/42 Wednesday. Up early after rotten night and off for flying. Three hours in the morning and took over a lot*. Nothing in the afternoon so left at 4.00 p.m. and home. Went into camp for dinner and along to Reggie's for evening. Bed 11.00 p.m. after mustard bath and whisky.

12/2/42 Thursday. Up late as not flying. Lectures all day. Evening stopped in reading and bed early.

13/2/42 Friday. Up early and away for flying. In spite of the date had good day with one bad landing. Off in the afternoon at 3.30 p.m. and home. Spent evening reading. Had gram from Peter – going on draft. Bed late.

14/2/42 Saturday. Up early for flying and got in quite a bit in the morning. Afternoon off late and home clearing up for tomorrow. Back at camp 5.30 p.m. for lecture and dinner. Evening reading and playing Monopoly. Bed 11.00 p.m.

15/2/42 Up 6.00 a.m. and so was Margaret (the Landlady's

* Observers and other crew members were frequently taught the basics of flying the aircraft. This skill saved many crews when the pilot was killed or badly injured.

daughter) and she cooked my breakfast of grapefruit, egg, sausage and bacon and toast and marmalade, and off for flying at 7.30 a.m. Went to the Isle of Man. Afternoon off for 48 hour pass. Did all necessary and by car to Carlisle. Night train to London.

16/2/42 Monday. Arrived London 6.20 a.m. Booked into Strand Palace Hotel and sent telegram to Peter to come up. Had bath, haircut and shampoo and to Moss Bros. Had lunch and still Peter not arrived. Then at 3.00 p.m. telegram from Margaret to say he was at Farnham and rang there and told he had caught 2.07 p.m. train to London. Rushed to Station in taxi and just met it. Spent quiet afternoon and had photos taken. Evening to dance at Astoria but not much good, so back to hotel for a drink and bed 11.00 p.m.

17/2/42 Tuesday. Breakfast in bed and up at 10.00 a.m. and off shopping etc till 1.00 p.m. when I caught train at Euston. Slept for three hours and then spent trip reading etc. Arrived Carlisle 7.30 p.m. and off for drink with Freddie Albion till 9.15 p.m. train which arrived 10.10 p.m. Popped up to camp for mail and found was flying tomorrow. Bed midnight. Letter from Mrs Acton to say that Joan was not going to write any more.

18/2/42 Wednesday. Overslept and did not get up till 7.00 a.m. so had terrific rush and did not shave. At camp did not fly and so sent away at 11.00 a.m. Went home and had shave and wrote letters. Afternoon had one short trip and home at 4.00 p.m. Yarning and reading and writing. Bath and bed 11.00 p.m.

19/2/42 Thursday. Up at 6.00 a.m. for flying at 7.00 a.m. and when I got there found that was not till 8.30 a.m.! Did one trip in the morning and in the afternoon I was told I could go again at 8.00 p.m. So went home and reading and writing till Mrs Birnie and Margaret came home and Margaret and I went for walk along sea prom past Skinburness. Into camp for dinner and then along to Reggie's for evening. Bed 11.00 p.m.

20/2/42 Friday. Up 7.45 a.m. and to camp for flying at 9.00 a.m. But did not fly. Spent the morning in the crew room. Afternoon in Synthetic Trainer and made rotten boob. Evening stayed in reading. Bed 11.30 p.m.

21/2/42 Saturday. Up 7.30 a.m. for lectures all day. Nothing entertaining – just missed night flying. Evening studying and Monopoly. Bed 11.20 p.m.

22/2/42 Sunday. Up at 6.00 a.m. for navigation trip at 7.00 a.m. but recalled due to bad weather – was snowing. Then up on ASV trip but turned back. Afternoon did ASV Mull of Galloway, Isle of Man and Base. Home early changed etc. and reading all evening. Bath and bed 11.30 p.m.

ASV was short for Air to Surface Vessel, which was the first effective air to surface radar used in the RAF. It had been fitted in Hudsons of Coastal Command since early 1940, and was by now widely fitted. It could give ranges of up to 12 nautical miles on large ships, and greatly enhanced the search capability of Maritime Patrol aircraft. Clearly Charles was not going to put any more detail on the use of this highly classified equipment in his diary.

Training in the Maritime operations continued, with much more success in flying than had been achieved at Blackpool on the School of General Reconnaissance. However, not everything went smoothly for the course.

25/3/42 Wednesday. Up late and navigation trip in late morning which took till 3.30 p.m. Rest of time off till night flying and this time actually flew. Did one and a half hours till 3.30 a.m. Lost two planes on night. Passed over convoy in North Irish Sea – might have been Peter's.

26/3/42 Thursday. Did not get up till 11.30 a.m. Bath and to camp for dinner. Afternoon up for drogue firing but guns not harmonised so down again. On a night navigation trip but weather came down again so was cancelled. Spent rest of time indoors. Bed 11.00 p.m.

27/3/42 Friday. Did one hour flying in the morning and two hours drogue in the afternoon Evening down for night navigation, but cancelled and so had to do local flying and we were up for two and a half hours. Bed 1.40 a.m. very tired.

28/3/42 Saturday. Up 8.30 a.m. and spent the morning quietly indoors. Afternoon not wanted in flights so home again. Postings through. Had choice of Wick or East, so chose 459 Squadron! Evening on night navigation, but back by 10.00 p.m. and home by 11.00 p.m.

29/3/42 Sunday. Up early and to the aerodrome, hoping to get flying in and cleared but did not fly till the afternoon and then only dropped live bombs. Got nothing cleared. Evening with Reg till dinner then to Queen's with lads, but left early and home at 9.30 p.m. and spent evening in. Had rotten night as had had injection and just feeling it.

30/3/42 Monday. Had rotten night and could not sleep for aches. Up at 9.30 a.m, hot bath and to camp. Got lot of clearances done but could not finish as our posting dates had not come through. Afternoon saw Reggie and Eve off to Wick and had to stay behind myself! Spent evening quietly indoors and got lots of packing done. Bed 11.00 p.m.

> 31/3/42 Tuesday. Wandered up to camp late in the morning but still no news of when we go. Wandered back home after lunch and stayed with girls a bit. Back at camp played darts etc till got tired of waiting and Bedwell and I went to see the Adjutant. Learnt that posting had been diverted to Stornoway. So rushed round finishing clearance and getting warrants. Said farewells and caught 7.20 p.m. train. Got to Manchester 12.30 p.m. but no connection to Huddersfield! So caught paper train to Crewe and slept from there to London.

Finally Charles and his crew had completed the operational training and could be posted to a squadron. The choice of 459 Squadron seems at first sight a strange one, for 459 Squadron was a Royal Australian Air Force unit, and was currently based in North Africa flying Hudsons. However, it was usual for a number of British crews to be on Commonwealth squadrons, and indeed it was common for Commonwealth personnel to serve on Royal Air Force squadrons. Plans in wartime have a way of changing unexpectedly, and in this case their operational debut was to be further delayed by their temporary posting to No. 500 Squadron at RAF Stornoway.

The Hudsons that equipped both No. 459 Squadron and No. 500 Squadron were the workhorse of RAF Coastal Command. Ordered from the United States Lockheed Company in the urgent re-equipment programme in 1938, more than 200 had been delivered to the RAF by December 1939. Just over 2000 Hudsons of various marks were delivered to the RAF over the six years of the war, and it proved a great success as a Maritime Patrol and Attack aircraft as well as being used in a transport role. Developed from a civil passenger aircraft, the Hudson Mk III was widely in use by 1941 and had two Wright Cyclone 1200

Horsepower engines giving it a top speed of 210 kts, a cruising speed of 193 kts and a service ceiling of 24,500 ft. It was much larger than its predecessor, the Avro Anson, having a wing span of 65 ft 6 in and carrying a bomb load of up to 1600 lb. Its range of nearly 1900 nautical miles and endurance of well over 6 hours allowed it to carry out long range surveillance and convoy protection. Armament consisted of two fixed forward-facing .303 in machine guns, twin .303 in machine guns in a dorsal turret and single .303 in guns in each beam. Some aircraft also had a retractable ventral .303 in machine gun. The crew consisted of a pilot, a navigator who was also bomb aimer, a wireless operator and an air gunner.

Charles had a few days of his leave at home on the Isle of Sheppey, then he set off to see various friends on his way to join No. 500 Squadron in Stornoway on the Outer Hebrides. After a night in Huddersfield he went to see Olive in Barrow.

> 6/4/42 Monday. The blackest day for years. I had bath and shave in the morning and caught 9.00 a.m. train to Manchester, arriving at Barrow at 2.00 p.m. Called at Olive's after lunch and noticed a slight coolness which worried me not. She suggested making four at a dance in the evening with Billie and a friend of hers. There I realised things were not what they were and challenged her with it. She said she still looked on me as a great friend, but the other seemed to have died in favour of one "Leonard"! I decided if the situation was such it was but life. After the dance we parted with handshake and I went back to the Hotel feeling rotten.
>
> 7/4/42 Tuesday. Woke at 10.00 a.m. but when I left Olive had not bothered to communicate and so it appears that is best for me to just fall out. Called to see Billie as train did not leave till 3.30 p.m. and had lunch with her. Had

good journey through pretty country and arrived at Glasgow at 10.00 p.m. Phoned Uncle and Auntie, but Uncle out. Anyway went up to them and spent night there.

8/4/42 Wednesday. Did not get up till latish and had the morning in. Then to town for lunch and caught 1.40 p.m. through train to Inverness. Was fairly slow, but passed through grand scenery via Pitlochry and the Grampians. Time passed quickly with passengers and a book and arrived at 8.00 p.m. Stayed at Caledonian Hotel and after dinner went for stroll round town before it got dark. Then in lounge till bed. Looked through Olive's last letters and it does not seem possible she has changed. Bed 11.00 p.m. Wrote to Olive

9/4/42 Thursday. Did not get up till 10.00 a.m. then down to Station to catch 11.45 a.m, but found it was running late and so went out for lunch. (Got two 2 star meals!) Train left at 1.30 p.m. and we had quite an interesting journey through the Highlands. Arrived at Kyle at 5.20 p.m. and left in the "Loch Ness" at 7.00 p.m. Interesting trip till we left land and it got dark and I then went below and slept till midnight when we arrived. Transport took us to camp where we were not expected and had to sleep in hut with no sheets or furniture. Everything seems very unsettled and disorganised.

10/4/42 Friday. Up about 10.30 a.m. Wash, shave etc down at mess and after breakfast went along to see the Adjutant, who has no accommodation for us. Saw CO who told us same among other things. Whole camp incomplete and Officers sleeping in tin huts with no washing facilities and had to go to mess to clean teeth even. After lunch met Atkinson and Mason who had come up with a Squadron Leader from Brize Norton and shot a big line. Waited in mess all afternoon till evening when we had to fix ourselves up with beds etc in an unoccupied hut. Dashed round collecting all kit and trunks and settled in. Bath and shower and bed.

11/4/42 Saturday. Up at 8.20 a.m. and wash and shave before breakfast. In the morning to see the Adjutant again but he still did not know what to do with us and told us to wait in mess again. And so we waited all day. There was some talk of another posting. Spent day just reading and writing. Evening went to Stornoway to look round and for a drink with the boys. Also called on a Sub Lieutenant I met on way over and he showed us over a motor launch. Back in time for dinner and bed early.

12/4/42 Sunday. Up early again but spent all morning in the mess again. Late in the afternoon four crews were sent for to the flights and when we got down there we were told we would stay and there would be a trip for us on Tuesday. So that is a move in the right direction. Stayed in for the evening and bath and Bed early.

13/4/42 Monday. Up for early reporting at flights. But did not have anything to do except collect a few navigation instruments. Afternoon had sleep and read and wrote. Same in the evening. Bed late.

14/4/42 Tuesday. First day of parades they are starting here. Afterwards we went for lecture on signals organisation of 15 Group, and then lunch. Afternoon I wandered across to intelligence office and read some reports and then back to the mess. After dinner went for stroll along cliffs and back early.

15/4/42 Wednesday. Up for the parade again and then had to go and censor letters! But spent rest of the day waiting in flights and in the mess and did nothing else. Evening bath and bed early.

16/4/42 Thursday. After parade nothing doing so I answered some letters and then back to the mess. Spent the afternoon in the mess and from 4.00 p.m. to 11.00 p.m. there was an aerodrome attack exercise and I was an umpire. Had a look round at 4.30 p.m. but no activity. Had game of billiards and at 8.00 p.m. went round again to all ports. Then got transport and when it got dark all sorts of isolated action started all over place. Did not finish till 3.00 a.m! Saw the northern lights.

17/4/42 Friday. Up 9.30 a.m. and down to umpires conference in town. Afternoon walked to town and back for look round and hair cut and back for tea. Had a nap before dinner and afterwards walked to town again to call on Rev Carmichael for yarn about Lewis and Stornoway. Back in transport. Bath and Bed early.

This state of inaction continued for several more days. The crew did not get to fly, but instead were given odd jobs to do, and were otherwise left to hang about in their messes. Charles was not pleased. But change was on the way.

22/4/42 Wednesday. Up early to take flight parade and then went down to see about a flight and was roped in for Orderly Officer. I spent all day looking round in transport till midnight when I had to meet the boat. Bed 1.00 a.m. Heard that we are to be posted on Friday to Bircham Newton! So all sorts of guesses why.

23/4/42 Thursday. Up early to do breakfasts. Filled in Orderly Officer's report and gave over to the Adjutant. Spent the day reading and starting clearance. Did some censoring. No packing done yet. Bed midnight.

24/4/42 Friday. Up late and spent day mucking about and

94

packing. Got kit off early and organised transport for Officers down to boat at 2.00 a.m. and then relaxed. Evening dance in mess, but did not dance, only drank with the lads, but eased up before got too late! Afternoon bought some Harris Tweed for Margaret and Aunt Marie and myself (trousers). Left at 2.00 a.m. for the boat and railway.

25/4/42 Saturday. Had bit of sleep on boat which did not leave till 5 a.m. Arrived at Kyle 10.15 a.m. and on to train. Warrant for five Officers exchanged for one ticket for the lot! Normal journey to Inverness. Reading and yarning. Then tried to change ticket for separate ones, but no luck. Lovely weather down and good views. Read, sat and played cards and in evening went to sleep. Arrived Crewe 5.30 a.m. where I got out.

26/4/42 Sunday. As I had no ticket had a job getting off station, but did eventually convince them. Had bath etc and cleaned buttons etc at Crewe Arms LMS Hotel. And on to Shavington. Went for walk till 9.30 a.m. and called on Joyce. Both went for walk after breakfast and again after lunch and again a sit down in fields after tea then indoors yarning till I caught last bus back to Crewe Arms for night. Bed midnight.

27/4/42 Monday. Did not wake up till 11.00 a.m. and got straight up. In the morning I got my case onto station OK and put in cloak room. Then to town and cashed a cheque and after lunch small shopping and down to park where I lazed on river bank and sunbathed. Met Joyce at 5.00 p.m. and went to a film. Then to hotel for dinner and collect my greatcoat and my hat and for walk till 9.00 p.m., went on bus at 10.15 p.m. Got myself onto station with platform ticket and waited for 12.20 a.m. train.

28/4/42 Tuesday. Got on OK and ticket not asked for on train all way. Slept off and on all way. Change at Rugby, Peterborough, Kings Lynn where I had three hours wait, so had a look round town and some breakfast. Change again at small station on way here and arrive 1.00 p.m. Transport up to camp but took us a long while to find anyone who knew of our posting arrival! Waiting in mess all afternoon – a grand palatial affair – and in evening down to Docking mess where we are billeted on dispersal! But we had single rooms each, a batman and very comfortable. Settled in and bed early.

29/4/42 Wednesday. Up at 8.00 a.m. and after breakfast wandered up to flights but the CO there said they did not know definitely what we were to do yet and we were to hang around mess. Afternoon went to Bircham to see Accountant Officer and argument arose between him and the Adjutant as to whether we were attached or posted here. So we drew no cash. Evening at Docking unpacking baggage which arrived and writing and yarning.

30/4/42 Thursday. Up late and had good bath in the morning and read. At 2.00 p.m. we were told we should go on 48 hour till Monday night! So three of us dashed off to catch 2.30 p.m. train and did it. Got to London at 7.00 p.m. with just time to cross over and catch 7.25 p.m. to Farnham. Bus to Rowledge and walked to Auntie's by 9.30 p.m. Great excitement when they all saw me and tons of chin-wagging. Bed 11.30 p.m.

Once again the crew found themselves surplus to requirements and were sent on a few days leave till someone could find out what to do with them. He spent the leave at Farnham with his Aunt Marie and other relations and on

Monday 4 May he and his crew returned to RAF Docking.

> 5/5/42 Tuesday. Rose at 8.00 a.m. and went to Bircham in the morning, but all we had to do was give our names and parties. So went into mess for game of billiards till noon. After lunch wrote letters and read. After dinner Madsen and I went for walk through Docking and back across lots of fields in evening darkness, arriving back at 11.00 p.m.

Not much change there! So for another week it went on. They were going on a 48-hour pass, then it was to be four days' leave, but that was then cancelled. Some crews were going overseas, but only Australian crews, but Charles might have a crew change, but he didn't. His diary shows his frustration.

> 13/5/42 Wednesday. Got up early and to Bircham at 8.40 a.m. Had breakfast up there and then went round to find out about posting. And the shock was that seven only could go on leave and rest had to stand by in case any of the others did not return. Then the rest arrived and I left for Docking. Also no chance of changing crews. Then at noon I learnt that some of the other three crews had gone. So after lunch I went back again and got in a terrific argument as to whether call them back or let me go and I won. But alas I missed the last train so had to wait till tomorrow. Spent the evening in the mess and my room and bed early.

So it was another four days' leave. This time he went back to Silloth to see the family he had been billeted with while on the OTU, and then to stay in London for a couple of days.

18/5/42 Monday. Got up at 8.30 a.m. Bath etc and down to catch 10.25 a.m. Met all lads on Liverpool Street Station and travelled up with them. Arrived at 4.30 p.m. and down to mess for tea. Learnt that we definitely were not going anywhere. The rest went up to get their tropical kit etc and I stayed in mess writing. Very tired so bed early. After a grand weekend weather changed again to rain.

19/5/42 Tuesday. All the gang went off this morning for Horsham and overseas and I watched them. Then went up to Station HQ at Bircham to see what they were going to do with us but no one knew a thing. So I came back and spent the day in the mess reading Masefield's The Square Peg – and got fed up as I was alone in the mess most of the time and slept a lot. Bed 10.30 p.m.

20/5/42 Wednesday. Started day as usual by sitting in mess. Afternoon the Sergeants rang from Bircham to sat that they had been told they could have fourteen days leave if 279 Squadron agreed, so I dashed up to organise it for them. By rushing round trying to get their pay I missed the evening bus and so got back and had to wait. Put in application for overseas.

21/5/42 Thursday. Up at 5.20 a.m. and caught 6.15 a.m. to London. Travelling continuously without sleep till arrived home at 2.00 p.m. Had meal and spent the afternoon wandering around doing odd jobs with Dad who was still out sick. Bed early tired.

A fortnight of leave was spent mostly at home on the Isle of Sheppey. Charles took the opportunity to relax and help his father in his garden and field. But he also saw a lot of Dil.

27/5/42 Wednesday. Up 6.00 a.m. and caught 8.00 a.m.

bus from Sheerness with Dil. Arrived in London 10.15 a.m. Taxi to New Theatre and Cumberland (but could not get a room) and back to Victoria Station where we met her friend Bet. Lunch at Strand Palace and along to show to see Ballet. The Gods go abegging, Les Rendezvous and Orpheus and Eurydice – a jolly fine one. Saw Dil off on bus and we went to see Ivor Novello's Dancing Years. Dined at Strand and saw Bet off. Then to Bonnington Hotel and bed 12.20 a.m. Bet introduced me to the Welsh Nationalist Movement.

28/5/42 Thursday. Up at 8.00 a.m. and after breakfast sat in park by Buckingham Palace reading Homer's Odyssey till noon. Lunch at Victory Club and caught bus to Sittingbourne. Went to Borden Grammar (*Charles's old school*) and saw all the old masters and look round. Back home at 7.00 p.m. and after tea went along to Rutland's House with Margaret for evening. Back at 11.00 p.m. Letters from Uncle Nigel about America. Took out £100 Policy. Heard of fox breeding in Ireland.

29/5/42 Friday. Did not get up till 10.00 a.m. Then to bank for more cash, got my films from chemist and some of them were good. To building society and to see Eileen and her baby and Margaret. Afternoon opened all bees with Dad and got two stings! In the evening to see Dil. She was very yielding, but her nature is contrary. Did not leave till late.

30/5/42 Saturday. Up at 6.30 a.m. and into shorts etc and down to meet Dil. Took bikes on train to Sittingbourne and went for a nice easy cycle ride all round the county, finally at Sittingbourne Bull Hotel for dinner of fish and lobster salad. Back on train and stayed talking to her till 8.45 p.m. and home after jolly good day out.

31/5/42 Sunday. Up late and mucked about in garden,

then down town to find about trains and see Dil. Afternoon bees and reading. Evening to see Auntie Nellie and Margaret. Bed late.

1/6/42 Monday. Into town early for times of trains, paint, more cash and see Dil, and rest of the morning pottering about. Afternoon – bees, digging, mowing lawn and sawing wood. Then after bath and tea along to see Auntie and Margaret. Gordon still very bad. Down to see Dil and !!! Home 11.30 p.m. and bed tired.

Charles had another day at home then went to Huddersfield to see his friends there before returning to Bircham Newton.

4/6/42 Thursday. ... Arrived Docking 6.45 p.m. having slept off and on all way down. Spent evening sorting things out. Bed late. News waited that we are wanted at SHQ!

5/6/42 Friday. Rang SHQ but no one seemed to know anything about us, or why we were wanted. So went up and started binding. Stayed to lunch and continued to the afternoon and waited while they rang group. Back at 3.00 p.m. and reading. In evening phone message through that we were going out at last and had to report tomorrow for draft leave! So after bath and dinner went out with Sergeants for a drink then packed and bed late.

6/6/42 Saturday. Up early and away to SHQ. Did everything except get money and caught 2.30 p.m. train. London at 6.30 p.m. and spent ages trying to get Vi on phone with no success. So decided to get away to Chepstow. Spent time waiting till midnight by wandering around Piccadilly and things appear just the same. Had dinner at Paddington. Slept all the way down on the train.

Charles spent three days walking by himself in the Chepstow area, much as he had done in the pre-war days. As the crew had been sent on "draft" leave, it seemed that at last they might expect to get away and get on with the job. At the end of the week, after a visit to Auntie Marie he returned to RAF Docking.

12/6/42 Friday. Up at 7.00 a.m. and caught train to Town. Spent the morning looking round book stalls in Tottenham Court Rd and then caught noon train to camp. It turned to rain today after weeks of fine hot weather. Back at camp at 4.00 p.m. but they didn't to want us till tomorrow morning. Spent evening writing and packing. Bed late.

13/6/42 Saturday. Up early and to camp. Got all troops etc and caught 4.00 p.m. train to Norwich via Wells. Arrived Horsham St Faith at 9.30 p.m. got my room and dinner and then found I had lost my key of my trunk! Bed 11.0.

14/6/42 Sunday. Up early and came up to see the Adjutant and the CO. They had not got organised on us yet, but had a spare kite we could have and so get away early (in seven days). But there was nothing we could do today so they told us to have day off. Alas it rained all day, and I could not get Jack Hepworth on phone and so I stayed in mess all day and read etc. Bath and bed early.

15/6/42 Monday. Up early and away to flights, but alas weather too bad for trip. So went and saw about kit and spent rest of the morning in the mess. Afternoon up to crew room for some gen and back to mess again. Evening old Group Captain's farewell do, and as I did not know anyone did not stay long but went to bed early.

16/6/42 Tuesday. Still too bad to fly in the morning so went and had look round the aircraft and then back to mess.

Afternoon got a bit of gen and then Bryan up for a bit of dual. A treat to get in the air again. Evening in mess reading and writing.

17/6/42 Wednesday. Up early and did initial swing of compass* in morning and corrected "R". Then drew all navigation equipment and instruments including sextant and Astro graph. Afternoon local flying then to see MO re life assurance report. To mess. Reading and writing.

18/6/42 Thursday. Up extra early for long navigation trip. Took off 9.00 a.m. out to sea, form up at Rattray Head then to Fair Isle. On way back diverted to Driffield – weather. Had lots of snags with navigation and had to ask for fix as Loop all wrong and above 10/10 cloud. So miles off track. So in evening went out to kite and went over it all and found I had misapplied variation! Checked loop and astro bearings and not too good. Landed 5.00 p.m. Spent evening reading and bed early.

19/6/42 Friday. Up early and pottered about aeroplane till others arrived at 10.00 a.m. and then off back to base via Goole and Peterborough. Arrived 12.45 p.m. and to lunch. Afternoon changed Dalton†, went to see MO but out, so to dentist and had tooth filled. Then to Accounts and back to mess. Stopped in again writing and reading. Filled in income tax and will.

20/6/42 Saturday. Up early and away for a three hour trip testing guns and fuel consumption and then brought

* The magnetic compass is affected by all the metallic components in an aircraft. In order to allow for the deviations induced, the reading of the compass on known magnetic headings is measured, and a correction card is placed in the aircraft so that a corrected magnetic heading can be obtained in flight.

† The Dalton computer is a mechanical device that allows the aircraft's track and speed over the ground to be calculated when the effects of wind are applied to its heading and speed through the air.

aircraft in for inspection and overhaul. Afternoon did several little odd jobs and at 3.30 p.m. told we were to go to London and Halton for Yellow Fever. Sent gram to Dil and met her in town at 9.30 p.m. We could only get in at Grosvenor Hotel and then all went out to a French restaurant in Piccadilly – L'Auberge de France – for dinner. Back at Hotel stayed in Dil's room till 1.30 a.m. then down to mine. Bed 2.00 a.m.

21/6/42 Sunday. Up at 9.00 a.m. and caught 10.30 a.m. to Windsor. Said goodbye to Dil. Had grand trip down and very quickly jabbed. Tried to see Squadron Leader Cross about my eye, but he had gone. Lunch in Windsor and back to London 3.30 p.m. to Regent Palace and then to Quality Inn for hot tea. Went and saw Jungle Book, a film of Kipling's stories – very good. Then for dinner at Scott restaurant £3-1-0 for four! Regent for wash etc and out for drink and wander round Piccadilly etc. Très intéressant. Bed 1.00 a.m.

22/6/42 Monday. Up late and after baths and breakfast too late for 10.00 a.m. train so rang Adjutant and spent the morning wandering round and cashed a cheque. Lunch at Lyons and afternoon to the Windmill. Caught 5.10 p.m. back to camp and arrived 9.15 p.m. Late dinner. Spent evening sorting out photos and sending them off. Bed midnight.

23/6/42 Tuesday. Up early and away up to crew room. Had air test and drew all tropical kit and handed in flying kit. Afternoon final swing and then learnt we were for dispatch tomorrow! But had met Jack Hepworth, so had last evening with him in Norwich. Back at 10.20 p.m. for final packing and letters till 3.00 a.m. and then not finished.

24/6/42 Wednesday. Up early as we were for despatch

today for overseas. In the morning we did all weighing etc, and then it was cancelled. Then later we were told to take off at 4.00 p.m. and so took everything up to "C" and found it all cancelled again and we had all cleared! So in evening whole crew went out with Pilot Officer Millioms on last binge – and what a binge! Ended in a dance hall and taxi home. Bed midnight.

25/6/42 Thursday. Up early and took everything up to "C" and set off for Lyneham. Had good trip down, though weather bad and arrived in time for lunch. But as all 1444* had come down by road everything was disorganised and so we could not get off to Portreath. So afternoon we repacked all kit into "C" and caught 5.30 p.m. to Swindon. Had meal, drink, look round and to a third rate theatre. Then caught 11.30 p.m. home and after walk of one and a half miles from station arrived back 12.30 a.m. and bed very tired. Swindon was dead - no theatres, two cinemas, no good pubs or eating places.

26/6/42 Friday. Up early again and out to "C". But still everything disorganised so spent day mucking about in "C" and lying on grass asleep. Evening tea and played snooker. Bath and bed early.

27/6/42 Saturday. Up early and over to flights as I hoped to get off this morning. But Bryan and others late and then had to get paid, so just lazed about. Off in the afternoon and had a good trip down over Frome, Taunton, Bodmin Moor etc. Portreath looked lovely from air. Sea blue and land green, but on ground everywhere was white dusty. County lovely! Tea then briefing and spent evening on "C" and drawing in track for tomorrow, then

* 1444 Ferry Training Flight. It was under this unit's auspices that Charles and his crew made the flight to North Africa.

Ready for departure overseas. The aircraft is Hudson Mk III "C", probably at Portreath. Note the horizontal aerials on each side of the nose and the aerial below the cockpit window for the ASV. Two .303 inch machine guns can be seen on the top of the fuselage, forward of the cockpit.

bath and sit in mess and bed at 11.00 p.m. in old farmhouse. Tomorrow change to GMT instead of BDST.

CHAPTER 5

Transit to War

Charles's diary was supplemented by a journal while he was away from UK. In it he recorded impressions and observations on events and scenes that he saw during particularly interesting periods of his life, continuing a habit he had started in his pre-war walking days with Rovers.

A few notes on my travels in "C" for Cupid

with

Bryan Rostron – Pilot

Lee Barrett – W/Op

Jimmy Craig – A/G

(Signed) C. A. Collins – Navigator

Please send to Miss E. D. Jones BA, 2 Neptune Terrace, Sheerness, England if I am killed

(signed) C. A. Collins P/O

Portreath, as our last sight of England could not have been better. The previous day we had seen it on a sunny summer afternoon with its green fields, its white dusty narrow winding lanes, its cliffs and the nestly town at the river mouth.

Now, in the early morning, at 0700 GMT in the first morning light, it looked a little gem. But it was the last gem we saw. We flew into cloud almost as soon as we set off. True, after a while, through breaks we did see a few rocks and islands in the sea, but did not think of them as the ends of England, but only as points where I might get a navigational aid.

And so began our great adventure! But to me it meant nothing in the way of a thrill. You hear of people leaving England who stand at the ship's side and watch it fade away and think of something they are leaving and how long it will be before they return. But all my thoughts were on the trip itself. To me it seemed, and I treated it, just as another flight. Maybe it is because I was busy with charts and things. But even when I sat back and tried to make myself realise I was leaving England for a long time, on what was not to be a safe trip to strange lands, I was unimpressed and could not produce a spark of excitement.

We flew out of cloud over the Bay but saw the sea only. And then when we were approaching the Spanish coastline we were above 10/10 cloud and all that could be seen was a mountain protruding in the distance.

When I estimated we were well south we came down below cloud and flew in South East to make a landfall and when the coast came in sight through the mist we were somewhere just North of Cape St Vincent. So we flew southward keeping the coast in sight to get a fix point. Now the cloud began to clear and we were able to get a better idea of the type of country it was. Steep, dark, barren cliffs, and behind high, black, bleak moors. It looked bleak and uninviting with no point of interest at all.

But this led us down to Cape St Vincent, and what a contrast: the white cliffs capped by green and standing in clear blue. A clean and impressive sight especially with the stumpy white lighthouse there. But then we left the land again and our next close up was of Cadiz. This is a town that I should like to visit. It looked a friendly place but

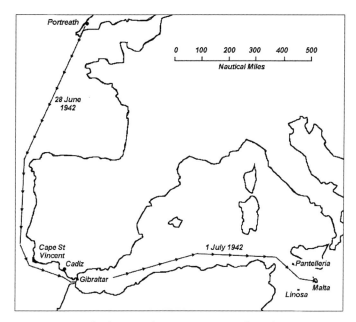

Charles's Travels – 28 June to 1 July 1942

owing to its semi-hostility we could not go too close. What could be seen was the long quiet water front, with numerous fishing and other vessels in the bay. Behind was a clean, white, lazy looking town, with the outstanding feature being the golden dome of the opera house. Then behind that black, steep hills.

But now we were approaching the all important straits. On the left the black hills had turned to brown and had come down to the sea in many long narrow ridges, while on the right a lofty, white, streaked mass loomed – the hostile side of the straits. What a striking contrast.

Then as we flew through, the Rock came in sight round the corner – just as we expected, but I suppose far more impressive from the sea. As we approached and circled it a more interesting vision was obtained. First of all the narrow strip of high rock (1400 ft) connected to the mainland by a narrow flat strip of land. But how insubstantial it looked. I had heard lots about its solid, permanent appearance but it had the opposite effect on me and the feeling was not improved on the ground. I thought as I looked at it that in a few years from now it could be gone, its importance and power lost, despite all the time, money and lives we had spent to get and keep it. What would posterity think of our tenacity?

Then we saw the town dominated by the fort and lighthouse at the tip. Just ridge on ridge of houses, all yellow, rising up from the water about one third of the way up the rock side. Then across the flat sandy isthmus the eye was caught first by the large Customs House and then the town of La Linea with its flat square houses and the large open bull ring in the centre.

Then we landed, the harbour full of various shipping and the first stage of our trip had been completed without incident.

In first arriving at a strange town it is difficult to say definitely what are the first impressions. They are so many and crowd in on one. But here I think it was the dust, the heat, the flies and the smells. And I was glad to get out of the RAF blue into tropical kit. Having dispersed "C" for Cupid we left all our stuff aboard and took only what we needed for a short stay and our nav kit, and went to be debriefed. But being one of many who had come out and were still to come we were met with no excitement, though they enquired after the condition of the aeroplane and performance and lapped up a "sighting" I had.

And so we prepared for a bit of comfort for our stay here, for how long no one knew except that we had to go and be briefed next day.

Impressions were mixed and sporadic. While here –

three days – most of the time was spent in the camp, but I went into the town itself on two occasions.

The Rock itself still had the unstable appearance that we saw during the three circuits that we did of it as we arrived. From the land the promontory certainly did not have any more lasting or permanent appearance, and the impression formed in the air of its potential early collapse was not lost. Standing here on the east side one gazes up at an almost sheer wall of solid white rock. It could easily be likened to a wall, with a thin steeply sloping buttress on the west. I wondered how long such a slender promontory would stand up to the forces of the rush of water through the straits. Knowledgeable men must be confident, as daily at 12 o'clock, the side of the rock was blasted to make room for a new runway. And I gathered that it is itself almost a warren containing in its interior such things as hospitals, ammunition dumps and reservoirs, not to mention the catacombs of tunnels to the various gun emplacements, the outlets of which could be seen from the road. Some are even in a narrow tongue of rock that runs permanently down the face of one of those sides.

I was lucky to hear some of these guns fire, the anti-aircraft variety at any rate, and the way the noise echoed and reverberated round and through the rock would have made one think the rock itself was falling. It is no wonder to me that one face has had to be reinforced with a steeply sloping face of concrete.

The population itself seems to consist mostly of service men and women – all in khaki with the exception of the navy, and the smart lily white uniforms of the naval Officers were a joy to behold. I had heard that the rock had been evacuated of women, except service personnel. There was a fair number of WRNS and nurses but there were also plenty of Gibraltar women and Spanish women from across the border.

These last, however, are very restricted. There are about eight thousand men and women who come over daily but they have to be back in Spain by a certain time. The women are not allowed to have any communication whatever with the forces and as they very jealously guard their permits they rigidly observe all the conditions. In any case the general attitude of the Spanish to the British is very hostile. These people it appears are living in poverty over at La Linea and rely only on their income from the rock. Food is very scarce and as a temporary privilege, they are allowed to take back with them a percentage of their wages in food. It is an odd sight to see men and women returning daily with loaves of bread etc under their arms. On this account La Linea is the most well-to-do town in Spain. They tell me the people in northern Spain are on the verge of starvation. But I wondered then, what else they took across and left with the German embassy there!

The Gibraltarians are a different people. Somewhat similar to the Spaniards in appearance with a dark oily skin, they are closely allied to the British through marriage. It is a queer sight to see the bands in the cafes which are composed almost entirely of girls and seem to play there all day, from morning till late and night, and to be able to consume any amount of liquor without too disastrous an effect. Though I have not seen it, they tell me that at closing time isolated fights often develop in the street, mainly among the forces.

The streets are in the Spanish style. Narrow and with upper stories overhanging in places. With the walls mainly yellow and white, and with latticed windows, the town itself nestles along the back of the rock with one main street and steep side streets leading up to one or two smaller ones higher up the rock face. Into this narrow street crowd the pedestrians, overflowing into the road. The traffic is scarce and drives on the right, and includes horse carriages, cars and service vehicles. The fact that they are not allowed to use their horns, however, causes a lot of shouting and banging of hands on the outside of the door. An effort is made to keep the streets clean by sweepers who use only a besom. There appear to be no brooms.

The policemen are another unusual feature, as they wear the normal English blue uniform with the helmet, and among khaki and white shirts and shorts make a sharp contrast.

In the camp itself incidental differences between home life were noticeable. The dust or fine sand which was everywhere. The myriads of flies and the variety of smells were most annoying and objectionable. But white bread, real butter, cheap tobacco and beer, and chocolate to order, though expensive, were a welcome luxury after rationing and shortage at home. Here there are fruit – oranges, bananas etc. But the water! True we had cooled fresh water to drink, but washing, bathing and above all shaving was in salt water!

Other impressions:

The mules and mangy little horses used for transport.

The mess and the restrictions there that Officers must wear trousers, tunic and tie to dinner and in the evening.

The Wellington that overshot the runway and put its nose down on the beach.

The glorious swim one afternoon in the blue, buoyant, warm Mediterranean and the sun-bathe that followed. But how hot – in fact too hot – was the sand to walk on! (Why doesn't it get as hot as that in the desert?) To stand barefoot on it we had to work a small hole a few inches deep.

On the first evening how I was struck by the clear eggshell blue sky and the rising of a full orange moon. With this peaceful scene we retired to bed for our first night. But how rudely we were wakened by the echo of heavy gunfire, then the falling of shrapnel and then the falling of bombs. We had arrived in time for the first air raid for months and months. Like animated fools we must go out and have a look and there was a Ju 88 in the searchlight and shell bursts all round. The shrapnel then drove us inside. But when the bomb went through the next but one hut, several of us ventured out to assist in moving the injured. Fortunately no deaths.

An aircraft dispersed off the runway was hit and burnt out – a Hudson on its way out east, the 'Spirit of Moscow'.

This dispersal area is what was the neutral zone, now equally divided between Spain and Gib, with a dividing thicket of palms, cactuses and various other trees. But these were some of the few trees here. And I saw very few birds and only one butterfly and no flowers or bees.

Charles and his crew arrived at Gibraltar at an interesting time. The Station Operational Record Book (RAF Form 540) for 28 and 29 June 1942 states:

28/6/42 <u>Transit Aircraft</u>. In. 4 Hudsons, 3 Wellingtons (of which one overshot on landing and ran over the sea wall, crew unhurt)
Weather moderate westerly becoming light ESE.
29/6/42 <u>Air Raid</u>. Unidentified aircraft were plotted at 0120 / 29. Sirens sounded. An Air Attack from 0145 to 0215 was made on Gibraltar, the main objective being

this station. Three or more aircraft attacked in three waves. One aircraft during the third attack was picked up by searchlights and identified as a Piaggio 108 – 4 engine bomber. It is estimated that 7 HE 100 kg and 55 small anti-personnel bombs were dropped in the aerodrome area, one aircraft also attacked with M/g.

Damage. To Runway – nil. One Hudson (24 Sqn) destroyed by fire. 1 BOAC Whitley slightly damaged by splinters and / or M/g bullets. 4 craters about 15 ft across by 4 ft deep were made in the dispersal area north of runway. One Nissen hut in which Officers from aircrews in transit were sleeping suffered a direct hit from an anti-personnel bomb.

Casualties to Personnel. (i) Killed – nil. (ii) Seriously Injured – 6. (4 Officers sleeping in the hut which received the direct hit and 2 Sergeants – all transit aircrew.) (iii) Slightly Injured – 5. Attack was carried out at Full Moon period.

Charles's diary is not detailed on the events; simply:

29/6/42 Monday. Had terrific air raid at 2.00 a.m. and one or two holes in Hut – Nissen. Next hut direct hit and I and two others went in to help them. Bad. Put up terrific barrage and got one a/c in searchlights. Up early and to initial briefing then pottering about and drawing in tracks, swinging compass etc. till final briefing when were told that it was off as LG 15 had been taken.

Landing Ground 15 was Mersa Matruh, which was to have been their next staging post on their route to the Cairo area. However, the pace of events in North Africa deprived them of that option.

In 1940, when it was clear that France was about to fall and it seemed likely that Britain would soon follow, Mussolini brought Italy into the war on the side of the Germans, forming the first leg of the 'Axis'. He hoped particularly to pick up the spoils of war in the form of territory in Africa. In September 1940 he attacked British forces in Egypt from the West, hoping thereby to gain control of the strategically important Suez Canal. The odds looked good, for about quarter of a million Italian troops faced just thirty six thousand British. The British under General O'Connor retreated to Sidi Barrani, and the Italian Commander, General Graziani, wisely recognising that his lines of communication were stretched and that the British force, though smaller than his own outnumbered and outclassed him in their tanks, stopped his advance there to consolidate and to dig in. However, General O'Connor made a bold move to break through the Italian lines and encircled them capturing nearly forty thousand prisoners. The remainder of the Italian force retreated and were soon driven back beyond Tobruk. In a further bold move, O'Connor sent the 6th Australian Division to chase the Italian retreat and the 7th Armoured Division (the Desert Rats) to circle to the south to cut off the retreat. By early February 1941 O'Connor had

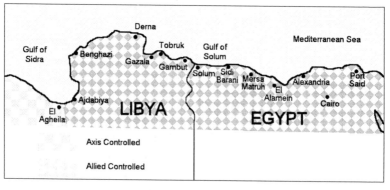

North Africa December 1940

captured one hundred and thirty thousand Italian troops and huge numbers of tanks and guns.

The Axis front line was driven back to El Agheila, and it was to defend that line that Hitler sent General Irwin Rommel. However, Churchill had to withdraw large numbers of troops for the defence of Greece, and Rommel saw the opportunity to attack and regain lost ground. This he did in March 1941, and effectively drove the Allied armies back to the Egyptian border by April. Adding insult to injury, Rommel also captured General O'Connor and his staff at Derna. The only bright spot for the

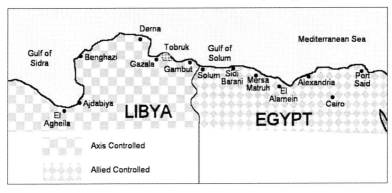

North Africa April 1941

Allied forces was that the strategic port of Tobruk remained under allied control as the Australian 9th Division and the 2nd Armoured Division dug in there and held out against all odds.

In June 1941 General Wavell, who was in overall command of the North African area, made a counter attack which failed disastrously when Rommel ingeniously adapted his 88 mm anti-aircraft guns to fighting tanks, and wiped out half of Wavell's force.

Churchill sent out reinforcements to the area, and replaced Wavell with General Auchinleck, putting General Cunningham in operational command of the newly christened 8th Army. In a closely fought operation in November and December 1941

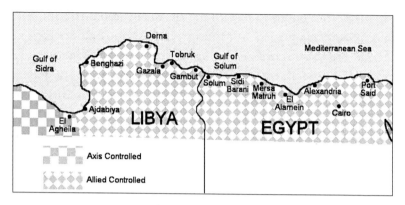

North Africa December 1941

Cunningham and Auchinleck pushed Rommel back, and the job was finished under the operational command of General Richie, who replaced Cunningham in late November. Rommel was back at El Agheila – more or less where he had started the previous year.

The British force in North Africa had, however, once again to be depleted to fight the war elsewhere, this time in the Far East. Again Rommel seized the opportunity to strike back and in January he drove the depleted British force back to Gazala, where they dug in in strong defensive positions in February 1942.

In May Rommel, the master of desert warfare, outflanked the

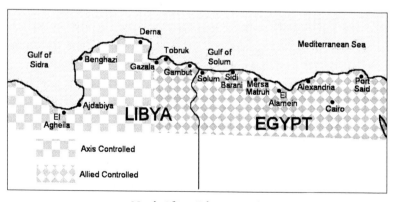

North Africa February 1942

British positions and on 21 June he finally took Tobruk, the target that had eluded him during his previous advance. The British forces fell back all the way to El Alamein. There, while the embassy staff in Cairo were frantically burning secret documents, General Auchinleck finally halted Rommel's advance on 30 June 1942.

It was this rapid advance that had deprived Charles's crew of their planned landing ground on their journey to Cairo. Alternatives were to make a huge detour to the south via Bathurst in Gambia, or to take the more direct but more

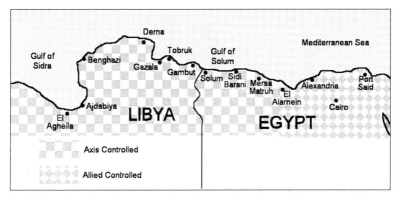

North Africa 30 June 1942

hazardous route via Malta. Malta had been under almost unceasing air attack for many months and was being starved of supplies by constant attacks on convoys bringing in vital supplies.

> 30/6/42 Tuesday. Up early but at briefing were told that we were not going by Bathurst after all and were briefed for Malta. Spent the morning putting in tracks etc. and getting gen! Afternoon sleep and bathe and sunbathe. Then after tea down to town for look round and drink and back to dinner. And then just lounged till early bed.

1/7/42 Wednesday. Away up for briefing and we were definitely to go via Malta. In the morning packing etc. and off at 1030 GMT. Flew in formation – two of us – at 200 ft, but down to sea level between Pantelleria and mainland to avoid fighters. Arrived Malta 6.30 p.m. Passed over Linosa. Malta looked very bomb scarred, but the towns are chalky and square with one main building like a mosque with minarets. Valletta looked modern with tall buildings. Air raid when landed and took cover. Taken to mess and bed 11.00 p.m.

Charles goes into much more detail in his narrative:

Slowly Gib and the Spanish coast was left behind and nothing was seen till the African coast appeared in the distance, sandy and deserted. As we followed this round we passed Italian Pantelleria on the port looking white and attractive in the distance. Then we turned to Malta and passed close to the semi-desolate island of Linosa with its two peaks and two white light houses which seem the only justification for any habitation at all. However, there were several farmhouses dotted about and a few yellow sandy roads around the coast. Sleep and a little cultivation in small compounds seemed the only occupation though a recent effort appears to be made in afforestation. But, with no town, the life on such an island far from Malta on the African coast must be very restricted. There was nothing impressive or interesting about the island even as a redeeming feature.

It was dark as we approached Malta, and therefore unsuitable for photography, which was unfortunate as there were some excellent subjects. We flew straight in from the coast over the eastern high land, with its edge of sheer white cliffs. Inland this plateau appeared labyrinthine with terraced valleys, but I could see little or no evidence of crops, instead the land seemed light brown or sandy and barren, spotted with numerous shell holes.

The small towns which were dotted about were similarly marred by bomb damage, and appeared to consist chiefly of small flat topped square houses of a sandy colour. And with one or perhaps two outstanding buildings with a dome of spire like a minaret.

The most striking thing about Malta was the innumerable air raids. We landed just before dark and a garry led the aircraft across the aerodrome for dispersal. The alarm went and immediately everyone was on pinpoints. As soon as we arrived at the blast shelter the driver and ground crew vanished and left us there with our kit.

Bryan Rostron's account of the crew's arrival in Malta indicates that it was somewhat more exciting than Charles described:

It was dusk and we continued towards Malta – there was no difficulty in finding it as the air raids were almost continuous at that time and Malta was one long firework display, dispensing with the need for navigation. The Luftwaffe were doing the bombing based in Sicily, about thirty minutes flying away, and could make a round trip every couple of hours, which meant that Malta was getting a terrible pasting. When I called up the tower at Luqa I was told they couldn't put on the runway lights as the airfield was being bombed continuously and would I circle a rock about ten miles to the south of the island until it was safe to land. I did this for about half an hour, having a bird's eye view of the bombing but, interesting though this was, the fuel situation was beginning to get critical and I called up again to say that, unless I could land in the next fifteen minutes, I would have to go into the sea. We were given a course to steer to take us over Luqa and when the controller saw us he put the runway lights on for thirty seconds so that I could line up the gyro. We then did a short low circuit and when we were about 100 feet on final the runway lights came on and we landed more by good luck than good judgement. The lights went off the moment we touched down and we taxied to the end of the runway but nobody wanted to know us as the bombs were still coming down on the airfield so we just had to sit there, scared to death, hoping the aircraft wouldn't be hit.

Charles's journal goes on to describe his impressions of the beleaguered island.

That night I had my first experience of mosquitoes. But the chief disturbance was air raids. I could not make out at the time why everyone kept getting up and going to the shelter. Later in my stay I understood it.

When the raids first started here the island had no AA defences and only three Gladiators and they used to send over twenty aircraft at a time every day and sometimes twice. Now they have their defences but the damage has been done. During our one day there, there were ten raids and seven brought down. But the raids are only five or six aircraft now.

We followed the ground crew in these raids and they certainly had the right idea. They dive for blast shelters till the bombs have fallen and then nip out and under cover or an aircraft until the shrapnel had fallen. But what a life.

During one of the raids I was in the mess and we all went

out to see the fighters bring one down. But alas a bomb fell nearby and all dived in again. I went through the window and left half my skin outside. I decided to wait some little time before going up to the MO to give him time to clear the major casualties. But half an hour afterwards ambulances were still coming in. When I did go I found just one or two minor injuries, and one Maltese. He was big and fat and with a stolid expression on his face. He had a scalp wound in among his thick matted dusty hair and a large gash in his broad flat thick feet. (A number of them never wore shoes.)

The MO brought a bowl of some disinfectant cleaning stuff and told him to just put his foot in it. On such occasions I have always found it usual to sort of test the feel of the water and then slowly immerse the foot. But not this gent! Just like an obedient animal he lifted his foot – more like a pad – and dropped it straight without a twitch or even a momentary change of expression. His head was then stitched and again, apart from one solitary grunt, there was no mention of pain. This sight rather impressed me and it seemed to me to rather typify the life of the people and their acceptance without question of life as it comes.

While I was waiting the SMO came in with his uniform covered in dust. It appears he always goes out with the ambulances, and on this occasion had to dig for victims. Of one they had only been able to find a finger with a ring. Frankly this island deserves the George Cross it has won and high mention in the annals of this war.

Another thing that mystified me was how they had managed to last so long for supplies. Apparently convoys are very scarce and almost a rarity and they exist on their stocks. Talking to a soldier at Luqa he said he would rather stay there than take the risk of a journey home, even though he had been there since the beginning of the war. The last lot to leave had been sunk thirty miles out and only a few saved. One big shortage that was pathetically obvious was cigarettes. At Gib they told us to take as many as we could and they would be bought from us, but if we had realised the situation we should have taken ten thousand.

We went into the nearby town of Luqa in the morning and found all the houses – what was left of them – built of the white rock of the island hewn into large square blocks. But in spite of the solidity of it and the thickness of the walls, there was hardly a house undamaged and most of them a complete wreck. In every street there were heaps of debris and yet people still lived and worked there. The centre square has the appearance of a Hollywood set, with its clean white blocks in the sun and the square broken buildings. Although the church was damaged the figures of Christ and the Saints remained. The houses that were still habitable opened straight onto the street with a clear open space right through to the back garden with apparently no rooms on either side. Although they were poor dwellings they looked clean and cool inside with tiled floors and green large plants in plenty in large pots or tubs.

We were able to go into one of the back gardens of one of the houses that was not there and here we found the plants still intact. Tomatoes well ripe, potatoes, vines and figs and a flat cactus bush. What a struggle to get crops from such a dry, rocky soil. The shops were like the houses, small and narrow and cool. We went into one for a drink and watched the people outside and the children coming from school all quite normal, and meditated on their lot and what they had been through in the last two years as a result of British dominion.

One other strange feature was the dress worn by the women and a black sort of gown gathered in, and with a full black sort of shawl affair with a long cane in one hem. This could be worn across the forehead so as to form a sort of sunshade, or it could be worn so that it hung down one side.

That evening after dinner we left for Egypt.

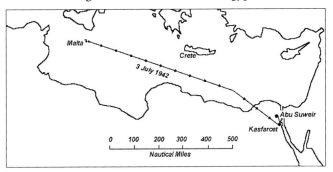

Charles's Travels – 3 July to 4 July 1942

3/7/42 Friday. Rotten trip. No loops, No ASV, sextant u/s, GMT wrong and could take no drifts! Had to pass Crete in dark but could not cross Egypt coast till daylight. Got there one hour earlier so had to stooge up and down for an hour. Then flew all across the Delta and down to Kasfareet on the Great Bitter Lake. Right out in desert. First Transit crews there and did not know what to do with us. Spent the morning and afternoon washing, feeding and sleeping in tent and getting comfortable for night as nothing for us to do and sand very hard. Mess lousy and flies terrific. Evening for bathe in Great Bitter Lake. Very warm, salt and shallow. Bought melon and ate it in the mess – lovely. Bed late.

The sequence of events that led to the crew's arrival on 459

Squadron becomes rather confused at this point. Charles's service records show that he was posted to HQ RAF Middle East on 28 June 1942 – the day they left UK – and a further, probably retrospective, entry shows that he was posted to 459 Squadron on the same date. However, Bryan Rostron's story makes it clear that the plot was not as simple as it appeared:

I had been given a movement order at Lyneham to deliver the aircraft and crew to HQ Far East in Delhi and we had talked about it during the trip... We didn't know when, if ever, we should be able to return home and the thought of going even further away to India didn't appeal very much.

The next day I went along to the Movement Office to ask for a further briefing but before I had the chance to say anything, a very young Pilot Officer asked me if we were going to 459. All the Australians had come through during the previous week and he thought we were the next instalment. We had heard that HQ Middle East was in a complete panic with Rommel being so near and were supposed to be moving down to Kenya (this may have been a rumour) but we thought quickly and I said "Yes, we are going to 459 Squadron. Where are they?"

... We felt pretty safe as apparently something like twenty five percent of reinforcement aircraft fell by the wayside, either crashed, shot down or delayed for other causes and they probably wouldn't miss one more so off we went to LG Z, which was situated about thirty minutes flying time away in the desert east of Cairo and north of the very mis-named Sweetwater Canal. LG Z was just a flat piece of desert marked out by oil drums and a few tents. When we landed Wing Commander Hennock, whom we had met at Horsham when he was forming the squadron, came up and in typical Aussie fashion asked us what the hell we were doing there. When I told him we were supposed to be going to India but would rather stay with our Aussie friends he wasn't very impressed until I told him the aircraft was full of spares. He took the movement order, tore it up and said "You're in". And that was how we came to find ourselves the only RAF crew on 459 Squadron RAAF.

Charles's journal describes their arrival:

> The second afternoon we were sent for in a hurry and took off for 459 Squadron at Abu Suweir. To get there we flew up a small portion of the Suez Canal and though we were perforce some distance away, and it was sand-cloudy we were able to see its straightness and narrowness and seeming hollowness.
>
> We landed in the evening and the first person I saw was Freddie Madsen. He would not believe it! I drove to the mess in style and there received a terrific welcome. I can see Eric Bedwell now, running from his tent, and George Holby with his infectious grin. It was all "Hello Chuck, are you posted?" And those who did not know me, about forty percent, soon wanted to find out the whys and wherefores. What a night in the mess.

At last Charles and the crew had got to an operational squadron. Their war proper could now start.

CHAPTER 6

Operational

In the modern Royal Air Force, postings to a maritime squadron are on an individual basis, and a new arrival will usually join an experienced crew to learn the ropes. In 1942, however, it was customary for individuals to form a crew at their Operational Training Unit, and for that crew to remain together. This had great advantages from the point of view of crew cooperation, for each man knew the strengths and weakness of the others, and a strong bond between individuals was formed. However, it meant that the first operational sortie was new to everyone on the crew, and there was little experience to fall back on. For this reason the Squadron Commander had to ensure that the crew was properly prepared and briefed before they went out on operations. For more than a week, therefore, Charles and his crew stayed on the ground.

> 5/7/42 Sunday. Up 7.30 a.m. and got cracking on various jobs – i.e. Adjutant and CO, Accounts and applied for allowances as I got 7/6 a day allowances! Then Navigation Section and handed in my stuff and collected more. Stores to try and get camp kit, but they had none. To photos for identity card etc. etc. Afternoon siesta and slept, then tried to put up our tent, but wind too strong and pegs too short so slept with Bill and Keith again. Bed early.

The identity card for which Charles was photographed was the Middle East identity card. As well as the normal function of

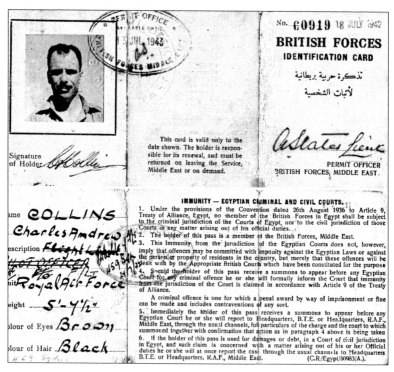

Charles's Identification Card for the Middle East.

providing identification, it served as something of a 'Get out of Jail Free' card, for it provided the British Servicemen with immunity from prosecution in the Egyptian courts. This, of course, did not give free licence to commit crimes. Indeed, those servicemen who did transgress the laws of the country could expect swift and firm retribution at the hands of their Squadron Commander. It did, however, mean that those who were tied up in the business of war could not be diverted from that duty by the long-drawn-out processes of civil justice in a foreign land.

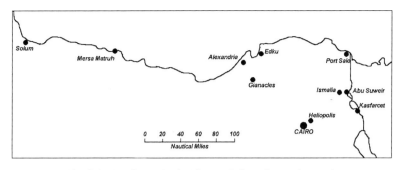

Charles's Travels in North Africa – July to September 1942.

Charles's impressions of the camp and the nearby towns and cities are recorded in his journal:

> This desert is worse than at Kasfareet, with patches of scrub, patches of stray areas and then the land beyond; and so it stretches for miles with nothing on the horizon. Here again are the pestilential flies and the heat, but there was more comfort than at Kasfareet. The mess was large and airy with good seats and good food and service. I had my own tent with camp bed, chair, wash stand and bath etc. The squadron had only just moved here and things were still in the process of erection, and at the moment to go to the lavatory one had to take a spade and go for a walk in the desert.

Abu Suweir – Officers' Mess.

Charles at his tent – well tied down!

The horizon is lost in what I suppose is the mirage that travellers used to imagine was water. It appears to end in a lake with just a sand bar across. In one direction there sometimes appears a forest or a village of houses. In truth it is a few distant telegraph poles. The wind is hot, nearly always from the same direction (about North West), but varies a lot in strength. The first time I saw a sand spout or willy-willy as they call them I was quite intrigued. It is a swirling thin column of sand, slightly curved at the base, with a thin continuous core and just disintegrates at the top. The height varies, the average being I suppose between 500 and 700 ft. But when flying once at 1500 ft a large one went right up beside us and I suppose for a few hundred feet above. They travel in the direction as the wind at the wind speed, i.e. about twenty to thirty mph, and last about twenty minutes, but anything light in its way goes with it. One passed over my tent just after it had been put up and just lifted it and laid it flat. This of course occasioned great hilarity in the mess. Now it just gives it a good shaking. When a good steady wind blows it lifts the lighter sand up in an evenly distributed fog of about ten to fifteen feet thickness.

There is no water here and all has to be brought in by tank bowser. How what life there is exists I don't know. I have only seen one carrion crow, one chameleon, like a lizard with frog's head, a bird like a thrush with longer legs and beak which I thought a quail but they tell me it was a plover. I saw its nest, just a few twigs flat on the stony sand with no attempt at concealment except its natural camouflage and it really was most difficult to find. They tell me there are snakes and scorpions but I have heard no reports of any being seen. The water, when we get it, is tepid or warm and is cooled to quite a low temperature by keeping it in porous jars or bags. The bathing problem is solved by a daily gharry to some showers about two miles away and is very crowded.

These gharries are sturdy little trucks and seem to run anywhere on this sand. After I had been here about a week I took one into Abu Suweir. It was only the camp area, but to see the stone and brick buildings and trees and shops was a change. But the Officers' mess was paradise found. A beautiful cool mosquito and fly proof solid building, with all mod cons and electric fans to scare off the flies. Made me envious. Two more animals here – grasshoppers about one to two inches long who whistle like ours but when they jump can stay in the air longer and steer their way about, and a few small sandy butterflies. Also a small dun coloured bug the same shape and twice the size of a Ladybird, only it does not fly, and a few ants, two breeds: one the same as ours and the others black and three eighths of an inch long.

The work here in the mess is done by the orderlies assisted by Italian prisoners from a nearby camp which is well lit at night and gives quite a glare in the sky reminiscent of towns at home in peace time. It is difficult to tell what these chaps think of things. They have no option in their lot and mostly can't speak English, but they look a poor lot and contented enough with life.

The sky throughout the day is almost always clear, occasionally a heavy layer of low cumulus moves in from the sea, but it is soon dispersed. The glare from the high sun on the sand is at first hard on the eyes in the day. At night there is no colourful sunset as there are no clouds. It is just a dull localized glow. And at night the clear blue sky brings out the beauty of the stars a treat.

One night the mosquitoes came. We had been free till then. I lay there and heard one. I killed it. I heard another and killed that. And still they came. I thought that I must be the unluckiest bloke that a mosquito should pick on me. But in the morning I learnt and saw that I was not the only one that had been favoured with their attentions. The whole camp had been invaded. Then of course began the panic for nets. And all the usual tales of the unusual feats of the mosquitoes. They had been holding up the edge to let their pals in. They had been seen gnawing a larger hole with a sickly leer on their faces. Nets should also be sound proof so that the mosquitoes could not be heard from within.

A few extracts from his diary show the way in which the crew were introduced to the squadron routine:

> 7/7/42 Tuesday. Up early and was duty controller – quite a good job when I got used to it. But there was little aircraft activity and I was not too busy. So I wrote a few letters. The only snag was that I had to be there all day and so no afternoon rest. Was it hot! First part of evening talking about Australian fruits and sheep shearing. I went to bed at 9.45 p.m. due mainly to lack of lights and nothing to do but drink.
>
> 9/7/42 Thursday. Bags of activity as everyone off on a strike in the evening. So I contented myself with astro for a bit and then back for letters and reading. Afternoon for a shower and evening yarning and letters. Had a rotten night as mosquitoes now getting very busy.
>
> 10/7/42 Friday. Spent a pretty idle day as usual. Went down to flights in the morning and evening but nothing doing so back again and sat in tent reading. In the afternoon a willy-willy took my tent away! Evening in the mess. Australians saying how England was so feudal with its 'sirs' and squires etc. Then George Holby and I went for a walk and discussed the power of faith in view of the three crews we lost last night.

The squadron Operations Record Book (F540) records that there was a major operation on the evening of 9 July, with three squadron aircraft having been lost on a strike on enemy shipping inbound with supplies for Rommel's forces in Tobruk.

12/7/42 Sunday. Went for first flight with Bryan only and did radio as well. Just local and had a look at Ismalia canal area, saw some goats and mules, small wadi areas crops and poor flat oases. Collected some camp kit and got my tent formatted. My projected trip to Cairo tomorrow was cancelled as it was temporarily out of bounds. Afternoon and evening just wandered round and in mess yarning till early bed.

13/7/42 Monday. Up early to flights. Went out on bombing trip in the morning. Afternoon shower. Evening night flying but just as we were going off lights went and so we packed up. Bed early.

The next day Charles had a two day visit to Cairo. His journal records:

Came the day when I got out of the desert for a break. Two days in Cairo on business. And going up in the gharry I saw a lot of what was superficial in Egyptian life. The women all wear the long black robes and shawl and mostly are veiled. They never appear to take off their clothes as I have even seen them bathing in the canal with them all on. They seem to spend their time carrying water or boxes on their heads, driving goats in herds or bathing in the canal. The men wear a long dirty gown affair with no shape, just like a night gown down to the ankles. Sometimes it is shorter and tucked up around their waist to show a garment down to the knees which might be trousers. They don't mind taking their clothes of to wash. In fact they strip on the side of the road and bathe among or near the women. They seem to spend their time doing nothing. Those that were working were on the land or on dhows or driving laden camels or mules. The children are all dressed the same, just a long gown. The younger ones are carried astride their mother's shoulder, the rest can walk. The dividing line between youth and age is difficult to see. All the children are well taught in the art of begging and practise it. Others help on the jobs.

Their houses are nothing more than poor mud brick walls about 7 ft high, and roofed over with plaited reeds, the roof normally being broken and full of holes. They appeared to be one room only with scanty furnishings and very dirty. The shops are more solid, having a framework of wood, two stories and facing the road. The door seems to be the whole of the front gable which has been removed, and anyone and anything can wander in and out at will. In the evening they seem to be full of Arabs sitting about drinking. They have a very easy was of sitting, i.e. sit on their heels. Easy if you can do it.

The land near the canal is cut up into small patches and well irrigated. The main crop as far as I could see was maize. From the air the impression is of a straight canal, a road and a railway and rectangular patches of various colours. The villages look like a lot of broken down boxes thrown on the ground. The dhows on the canals are all of the same approved pattern, with tall mast and large crossbar with sail. They are broad of beam, have a flat tall bow, and are able to carry a large deck cargo. Going down wind it is easy, but up wind the sail has to be stowed and they are hauled along by two or three men by a long rope from the mast head, and with a loop at the far end which is padded and goes round their shoulders and chest.

The canals are mostly fringed with rushes or just a shallow sand embankment, and then continues a narrow margin of well-irrigated sand. The water is raised by the age old methods: the spiral cylinder which is operated by a boy or woman and lifts the water on the inclined plane principle; the water wheel operated by one ass, mule or camel where a large wooden horizontal cogged wheel operates a similar vertical wheel fitted with scoops, the water being emptied into a trough just above the hub; and the weighted bucket which is just a long pole on a fulcrum, with the bucket at the canal end and a load at the other.

At intervals along the road are small three sided sand enclosures with two large earthenware jars containing water, presumably for the traveller who replenishes them from the river. And all along the road are these wanderers, mostly men and mostly barefooted and very few with any bundles. Sometimes a man or woman will be leading or driving a mule. Sometimes mules or camels are heavily loaded with panniers. The more prosperous will be seen riding their own mule with their legs swinging well out sideways in a regular rhythm – men only of course. The really well-to-do even carry a sunshade and have clean robes and turban.

Occasionally along the canal are modern, mechanically operated lock gates. On the road itself were various classes of service transport, all on the right, with an occasional private car. I also saw one steam roller making a strange contrast. The ploughing is done mainly by a heavy, wooden, one sheared plough, slowly dragged along by two yoked oxen. The road is edged for long distances by gum trees or date palms. At one remote village was a well-kept British war cemetery.

After a while the isolated villages ceased, the cultivation became more ambitious and scattered small houses heralded the approach of Cairo, the tall white buildings of which could be seen ahead. The road leading into the city was straight, walled on one side and lined with palms and a bright red-flowering kind of mountain ash, and ended in a domed mosque. The streets at first are wide and tree lined, and with large pleasant looking houses standing back. But the centre of the town is the opposite, like all the other towns. Streets appear narrower and everywhere are shops, hotels, offices etc. Despite the efforts to keep the streets clean and tidy and their more or less clean and tidy appearance, one still has a feeling that they are dirty and untidy. The flies still abound and it is still as hot. Eighty percent of the shops appear to be watch shops.

There are all varieties of transport: trams, buses, taxis, hansoms, the latest American cars down to old fashioned English cars, motor bikes, cycles, lorries and all types of service transport. The trams are single decker and open and nearly always crowded, with people sitting on the running board or hanging on there. The urchins have a habit of running behind and sitting on the bumper and many is the maimed child or man seen about. The taxis are mostly Fiats. The hansoms are dirty and decrepit. They all drive on the right and sound their peculiar warning under the slightest provocation. There are various types of car hooter. Bells on the hansoms, and whistles on the trams. And added to the general clamour it is terrific. In fact the noise is the first thing you notice on arriving.

Many of the Arabs in the streets have adopted western ideas and wear the casual trousers, jacket and light collar and tie, and a red fez and tassel. The women wear a light summer frock, not stockings as a rule, high heeled shoes and even powder, paint, lipstick, rouge and nail varnish. From this standard there were various grades down to the old night shirt and gown. The streets abound with Arabs in their dirty shirts of all ages. The youngest, just begging, or offering to clean shoes or sell papers. Some of the older youths sell various coloured drinks which are in large pitcher shaped glass jars and are slung on leather straps round their waist and shoulders on a sort of pivot. Attached to the waist band is a small container of water and a tray of two glasses and small change. The liquid, when the jar is tilted, is poured from a thin tube at the top in a long thin stream to the low held glass. On the glass being returned empty, it is summarily rinsed with a drop of water and returned to the tray. To attract attention to their wares these fellows carry a pair of brass quoit shaped stoppers in one hand.

There is quite a large well trained modern police force. And when I wandered once into the poorer quarter they contrasted strangely with the child labour there. There are numerous small workshops – cobblers, farriers, carpenters etc, opening onto the street and apart from one or two adults the main payroll is of youths or small children. It somehow seems the natural thing and quite accepted by everybody. Lord Shaftsbury's difficulties are more easily realised having seen this.

The only really pleasant spot I found was the New Zealand Club, where it was clear and cool and friendly. At the Grand Hotel the food, in fact the whole hotel, was typically Arab and that is the only way to describe it.

In the evening, although a blackout was supposed to be in force, there were many lights at hotel windows and many people would sit out on the veranda and watch the traffic below in the still warm air. There was nothing unusual about it, except that it was Cairo – and the noise! A dance band played in the lounge, but not attractively and as there was a curfew for forces the only thing was bed! And such were my first impressions of Cairo. It was all too crowded to pick up small details. It just merged as a whole when I got back to the desert.

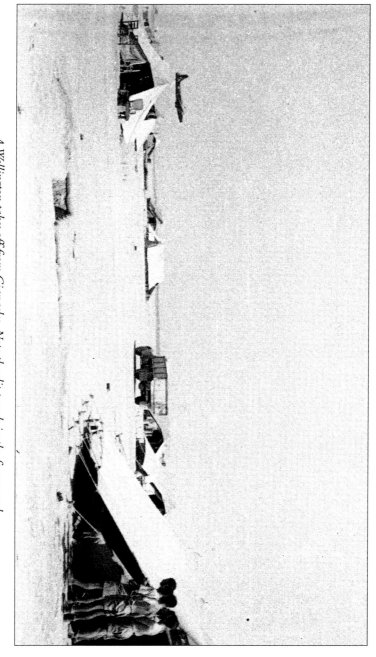

A Wellington takes off from Gianacles. Note the slit trench in the foreground.

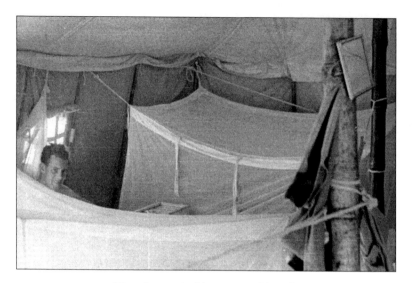

Mosquito nets inside a tent at Gianacles.

Back at the squadron there was still nothing for his crew, so the next day:

> 17/7/42 Friday. Up early and caught Gharry to Ismalia. Had short, interesting run, but did not stay long in town. Did a bit of shopping and then caught taxi out to the United Services club on the lake side and spent the day swimming and sun bathing. After dinner went to the French Club for a drink and watch dancing. Back in Gharry at 10.30 p.m. and bed late very tired.

Then at last:

> 18/7/42 Saturday. Started out as a quiet day but at noon were told to pack up and go off to Gianacles in one hour for a strike. Got to Gianacles and were not wanted, but told to stand by. Settled down and did nothing all afternoon and then went to bed early to wait developments.

19/7/42 Sunday. Up latish and spent all day waiting about in tent and had a sleep in the afternoon. Then told we were for briefing at 8.00 p.m. and due off at 10.30 p.m. on an offensive patrol along coast as far as Derna! Not too good. Very dark and at Matruh a big attack was going and we had to take avoiding action. On way back I lost one hour somewhere and on ETA the coast not in sight. After a while turned south and landed near Alexandria 6.00 a.m.

Charles's account of this flight is, perhaps understandably, reticent about the extent of what went wrong. Bryan Rostron's account goes into much more detail:

We took off at ten o'clock at night to fly off the coast and do a sweep in a north-westerly direction from Tobruk to Derna, our objective being to find any shipping which might be in the area. All went well and we duly reached our patrol area and carried out the search. The weather was clear with no clouds and the visibility very good even thought it was the middle of the night. When we finished the patrol we were somewhere off the coast of Cyrenaica at its most northerly point and everything was going to plan. I remember thinking then that this operational business wasn't perhaps as bad as we thought – little did I know!

Although I didn't realise it at the time, the seeds of disaster were already being sown. I asked Chuck for a course to steer to bring us to a point twenty miles out at sea roughly due north of LG 226 so that we could then turn south and return to base keeping well clear of the front line at El Alamein. He gave me a course and an ETA to the turning point and off we went. The resulting shambles taught me a lesson I have never forgotten and for all future flights, however insignificant, I always made a note of the approximate courses and leg times so that I could make a rough check on the navigator's instructions. Chuck somehow misapplied the variation and the direction of the wind so the course he gave me, instead of running roughly south-east parallel to the coast, was almost due east and we headed off into the middle of the Med. He also made a mistake in the ETA which he gave as one hour sooner than it should have been. When the time of ETA duly arrived we flew on for about ten minutes but could see no sign of land on our right so, thinking that we might be a little further out to sea than expected, we turned due south expecting to hit the coast somewhere near Alexandria in a few minutes.

We flew south for about an hour with still no sign of land by which time we hadn't the faintest idea where we were but the only solution was to keep on a southerly course until we eventually made landfall somewhere on the African coast. After a further twenty minutes we saw the coast (it was about thirty minutes before first light by now) and the coast appeared to be running North West to South East so we did a bit of quick thinking and, bearing in mind we had flown for an hour and a half beyond our calculated turning point, came to the conclusion that we had overflown the Nile Delta and were running down the coast towards Port Said at the entrance to the Suez Canal. In the hope of identifying where we were, we came down to 200 feet and flew south east. After a few minutes we began to fly over large quantities of tanks, guns, tents and all the paraphernalia of a large army. So we thought, "This must be the build-up of Eighth Army reserves waiting to go up to El Alamein". When they started shooting at us our immediate reaction was "Bloody pongos, they don't know their own aircraft when they see them". So we carried on eastwards at 200 feet in the hope that they would see the error of their ways. After a mile or so the shooting stopped and there was a stretch of empty desert and then a further concentration of tanks and guns. These did not fire at us so we assumed they had seen the light.

Dawn had broken by now although it was quite hazy and we suddenly realised the coast had turned north east. This threw us completely and we assumed we were flying up the coast towards Palestine! What had happened to Port Said and the Suez Canal in the meantime we couldn't understand. Suddenly, out of the murk appeared a small airfield so I did a quick circuit and landed with the intention of finding out where we were. The place appeared deserted except for a few strange looking biplanes, there was not a soul in sight and nobody took the slightest interest in us. There was a small control tower and we thought we might even be behind the German lines as we didn't recognise the aircraft, so in best Wild West fashion I drew my revolver and went into the building. There was a man asleep on a camp bed in a strange uniform, so I stuck the gun in his ribs and shouted "Wake up!" The resulting burst of British profanity made me realise we weren't in enemy territory, so I quickly pocketed the gun before he saw it. It turned out we had landed at Maryut, a very small Fleet Air Arm station on the outskirts of Alexandria and the aircraft were Swordfish. We quickly climbed back into the aircraft and headed for LG 226, about thirty miles away.

When we were debriefed we conveniently forgot to mention that we had flown right over the German reserve and front lines at 200 feet and nobody ever found out that we had landed at Maryut so, from an official point of view our first operation with 459 was quite uneventful whilst, in actual fact, it was a complete shambles – the landing at Maryut never appeared in my log-book! It did teach us a number of lessons which stood us in good stead on later operations – it was a very good learning experience, particularly as we lived to tell the tale. I felt very sorry for Chuck and he certainly didn't get his lines crossed to that extent again.

Their first operation could so easily have been their last, but fortune seems to have favoured them.

> 20/7/42 Monday. Refuelled and back to base at 7.30 a.m. and de-briefed. Breakfast and bed. Slept fitfully from 9.00 a.m. to 5.00 p.m. then just laid around till bed late. Had a trip out to the vineyard and bought back several bunches of grapes to the tent.

During this period, Rommel had been consolidating his position, and the allies were desperate to intercept as many of his supply ships as possible. They were particularly engaged in attacking the freighters and barges running supplies from Tobruk to Mersa Matruh. Ground forces had also kept Rommel on his toes, with an attack by the Australian 9th Division on Italian positions near El Alamein starting on 10 July, and other attacks on two further Italian Divisions on 15 July. General Auchinleck made a major offensive on 21 July, but again was held by Axis forces. The pressure had to be maintained on Rommel.

> 21/7/42 Tuesday. Up early and started to rest, but at 10.00 a.m. they called us out for a strike. Six of us with fighter escort. It was a hazardous trip and we were all apprehensive but when I got in the air I was quite keen about it and somewhat disappointed when we did not see the target. Spent rest of day idling and bed late.

459 Squadron's first formation strike. Two Hudsons in the foreground and a Beaufighter fighter escort in the distance.

This formation strike was a new procedure for 459 Squadron. The escort of fighters must have been very welcome in a theatre where the German forces were very strong. The squadron Operations Record Book records:

21/7/42 The squadron performed its first sortie in formation. Pilots were as follows. Sqn Ldr Howson, Sgt Staines, F/O Proctor, Sgt Rostron, F/O Beaton and F/O Wetherby. The first aircraft was airborne at 1012. They took off in threes and maintained close formation in 2 Vs and set course for Edku picking up 4 Beaufighters as escort. One of the Beaufighters returned but the other three went through the patrol. The formation went along to Cape Azzaz area and searched at 300 feet but sighted nothing to attack so returned, the last aircraft landing at 1537 hrs.

That was the end of the crew's introduction to war:

22/7/42 Wednesday. Up early and dashed out for Ops, but it was cancelled at the last minute. So we did thirty five minutes formation flying and bombing. Afternoon briefed for standby for strike, but did not go. Evening in tent yarning. Bed early.

23/7/42 Thursday. Up early and idled for the morning, until we were told to pack and return to base – a big relief. Spent evening in mess playing cards and drinking and went to bed late with sore head.

24/7/42 Friday. Up late and was grabbed for Orderly Officer, so kept busy all day and most of night as had to visit guards twice after midnight. Spent evening in Sergeants' mess drinking which was unwise as I have a gippy tummy. About five hours sleep.

25/7/42 Saturday. Up early and caught gharry to Ismalia for day. Did a bit of shopping and then to United Services Club. Had glorious day and in the evening dancing to a band in beautiful full moon was a marvellous setting. Bought Tennyson, and reading and writing.

One of the letters he wrote that evening was to his old school at Borden – the Old Bordonians Association. Clearly censorship would not allow him to go into too much detail, nor to name any places. But his letter conveys his impressions of war so far:

July 25th, 1942.

Dear Mr Editor,

To commence in the approved style, I have arrived here safely and am stationed with an Australian squadron miles out in the desert. We are flying the same aeroplanes and doing pretty well the same job, only under somewhat different conditions.

We had a very interesting trip out, and where we had to

stop I had a good look around while I had the chance. Of course, there is not much to see out in the desert – just miles and miles of sand – the only life consisting of flies, grasshoppers two inches long, chameleons, and I've seen one quail. The monotony of the scene is relieved only by tents and aeroplanes.

But in the country things are a lot more interesting. All just the same as they tell us in geography books, but still very interesting to see. The people for the most part are living as they must have lived for years, in single-storied, one or two-roomed square mud-walled houses. The roof, if there is one, is made of thatched rushes, and very dilapidated. All mod cons, and even primitive sanitary arrangements appear to be lacking.

They wear the same clothes year in and year out – the men, a dirty gown, like a night-shirt, right down to their ankles; the women wear all black and are mostly veiled.

The women seem to spend their time with the goats or carrying water in jars on their heads. Occasionally they are seen on the land or helping with the various primitive means they have of lifting water from the canals. The men work in the fields with their yoke of oxen and a one-shared wooden plough or on dhows, or mostly they seem to do nothing except beg and sell odds and ends.

Cairo would take a whole letter to describe. It is the noisiest town I have ever been in. But the most noticeable thing is the contrast between East and West. Westernisation has overtaken them before they have got out of their eastern traditions. I found telephones where there was no drainage or sanitation; child labour, with a modern, efficient police force; the latest American cars and hansom cabs; electric trams and donkey carts. Egyptian women in summer frocks, high-heeled shoes, lipstick and nail varnish, and in various degrees down to the traditional black. The same with the men – from their night-shirt to trousers, jacket, and collar and tie. And so it went on – a strange city of contrasts.

I have just returned from an advanced 'drome, where we were in it pretty hot, but as I have a day off I have come to the nearest town for a change of scenery. Here there is an excellent Officers' club on the side of a lake. From the veranda there are the gardens and lawns, the seaboard, then the shining blue water and a moored diving-board. In the background, yachts, a green fringe of trees and palms, and the dazzling yellow undulating sand. I have been in the warm, buoyant water nearly all day, and am now enjoying the evening scene and catching up on my mail. In a few days now I shall be back in the thick of it, and all thoughts of this peace and tranquillity destroyed by shell-bursts and tracer bullets.

Conclusion now, and I hope everything is still going well in England – in Kent – at Borden.

Yours sincerely,

C. A. COLLINS

26/7/42 Sunday. Up early and down to flights but nothing. Belly ache all day so in the afternoon went to see Doc. Diagnosed gippy guts and had dose of castor oil. Running all night and had had no food since tiffin.

27/7/42 Monday. Up late and running all day. Still off food till dinner when I was able to eat meat but no vegetables or fruit. Evening started writing letters when warning went and all lights out, so yarning. Bed early.

28/7/42 Tuesday. Up early and still a bit bad inside. But then Bryan came and said they were sending him to Gianacles with another observer. So I tightened belt and said I would go, and thither went I in trepidation. And got there to hear that Wickham was down in sea. That's Livingstone and Dig O'Brian, Gunny, Kemp so far. Nothing tonight and bed early.

29/7/42 Wednesday. Up early and spent day hanging about and reading and writing. Afternoon went for briefing and took off in evening for strike in Bay of Solum. Had good look round and along coast but could not find ship. Back at base at 11.30 p.m. and bed 2.30 a.m.

30/7/42 Thursday. Up late and thoroughly bitten by mosquitoes and sand flies. Had idle day reading and battling against flies. Nothing on today. Bed at dark – i.e. 9.30 p.m.

31/7/42 Friday. Up late and spent all day in a mosquito net to keep away the flies and reading and writing. Evening stand by for a convoy escort at 10.30 p.m. to 4 30 a.m. No fun having to get up at that time as my blankets were flea ridden and I put them out but when I came back they were dew soaked. So I had little sleep.

1/8/42 Saturday. Spent all day reading and trying to sleep. Briefing at 8.45 p.m. for dawn patrol along coast from Solum to Mersa Matruh. So straight to bed but got no sleep due to flies again.

2/8/42 Sunday. Up 2.00 a.m. and had uneventful but interesting trip along coast only about two miles off. Arrived back 8.30 a.m. and found letter from Arthur. Washed etc and bed for sleep. Had arranged to go into Alexandria with Magnus to try and locate Arthur, but slept till 3.00 p.m. Spent the afternoon lazing and then to briefing at 6.30 p.m., as on standby and had to get up at 1.00 a.m. and did not get off after all.

3/8/42 Monday. Slept till late and spent the afternoon in tent till 5.00 p.m. when told to get back to base and away we went. Arrived 6.30 p.m. and then we were told

to get a 48 hour pass in for the Sergeants. To bed at
midnight after I acquired passes and did everything.

4/8/42 Tuesday. Caught 8.00 a.m. gharry to Ismalia and got
off at main road and hitch hiked into Cairo. Arrived at
11.30 a.m. booked at Grand Hotel and then to Officers'
Club for various purchases. Tiffin at Grand and then to
Metro to see Come Live With Me! Then shopping till
dinner. After dinner to Cabaret Birat. It is for other ranks
only, and I saw Arab shows, as they are on till midnight,
then back in a horse gharry. Bed 1.00 a.m.

5/8/42 Wednesday. Up early and at New Zealand Club at
9.30 a.m. and picked up a guide and car to pyramids.
Went all round on camels and had good shufti and we
were told everything. Then back and round crowded
bazaars and the Blue Mosque. Lunch at the Metro Cafe
and afternoon at a film and then caught a gharry to
Ismalia at 6.00 p.m. and arrived there at 9.00 p.m. Spent
the evening at the French Club and caught gharry to
base at 10.20 p.m. and bed late. Sgt Staines missing.

Charles went into more detail in his journal. On his visit to
the 'Cabaret Birat' he wrote:

This was nothing more than a big open area. The side
was a raised portion for a few tables, and ending in a shelter
in one corner for more tables and the bar. From here was
another shorter raised edge for tables and then the orchestra
in the other corner. The far side was taken up mainly by a
stage, having the entrance and surround on the remaining
side. The music by the orchestra had a modern western
rhythm and they even played fairly modern tunes. A space
was kept clear of chairs and tables in the centre for dancing.
Hostesses of an obviously indifferent character and obvious

designs, but not withstanding a few fairly attractive, were well in evidence and forthcoming at the slightest sign of interest from a client. Prices appeared little if any dearer than elsewhere.

Late in the evening the stage show commenced. First of all a play in Egyptian, which had the appearance of being a serial, like the Chinese ones. It was just a constant procession of characters on and off the stage, and without their seeming to stay long enough for any sustained piece of good acting. From this the scene changed to short sketches. First musical and vocal with the typical Egyptian lulling dirges. Later it slowly evolved into various single and cooperative sensuous eastern dances, in scanty or thin attire. To me there appeared little grace of movement. The whole dance being centred in the movement of the hips and the sensuousness was accentuated in the lifting of the bulging belly. Maybe that was all I noticed though, as I did see one occasional fine shoulder and arm movement.

The show finished at midnight and we returned with the assistance of a hansom. On the river bank things were very quiet but in town the usual noise prevailed. Blackout regulations seemed to be very lax as traffic lights were not hooded and a few shop window lights still burned with the whole producing a very coloured effect that I have not seen for years. The vendors with the flat doughy pancake affairs in glass cases on barrows work all night and when they put a candle in the glass case it looks like a firefly moving along – or better still, a glow-worm.

He describes in some detail the sights in and around Cairo:

The next morning we went to the Pyramids. We took a car and a guide out there and then hired a camel each. A

The crew visit the Sphinx and the Pyramids using local transport.

slow and monotonous means of progress but they can trot if you can stand the jolting. The taking off and landing is the worst part. They land by placing the fore and the hind legs fairly far apart and then dropping forward onto the front knees. The back legs have two joints and sort of slowly fold up with the knees at the upper joint. The take off is the opposite movement. These camels took us round the Great Pyramids of Gisa (one for the King, one for the Queen and the others for the princes and princesses), the Sphinx and the tombs. By the time we had finished we had had enough of camels and we knew how to land them, drive them and start them. If you cluck they stand up, if you click your lips they move and if you hiss they kneel down.

The Pyramids themselves were very interesting and well worth seeing. But they were more or less what I expected to see, and one is enough. I like seeing the unexpected.

Everything that has been said about them has been said before, but the points that interested me were the size of the blocks, the size of the whole and the fact that having seen them it makes me wonder all the more at the number of slaves that must have been employed to get them here and build it.

Each block was quarried by drilling holes into the rock, plugging in wood pegs and soaking in water to make them swell. They were all cut to shape and size in this way and they all perfectly dovetail together. The site is now close to a main road, a large hotel and town. But I imagine that originally it was right out in the desert. They are all built on a solid limestone base. In fact the Sphinx itself is cut straight out of the rock. This has kept its shape (a lion's body for strength and a man's head for wisdom to represent the King) exceedingly well seeing as they were all built 1300 years BC. (Took thirty years to build). The Sphinx's features are almost perfect except for a missing nose removed by a cannon ball from Napoleon. I was surprised to hear that he spent three years here.

The Romans while here made great efforts to destroy the tombs and the murals, but apparently did not get far enough below the surface of the sand and a number of the blocks still have the various figures and cryptic signs well preserved, some in relief, some carved. In places traces of the old colouring still remain, even though it has been exposed to the open for so long. All these are limestone. Inside corridors are supported by huge granite columns and cross pieces. The floors and walls are of white alabaster blocks. It is unfortunate that all the mummies and untold wealth had been stolen from the pyramids before we discovered them! Now it is just a bare interior with just the empty sarcophagus.

Having seen the whole of the pyramids we went back to town and were taken round the old bazaar quarter and the Blue Mosque. The bazaar is the native quarter as seen in pictures and made of dirty, very narrow streets with the shops straight over the street. They are cool inside and some of them have various odd rooms, small and dark leading off the main hall, which usually opens out into another narrow street. All the work here is done by hand, by the natives and on the spot. Leather work, brass work, pewter, ivory, cloth and silver: really an amazing sight. The difficulty was that everywhere we went the shop keepers swarmed round pestering us to buy. Some of the work, however, was unbelievably wonderful.

From here we went to the Blue Mosque. Cool, quiet and shady inside, with the usual awed, sacred silence. The general construction was square with the centre occupied by the tomb of the builder in the thirteenth century. The body being four feet below the surface and the tomb of cedar wood about seven feet high and surrounded by a cedar wood sort of square lattice work. The floor space for the congregation appeared small, but there were no seats or pews to take up a lot of room. The shrine was in the eastern wall so that everyone faced east – to Mecca. It was a small alcove beautifully inlaid with mother-of-pearl. Various parts of the wall were also inlaid with mother-of-pearl, or scripts from the Koran. The lighting was from high small windows mostly of ivory and looking blue and gold. They look like stained glass windows, but only one or two of them are glass. None of them has figures, just straight design, as it is contrary to the Koran teaching.

And again Cairo was left behind for the desert. And again we think of Gianacles with foreboding. All it means to us is possible tragedy and discomfort. Being our advanced striking base we only go there for about a week, or two or three ops trips and then back to base. Therefore we only take a minimum of kit. There are no bathing or batting facilities. Tons of sand. Temp about 110° in the shade. Mosquitoes, sand flies and ordinary flies and worst of all fleas. On one occasion I came back with lousy blankets! If we are not flying I lie on my bed naked, under a mosquito net to keep out flies all the afternoon. The mess has nothing to recommend it and I don't know many of the fellows there.

Charles and the crew spent the next few days at Abu Suweir waiting for another mission. He did spells as Duty Controller, took some practice astro shots, but spent most of the time reading.

11/8/42 Tuesday. Up early to be told to go to Gianacles at 10.30 a.m. So did a Beach patrol on way and arrived at 1.00 p.m. Quiet afternoon yarning and bed early in evening as due for morning patrol.

12/8/42 Wednesday. Up 2.00 a.m. and take off 3.30 a.m. Very tired. Arrived at Cape Azzaz at 6.15 a.m. and ran in on wrecked schooner. Then patrolled all along coast. Enemy aircraft at Sidi Barani! Turned off at Taifa rocks. Then saw first boat and attacked! Two hits and one flash, and did she rock! Back at 8.30 a.m. and bed 10.00 a.m. Wake at 4.30 p.m. Spent afternoon reading till 6.00 p.m. when we briefed again. Bed early.

13/8/42 Thursday. Up 2.00 a.m. again and away at 3.30 a.m. Usual patrol Cape Azzaz at 6.00 a.m. and saw a terrific explosion to the east. Went for it and found another barge left and one down. Attacked and sank the other and back to base at 8.30 a.m. tails up. Bed 10.00 a.m. Up at 4.00 p.m. and briefed again at 6.30 p.m. for shipping strike. Did not find ships but got some very accurate AA from Matruh! Back midnight and bed 1.00 a.m.

14/8/42 Friday. Spent day sleeping and reading and afternoon in the mess yarning and drinking.

15/8/42 Saturday. Two more barges this morning. Left Gianacles in the morning and back at Abu Suweir for lunch. Afternoon wandering round doing things, reading and writing. Evening in Sergeants' mess on celebrations and had a good time.

16/8/42 Sunday. Up late and swing an aircraft, then reading and getting things arranged so that we could get away on the evening gharry to Ismalia. Arrived there at 7.00 p.m. and waited till 8.00 p.m. but could not get a lift to Port Said, so took a train. Had meal at YMCA while waiting. Arrived at midnight and had loose gharry take us to hotel, only very poor one!

17/8/42 Monday. Up early and after breakfast got away and booked at Hotel de la Poste which was a little better. In the morning looked around and afternoon across on the ferry and bathed on a private beach then back to dinner and spent the evening with George Holby's gunner and his father. Bed midnight. Sergeant Cadel missing.

18/8/42 Tuesday. Up late and then went out to bathe over the ferry. Back for lunch and then back again to bathe. Caught 6.00 p.m. train to Ismalia and spent rest of evening at the United Services Club. Back at camp 11.30 p.m. Bed. Pilot Officer Terry missing.

Charles describes Ismalia and Port Said in his journal:

What a treat Ismailia was in the days when leave was cancelled! We would get a day off and go there in the morning gharry, to return at night at 10.20 p.m. The town itself had nothing to offer. The usual Arab shops, heat and palms, two cinemas and one or two hotels. But the United Services Club – there would I go, some way out of town and on the lake side. It was built for coolness and comfort, and to the exclusion of flies. From the air-conditioned lounge, netted french windows opened out to a wide shady veranda, with a just sufficient sprinkling of wicker tables and chairs. From here one looked out across the garden edged lawns to the lake side. The light blue water was almost always studded with bathers and the white sails of yachts. In the distance rose the pale yellow sand from the palm edged lake. Most of my time there would be spent in the water, just splashing around or laying on the moored diving raft. Between times I would sit under a table umbrella on the lawn and smoke and sip iced drinks and read. It was a wonderful peaceful change from the desert life.

A moonlight evening here was an ideal setting. The full moon shining across the far yellow sand and reflecting in a broad rippling band across the water to the dark lawns. Here the parties sitting on the lawns, smoking and chatting, were surrounded by a romantic setting of swaying silhouetted palms and gum trees. An orchestra played, softly it seemed, from a corner of the veranda for dancers on a semi-floodlit mosaic square on the corner of the lawns, and added just what was needed to the scene. The food and service were good and made it a perfect retreat.

Another club, the French Club, was after the same style except that it was in the town and had no bathing facilities. But there was a larger dancing square, dining room and bar, and library and writing room.

Port Said is a nondescript sort of place and obviously owes its importance only to the Suez Canal. As far as I could see it was all of fairly modern building, and none of the dirty Arab houses and shops. It is hot, it smells, it is dirty, dirtier than Cairo, though not so noisy or busy with traffic. More of the streets are tree lined and there are more small restaurants and cafes, but only one good hotel. The population is mainly French and Egyptian again, but there are some of everything. The harbour was pretty full of shipping of various denominations, and with any number of small craft, cutters and motor boats nipping about. The two most prominent buildings on the water front appear to be the Harbour Master's Office and the Office of the Suez Canal Company. A regular ferry service plies across the harbour continually – two boats, for pedestrians and traffic. We used to go across to a private bathing club on the Mediterranean shores and it was grand.

There now followed a period of comparative idleness for the crew. On 27 August they flew to Gianacles for operations, but nothing was needed. They flew two operational trips on 30 August, but encountered no enemy vessels or aircraft. The whole theatre of operations was settling down after a period of rapid change. At the beginning of August Churchill himself had flown to Egypt to join General Alan Brooke (Chief of the Imperial General Staff) who was also there. Unhappy with the performance of General Auchinleck, they replaced him with General Alexander, and the 8th Army was to be commanded by Lieutenant General Gott, replacing General Richie. In a cruel turn of fate, the day after his appointment the transport aircraft in which General Gott was flying to Heliopolis, near Cairo, was shot down by a German fighter and the General was killed. His command of the 8th Army then went to Lieutenant General Bernard Montgomery. Churchill was anxious to attack Rommel's forces, and Alexander and Montgomery set about preparation for that aim. Rommel made an attack to the south

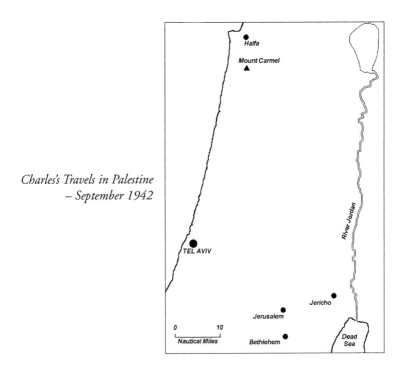

Charles's Travels in Palestine – September 1942

of El Alamein on 31 August, attempting to outflank the Allied forces. Intelligence from the intercept and decoding of enigma messages meant that the Allies were ready for him. His attack faltered in the Allied minefields and in the poor condition of the desert sand. Now ill with jaundice, Rommel's luck seemed to be failing him.

Meanwhile on 31 August the crew were sent on seven days' leave to Tel Aviv.

> 31/8/42 Monday. Up early and took off by air with nine others for Tel Aviv in Palestine. Arrived at lunch time and fed. Afternoon went for a walk around shopping.

Charles's journal describes the rest of the day's events:

The first day was Lee's 21st, so in the evening we went out to a posh dinner and then to cabaret. The trouble was that there is no beer here, or very little and so we had to drink short fancies. But at midnight when we left I was still pretty well OK and so suggested to Jimmy that we went for a dip before returning. It was quite dark and we decided to go in the nude and for the first ten minutes it was jolly good fun. But we were bathing round a pole with some indistinguishable notice on it. We were soon to find out what it was. Quite suddenly I felt a very strong undercurrent and Jimmy shouted at the same time. When I put my feet on the bottom it just sifted away out like quick sands, and there was no footing. I gave Jimmy a quick shove in and turned over to float in on the breakers. But no – out I went. Then I realised the worst and was inclined to panic. I swam as hard as I could but it soon became evident that I was making no headway, I was getting tired and swallowing a lot of water in the breakers. It was borne in on me that it was hopeless and that I should not reach the shore again, and yet the thought was not abhorrent, I felt no horror and yet still struggled.

It is difficult now after it is all over to recall all my thoughts. I realised I should be killed on active service but not in action, but that was forgotten. The two main thoughts as I remember them now were what Jimmy would do, and what Bryan and Lee would do when told and how they would feel. Soon I was reaching the stage of exhaustion, and the knowledge that I was pretty well full of salt water and spending most of the time under water and yet it did not appear an unpleasant death. Suddenly and quite unexpectedly my feet touched solid bottom. I came to the surface and saw the silhouettes of the houses quite close. I cannot remember getting ashore except dragging myself up onto the sand and flopping out, thoroughly done up and wondering if Jimmy would find me or how long I should stay.

Salt water is a good emetic! I was sick continuously and it was a pleasant relief. Jimmy arrived shouting for me, much relieved and I was soon helped to the hotel, a cold shower and bed. But I spent most of that night going to be sick and drinking water.

The following day Charles felt the effects of his exertions, but the local Doctor said no permanent harm was done. He was full of salt water and had strained his heart. It can't have been too bad; his diary merely complains that it stopped him drinking too much beer! The rest of the leave is described in detail in his journal:

The next day we took a car to Jerusalem. The first part of the journey was through the coastal cultivated area, of ploughed red soil or dull green orange trees etc. After a while we left this behind and the road begun its wind and climb up the inland hills. The aspect now became less and less green. The hills were the same ruddy-brown but liberally strewn with splashes of white. Woods and trees were frequent on the lower slopes but as we got higher, they thinned out, soon only occasional on the slopes – a few dotted about. At the top could be seen a huge white figure of Christ, actually outside an orphanage. Over the top the valley stretched in front of us winding among the hills and all the slopes regularly and mathematically terraced, with a row of olive trees on each terrace.

We wound down through this valley and over another slight ridge into a white arid hollow and Jerusalem. It stuck out like other eastern towns' outskirts: hovels, squalor (though not a much as usual) and later built up streets, crowded and hot. The Australian Club where we stayed was an old hotel, I imagine taken over by the Australian comforts fund. There is no doubt that this combined comfort fund does them well. It was a spacious comfortable place with excellent food and drink.

The 'Old City' contains all the historic places of interest. But what a disappointment. The place is I suppose much the same as it was two thousand years ago, except perhaps the dress of some of the people. The streets are narrow, cobbled and steep. There are no pavements and people just crowd up and down between the shops, which are small and open straight onto the street. Flies, heat and smell are overpowering – smell especially. In places awnings are spread over the street to keep out the sun, and they concentrate the smell. One street we went down was arched over like a cloister and on either side were metal workers' booths. The heat was less oppressive under the stone covering and there was less smell, but it was noisy and dark. Yet in this thick gloom, old men and young children worked at intricate turnings.

In other open streets individual itinerant vendors are found in places sitting at the sides with their wares. Why they are never walked on amazes me. And here was a surprising sight: a loaded camel being led up by a loud shouting Arab, followed by a mule. I should hardly have thought there would be room. These ways lead away from shops to small stone hovels and then to the Wailing Wall – a solid wall of huge blocks, not very long, but all that is left of Solomon's old temple. Here the orthodox Jews come to "wail". I assume they are praying, but they stand there holding onto the wall, swaying to and from and reciting from some book in their hands or just crying or walking up and down reciting. It is a strange sight.

Jerusalem, Street Sellers.

From here the Way of the Cross winds up to the Church of the Holy Sepulchre. But it is nothing like I had imagined. I pictured open fields to a hill. But the whole area is built up, and the church itself surrounded with hovels. The church is a huge building, and is composed of numerous small rooms. The main ones are 'neutral' ground, and here is supposed to be the place of the Crucifixion somewhat above floor level, and one is told to put a hand into a hole and feel the wood of the cross! Down again on the floor level is a marble slab where Christ's body was laid for anointing, and in a corner is the place where Mary stood, and only a few yards away is the tomb – a small stone building over a marble slab. Over all there are hung numerous lamps, one for each Christian Church, and a few ardent Christians come and go and kiss the stone. The other rooms are each devoted to one of the different Churches.

One of the many things I did not like was that even here, strangers are continually pestering travellers to show them round. They start at the city gates and are met the whole way. We saw some of these gates – pretty solid masses and almost complete. And we at home reckon sixteen hundred years to be old.

Solomon's caves, from where he is supposed to have got the stone to build the temple, extend right under the city and are wide, cool and airy. The stone is fairly soft but hardens in the weather.

Bethlehem is only a short run from Jerusalem and it was a pleasant trip across the white limestone valley with occasional trees and a few houses here and there. In the distance in the heat haze are the mountains on the other side of the Dead Sea. It is a charming village from the distance there, on the side of the hill, and then again as the road winds round into the village. The Church of the Nativity is again on the same idea as the Holy Sepulchre. The place of Birth and the Manger are neutral ground and hung around with various lamps. Also numerous small rooms are used by each Christian religion. In one – the Armenian – the bearded priests were conducting a service. The singing was quite melodious. In the Roman Catholic was a fine wall sculpture of St George and the Dragon. But here again we were beset with willing but unwelcome guides.

The run to Jericho proved most interesting. The start, in the proximity of Jerusalem, was a bit confusing where the history of the various gates and streets was explained, as was an odd looking skull formation in a limestone cliff which is supposed to have some significance. Then the car came to the Mount of Olives and half way up stopped at the Garden of Gethsemane and the Church of all Nations. Here was a

Bethlehem – Church of the Nativity.

pleasant change. Peace and quiet, free from smells and crowds and worrying guides. The surroundings are pleasing and across the valley the old walls of Jerusalem can be seen and Abraham's Dome. The Garden itself is pleasantly laid out but railed off. In it are the rotten, decayed, but still alive old trees alleged to be the 2000 year old Olives.

The Church of All Nations again is a very inspiring place, beautiful, peaceful and cool inside. It is built straight on the rock which can be seen cropping out in places at the base of the walls. The floor is an imitation of the old Armenian or Grecian Church tessellated floor that stood there in the dim past.

The rest of the journey was much the same, from 2000 ft above sea level to 2000 ft below in forty miles. But it is a striking type of country. All completely bare and composed entirely of deep steep valleys, the white limestone rocks gleaming in the sun, but looking clean and pleasing. The road of necessity is very steep and winding.

The first point of interest was an old brick shelter over the one and only spring in the whole journey. Here Christ was supposed, and no doubt did, stop on his travels. The next point is the Hill of Blood. A striking outcrop of red stone like a patch on the hillside. Just near is an icon, an old one and a new one, at what is supposed to be the site of the parable of the Good Samaritan. For most of the route down one can see various military works. Also some craters of the last war's bombs. Then rounding one of the corners, the first sight of the Dead Sea appears. Very low and blue and we descend to the flat Jordan plain and go straight to Jericho. At the present it is just several piles of stones, or at least the old city is, but walls are pointed out that were marched round. Also charred rocks and ashes, supposed to be the result of the sack.

We stopped here for a drink and a cool down, and then went on to the Jordan, an uninspiring narrow muddy strip with a few trees on the bank. They tell me it floods though. Near a bridge is supposed to be the place of the Baptism. We walked over the bridge to say we had been in Trans Jordan, and then left for the Dead Sea. Here again we stopped for a drink and then went in for a dip. The water is strangely warm and dense. It is shallow at the edges, but when out far enough it is a strange sensation to feel its buoyancy. Then to get further out and realise the difficulty of obtaining and maintaining the vertical position. The feet will not stay down. To try and swim is equally difficult, the feet will not stay below the water, and the salt burns lips and eyes. If you lay flat out with hands at sides it is possible to just roll over and over. But when we came out we felt so clammy that even a shower did not thoroughly dispel it.

And so we returned to Jerusalem having seen all that we had time for.

The thing that struck me most about the whole trip was that a man could have had or received inspiration in such a country, in an out of the way place, in dirty, unhealthy, unpleasant environment and uninspiring countryside, to evolve or further a doctrine which has stood the times of change and been accepted by numerous other countries and peoples. Just one of life's mysteries.

Back at Tel Aviv, I had a day's run up to Haifa through the cultivated coastal area. Mainly this was orange orchards, but there were cultivated patches of red brown earth for root crops and cereals. The taxi driver told me a lot about the oranges. Firstly that now there was no export trade, owing as he said to lack of packing cases, but of course there is the shipping situation. The oranges have to be picked though, or the tree is spoilt. Further, the life of the tree is five to seven years, then they have to plant fresh ones.

Haifa was a typical Eastern naval port, with the distinction that the Arab section is separate from the Jewish. Therefore there is a clean and dirty section! There are the usual open shops and the dry heat. After a very good lunch I started to walk up to Mount Carmel but half way up I was lucky enough to get picked up by a Major in a car who was also sightseeing. We got to the top and then went some long way inland trying to find the Carmelite monastery. In this quest we had some really good views and eventually reached a pretty high point somewhat inland. The mount appears to be a solitary hill on the west and commands a fine panorama in all directions. The houses run all the way up, but not crowded – just isolated clumps of houses among the trees. From the sea level they stand out more prominently, especially the hotels etc. Up at the top there is was of course a lot cooler and very pleasant. Therefore we found various headquarters buildings.

Eventually we found our way to the monastery, lower down on the seaward side of the mount (in fact next to Admiralty House). Actually it is a modern building on the site of a much older one that appears to have had a very chequered history. But I did not get the whole story. The present effort has a most imposing and impressive interior decoration. Intricately and colourfully beautiful. It took one of the monks four years to paint the ceiling! The figure of the Virgin Mary was a masterpiece. I bought a photo, but parted with it later. While there we witnessed the baptism of a peasant mother's infant.

Returning I travelled with a young newly married Pole. Her husband was in another taxi, but it did not worry her. She was only eighteen and had only been married the previous day. She was full of life and happiness. We had some fine pleasantries on the journey. Marriage she seemed to think really wonderful. She asked me to call on her when I came again and wrote her address in Arabic. She could speak fluently Arabic, Hebrew, Polish, Russian, German and English. It was to her I gave my photo of the Virgin Mary as she appeared very attracted to it.

To return to Tel Aviv. One night I went with Bryan, Lee and Jimmy to the San Marino cabaret. The dancing was crowded and tables taken mainly by servicemen. One item in the floor show was particularly noticeable. I imagine most of the artists to be unfortunate refugees (in fact most of Tel Aviv appeared to be). But one singer was Polish and was rather high class and had clearly sung in better places. It must have been a come down for her to have to sing in such a contrasting place and unfortunately she showed it. If anyone 'barracked' or stood up and moved about she would stop and wait. On one occasion while she was singing, a Polish Officer walked on and gave her a bunch of flowers and returned. But afterwards when one of his pals shouted some obscene remark she threw the flowers to the back. After a pause she continued, only to break down when she left the stage.

Aspinal and I left here early – about 11.30 p.m. – and on the way out bumped into two girls running up the drive. They said they were running from a drunken Pole and when he appeared we offered to take them home. They spent the rest of the time talking in some strange lingo, but I discovered they were White Russians. We got to a corner and the girl I was with asked "What time we meet?" At first I thought she meant at what time would I meet her tomorrow, but I discovered she meant what time I would meet my friend. I told her we lived at the same hotel and it did not matter. So they drifted off. I asked my girl if she wanted to go for a walk, but she said "No". Her house was only next door or so but she did not seem to want to go there yet.

A few minutes fruitless discussion followed. I got fed up and said I would see her home. We got there and she asked me how long I had. I said a few days, but that did not appear to be the answer she wanted. I cottoned on and said the whole evening as long as I got some sleep. Then she asked how long I wanted, and I tumbled to what she meant and was profoundly surprised. Having surmounted this surprise, before I decided to pursue it further, she offered an hour at £2. This thoroughly shook me and I remonstrated and took my departure.   Later that night I wished I had beaten her down a bit and gone in to try and find out a bit about her and why these people did this sort of thing.

We returned to the desert by air over the sea – doing an anti-shipping patrol on the way.

From time to time Charles jotted down thoughts and descriptions of scenes in his journal:

On the squadron we have some Basutos who do the labouring in the camp. They are a cheery crowd of boys and pretty intelligent. We watched them at work one morning digging a trench. Six of them in a row are armed with picks and shovels and one stands by. As they begin to dig the leader begins to sing and the picks rose in time and thudded down as they joined in the chorus. It's a pleasure to listen to. The leader sings a short phrase and then the boys join in with a sweet and lovely harmony as they swing their picks. One could almost visualise them in a canoe on some jungle river swinging paddles instead of picks. I guess the harmony must be a natural gift but they certainly can sing. Their tongue has a broad babbling sound with its vowels predominating. This combined with the deep timbre of their voices and harmony gives a music rich indeed.

There is a peculiar lake, just inland from Edku, near Alexandria, which every time we fly over looks a rose red, and that is at all times of day, so it is not a light effect. The desert is all round so it is not rocks. Therefore it must be the colour of the water or some weeds. It only appears to be shallow, but why red?

Last night Iffy Rose introduced us to "Spendules". "Gremlins" I had heard of. An exact definition is difficult. A Gremlin appears to be a "something" that accompanies one on expeditions and is either lucky or unlucky. A Spendule is not a necessary appendage. One is just lucky if one has one, and they appear to be anti-enemy gremlins.

On a more philosophical note:

What are we fighting for? That is a question I have often asked myself in my idle moments. Why am I a willing participant in this war of destruction of things and thoughts? At first I suppose it was simply because this island home of ours, which is really more to us than just our homeland, was attacked. That the inviolable traditions, which had been built up for years and had been taught to the children till they were part of their being, were threatened. Yes, I believe that was it. But now I look further. I am not fighting merely to prevent, on the defensive. But then what will be the result, the benefit of victory? What good thing will come out of it? All the best men and the youths of the nation are being destroyed. All high ideals and thoughts have been proved false. The foundations of belief and confidence are being undermined. And even the keystone of our "war aims" – democracy – is beginning to assume a doubtful, even unsavoury meaning. And I even ask, is democracy practical in a modern world? If so, a radical change will have to be made in policy. But then what is going to be the policy after the war? What have "they" to offer us if "we" bring it to a successful conclusion? There is a whole lot of talk about, but I have heard nothing satisfactory yet, and what I have heard I don't like. Unsatisfactory half measures, only making for bigger confusion. Yet our enemy has a clear cut policy and plan of action if he wins and he has unashamedly broadcast it for years and even proved it. And to all intents and purposes to the economic benefit of the country. The happiness and success of the people I know nothing of, but I am not half as sceptical as some people.

Then what am I fighting for? Well, I prefer a doubtful post war plan to the plan Germany offers. Excellent it may be in many points, but it would involve England in a way quite contrary to the ideas and principles of her people and no one would be happy. Whereas, on our own, we would muddle through somehow, trying to please everybody and pleasing only a few and making a lot miserable. We shall make some mistakes and be excused. We shall be condemned by other demagogues and frowned on by the dominions. But we shall continue to hold our heads up and wave flags and yell "Good Old England". But for how long?

They were soon into the routine of squadron life once more:

8/9/42 Tuesday. Up early as Orderly Officer and between rounds slept, read and wrote letters. Evening went down to develop films but just as I started an ops film came in and we had to pack up. Bed early.

9/9/42 Wednesday. Up early and down to flights, but back early, reading in tent and writing. Same in the afternoon till Bryan called for me to say we were going to Heliopolis to collect a kite from the Maintenance Unit. We were flown down but the aircraft was not ready so Bryan and I stayed the night in Cairo at the Grand Hotel. Evening went to pictures. Then bed late but could not sleep on account of noise.

10/9/42 Thursday. Up early and to aerodrome. But when we got in the kite, the engine cut and failed. We went and saw The Engineer Officer and were told it would take all day to fix it so went back to Cairo and stayed at the Grand. Spent the afternoon wandering around. Same in the evening and then to pictures again. Bed late.

11/9/42 Friday. Up early and away to the aerodrome, but the aircraft was still unserviceable. They had to change the carburettor again and would take another day. So back to Cairo. Did nothing in the afternoon except get

£2 from base Accountant. Evening very tired so late dinner and bed early.

12/9/42 Saturday. Had good night and up late. Aircraft again not ready so as we had no cash and the Squadron Leader Accounts would not let me draw any more as I was overdrawn, I rang the squadron and asked for an aircraft to bring us back. Had lunch in mess with last 10/- and waited for the aircraft. Back at Abu Suweir with sigh of relief at 6.30 p.m. and then after dinner across to Sergeants' mess to drink in celebration of Colin Stuson's birthday and drank plenty. Bed late with bad head.

13/9/42 Sunday. Up early and had quiet day reading and writing. Evening down to photo section and developed more film. Wrote twenty eight Xmas cards.

14/9/42 Monday. Up early and took off to Heliopolis again for the aircraft. But when we got there it was still not ready so we came straight back! We were not waiting again. Rest of day as Duty Controller and most of time reading.

15/9/42 Tuesday. Signed on at flights and then got a gharry and went to No. 6 Hospital to see George Holby. Afternoon reading, sleeping, writing. Evening CO leaving and Squadron Leader Howson promoted to Wing Commander. So had high dinner – very good with guests from 203 Squadron. Then drinking. Someone got a shirt torn and that started a shirt tearing mania. Nearly everyone was torn off. Some however were quick enough and took them off – me included, and the evening was spent semi nude. Bed 12.15 a.m.

George Holby seems to have been one of the squadron characters. The narrative describes the events leading to his hospitalisation:

George Holby

George – i.e. George Holby – was for some days a celebrity in the mess after his promotion to Squadron Leader and he gained notoriety by being hit by a piece of our own shrapnel from shells being fired at one of the high flying 'shufti kites' that occasionally came over. Then his pilot Jimmy McHale piled up an aircraft on landing but they all got out OK! The same evening on the way over to the showers in the gharry, George fell and a bolt went through his leg. This necessitated a spell in hospital where I went to see him before leaving for Aden. His leg had healed, but he was remaining in hospital with gippy gut!

On life and revelry in the desert, Charles writes:

To celebrate the CO's departure, or rather as a parting gesture we invited some of 203 Squadron over as guests and had a "dinner' – a real dinner à la style and the cooks really did excel themselves. After dinner the drinking really began. Norman Pottie I think started it, and he was the king pin of the evening for liquor effect. But before long there was a shirt tearing mania developing in the mess. The number of Officers who had their shirts torn from their backs I don't know, but John Sharply lost two. I was quick enough to remove mine before it was torn, and by 11.30 p.m. everyone was in the nude from the waist upwards. The next night the CO went to the Sergeants' mess and the same thing happened and then when he got back to the Officers' mess everyone took off their shirts. So he anointed us all with a pint of beer. That's what goes on in revelries in the mess in the desert.

16/9/42 Wednesday. Spent whole day idling, writing, reading and sleeping. Evening in mess and drinks again but bed early.

17/9/42 Thursday. Up early to get to Ismalia to bank to collect money for pay parade. Had tour round shopping and to United Services Club for a drink. Afternoon stayed in tent till dinner and then told that we were going to Aden on detachment tomorrow. Saw Bryan and fixed it all, and then drinking in mess.

CHAPTER 7

To Aden and Back

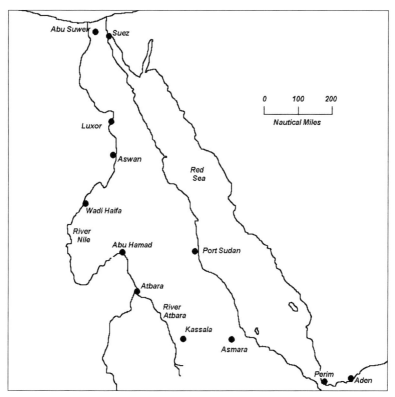

Charles's Travels to and from Aden September and December 1942.

We left Abu Suweir and flew across the desert to Suez over a small plateau of black brown rock with a hard craggy edge dropping down to the desert flat. In hollows the sides were patches with drifted sand. Suez appeared a pretty busy port in the distance, with plenty of shipping out in the bay, or rather in the arm of the Red Sea. Flying down over the sea we passed a veritable mountain range on the West coast.

Described in Charles's diary as "Kite Ready for Aden".

Flat on top, but the edge, though craggy, did not present an ugly black face but rather a beautiful blend of tones from black and purples, browns, reds to pale yellow. A narrow border of orange sand met the blue sea with the shallows a mixture of greens to yellow where the sand banks were above sea level. These shallows, sand banks and islands continued all down the coast in patches. Sometimes the islands were quite large, one or two having lighthouses, and on one beach were oil wells. At one place on the Red Sea coast was a small oil station. But for the most part it was deserted and uninteresting. The mountains were always there, sometimes close to the coast, then gaps of yellow plain, but mostly well back from the sea where colour was lost. Then they appeared again as dark brown rugged masses with sharp hard jagged tops.

And so we arrived at Port Sudan. This was only a small town but from the air presented quite a pleasing effect as of a town of lots of bricks on a brown setting. Along the sea front were docks with oil containers and slips. Round the town were scattered collections of huts and tents. From out of the town a railway line ran west and disappeared into the mountains. When we landed we were told that we should still be in the air! We had sent an ETA but the time here is an hour behind Egyptian time.

The mess was new, very cool and airy and pleasant. (The temperature outside was noticeably higher than Egypt.) And we could sleep out on the balcony without fear of mosquitoes. The sky above was a pale blue but long before it reached the horizon it blended into a sort of pale purple haze which ran as a wide margin all along the top of the dark purple hills in the distance. It was quite a pleasant sight to see the hills after an expanse of flat sand, and when the sun set, sending pale yellow rays darting out from behind the flaming clouds right across the sky, it reminded me of looking at the sunsets at home.

We went into the town after tea. It was only a small place, and quite pleasant. It appeared to be British built and controlled with wide streets and the locals well organised to conform to our standards. But that did not prevent them having their own houses and shops, dirty and dark. The park was a good effort having the usual gates and drives and a number of various trees. But grass seemed out of it at this season. There was also a fine white bandstand, a memorial to something or other and a fountain. The notice at the gates forbade the asking of baksheesh, which was a good thing. For the first time I saw a real "Fuzzywuzzy", and only one, with his hair sticking up in a thick wild mop on top and a thick fringe about six inches long down the back.

I lay on the veranda that night listening to crickets instead of mosquitoes and watching the lights of the town as there was no blackout. The half moon was on its side and very pale. In the morning I was woken at 5.20 a.m. as working hours here are 6.00 a.m. to 8.30 a.m. and 9.00 a.m. to 1.00 p.m. and I watched the sun rise steadily like a balloon over the clear-cut edge of the sea – a glowing dull oval. The only interruption to its light was an early flight of flamingos.

The flight from Port Sudan to Aden was about the same, but we were out of sight of land for most of the time. Once or twice we passed islands or shallows and on one particularly large patch were a number of sailing dhows. The temperature was noticeably rising now and after a while the rocks at Perim loomed out of the heat haze. The distant view looked just like Gibraltar. But on approach they were seen to be not just one rocky peninsula, but several huge rocks and one or two rocky islands of varying size. But round it all I saw no town of any size. Here we turned east and flew along the coast to Aden. The hills rose steeply in the distance out of the flat, arid wastes tracking down to the sea. Once only did I see any signs of habitation.

When the rocks appeared we turned inland as instructed and flew over the flat sand till we came to a desert town – Lakej – of fairly large substantial looking buildings, but all windowless and surrounded with what looked like straw tents. This town was on a dry wadi. Apparently inland the same river always has water in it, but it dries before it reaches the sea. There are quite a number of trees about and patches of cultivation and greenery.

We followed the road from here into Sheik Othman and landed, the most concerning thing being the heat.

Sheikh Othman airport was a small airfield about 15 nautical miles north of Aden town. Crews from 459 Squadron were sent here to patrol the strategically important waters of the Gulf of Aden, which gave access to the Red Sea and thence to the Suez Canal.

19/9/42 Saturday. Landed before lunch at 2.30 p.m. Wizard mess etc. Afternoon went for a bath at the club with some fellows. Eighteen miles to town. Evening drinking and at ops room to gen up etc. Bed late.

20/9/42 Sunday. Up early and shower and breakfast. Then to Accounts and Adjutant to fix up etc. Spent rest of day sleeping and reading. Evening drinking but bed early. Queer thing was that there was 10/10 cloud most of day but no rain and terrifically hot. Feeling the heat here more than I have ever done. It never gets cool and fans in rooms have to be kept going all the time.

21/9/42 Monday. Up early but did nothing all morning except read and write. Afternoon booked a taxi to take me Bryan, Lee and Jimmy to Aden for the afternoon, but then later told we were to fly and so cancelled it and took trip along coast and back. Evening briefed for ops trip. Anti shipping patrol to Socotra in the morning. Bed late.

22/9/42 Tuesday. Up 4.30 a.m. and set off at 6.00 a.m. as aircraft not ready till then. Uneventful trip save for bags of wind changes. Landed on bleak and lonely Socotra before lunch. Only a small detachment there and short of rations etc. Fed on bully beef in our stay. Afternoon jobs in the aircraft and then Jimmy and I went down to shore for walk and collect shells. Back to early dinner and then on an improvised bed for night. Although island in the tropics, it was not hot as monsoon wind was strong.

For some reason the squadron Operations Record Book summarised the navigation log that Charles kept of that sortie.

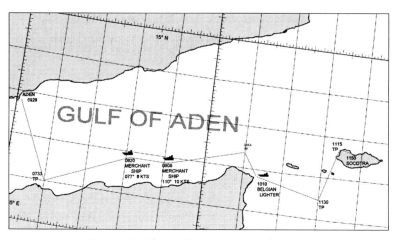

Crew sortie Aden to Socotra 22 September 1942.

It is interesting to see just what was involved in one of these patrols, and the route and timings are reproduced below.

In a sortie that lasted five hours and twenty-five minutes, they made just eight changes of track and saw three vessels; no wonder they were pleased when they saw some action! They were supposed to be at Socotra for just one night. However, when they taxied the aircraft the next morning the tail wheel burst. They were therefore compelled to stay a further night. Charles and the air gunner Jimmy went for a walk – carrying, Charles comments, guns – and he recorded his impressions in his journal:

> The island itself appears to be a barren mass of rugged peaks, with no vegetation. But actually there are lots of stunted trees and some grass which gave us that impression. The trees are all only about six to eight feet high. The majority of the orthodox shape, but smoothly barked and fleshy. When cut or broken, oozing a yellow sap which is supposed to be poisonous. (Is it Frankincense or Myrrh?) The other variety is very strange, being very thick at the

base, about eighteen inches to thirty inches and tapering rapidly to the top to about six inches. From here about three or four branches jut out about three inches wide. The leaves and few flowers I saw are similar to Rhododendrons, but with little smell. The trunk at the base curves in at ground level to one or two totally inadequate short roots, and does not enter the ground itself. The bark is smooth and soft and fleshy about one and a half to two inches thick with the same yellow sticky sap in abundance.

The natives of this place are Arabs and Bedouins or types of such! They are few and live in scattered villages of thatched framework houses or houses of stone. The boss is a sort of Sheik. They appear to have no boats of their own, but rely on outside navies for their supplies. Goats and donkeys seem indigenous and some camels have been imported and few grain crops are grown I believe. Gold is supposed to be on the island. Some years ago (1830) a special currency was issued of large silver coins with a queen's head, but they contained a high percentage of silver and most of them the natives have melted down for trinkets. Water comes from shallow artesian wells.

At monsoon times the sea round is thick with weed and impossible for swimming. The shore is mostly silver sand with an abundance of large and small strange shells. Sharks abound in the Gulf here, and whales have been washed up and amber is traded. There is a small detachment of Aden levies there under a Major and a Lieutenant and an Indian Doctor. Also there is a small RAF detachment and WT station of fifteen men under a Pilot Officer who have to look after everything. At the time we landed the Doctor had an outbreak of scabies to attend to. Also supplies of food and tobacco were very short as the supply ship had not arrived.

One afternoon we went climbing up into the wild craggy hills. It was hot work but the breeze – thirty knots – at least cooled us off at the top. The rocks were hard, black and hollow, like a sponge. Volcanic origin I should imagine.

24/9/42 Thursday. Up early and prepared for lazy morning when a Blenheim arrived with our tail wheel. So got to work and fitted it and took off at 11.40 a.m. for base. Uneventful trip and landed 5.30 p.m. Shower, shave, drink, dinner, more drink and bed.

25/9/42 Friday. Up early as usual. It is impossible to lie in bed here as it is too hot. Morning pottering about and reading etc. Afternoon sleep and then with Bryan, Lee and Jimmy to Aden and did some shopping. Back at 6.00 p.m. and party in the mess started at 6.00 p.m. Some nurses from the Hospital came and I managed to dance with two! But most of the evening was spent drinking.

Charles's impressions of Aden are, as usual, recorded in his journal:

Aden harbour is formed by low hilly promontories with the harbour between. The smaller – with the town of Little Aden – is a mass of needle-like peaks. The other in which is the actual port town is an extinct volcanic mountain. The port, Steamer Point, is built on the solid lava deposits. All inland along the coast is flat and with black sand and in the distance the Yemen mountains loom up. What little vegetation there is grows in dried or semi-dried up wadis and is only stunted trees and coarse patches of grass. We were stationed first at Sheikh Othman fifteen miles from

Aden in the flat sand. However, a very comfortable, spacious mess had been built with grass lawns in front and surrounded by gum trees and creeper like clematis over the veranda. The mess and billets were only kept cool by having a second roof, usually of rushes, over the first, and overlapping about six feet to form a sort of umbrella. Also in each room was as electric fan.

Batmen, waiters, mess boys, what ever you like to call them, were the local Arabs duly instructed and attired. Two Officers shared one, who not only did batman's duties, but waited at table as well. Food was up to a point English, but with the inclusion of native fruits.

The first attraction of Aden I found was Gold Mohur bathing beach in a small bay beyond Steamer Point. The sea was beautifully warm and protected from sharks and dolphins by wire netting, although various multicoloured smaller fish entered.

The crater of the volcano is now a huge flat plain and can be approached only by a narrow cut in the mountain rim, sufficient only for the road. The Queen of Sheba is supposed to have built her town here. The present town is called Crater, and wells or tanks have been discovered in a narrow rocky valley leading into the centre. Each well overflows into the next lower as it fills up. When these tanks were rediscovered they were cemented up and were in use until recently, when the Sheikh Othman artesian wells were sunk – the only water supply, though where the water comes from I don't know.

Further back, the Garden of Eden is supposed to have been in this district and a cave in the hill is pointed out as the grave of Cain (or Abel). Along the ridges of the mountains are strong walls and one or two forts, the limit of the Turkish approach to the harbour in the last war.

Another feature of the landscape are squat white windmills used for pumping sea water into the salt beds for drying.

I found the climate generally very hot and moist. But one morning soon after my arrival I woke to find it dull, cloudy and heavy, and outside the mess numerous small birds, like tits, were singing for all their worth in the trees. It was a very pleasant sound and the only time I heard it. Later on the clouds burst and we had a short heavy downpour – the first for two years they said. The result was that very pleasant smell that I used to love in England of rain after a dry dusty period. Noah's Ark is supposed to have come to rest on one of the hills here!

Muala, a town not far from Steamer Point, is said to be the oldest ship building yard in the world, and here they still build large dhow like ships, about forty feet long and fifteen feet wide, very deep and with a deep draught. Some of them have two masts with the usual crosspiece for the sail to hang from. In these ships the traders have sailed to and from Java since the year dot with no compass. Another remarkable craft is a small one between a canoe and a kayak, a one man affair and with no keel. The remarkable part is that they manage to propel them without capsizing and even put up a sail, and in these they go across as far as Bilbera.

Crater is at the bottom of the valley. On the walls is a sort of garden with mainly gum trees and a few creepers and several varieties of flowers, like cosmos and Chrysanthemums. In the town was a bazaar like all other Arab bazaars. Also a prison for whites as well as Arabs, and incarcerated there was a British Tar aged about thirty two doing a life sentence for murder, poor devil.

The Arab headgear is interesting. Here it is a turban sort of thing, in Egypt the fez and in Palestine the picturesque flowing type. I have been told the fez is thus because when they pray they must have the head covered and also hit their foreheads on the ground. Also it is cool and comfortable. The same applies in Aden I suppose, as here they unwind the turban and use it as a kneeling mat, and under it they wear a small skull cap. I don't know about Palestine.

26/9/42 Saturday. Had another hot idle day just sleeping and reading and yarning in mess. No trips came through. Bed early.

27/9/42 Sunday. Another idle day doing nothing except read. Evening out taking sights of stars. Bed late. Quarter of an hour heavy rain in the morning! First for two years.

28/9/42 Monday. Up early and pottering about but felt bit queer so went to see Doc. He sent me to bed with temp. But afternoon an ops trip came through and I went to town for briefing. It was a five day effort from three different stations and really good. But I was crook by the time I got back and the Doctor said I could not go!

29/9/42 Tuesday. Had lousy night and woke pool of sweat and did not feel so good in the morning. Still temperature of 103°. Bryan did not go on ops as I was not with him. Felt weak all day and did not feel like doing anything.

30/9/42 Wednesday. Felt heaps better during day. Morning temperature normal and same in the evening and the Doc said I could get up for an hour. Went to mess and drank too much and had to go to bed feeling bad. Bryan has now gone sick, so it is just as well I am getting up as I am detachment commander for a few days and have tons of returns to do.

Unfortunately Charles's apparent recovery at the end of September was short lived, and his condition got steadily worse over the next ten days or so. His skin took on a yellow pallor, and the Doctor became increasingly worried about him.

> 12/10/42 Monday. Doc decided to send me to hospital, so I packed up everything and sent it all to Khormakser and then went by ambulance to hospital. Seems as though I shall be better off here but how long shall I stay?
> 13/10/42 Tuesday. Somewhat uncomfortable day. But I had more to eat. Also had to swallow cartwheels! Did nothing all day except read.
> 14/10/42 Wednesday. Today had two blood tests and stools and urine. Felt lot easier and ate more.

So it went on for a few more days. Then:

> 17/10/42 Saturday. Bryan and crew sent back to base! Just the same day.

To be separated from the crew was a nasty shock, and it indicated that it would be some time before Charles could expect to be back operational once more. In his journal Charles refers to his condition as 'Sand Fly', and his service records use the generic term 'Jaundice'. Whatever disease he had contracted, it was not getting any better.

> 18/10/42 Sunday. Still eating next to nothing and no signs of improvement.
> 19/10/42 Monday. Hadn't energy even to have a bath today. Getting lethargic.
> 20/10/42 Tuesday. The old tum very painful today.

For the next three weeks his diary entries became more and more brief, and on some days nothing was written at all. His writing – already bad – became almost unreadable at times.

> 5/11/42 Thursday. Feeling better but still yellow. Doc said I could now smoke my pipe. First time for six weeks!
> 6/11/42 Friday. No change in treatment or condition.
> 7/11/42 Saturday. Irritation and scratching very bad and tearing myself to pieces, so asked to have my hands bound at night!

Charles recovering in hospital on the veranda. Note the fine handlebar moustache.

For some days there is little, if anything, in the diary; then:

> 12/11/42 Thursday. Thoroughly cheesed, browned, chocker.
> 13/11/42 Friday. *(No entry)*.
> 14/11/42 Saturday. Weighed myself 8 st 7lb! Lost 2 stone.
> 15/11/42 Sunday. Doc said I could get up for two hours. But what good is that when I want to get back.
> 16/11/42 Monday. No change.
> 17/11/42 Tuesday. As before, but trimmed a terrific moustache.

Charles became quite proud of this moustache, which became a full RAF 'handlebar' appendage. He even had it photographed.

22/11/42 Sunday. Complained bitterly to Doc. It looks as though I might be in for Christmas! He put me on a pint of stout per day! And now beer is rationed to two pts per week.

23/11/42 Monday. Last night stout was flat! After two mouthfuls was terrifically sick and wasted all dinner! Had lousy night, could not keep cool, skin burning worse. New patient in and so could not have the fan on. Conceived the idea of getting out in time for Xmas leave in Jerusalem.

24/11/42 Tuesday. Yesterday irritation suddenly stopped. I had a good night and it has not returned today.

25/11/42 Wednesday. Irritation returned in fine form. By evening very bad.

26/11/42 Thursday. At 3.00 a.m. suddenly had shivering fit from burning skin. Had to ring for sister. Took temperature and put me to bed with two blankets! No irritation now! Bad fever and slept till morning. Doc came in early and temp 102.8°! Gave me a thorough overhaul but found nothing. Blood tests! By noon felt a lot better and fever passed by evening.

27/11/42 Friday. OK now and burning returned as bad as ever. Usual day. Still hoping for Christmas. Ali still wanting to come to England.

Ali is mentioned in his journal, in which he describes his stay in hospital very briefly:

Then I went into hospital on 29/9/42 with sand fly and jaundice – sickness, loss of weight, weakness, indisposition, foul taste in the mouth and stomach and finally skin irritation. For the most part I lost all interest and did not even want to read or write. All I did was think. I had no variety of food for about two months except when I sent out for biscuits, carrots and for nuts. I grew a moustache to a colossal size. I noticed particularly the chlorination of the water, could not drink it and disliked washing shaving and bathing in it. I got on very well with the bearer – Ali – who told me about his religion etc, and wanted me to bring him back to England with me as my man.

Alas for Ali, Charles was not in any position to do such a thing. When he got better he still had a war to fight. And now he did start to get better.

28/11/42 Saturday. Yellow slowly disappearing. Sweating at night makes itching worse.

29/11/42 Sunday. Yellow less. Not so irritable except at night.

30/11/42 Monday. Some more improvement. Better night.

1/12/42 Tuesday. Yellow as good as gone. Weight 8 st 6 lbs. Sips of stout.

2/12/42 Wednesday. Doc said vast improvement and should be out in five days.

3/12/42 Thursday. Nothing consequential. Bill and Mac came in with news that 459 Squadron had moved westward. Also rumour that St Jeans detachment closed, therefore hopes of getting to Palestine for leave are slight.

4/12/42 Friday. Went for walk in evening.

5/12/42 Saturday. Doc said I could go out in seven days. Rumour that all Aden detachment going back to base.

6/12/42 Sunday. A lot better today. Afternoon I went to Crater with some others in taxi and got fagged out after about half a mile. Therefore I must be very weak.

7/12/42 Monday. Doc actually asked what day I wanted to go out.

8/12/42 Tuesday. Norman Potter was brought in after a crash at Socotra! His leg is broken in five places etc. and he was even put on the danger list. I had a pass out and went to see boys at Khormakser for evening and stayed to dinner. Bed late. Bad night.

9/12/42 Wednesday. Learnt that I was now paying – or losing – 4/6 a day, so decided to ask for discharge. Afternoon I went out for two hours to see football match.

10/12/42 Thursday. In the morning the Doc said he would board me tomorrow and discharge me Saturday as I wanted, with a recommendation for leave. Afternoon pass into town and bought big leather case. Evening teaching English to Ali.

11/12/42 Friday. Morning discussion with Padre re-baptism. Should I or not? Afternoon out again with a Pole for look round. Developing tanks which were 15 Riyals when I went sick now cost 25 Riyals! Then to Scots mess for dinner and evening. Bed late on veranda.

Charles commented in his journal on the high rate of inflation in Aden. With his increasing interest in photography, he had been seeking equipment to do his own developing and printing:

Cost of a developing tank before I went into hospital was 15 Riyals, before I came out 25 Riyals, and when I left 30 Riyals, and that is an example of what is happening to prices of everything in Aden, with the exception of tobacco which is cheap, due mainly to the lack of supply and increase of demand, aided and abetted by the income of wealthy Yank forces. In fact they are spoiling everywhere they go with their greater spending power, so much so that taxi drivers have refused to take us, but prefer to wait for a Yank!

12/12/42 Saturday. Up late after good night. Got packed and wandered round in the morning. Boarded A4B* and to return to unit forthwith. But when I got to Khormakser found the plane would not be going for several days. Evening went to open air picture on camp.

13/12/42 Sunday. Morning I saw the Adjutant, Mess Secretary and Doc and reported to flights. Then lay on bunk for rest of day reading. Evening to camp cinema again, as there was a change of programme.

14/12/42 Monday. Up early. Still chasing up my laundry. Signal from base that Hudsons are to be attached to 8 Squadron. Hence it appears my chances of getting back to base in time for leave in Jerusalem going. Most of day on bed reading.

15/12/42 Tuesday. Up early to flights. Still no news of how I am to get back. Got my laundry but some missing. Evening celebration of Dave Beaton's DFC. I had to make a speech as only English Officer. Had a lot of whisky. Snooker and bed late with head.

16/12/42 Wednesday. Usual morning. Got some more cash from Accountant Officer and spent the rest of the day on bed till 4.00 p.m. when I went down to town shopping. Baccy (Punch Bowl only 1/- an oz). Developing tank now 30/-! After dinner to cinema again. Bed late as talking about South Africa and jobs there after the war.

17/12/42 Thursday. Still no further forward with getting to

* A4B is a Medical grade. It would have allowed him to fly, but not to go onto operations.

base. Spent all day in bed reading. Evening to cinema. Bed late.

18/12/42 Friday. Usual day, lying on bed reading till I was told I was leaving by Anson tomorrow at 6.15 a.m. Packing and pictures.

The return trip to find 459 Squadron was a long and tortuous journey. The journal tells the story:

We left Aden on 19/12/42 and flew along the black sandy coast to Perim, climbing all the way. Perim looked yellow and white and sunny away out from the coast. Here we crossed to the African coast and flew north. The coast is flat and sandy, not above 100 ft as far as Barasoli. Beyond here the hills rise slowly, higher, brown above the yellow sand and in places with strange red tops to them. By now we were up to 10,000 ft so as to cross the Mountain ranges that separated the coast from the plateau. The yellow coastal fringe of varying depth all up here is bare and irregular with some very steep wide bays and contrasts well with the green and the blue of the sea.

The mountains are bare black and pointed and run in regular ranges enclosing steep narrow valleys, very deep and mostly in shadow. At the bottom of one of them I was able to see a narrow rapid stream, with a very rocky bed and just a trifle of vegetation. These ranges are also deeply and regularly cut with small narrow valleys, giving them somewhat the appearance of being striped, like a zebra. These mountains dropped away to a large plateau with Asmara in the middle. It appeared a large modern town well and spaciously built (7000 ft above sea level). The plateau around appeared to be divided into plots, with the usual varying colours from brown to green, showing obvious signs of a great deal of cultivation. Also I saw small herds of cows on stunted grasses. The plateau ran out into wide pleasant green valleys, which somehow seemed to end suddenly in a rapid wooded descent into the desert. With little odd bits of vegetation to Kassala (the first place we saw water) and then we flew along the Atbara river to the Nile.

This river, like the Nile, runs all through the desert surrounded by vegetation. Around here the hills look very strange, rising up, sometimes singly, sometimes a few together, sometimes in a range, smooth and brown from the yellow sand to about 100 ft. And so we came to the town of Atbara itself and the Nile. Here the narrow green marginal fringe of the Nile widens out and trees and palm grow. Whether due to irrigation or naturally I don't know.

All along this leg, at least as far as Asmara, being high it had been perishing cold and we had tried to wrap ourselves up with what we had without unpacking. We had hot tea, but the pilot, Squadron Leader King, had whiskey added to his for more warmth. Also all the way to Cairo he chain smoked cigarettes. We were flying in Ansons, five in formation.

We stopped at Atbara the night. It is a large town – scattered and covering a wide area – but the population is not large. It is quite a large railway centre – repair shops etc. – of the Sudan Railway. The mess is a pleasant place among trees on the river bank, but we had rotten sleeping quarters, like cells. In the evening we went to the cinema in the open air like Khormakser, and ate a nut like peanuts but with a shell like a beech nut and a name something like puma nut.

From Atbara the next morning we flew along the Nile, flowing through desert with just a narrow fringe of green, and here and there the same sort of hills. I was interested in the fifth cataract on the map, but when we got to it all I saw was the river split in two to surround a large island and the two river beds contained sandbanks and in places smaller islands with some vegetation. When we got down sun, the water did appear to be flowing more rapidly round these banks, and what looked like some smaller obstacles which may have been rocks, but I think were tree trunks.

We left the Nile at Abu Hamed where it makes a big detour and cut straight across the desert, more liberally scattered with the brown hills. For the most part we followed the railway line and it did look odd to see a long black train smoking across the sand.

We joined the Nile again at Wadi Haifa and while the aircraft were being refuelled here went into the town for lunch. We did not stay long enough to have a look at it but in general appearance it was like all other small towns – square white and yellow houses and wide roads. But I did see a pile of cotton bols or husks which are used as fuel. I suppose in the form of the common camel cake which in past times was also sent to England to mix with cattle fodder.

From here we flew over hilly desert till we came to Aswan where we came down low leaving the convoy to have a shufti and take snaps. It certainly was one extensive piece of engineering, both in length and breadth. Below it is an extensive muddy delta and above it a lake, though nothing like the extent I expected. The town was also large and with many modern large buildings. But what was most noticeable was the gorge that the river entered here. We flew all down it with its various heights and widths, in places going down low to 'shoot up' Arabs who would scatter, duck or even throw themselves in the river, or flying up to get over two lots of high power cables. The sides were all the way steep rocky and yellow. On the right

Edfu Temple photographed from the Anson.

a railway line ran unless the river actually lapped the foot of the cliff as it often did, when the railway went round the back or underneath.

In places temples, tombs or perhaps houses were cut in the rocky sides. At others real old temples of very odd shape were left in the plain. The plain was flat and green right to the foot of the cliffs with trees, palms, corn, the river with white sailed-dhows, irrigation etc. And the usual Arab villages of mud houses and sometimes a white domed mosque. Along the top edge of the left cliff would sometimes be left rocky crags of various shapes and sometimes precarious. At Luxor we circled to have a look at the town and temple of Thebes. I took two snaps of the two main ruins. They certainly looked extensive and impressive with their huge columns and arches, wide avenues etc.

Transport from the camp to the town was scarce, and as it was a long way we decided that it was too difficult to go and have a better look and so spent the evening in the mess playing monopoly. But also we slept in tents and gee was the temperature and the water cold! I had to fish out my slacks.

From Luxor the valley widened and the river meandered about a lot, leaving ox bow lakes and odd islands. The cliff sides widened and disappeared from view. The valley became more intense in cultivation, and widened to merge in with the sand of the desert. The various pyramids appeared as we passed them.

We turned off east to avoid Cairo which could be seen in the haze. We flew along the Suez road and landed at LG 204, a cold, desolate aerodrome on the road side, so here I had to stay till the next day and it was most uncomfortable. It is a new place and they were cementing the mess and generally reorganising it. So I was very much in the way. By evening they settled down and I went in to read and yarn with a WO2 I had met. Three young fellows were playing Cardinal Puff and got hopelessly full. But continued till they were sick and did not bother to go outside, just turned their heads over the side of the chair and continued, just covering it with sand. One or two others registered disgust, but mostly it was ignored. I left and went to bed.

The next day I left via Kasfareet, Heliopolis and two Landing Grounds near Cairo and was dropped at Gianacles where I was told 459 Squadron were. But alas, they had moved again and left only George Holby and crew. They were surprised to see me arrive from nowhere, and I was pleased to see them, and went with them the next day to Gambut and 459 Squadron, where they were surprised to see me, but I was handsomely received.

This trip over once Jerry territory and the battlefields was interesting, though having a heavy load we were not able to go low to have a look. But I could see slit trenches, gun pits, shell and bomb holes, blown up and burnt out transport, tanks and planes. Sometimes they were in bunches where battles had been. In places along the road wrecked transport lined the road edge. On the coast I saw an odd wrecked F boat of notable memory. I wondered if it was one of ours. Solum was the only town we saw, and in the distance it hardly looked a town at all, and wrecks could be seen in the harbour.

Gambut – 459 Squadron's new base – was close to Tobruk, which had been firmly in the hands of Rommel's Afrika Korps when Charles left for Aden. Events had moved swiftly in his absence. General Montgomery had built up his forces in preparation for the inevitable battle. With a nearly quarter of a million men, twelve hundred tanks and more than seven hundred aircraft, the Allied forces massively outnumbered those of the Axis. On 24 October Montgomery's assault on the German positions began in Operation Lightfoot. By 29 October, both sides had suffered severe losses in tanks and manpower, but the Allies could sustain the losses while to the Axis forces they were crippling. The advantage was soon pressed home in Operation Supercharge on 2 November, and by 4 November Rommel and the remnants of his army were in full retreat. With just 36 tanks remaining, Rommel had lost more than 90% of his tanks to the Allied assault. The retreat was prevented from becoming a rout by Rommel's leadership and tactics, but by mid November he was driven out of Egypt entirely, and had lost half of Libya. Montgomery's advance was cautious but inexorable, and he allowed Rommel no time to regroup, while consolidating his own position at all times.

Meanwhile at the other end of the Mediterranean Operation Torch had started on 8 November 1942. Under the command of General Eisenhower, a force of seventy thousand men had

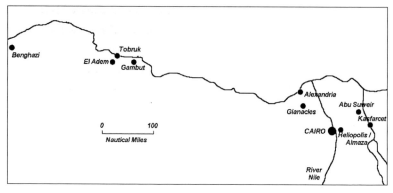

Charles's Travels – December 1942 to January 1943.

taken the Vichy French controlled territory of Morocco and Algeria, though fierce resistance had been encountered initially. The advance was again rapid, and by the year's end the Allies were squeezing the Axis forces from the east and from the west. Rommel dug in in Tunisia.

> 23/12/42 Wednesday. Left at 10.30 a.m. for new base out in the blue at Gambut near Tobruk. Just settling down in camp and this is the third time I have landed at newly settled camp! Everyone pleased and surprised to see me. Jubilation. Mail – eighty items for me. Two cables – (I have a niece!) Five parcels, three registered letters. Jigsaw from Aunt Marie, book from Margaret, book from Dil, periodicals from Olive, diary from Olive, notecard from Billie, hankerchieves etc from Vera. Spent all evening reading letters.
>
> 24/12/42 Thursday. Did bit more organising and decided to stay at base for Xmas. Spent the afternoon resting. Evening everyone drinking and getting tight. George and I sat talking to Padre and then I went to bed early. Air raid warning but it was over Benghazi I think.
>
> 25/12/42 Friday. Very quiet day wandering round camp

and to Bryan's. Afternoon serving airmen's dinner, then had our own, but it was a flop. Then lots of people went to 235 Wing and so the mess was very quiet.

26/12/42 Saturday. Up early and packing for fourteen days sick leave. I left by plane at 1.30 p.m. and stopped at Alex for evening and night. Went with others to cabaret and dancing club and very tired myself.

Charles's journal takes up the description of his sick leave:

Boxing Day I hastily packed and flew to Alexandria for fourteen days leave. I was only here two days but saw a little of it and it appealed to me more than Cairo. It looked cleaner, less crowded or hurried or noisy. The people seemed cleaner and not so much abject poverty. I found my way round a bit and did some shopping. I flew on to Cairo after two days and intended to go to Palestine or Luxor. Over Heliopolis this time I noticed particularly the fine houses, blocks of flats and hotels and one or two large houses – almost palaces – with spacious grounds and approaches.

I spent two days at the National Hotel and then moved to the Junior Officers' Club. Up to now efforts to get to Palestine had proved unsuccessful and as I found this a quite comfortable place I settled here and decided to spend the rest of the time here. While in Cairo this time I found my way around quite a lot and got to know places. Also I found where things could be got a lot cheaper than I had paid before. I went out to the ADU house boats on the Nile for dinner and to see a friend. These must be grand in peace time. Another thing I noticed was the weird vegetables they sometimes dished up, always palatable but odd. Some I identified as boiled melon, cucumber and celery, others I could not.

The local fire brigade rushed madly through the town once with their usual disregard of care – just half a dozen men on a box sort of engine like we used to have in 1920. It is strange how they all wear the fez from lowest to highest "Saville Row" tailored men, and all uniformed men. Police, firemen, bus conductors, Army, Navy and Air Force etc. I have mentioned the Arabs going about bare footed. I noticed one with a sole like a piece of cracked leather; the cracks were painful to see, deep and long up the side of the heel, but she did not seem to feel it.

One night I saw a plane in the searchlights, and it was great to see how it was held by at least twelve from one side of Cairo to the other. One day I went to see the Citadel but was unimpressed. The Mosque was more interesting, but it was in use and we could not go in. The minarets are great pieces of work.

One night in the Junior Officers' Club I was talking to the Liaison Officer of the Cairo Police. He was an Officer from the last war and had been here in the police ever since. Now he was paid by the British Government. He wore an Egyptian uniform and fez. Of course he knew lots about the place and was very interesting. He talked of the descent and mixture of the real Egyptian and their origins as Copts. (I had noticed how some of the girls now even in profile resemble the carvings on the tombs.)

How things have degenerated since the British gave up control (1926) and good positions were only gained by influence and graft. The hospital in particular, where administration had deteriorated so that it had become dirty since the British MO left. Yet the MO now is an eminent man who studied in England at Spilsby*. Also patients with no influence received scant treatment.

* Spilsby Hospital in Lincolnshire. It closed in 1948.

He spoke also of the way the British soldier had let himself down by his familiarity with the lower Arabs and general behaviour. The tradesmen and street vendors and boot blacks etc. were taking advantage of his ignorance and impotency and robbing him! These Arabs have only one idea of spending their money: on a holiday – the pilgrimage to Mecca, and this year there were three times the number that has ever gone before!

At the end of the leave I had to report for a medical board, but had to wait three more days for it and then the brilliant RAF organisation came into force causing all the unnecessary waste of time, energy and material. I had to go to HQ first and then to Heliopolis. The various departments I went to there for the board took a whole morning. They said I had to report to HQ P staff again in the evening to get transport back to base. They could not provide or suggest transport. All they could do was to post me to 22 PTC on the morrow, which they did! Then Accounts could not pay me any money, only in the mornings, necessitating my return in the morning. The Principal Medical Officer could not sign my temporary duty certificate and I had to go to the Camp Commandant and he sent me back to the PMO, who did sign this time. Fortunately I had no difficulty signing the movements Book!

The next day I went to HQ again in early morning and got some cash. Then I made various enquiries for transport and after a bit found a special transport was laid on every day at 2.00 p.m. collecting people for 22 PTC. They could not have told me that yesterday!

And thus I got here – the renowned Almaza that I had been told of, but had fortunately had not experienced. People come here for posting and are forgotten, live uncomfortably in loads of bullshit unless old enough to avoid it. As I have a squadron to go to I hope to avoid it and get away early. I have already avoided CO's and CGI's parades and found the Movements Officer. One thing about Almaza struck me besides the monotony and discomfort – a notice on the wall of the Latrines from Principal Medical Officer Middle East:

Men and Officers are advised <u>if possible</u> to avoid all contact with women. However, if it cannot be avoided to use only <u>authorised brothels</u> and not use women that are chance acquaintances or picked up in the street. To always use a "French Letter" obtainable in Sick Quarters and after each connection to go to the ET Dept.

Comment needless!

I left Almaza by road for Cairo Station, but when we got there we had several hours to wait and so went to a cabaret. On the whole the floor show was good and showed quite a lot of imagination. But again the theme was the hip wobble, belly lifting and udder shaking. We started journey at 1.00 a.m. and it took till morning to get to Amanyer and that was about the fastest part of the journey. Here our discomfort really started. A lousy breakfast that we had to queue in the cold for. The train was so slow that we did not get to our destination for lunch till 7.00 p.m.! And then it was lousy. We were woken again at 1.00 a.m. for dinner! Of course we had to break into our rations.

At odd places the train would stop for some reason or other and usually locals, mainly children, would dash along selling oranges and chocolate. As we got further away the quality decreased and the cost increased. On one occasion I got off and went right back to the end of the train – 3rd class – to see some Sergeants and the train started while I was there. I had to walk the whole tangle of the train and was disgusted with the condition of the 3rd class men lying on the floor which was nearly knee deep in dirt, a urinal in the corner of the carriage and no provision for washing etc.

The journey itself was fairly interesting though monotonous at times. It passed through all shades of desert from rocky to grassy, and all through the battle fields – tanks, lorries, trains and aeroplanes at a close up. Also in one place heaps and heaps of bottles. At Tobruk the outer defences were absolutely razed to the ground, but I could not go into the town and had to report at a transit camp again, and stay for night till a gharry came for me next morning.

The road was really good considering its history with just occasional bumps and potholes, and was lined again with destroyed transport and mine fields. But the noticeable things were the cemeteries, and the herds of hundreds of camels. How they have survived the passing of two fronts I don't know. The escarpment from the road to the camp was steep, rocky but fairly colourful and interesting. I don't know how the water bowser makes it each day. The desert here I found somewhat different in as much as flowers were definitely fewer and well on the wane. But it was still very cold, especially at night and the wind blew and we had some rain.

His diary records his eventual reunion with 459 Squadron:

18/1/43 Monday. In the morning I found transport had gone to El Adem aerodrome, so I rang again and transport arrived at noon. Arrived on squadron at 3.30

p.m. and had the usual unpacking and organising etc. Then in the evening reading fifty letters and in Sergeants' mess. Bed late. Flying Officer through.

Charles had been promoted to Flying Officer (on probation) with effect from 1st October 1942, though it had not appeared in the London Gazette until mid-December. However, such was the fog of war that it was not till mid-January that he was informed of his promotion. It would mean a welcome increase in pay, but would add little if anything to his duties. He now had to reintegrate into squadron life.

CHAPTER 8

Back to Work

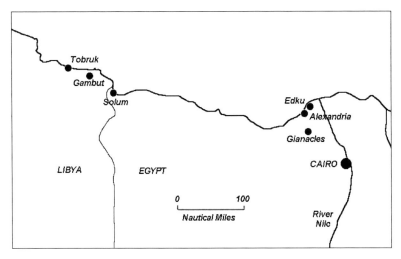

Charles's Travels – January to May 1943.

19/1/43 Tuesday. Up early and spent the morning dodging about organising things. Afternoon letter writing etc. and same in the evening. Spent part of time with Bryan.

20/1/43 Wednesday. Up early and Orderly Officer. But does not take a lot of doing these days. Morning censoring mail and usual. Afternoon reorganising and digging in the tent. Evening writing and reading. Bed early.

21/1/43 Thursday. Up early but idle day reading and writing. Evening briefing for CV escort and off at midnight. Lot colder today and bags of rain.

22/1/43 Friday. Had very long flight. Picked up convoy then flew round and round it. I dozed off to sleep. But it was a change to be able to fly in Solum bay without getting shot at. Landed 4.04 a.m. and did not wake till noon. Had desert bath in two pints of cold water. Spent the afternoon reading. Then for a stroll to Army AA camp nearby to look at predictors. Evening letters and bed early.

23/1/43 Saturday. Lazy day doing nothing but reading and writing. Evening briefed for another night trip and took off at 9.45 p.m. and back at 4.00 a.m.

While the crew were flying, events were moving fast on the ground further to the west. By 19 January the Allies had advanced to face the Germans' line of defence running south-west from Homs. On 23 January, Montgomery's forces entered Tripoli while Rommel retreated to form his new defensive line to the west at Mareth in Tunisia. He was dug in there by 1 February. By 4 February, the first allied units were crossing the border from Libya into Tunis.

It is interesting to note that four days after returning from three and a half months without flying, Charles is sent on operations once more with no apparent time to refresh his skills. The squadron Operations Record Book shows that these two flights were with a Sergeant Martin as Captain. Bryan Rostron's crew must still have had another navigator assigned to them. There then followed a period of two weeks without any more flying. During that time, Charles carried out normal squadron duties, visited Tobruk and complained about the weather, which now deteriorated. His journal describes what went on:

As I sit in my tent, way out in the desert, what do I see in the framework of the tent door? Yellow sand stretching away endlessly to the horizon, and finding no ending there even, but merging in a heat haze with the clear pale blue sky? No! Definitely not. That is a dream of some months ago. Now it is a dismal sight. The desert sand is there, but it is liberally strewn with clumps of scrub, this giving rise to solid lumps of sand. Between them the sand is flat and sodden, water logged, with numerous little pools and several very large ones, rippled by a cold north westerly wind that I know is reducing the temperature outside to overcoat level. The whole air seems permanently full of a steady shower of rain.

The horizon is still indefinable, but now it merges with the sky nearer and in the hazy grey of falling rain and rain clouds which sweep back from the horizon in a billowing grey-blue mass. In places it looks just too heavy to stay aloft and it can be seen falling away like a curtain and dropping to the desert. The only relief to this drab scene is a few stray disconsolate looking tents and one aeroplane whose wings can almost be imagined to hang down in dejection. This rain and wind have continued for three days almost continuously, except for the odd period when the clouds have broken away and a feeble sun has shone down from a very pale sky. Nearly every evening a break will occur in the west and as the sun goes down through it we are compensated by a very colourful and rapidly changing sunset.

This weather has also produced another blessing. The little dry grey scrub has blossomed with fleshy looking little pink flowers. In between numerous other green plants too have sprung up with a large variety of small flowers of all shapes and colours from daisy shape to antirrhinum shaped vetches, worts and grasses. It truly is amazing and a very pleasant change, but gee it is cold!

At last I have been into Tobruk itself. The trip into town had nothing particular to comment on. It was cold and bleak and windy, and we were in the back of a lorry. But we had a comfortable spring seat and our Irving jackets and flying boots. The general scenery was just the same monotony all the way, except for the now familiar wrecks on the road side. But I did see some real Flanders poppies among the flowers.

The road climbed steadily till we came to the first crest from where we had our first sight of the town. The sun had now come out and across a sunny waste of devastation and destruction a small white town stood on the far side of an apparently land locked bay, with quite a lot of shipping. But as we approached closer down first one escarpment and then another past wrecked aircraft, guns etc the general appearance took on a change. First of all, gaps appeared between the houses, then most of the houses were incomplete having whole walls or half walls missing. The ships in the harbour showed to be only semi-submerged wrecks. Then quite close heaps of debris appeared everywhere and the general devastation was fully apparent.

As we drove through the streets it was a pitiful sight. Not

Tobruk Harbour.

Inside the badly damaged Tobruk Church.

a house appeared habitable, yet several were "dished up" to house various service departments. Everywhere on the wrecked buildings were signs of the original Italian tenancy. Benito Mussolini schools, cafés, banks, cinemas etc. Obliterated directions to Axis troops with ours superimposed. The city centre gardens and town hall were a shambles. The church still had its steeple and four walls but there was hardly any roof and inside everything was bare and broken. Yet there was an air of solemnity and as we entered we removed our hats. The painted and gilded figure of the Virgin Mary had been knocked down from above the marble altar and recently stood up at the side.

We came out and stood for a while looking round at what was left of all these white buildings under a clear blue sky and tried with some difficulty to imagine what a truly picturesque sight it must have been in its prime. We walked down to the blue waters edge to get a closer view of the shipping past what was obviously the Port Authority building, with all the reinforced concrete hanging down by the iron reinforcing. Across the bay a bombed tanker was burning furiously – why I don't know, but it looked horrible belching out clouds of black smoke into the blue sky and against all this white background. It must have been a very frequent sight a month or more ago.

We had an interesting look over a balloon site, and indeed it seemed to me strange to see balloons again, though I had seen them recently at Aden and Alexandria. We drove into what was, and is now, used as the barracks, shrapnel peppered husks of buildings, and sat in the back of the lorry for our lunch, with a cup of tea from the cook and a fresh loaf from the bakery.

One of the star rooms was once, I should imagine, an assembly room of sorts. It had a tiled floor, the usual white walls with gilded columns, with one or two large murals of feats of valour in Italian history. A fresco depicted the taking or conquest of various towns and places in the Italian empire. At one end on the wall was a sort of scroll of honour 1914 – 18 and at the other on either side in an alcove was a small head and shoulders of King and Duce painted on the wall. Rex on left, and Duce on right. A large number of the occupying troops appeared to be Indian. Such was the fate of a once ambitious man's vision. What scenes of heroism, agony and death this town must have witnessed from both sides will never be known in full.

On the way back we called in for dental treatment at No. 10 Casualty Clearing Station, a small tented hospital, though I was OK. The dentist was a very pally type and took and introduced us to the Matron. They were all very friendly and made us very much at home in the Sisters' mess, a very comfortable place with a carpet on the floor and comfortable chairs and throws on a side table. We felt very easy there talking to the sisters and taking afternoon tea. Of course we extended an invitation and it was accepted for next Saturday.

Dated 3/2/43.

Yesterday was a wonderful change. After five days of

continuous rain the sun rose in the morning in a cloudless sky and throughout the day the few clouds kept well on the northern horizon over the sea. Leaving the sky above that bright clear blue that I like.

A slight chilly breeze from the north west kept the thermometer from rising high, but the sun was very warm and in the afternoon I went for a walk over to the escarpment and sat there for a while looking across the valley. The extra warmth after the rain had brought out more flowers of an even bigger variety of shape and colour, butterflies flitted about, lizards and chameleons flashed from rock to plant, and everything seemed bright and cheerful. But that little snag that spoils the otherwise perfect. The flies appeared! In the evening at dusk the wind dropped and the scent of the flowers could be smelt and felt, hanging over the desert.

This morning when I woke there was that familiar herald at home of a bright sunny day – a ground mist. And it looks as if it holds out here so far.

6/2/43 Saturday. Up early and with Roy and Del went in gharry to 80 Squadron near Tobruk for lunch and a drink. Then in to No. 10 Casualty Clearing Station for tea and to pick up 3 Sisters to bring back to mess for dinner. Only forty miles. Had very good evening with lots of fun. One of them said she was 34! Did not get back till 4.00 a.m.

No. 80 Squadron flew Hurricanes, supporting operations throughout North Africa. On occasions they provided escort for 459 Squadron aircraft on strikes.

7/2/43 Sunday. Up 7.30 a.m. as usual and wandered about

Collecting Sisters from No. 10 Casualty Clearing Station to visit the Squadron for Dinner.

all day doing nothing in particular. Then at 4.30 p.m. they said we were flying at 2.00 a.m.! So I went to bed after dinner and was called at midnight again.

8/2/43 Monday. Landed 8.30 a.m. Debrief and wash and shave and reading and writing outside tent. Afternoon Bryan's commission through so I helped him then had lots of drink in mess and also went to camp concert which was very good. Bed late.

9/2/43 Tuesday. Another hectic day doing nothing. Bed early.

10/2/43 Wednesday. Again did nothing except read.

11/2/43 Thursday. Windy and dusty morning. Afternoon played goal for the squadron against Wing but made a mess of it and also strained my wrist. Bed early.

12/2/43 Friday. *(No entry)*

13/2/43 Saturday. Did nothing all day, but in evening went to Toc H for a Spelling B. Bed late.

14/2/43 Sunday. Orderly Officer. But again very easy till evening when we had an air raid warning and so I had to get around. When I got back was told I was flying at 3.00 a.m. and so dashed off to bed.

15/2/43 Monday. Up at 3.00 a.m. Take Off 5.00 a.m. on sub-search with a destroyer. Found oil slicks off Azzaz apparently moving and stayed searching area with a

A destroyer drops depth charges on an oil slick that can be seen in the upper part of the picture.

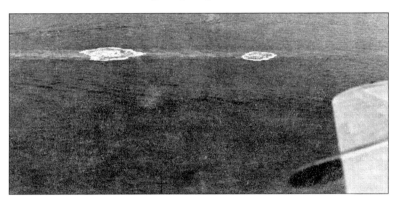

No results are seen from the depth charge attack, which was accurately placed across the line of advance of the oil slick.

destroyer but saw nothing. Afternoon and evening resting and reading. Bed late.

16/2/43 Tuesday. Had another quiet day sitting in the sun. Bed early.

17/2/43 Wednesday. Bryan back in the afternoon from Alexandria. In the morning a memorial service for K. O'Brian. Afternoon to see Doc and I now have to have treatment to my eye. Bed late.

A Flight of 459 Squadron. Charles is seated in the front row, fifth from the right. Note the mixture of 'uniforms'. The dark battledress tops are Royal Australian Air Force, the lighter ones are Royal Air Force. Charles appears to have opted for Khaki Drill!

18/7/43 Thursday. Another active day doing nothing. Morning lecture on SI. Evening writing. Twice to see Doc about my inflamed eye. He wants me to have another operation. Bed early.

19/2/43 Friday. Morning told I was posted to 75 OTU! Badly shaken but nothing I can do about it. Was wondering whether to have eye done now or re-muster to pilot now or just wait a bit. Had half hour flight dropping practice depth charges. Afternoon photo of A flight taken. Evening writing. Bed early.

2012/43 Saturday. Usual day dodging about and bath in the morning. Afternoon sitting in sun reading. Evening Toc H. Air raid warning. Bed late.

21/2/43 Sunday. Nothing doing in the morning but in the afternoon we had very entertaining sports meeting including races, jumps, hammer throwing, weight putting etc. and a Gambut cup for the winner. Evening quiet.

22/2/43 Monday. Still no news of date of our posting. Very windy all day with sand and rain. Spent most of day in tent and bed early.

Gambut Cup Tug o' War. Flight Lieutenant Freddie Madsen, apparently without sports kit!

The Gambut Cup is presented to the winner, Sergeant Pilot Tony Martin RAAF, by Wing Commander Howson, OC 459 Squadron.

23/2/43 Tuesday. Blowing hard and bitterly cold. So for the first time stayed in bed till noon reading. Afternoon and evening in the mess and for short walk. Bed late as the Padre arrived with lots of good records.

24/2/43 Wednesday. Up early and told that we (Bryan and I) were to take a Group Captain to Marriot at Cairo. Took off at 1.30 p.m. and we were soon lazing in hot soapy steamy bath. Spent evening with several fellows I met who I knew including Wing Commander Campbell ex 459 and a Squadron Leader and a Sister from Aden. Bryan went out with his lass. Bed late.

25/2/43 Thursday. Up late and met Jimmy and spent day wandering round and out to Group. Evening met some of Bryan's girlfriends and took them to the pictures and then to dinner, then left Bryan with them, and Jimmy and I went and had another meal. Bed late again.

26/2/43 Friday. Did a bit of shopping in the morning and then out to aerodrome at noon and to mess there before take off. Back at camp for evening but I went to bed early as I felt sick, probably from travelling in the turret.

27/2/43 Saturday. Spent all day collecting things, handing things on and generally getting organised for leaving tomorrow evening. Had Sergeants in mess for farewell.

28/2/43 Sunday. Up early and finished packing with getting things out to the aircraft and saying goodbyes. Had good fast trip down and landed Gianacles in usual sandstorm. Spent the afternoon getting tent and bed arranged and evening reading and writing. Bed early.

Charles and the crew left their operational squadron at an interesting time in the North African theatre of operations. The

The crew as they left 459 Squadron RAAF. Left to right: Lee Barrett, Bryan Rostron, Jimmy Craig, Charles Collins.

past fortnight had been a busy one for the Allied and Axis armies away to the West in Tunisia. On 14 February, the Axis plan to make a major assault on the US supply base at Tebessa in Algeria had begun. General Arnim with the German 5th Army had made a good start by attacking Allied forces and taking Sidi Bou Zid. The next day Rommel began his advance further south towards the Kasserine Pass. On 18 February he began his attack on the pass, and the next day he took control of it. Allied command structure in the area did not lend itself to coordinated action, with the French under General Louis-Marie Koeltz still resentful of the British action in sinking the French Fleet at Oran, and the United States II Corps commander Major General Lloyd Fredenhall having an antipathy towards the British in general and the commander of the British V Corps, Lieutenant General Alfrey, in particular.

Rommel was not, however, able to press his advantage, partly because General Arnim did not give the cooperation he needed, partly because of the arrival of Allied reinforcements and partly because of the need to send troops to bolster the defence of the Mareth line where Montgomery was applying pressure. He therefore had to retreat from the Kasserine Pass on 25 February. Though he continued to make spoiling attacks where he could, the situation for Rommel was not good.

The function of No. 75 Operational Training Unit to which Charles was posted was to train aircrew in Maritime Operations. It was a new unit, and was still being set up when Charles arrived at Gianacles. The Operations Record Book for 75 OTU records:

> 28/2/43 Flt M J Griffiths, Fg Off C Butterfield, Fg Off C A Collins, Fg Off A W Proctor, Fg Off C E Fergerson, Plt Off B E T Rostron, Plt Off A P Bowman and 14 NCOs arrived on posting for instructor duties. Remaining personnel of Flight on No 1 METS arrived. Two Bisleys arrived.
>
> Sufficient equipment now received to permit of training being commenced on 1 March 1943 and first pupils comprising 12 Officers and 20 NCOs arrived.
>
> 1/3/43 First course assembled and lectures commenced.

Charles and his fellows were certainly being thrown in at the deep end. It is interesting to note that Charles and Bryan Rostron at least had been given no training in instructional techniques before being required to teach on the OTU. Charles's diary records that they had a week to settle in before starting teaching:

> 1/3/43 Monday. Morning doing the usual jobs at Adjutant etc. Afternoon to Training Section to get gen on what I was to do. Picked three lessons on meteorology and one

on night navigation and that is all. Evening writing and reading. Bed early.

2/3/43 Tuesday. Spent all day sitting in ops room talking and reading navigation gen and getting thoroughly fed up with doing nothing. Evening in mess. Bed early.

3/3/43 Wednesday. Spent day blankly in ops room and wrote some letters there.

The Operations Record Book also records that on 3 March, two Blenheim IVs and two Blenheim Vs were transferred from No 1 METS for use by Conversion and Refresher Flight.

4/3/43 Thursday. In the morning flew to swing a compass then spent rest of day in Duty Pilot's tent learning the job. In the afternoon two Hudsons from 459 Squadron landed and so in the evening we went across to the Sergeants' mess (having first had permission from the CO). 459 took up the centre table and did well with bags of bottles till late at night.

5/3/43 Friday. Morning in section yarning and reading. Relieved Duty Pilot for lectures and lunch. Afternoon sleep in mess to see what would be said. Then to Sick Quarters to have ear syringed and relieve Duty Pilot again. Gale blew up – cold and sandy. Bed early.

6/3/43 Saturday. Up early and on duty as Duty Pilot all day and kept pretty busy between letter writing and reading. Also did some night flying, but bed early.

7/3/43 Sunday. Returned to my tent and spent bit of time getting washed and brushed up and then idled till lunch. Afternoon sitting in sun outside tent reading. Evening writing. Bed early.

8/3/43 Monday. Gave my first lecture which was not an outstanding success as it was supposed to last an hour, whereas I finished it in quarter of an hour and then worked round it for the rest of the time. Rest of day very slack and quiet. Bed early.

9/3/43 Tuesday. In the morning we had a lecture by the Air Commander about anti-submarine work. Afternoon I gave my second lecture on meteorology and spent rest of day reading. In evening 454 Squadron RAAF sent over a gharry for 459 Squadron fellows to visit their mess. Did not get back till 12.30 a.m.

10/3/43 Wednesday. Nothing particular all day, so sat outside tent in sun reading and writing and bed early.

11/3/43 Thursday. I was Duty Instructor and the Navigation Officer was off sick, so I stood in for him. The Air Officer Commanding came round. Evening writing and bed early.

12/3/43 Friday. Duty Pilot, and I was pretty busy on operations from here. In the evening a terrific storm blew up and moved several tents. Wind about 80 – 100 mph in gusts. Moved aircraft and roofs off buildings. Little sleep.

13/3/43 Saturday. Group called all through night. Did not finish as Duty Pilot till late! Spent the morning going round seeing Adjutant, Accountant Officer, Chief Ground Instructor etc and fixing a day off tomorrow. Afternoon had nap and busy in tent. Evening reading.

For the next two days Charles visited Cairo where he played golf and tennis, drank with friends and did some shopping. Returning to Gianacles, he continued the round of lecturing, being Duty Pilot and Duty Controller. He comments on how bad the weather was, and on a number of aircraft incidents. He was not enjoying his 'rest tour'. Extracts from the Unit Operations Record Book for the rest of March reflect some of the problems that were being experienced:

19/3/43 Owing to extremely adverse weather conditions six aircraft on navigation flights were recalled with instructions to land at Edku. Four of the aircraft landed here and two at Edku.

20/3/43 Yesterday's sandstorm continues and a signal despatched at 1430 hrs stating that aerodrome visibility was from 10 to 50 yards. All flying was cancelled at 1200 hrs.

21/3/43 Once again bad weather caused the cancellation of navigation flights. ..... .

On 22 March the author comments that 75 OTU cannot possibly meet its target output of thirty trained crews per month with the aircraft available. They would need one hundred and twenty aircraft to achieve it, whereas the serviceability on that day was just one quarter of the Ansons, no Bisleys and one quarter of the Baltimores. The one Hudson was serviceable, but had only enough hours to convert three pilots before it was due for a servicing. Then next day he records that they are regularly told that more Hudsons would soon be delivered, but they never were. Then on 29 March the ironic entry:

29/3/43 Cheers – one Hudson duly collected from BARU.

And on the last day of the month:

31/3/43 Signal sent to 201 Group Headquarters today stating that "Operational Training ceased with effect from 30/3/43 owing to NIL serviceability Bisleys and Hudsons".

This was not a happy unit.

Charles meanwhile managed to get a more interesting job as March drew to a close:

25/3/43 Thursday. Duty Controller all day and kept pretty busy. Tried to get the job permanently, but they said it would be too much, but I got the job of Officer in charge of the ops room, which took me off lecturing. Evening writing. Bed early.

26/3/43 Friday. Swung compass in morning and otherwise had lazy day. Bed Early.

27/3/43 Saturday. Morning conference where I was confirmed as i/c ops room. Evening busy with secret docs! Bed late.

28/3/43 Sunday. Pottered around all day. Bed late.

29/3/43 Monday. Duty Controller. Kept pretty busy all day and with ops room. Night navigation exercise and did not finish till 11.00 p.m.

30/3/43 Tuesday. New ops room taking shape and so organising furniture etc. Bed early.

31/3/43 Wednesday. Up early and spent the morning preparing orders for controllers etc, and getting plotting map in ops room. Noon changed and then had to wait till 4.30 p.m. for an aircraft. To Alex with Griff. First thing was a haircut and shampoo, then hot bath. Then for drink, dinner and to see film – Mrs Miniver about raids on England etc. Very good. Bed late.

1/4/43 Thursday. Clocks on one hour. Did not get up till 11.30 a.m. Had a good breakfast in bed and then went out to Sporting Club for golf. Left early and back for bath etc and out for drink just in time. Did quite a lot before we met Hughes with three girls for a big dinner – 30/- a head! Took two and a half hours, then on to Excelsior for floor show. Bed very late but biggest catastrophe was when I lost my best pipe. It spoilt the evening.

2/4/43 Friday. Up early and out to Sporting Club for golf. Went all round and did not do too well, but in the afternoon I had some practice first and then played holes a lot better. Evening Griff went to GHQ and I booked seats for cinema. Then while waiting for him at Cecil Bar met a Squadron Leader from the Aircraft Delivery Unit who said he could get me posted there. So I gave him all my particulars and he was going to see what he could do. After dinner and cinema I was still feeling excited about it and only hope it comes off. It will be great to fly again.

3/4/43 Saturday. Up late and then rushed to catch gharry back to camp. Did not like coming back to desert again. But I spent £10 in Alex so it is as well. Also I am still hoping for ADU, although I do not feel too optimistic about it now. Evening letter writing.

The routine of setting up the ops room kept Charles busy for the next few days. Things brightened up a bit on the eighth:

8/4/43 Thursday. Busy lining out wall map all day. Evening up to briefing and reading. In the evening some French people came out to give us a show, but I wanted to write letters. However, I got drinking with Griff and did not stop. When the French girls came in the mess I met and stayed with a very nice little one of seventeen years and I spoke French fluently enough for her to understand.

Another week of routine passed. Charles was clearly bored stiff, and there are a few days when his diary contains no entry – something unprecedented except when he was seriously ill in hospital.

15/4/43 Thursday. Duty Controller as well. Busy up till turned midnight. Had conference with Robby and he now wants us all to report at 0715. Gee how I hate this place. When I got back to mess the ENSA concert party who had given another show were still there. I saw my little French girl for a few minutes and she said she would write.

16/4/43 Friday. Up late and then had a very quiet day. Told Squadron Leader Robinson that I wanted to be posted to flying as I had heard nothing from ADU. In the afternoon had letter from 201 asking for more gen on my re-mustering as a pilot. So that may come off yet. Stayed up late listening to TSF.

17/4/43 Saturday. In the afternoon we had another "conference" with more bull and binding duties. But things have been piled onto me and I am just about fully cheesed! Oh to get away from here.

The Operations Record Book paints no rosier a picture. On 2 April it records that twenty Baltimores, ten Blenheim IVs and four Blenheim Is were allocated to the unit. What actually arrived during the month were one Blenheim I, five Blenheim IVs (of which one crashed on landing when being delivered), three Blenheim Vs and two Beaufighters (of which one also crashed on landing).

Flying was frequently cancelled because of the weather, and when the weather cleared on 11 April, there is a plaintive entry that the weather is fine, but three days of sandstorms have left all the aircraft unserviceable.

Despite everything No. 2 course got under way, and some flying was achieved, although on occasions there is a cryptic entry that flying in the Delta area was cancelled "on the advice of the Intelligence Officer." A number of aircraft crashed or carried out forced landings for various reasons, but there were no fatalities.

Charles's diary reflects the mood of the Operations Record Book. He too comments on the weather and the crashes. In the last week of the month he became unwell with a sore throat and very high temperature, and was consigned to bed for some days, followed by "light duties". By 1 May he was sufficiently recovered to go to Alexandria for three days.

> 4/5/43 Tuesday. Very busy day running round in ops room, but otherwise nothing special. Evening in tent reading and bed early.
>
> 5/5/43 Wednesday. Usual odd jobs all day and quiet evening in tent.
>
> 6/5/43 Thursday. Jogging along all day. Getting mighty hot now.
>
> 7/5/43 Friday. Nothing unusual.
>
> 8/5/43 Saturday. Night Navs. Lost one aircraft down in the drink.
>
> 9/5/43 Sunday. Bags of flap all day in ops room, sending out searches etc. for missing aircraft, but not found. Late night.

Once again the Operations Record Book notes a series of accidents and engine failures. The "aircraft down in the drink" was an Anson on a navigation exercise, lost about ten miles off Aboukir. One body was washed up on the shore four days later, but the remainder of the crew were not found.

> 10/5/43 Monday. Busy all day again and then in evening had to prepare sub exercises for tomorrow. Evening Eric Bedwell and George Holby and crews from 459 Squadron were posted here!
>
> 11/5/43 Tuesday. Bags of panic in morning preparing

report on the missing aircraft and getting a submarine exercise arranged for the afternoon. In evening doing astro till 11.30 p.m.

12/5/43 Wednesday. Quiet day with nothing special.

13/5/43 Thursday. Usual busy day but when I got to mess was told on QT that I was posted, but the chap did not know where or when. Bed late wondering.

The speed of events was to be breathtaking:

14/5/43 Friday. Trying all morning to find out something. Afternoon rumours came round that posting was to be on the 18th and to a Transport squadron. No definite news in evening.

15/5/43 Saturday. In the morning I was told that it was definitely on 18th and to 216 Group. Went to lecture by a Group Captain on anti-submarine weapons. Afternoon packing, shower and clearing. Then after dinner with Bryan and Lee to Jimmy's tent for feed of tinned stuff on premises and beer. Very good evening.

16/5/43 Sunday. Spent day getting cleared. Had tooth filled. Got new camp bed. Then in evening had farewell evening with the boys in my charge. And did I get rotten.

17/5/43 Monday. Up very early and finished packing. Left amidst farewells at 8.15 a.m. and took decent road via the pyramids to Cairo. Arrived 216 Group too late to catch staff. But duty Officer had no clues. So went to the Junior Officers' Club for the rest of day and night. Bed early and slept soundly.

18/5/43 Tuesday. Went out to Group early and saw Wing Commander Ryan and in five minutes he told me that I was posted to 117 Squadron! But the speed of the whole thing was mucked up by transport as I had to wait till 6.00 p.m. for it. Arrived at base at 8.00 p.m. in time for a party with free drinks and 36 ATS. But I left early for bed.

Throughout his time overseas Charles wrote frequent letters to friends and family. In some of these, particularly to his family, he expressed his feelings about what he did more freely than he did in his diary or journal. A letter written to his Father while at 75 OTU at Gianacles reflects this:

113923 F/O C A COLLINS
75 OTU
RAF
MEF

4/3/43

Dear Dad

You will have got my change of address by airgraph by now, and I have just written to Auntie Nellie to tell her I am here and briefly what I think of the place here, which on the whole is not much. But more of that later.

Since my last letter there is not much I have done to make news. Two things of interest happened before I left though. First was a sports meeting we arranged. It was a great success with all the usual sporting events and even a cup for the champion, which turned up from shell casing etc in the maintenance tent. They made an excellent job of it and the Sgt Pilot who won it should be very proud of it.

The other thing was that a Group Captain up in the desert had to go to Alexandria to HQ and we, my pilot and I, were given the job of flying him down. He was there two days, and so you can guess we made the most of our time and had a good look round. I think I have mentioned Alex before. It certainly is quite a good town as Egyptian towns go. But the biggest change was in the comfort. To be able to sleep again in a wide soft bed with clean white sheets, and in a well furnished room. And best of all to be able to lie in a steaming hot bath and soak out all the sand and dirt that we had been futilely trying to wash off in a tent with about a cubic foot of cold water for the last month. Gee it was good, and I had my share.

Also the change of food, plenty of variety and well cooked and no rationing. Then we would go out to a restaurant for a cup of chocolate, nice and hot, and take our choice of the biggest variety of cakes and buns I have ever seen, cream ones, chocolate ones, acid ones, in fact everything you can imagine and more. It would have given anyone in England a terrific shock.

Well, just after that I came here. It is still in the desert, which I don't mind so much, but I don't like the job. It is too slow and not exciting enough and I don't get enough to do. We did have a jolly good time on the squadron all together and I did not want to leave. Also I had got the job well buttoned up and we could do it well with a fair degree of safety. Now I don't fly at all unless I want to and then I don't always get the chance. I have to instruct people how to do the job I have learnt and how to get away with it. Well there is no doubt about it, we can teach them a lot and help them in many ways, but really it is a job you learn from experience and I wonder now as they go out to operations with the first zest and at the same time foreboding that I did, what will happen to them and how they will get on.

The first two or three trips are usually pretty shaking, but after a while you get used to it and accept it as an everyday event – even look forward to it. This easy attitude we have adopted did not dawn on me till now, and I look back and try to tell the fellows what to expect.

But even if I can help them, I would rather someone else do it who wants to and better get on with the real job. I am longing to get the whole show over and get back if possible to peace and normality and forget it all. But I fear I shall have to go out and have a stab at the Japs first. But I don't mind if only it will hurry the job on.

Well it is time now I got on with some work. I hope everyone at home is keeping well and fit, and work is not too much for you. Do take care and look after yourself. I expect to see you just the same when I do get home.

Love
　　Charles.

Now Charles was to get his chance to get back to 'the real job'. His rest tour had not been a great success. He had been taken off operational flying much earlier than was normal, for he had completed only a few hundred operational hours, mainly because of his long stay in hospital. It is likely that the need for instructors, a brief lull in operational tasks for 459 Squadron and the fact that the rest of his crew were probably due for a rest all conspired to have him posted early. No. 75 OTU, on which he had spent the last two and a half months was a new unit, and appears to have suffered from poor organisation and leadership. Certainly the Group Headquarters gave little practical support, making and breaking innumerable promises for resources. The Operational Record Book summarises May 1943:

It is understood that certain crews of No 2 course are being returned for further training and night flying.

Serviceability of operational type aircraft has never been above 40% and mostly below 25% since the opening of the OTU, otherwise crews would have left the station fully air trained.

As yet synthetic training, RDF etc cannot be carried out, owing to the almost entire lack of equipment. What is available is entirely thanks to the efforts and improvisation of the Officers in charge and reflects very strongly to their credit.

Training Unit Statistical Summary for May 1943 (F102).

Average serviceability for May

12 Anson serviceable	0 u/s
1 Baltimore serviceable	3 u/s
8 Blenheim serviceable	34 u/s
0 Hudson serviceable	2 u/s
1 Beaufighter serviceable	1 u/s
1 Beaufort serviceable	0 u/s

The tone of the document is always negative, and it is interesting to note that all the monthly entries are signed "on behalf of" the Commanding Officer rather than by the CO himself. It is usual for this type of document to be prepared by a junior Officer, but for the CO himself to add a few words of summary. Apart from a pointed signal to Group at the end of March in which he stopped all training, this CO appears to have done little to improve the situation. The final paragraph of the monthly summary would indicate that some Officers at least were able and willing to make the effort. Properly directed, this enthusiasm could surely have been usefully employed, for example, to protect aircraft during bad weather so that they were serviceable when the weather improved.

While Charles had languished in Gianacles, Allied fortunes in Tunis had been good. In the middle of March General Montgomery had assaulted the Axis front line at Mareth, while General Patton had attacked from the west. By the end of the month the Axis front line had fallen back northwards sixty miles to Wadi Akarit, and the United States forces were squeezing them into an ever narrowing strip of the coast, in places less than fifty miles wide. In mid-April Rommel asked Hitler and Mussolini to withdraw all Axis troops from North Africa, but they refused, fearing that a withdrawal would precipitate an early invasion of Europe. Outnumbered in aircraft by three thousand to five hundred and in tanks by twelve hundred to one hundred and thirty, the Axis had an impossible task. In two days alone in April the Germans lost over one hundred transport aircraft re-supplying Tunis; losses such as this could not be sustained, and Allied forces advanced steadily. Despite a counter attack by the German Panzers where they took Djebl Bou-Aoukaz, the end was inevitable, and on 6 May Operation Vulcan started, leading to the final surrender of all Axis forces on 13 May. Over one hundred and fifty thousand Axis prisoners were taken. From the North African theatre alone the Axis had lost about a quarter of a million men.

CHAPTER 9

Transport

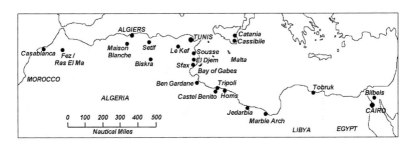

Charles's Travels – May to August 1943.

No. 117 Squadron, to which Charles now found himself posted, was a transport squadron flying Hudsons. The squadron had reformed in Khartoum in 1941 flying Bristol Bombays, though they soon acquired some Italian Savoia-Marchetti 79s, and later some DC 2s. In November 1941 they were moved to Egypt, taking with them just the DC2s to which were later added some DH 8s. By April 1943 they were re-equipped with Lockheed Lodestars and Dakotas (DC3s), but by November 1942 they had finally settled to being entirely equipped with Lockheed Hudson Transports. Seven aircraft types in 20 months must have been confusing both for aircrews and ground crew! In May 1943 when Charles joined 117 Squadron they had been supporting operations by the 8th Army as it advanced across Egypt, Libya and Tunis. The squadron Operations Record Book for May describes their work:

> This month saw the end of the Tunisian campaign and a landmark in the squadron's history. ...... A new phase in the squadron's activities commenced – its assistance in the

Bilbeis – Tented Accommodation.

general reorganisation and re-establishment of the numerous units scattered throughout North Africa. This work took aircraft on many runs, anywhere between Casablanca and the Delta, carrying a large variety of freight and personnel and many thousands of pounds of mail. There were a few instances of aircraft going unserviceable on scattered aerodromes causing some small servicing difficulty, but usually only necessitating a few days delay before it returned to base.

When Charles arrived to join 117 Squadron they were based at Bilbeis on the south-west side of the Nile Delta. Charles described his arrival in his journal:

> After one day in Cairo I went by gharry to Bilbeis, the HQ of 117 Squadron and a permanent camp with tented accommodation. It was off the main road from Cairo to Ismalia, on the fringe of the irrigation system and so

I found various flowers growing and even tomatoes. They appeared a grand crowd of fellows and I felt I was going to enjoy the job.

I was only there one day, however, flying up to El Djem the next. The first part of the journey was of course all across the well known uninteresting desert. Marble Arch, where we refuelled, being the first destination. Much has already been said about it and I concur with it all, but it does seem ludicrous

"Marble Arch"

standing there that Mussolini should have thought it necessary to go to that extreme to impress people with Italian pomp and grandeur.

From here to Tobruk took us over inland desert again, till eventually we came to the coastal plain east of Jedarbia, where irrigation has made it possible to grow widely spaced olive trees. At regular intervals along the roads, very wide apart are stereotyped houses, white with flat roof and at the side a small separate building. This was surrounded by a square enclosed garden of about quarter of an acre. Then we flew over the barren but colourful mountains to Jedarbia port itself. The port is only small however. Here there are one or two sunken wrecks in it. The town, again small, lies some short distance to the west.

We missed Tripoli and then cut across the Bay of Gabes and past Sfax. Unfortunately I dozed off at this stage and did not wake till we were flying over the acres and acres of

239

olive groves in Tunisia. Then the huge colonnaded Coliseum at Djem, built two centuries BC and now breached only in two places. From the air other small superficial damage was not visible. And we did not fly close but landed immediately.

Today I have been able to have a look around. It is irregularly undulating and though very dry, is quite green. The main product is olive trees, but I saw oranges, apples, walnuts, and a small shrub with red bell like blossom. Also flowering cactus and cornflowers, convolvulus, red poppies, rye and oats, straw stocks; and goats and camels. And a very wide deep well with primitive hoisting mechanism consisting of unshaped boughs of trees supporting a cross section of a walnut tree about two inches thick and grooved for the rope. The water was raised by buckets and tipped into a large concrete compound from where it drained into several successively smaller connected hollows.

Back to the diary:

> 22/5/43 Saturday. Up very late and spent uneventful day except for sleeping and reading. Evening packing for move and spot of drinking but bed early.

The "spot of drinking" would have been to celebrate Charles's 28th birthday.

> 23/5/43 Sunday. Up at the crack of dawn and fully packed and took down my tent and mess. We were airborne at 10.00 a.m. and landed at Castel Benito two hours later. Took my kit and put it in a room. Had wash and in to tiffin where told I was to take off for Malta at 4.00 p.m. Repacking etc., but did not get off

Well at El Djem, Tunisia.

till late and therefore landed at Malta too late to go anywhere, so stayed in mess at Luqa. Whole island looks lot cleaner, tidier and quieter than last time, but there is a suppressed feeling.

24/5/43 Monday. Up and away at crack of dawn again and back to Castel Benito in time for another breakfast. Spent day tidying up and settling down to things. To bed early.

Charles expands on the "suppressed feeling" in his journal:

Malta when I saw it last had a battered and harried look. Everywhere appeared shrouded in the disorder that comes of plans hurriedly made and of emergency measures that, though effective, have not proved tidy. The towns were broken and shattered, with the streets debris strewn and blocked up. The fields were also broken open and splattered about. The whole presented an almost cowed appearance, but nevertheless a sort of determined, pugnacious hanging on for the near future when it too would be able to turn again and deliver the blow. Now, not yet twelve months since, I have seen it redressed for this purpose. It looks peaceful, clean, quiet and even lazy. A small patch of beauty in a wide blue surround. The country and fields are healed again and producing as nature intended. In the towns, streets have been cleared, buildings are being rebuilt, and work is going on as man intended.

But what the people have gone through has left its mark. Though they laugh and chatter and the children play, there is a resigned, determined submerged part of them that is not obvious to the unobservant. In fact the general atmosphere of the whole island and not only the people is an undertone of rumbling, a feeling or sense of latent power, vital and tremendous as though to challenge the foe who tries again, and threaten even without another try being attempted.

For the next three weeks Charles did little but hang around. He observes in his diary that he was the "spare" observer, so being uncrewed he found himself doing many of the minor, though necessary, jobs that have to be done on a squadron. He described the accommodation at Castel Benito in a letter to his brother Peter in early July 1943:

We now live in a sort of barrack block vacated as far as names on the walls go, by Jerry, Ities, Aussies, NZs and Canadians. The pictures, or rather drawings, on the wall show also the surprising number of people whose sole idea of beauty and art run to shapely female bodies, dressed (scantily) and undressed. Usually I must admit, some of them are quite a joy to behold, and I wonder sometimes if girls really do look as beautiful as that. I've forgotten. But others, such as sketches round holes in the wall are neither artistic nor edifying, and tend to keep one awake at night. So we have removed them.

Some of the other drawings show the surprising confidence that Jerry had in his ability to reach Cairo. Perhaps it is not surprising though, because he should have done by rights, if he had had the odd clue. Also they were fond of their home town and suffered from a quite natural nostalgia. In several places there is a person's name and the name of their town in Germany. The Italians particularly were always saying "When I arrive in…" or at least that is how it reads to me.

During this period Charles was appointed as 'Gas Officer', and he also went to Cairo where he underwent a full medical examination and was passed as fully fit – including with respect to his eye, which had been giving him trouble. He saw something of the local area, went swimming in Tripoli when he could, and as always recorded impressions in his journal:

The other day I went into Tripoli by road. Through the countryside it is very sandy but grass grows there and it is tree bespattered much like our heathlands at home, particularly in Hampshire, and it is just as undulating. Some of the trees were strange, but mainly they were olives and walnuts, and with quite a lot of wattle along the road sides. In Tripoli I was surprised to find so little bomb damage. True there was some, but compared with Tobruk it was nothing. The shops, or some of them, though with considerably limited supplies, were still open and carrying

Bust of Il Duce in Castel Benito with RAF Officer's hat.

on trade, though I wondered what the people thought of recent events. Selling first to Jerry, and then to us. The buildings also were still the rectangular build with white or pale yellow plaster facade. From the glimpse of the harbour I had it looked very full and active. But we passed quickly in a hurry to get to the bathing beach. Very fine and all that, but cold and shallow.

The country from here to Homs I have only seen from the air, but it appears much the same, the coastal strip slightly grassed and with widely spaced orchards with large white homesteads and now and again a small village. Then at Homs the mountains come right down to near the coast.

However, in mid-June things livened up a bit.

16/6/43 Wednesday. Operations Officer all day, but not much doing. Late afternoon to conference at SHQ and found I was leading the contingent welcoming General Lion! But I got back in time for the party. The mess had been transformed and we received in grand style sixteen nurses and sisters from local New Zealand hospital. Very good. I drank a lot and danced a bit, then took them home and returned to Ops Officer duties.

"General Lion" was King George VI, who visited the victorious troops in North Africa at this time.

17/6/43 Thursday. Up early to get crews off then did two hours local flying. But that is all I can get. Getting fed up with having my feet on the ground. Afternoon down for usual bathe. Then spent evening quietly writing letters.

18/6/43 Friday. Spent the morning sorting snaps. Afternoon for a swim. Evening letters.

19/6/43 Saturday. In the morning did a three hour flight and then parade for HM King visiting Tripoli, but only saw a glimpse and so was unimpressed. Afternoon too late for swim. So spent rest of day letter writing and yarning.

Charles, alas, was unmoved by the visit:

One day the King came. Of course it was all very hush hush, and he came as General Lion, and no one was supposed to know it was him until they saw him. But there was so much flap and preparation that everyone was asking questions and the gen also leaked out. Then when we had all lined the road, the civilians had been confined to their houses and either side of the road cleared by the RAF Regiment. His plane came over – and what an escort, with loads and loads of fighters, top and bottom cover, and formation. Then he flashed past in his car with hardly a smile – all over in a second and forgotten. I hope he was impressed with his victorious 8th army, but from what he saw he will never know what they went through.

At this time Charles was finally crewed up, and began a period of intensive flying with his new captain, Flying Officer H. M. Carter – "Maggie" to his friends.

20/6/43 Sunday. Set off early for Sousse and Setif and back, but the aircraft went unserviceable at Sousse and though we tried twice could not risk it. So we had to stay the night in town. No accommodation and had to sleep on a marble floor.

21/6/43 Monday. Up early and after a restless night returned at 6.00 a.m. to the airfield through quite interesting country. Spent all morning on the aerodrome while fitters worked on the aircraft. I saw two Spitfires collide and burn. After lunch did an air test and took off for Setif. Went via Le Kef and Constantine in case, but engine cut past Constantine, but made Setif on both. Evening for walk through lovely country, just like home. Change to see red gabled roofs again and trees etc.

22/6/43 Tuesday. Off early in the morning but over the mountains we ran into storms so went south and flew over desert. We had to fly for about an hour on one engine! Landed in time to read Arthur Turner's note and dash down to meet him for the afternoon in Tripoli. Evening letter writing and preparing for trip tomorrow.

23/6/43 Wednesday. Off early again to Sfax, on to Tunis and then to Algiers. But we could not go direct as there were big cumulus clouds over the mountains. So we went out to sea. At Algiers, by the time we had got settled down it was fairly late, but I went on into town as I thought Peter was there. But alas no, so went for walk round. Very interesting, but back early and very tired.

24/6/43 Thursday. Away early again. This time it was over the mountains and it was lovely to Tunis, on to Sfax and across to base. Then I had a decent clean up and sort out and settled down and spent evening quietly, and bed early.

25/6/43 Friday. Morning up early and away to Malta and

246

back. Afternoon saw Arthur Turner. Went to gas department. I got a terrific jeep and then went in it to get John Stanwell over for dinner and evening's drinking in mess. Took him back in jeep. Very dark and very fast. Bed late.

26/6/43 Saturday. Had very good lie in till 9.00 a.m. Spent the morning on small odd jobs and in the afternoon I went for a swim and some shopping. Evening writing and reading.

27/6/43 Sunday. Up early for briefing but did not set off till 7.00 p.m. and went to Korba in Cape Bon for a Yank fighter group to be shifted to Gozo. In evening went down to beach and had a very good swim in fine warm water with fine silver sand and no costume. Then back to sleep under the aircraft as there was no accommodation.

28/6/43 Monday. Up at crack of dawn. Very sketchy breakfast and away with first load. Only had to do two trips (nine aircraft) and had a grand Yank lunch on return from second trip. At Gozo it was the first time aircraft had landed there, so the local populace were very curious. Afternoon we went to Luqa and then back to base. Had first wash and shave and bath, then writing and a good drink.

29/6/43 Tuesday. Up early and took off for Malta, Tunis and Algiers. Apart from some scares on landings, nothing special except a very interesting journey. In the evening at Algiers we had some trouble getting beds but got fixed up at some flats. Very tired, so did not go into town. Went to bed early.

30/6/43 Wednesday. Left early again after a grand night sleeping on a balcony. Went direct to Malta and had some lunch there before moving off again to Castel Benito. But we had to return then to do an airtest owing to a bad engine. However, we eventually got back in time for wash etc. and dinner but went to bed at 9.00 p.m. as very tired.

The squadron Operations Record Book shows that over the twelve day period the crew flew on every day except one and did nearly forty hours flying, usually doing three or four flights per day. Cargos varied, and they often carried passengers. In his journal Charles describes the towns they visited:

To Sousse we flew over the El Djem country, but failed to get off again from the Monastir aerodrome. So late at night we had to go into Sousse for accommodation, and at midnight bedded down on a marble floor. However, the next day on way back to the aerodrome we saw a bit of the place. It was as usual, white and dusty, with the houses still square. Here, however, nearly all the houses have strips of inlaid coloured glazed stone, mainly blues and greens, about three inches wide over windows and doors. There is an old fort there, somewhat knocked about, but plain, extensive and not interesting from the outside; it has thick tessellated walls, a dirty, dusty white facade with white stone blocks showing in places. The roads out are over salt flats or low pasture and cereal land. Monastir is a small village and is quite pretty with its palms and cactus and wide leaved cactus. The fezzes worn here are round, not with flat tops as in the Delta. The old part of Monastir apparently had a city wall, and some of the gates are labelled "Out of Bounds" and "Disease"! Probably the native area.

The flight from Monastir to Setif was over beautiful hilly country with the green of trees and grass in the valleys, the yellow of freshly cut crops and corn sheaves in the fields and the brown of the tops of the mountains and then white roads winding about. Setif produced a pleasant surprise. A perfect town. The usual white houses, but looking clean, not dusty, with red tiled gabled roofs, very wide straight avenues, all tree lined and a large tree avenued square. A really beautiful looking town. The aerodrome was out in the country, and an evening walk was more like home with the surrounding hills, the ripe corn, standing and cut, the poppies and thistles. The haymaking smell and the quiet of a country sunset.

Coming back we started over well wooded mountains, a lovely deep green, but we ran into a front and as our engines were bad we went south, over the salt pans to avoid it and so saw only the usual desert.

Dated 26/6/43

Sfax is not a town at all, at least it does not look like the usual concept of a town from the air, except for a small centre section round the docks. The rest of the very large area that comprises the town is made up of many large gardens apparently of about an acre, with one large house at one side, so that there appears to be a whole network of this round the centre nucleus.

Enfidaville, so much in evidence in the papers*, is only a small town with four streets. But these four streets are main arterial roads from the surrounding country. Hence its strategic importance. The country here is flat, with three large salt flats, but mainly open orchards. Tunis is a town truly in every sense of the word. First there is the outer harbour, really the bay. Behind this is one sort of shallow island lake divided from the bay by a sand bar. This has been breached and a

* Axis forces had retreated to Enfidaville to make a stand as they withdrew towards Tunis in April 1943.

channel cleared up to the town front. The town itself as a whole is conspicuous by its long straight very wide streets, almost all of them tree or garden lined. But it is clearly divided into three areas. The centre portion round the seaboard is all of tall business blocks and flats etc. Another large area is of the familiar square, flat roofed, two storey houses, probably used by the poorer classes and with no regularity or planning. Then round it all, except the west side, is a thick border of large gardens and houses as at Sfax. The west side is rather restricted for development by a large salt flat.

All those aerodromes up round the Gulf of Gabes are absolutely littered with wrecked aircraft. The bombers and strafing aircraft must have had a really wonderful time of it.

Oh beautiful, beautiful Algeria! A land of high hills and deep valleys. Woods and streams. And how like Scotland with the normal villages in the valleys and pastoral pursuits, then the deep green woods which roll up the hillsides. And the extent of it all! Though covered by tracks and mountain paths, the impossibility of appreciating it all on the ground was evident, and yet from the air, with everything in our favour I felt I wanted to get on my feet and wander round for an afternoon. We went into Algiers for a few hours in the evening. It is a very French town, with the usual open cafes etc. and in blanc and rouge etc with shops and amenities. It was grand to get into a town again, but I did feel out of place again as I always seem to in a town. A rather striking thing about Algiers is the way it climbs prettily up the hillside from the busy harbour. But I was glad I too did not have to climb up!

When we went up to Cape Bon to shift a fighter group to Gozo, I was surprised that there was not more evidence of the thousands of troops who had been trapped there. True most of the small towns had been very severely damaged and knocked about, and again there were large numbers of wrecked aircraft, but roads, bridges etc all appeared to be in very excellent condition. The crops were still standing or being reaped, and it was strange to see it being done, and stacked by machinery. Others were being gathered by the now familiar winnowing methods. But it was easy to imagine the plight of the armies with the narrow plains and the high fastness of the hills. Gozo was very interesting. It appeared the same as Malta on a smaller scale, the terraced blending valleys, the small towns with the predominant church in each and the white dusty walled roads. We passed over a very feudal looking castle on the outskirts of the town. In fact the town seemed to leak out of it as it stood high on a mound surrounded by successive horizontal terraces down to the level of the plain and then dwindle away down the road.

The natives had obviously seen many aircraft flying, but this was a new aerodrome, and they all streamed out to see the mighty monsters on the ground. It reminded me of how I used to dash out, full of curiosity, to see a grounded aircraft at home when I was only a child. One thing that is lacking round the Maltese Islands are the fleets of landing barges that are swarming in all mainland African ports. But there is plenty of other activity.

Charles at last was getting on with a job again, and could hardly complain of boredom now! At this time also the squadron started to receive Dakota aircraft once more, though Charles and Maggie continued to fly the Hudson transports for the time being. Meanwhile in June 1943 the preparations for the Allied invasion of Europe continued, and heavy bombing raids were carried out, particularly in Sicily. The movement of the American fighters to Gozo on 28 July was just one part of this build up of forces. The Maltese islands were once again in the front line, but this time on the offensive.

1/7/43 Thursday. Non-flying day, so spent time pottering around. Afternoon usual swim. Evening writing and party for a Squadron Leader's parting, but I went to bed early.

2/7/43 Friday. Pottering around on little personal jobs all morning again and afternoon down for a swim. Sirocco here with a vengeance. Wind very strong and temperature terrific. Evening bed early.

3/7/43 Saturday. Airborne early and took nearly all day on uninteresting flight and back. Arrived too late in the afternoon to go anywhere. Had good shower. Collected some of my kit. Bed early after late dinner.

4/7/43 Sunday. Up early and off to Cairo in the mail aircraft, but as it was Sunday I could not get all I wanted. Afternoon was stifling hot, so I went to Metro – air conditioned. Evening to Music for All for La Boheme on records and then straight to bed.

5/7/43 Monday. Up early and did some shopping including some silks for Margaret. The out to Heliopolis for lunch on the aircraft. Back to Bilbeis, had shower and change and into Cairo again in car with three others for evening, and saw French for Love – very good and back late.

6/7/43 Tuesday. Up late, but I was told I was to go to Castel Benito tonight so tried to get some astro kit. Into Heliopolis again for the afternoon and back at night. Then getting gen and took off at midnight.

7/7/43 Wednesday. Had quiet uneventful trip and landed 7.30 a.m. Spent the morning sorting out again and washing and shower. Afternoon down for swim. Evening letter writing. Bed early to catch up on sleep.

8/7/43 Thursday. No flying so had a quiet morning. Afternoon for swim and in the evening a mess meeting and letters.

9/7/43 Friday. Compass swing in air in the morning. Afternoon a swim as usual then letters. Hot spell now passing and far more comfortable without getting clothes wet through with sweat.

10/7/43 Saturday. Ops Officer today and as invasion now started bags of work organising stand bys etc, especially in evening when people standing by to land on Sicily. Up all night.

Operation Husky, the allied invasion of Sicily started on 10 July 1943. General Montgomery and the 8th Army landed at Messina on the east coast of the island, while General Patton with the US Seventh Army landed on the south coast at Licota. The Axis forces seem to have been caught by surprise, and the Italian resistance rapidly crumbled. Two German Panzer divisions, however, were also on the island under the command of Field Marshall Kesselring. Their resistance was stronger, but they withdrew to defensive positions around Mount Etna over the next few weeks.

11/7/43 Sunday. Quiet day.

12/7/43 Monday. Up early to go to Fez, but the aircraft was unserviceable till 10.00 a.m. Then we went first to Ben Gardane then Maison Blanche and on to Fez (Ras-El-Mar). Weather lousy so did not see a lot. We were put up in very comfortable billets in hotel and made welcome.

For the next two weeks the crew operated from Ras-El-Mar airfield near Fez in Morocco. They flew almost daily, logging over forty-five hours taking passengers, mail and supplies all over

Morocco, Algeria, Tunis and Libya. In their spare time they managed to see something of the places they visited and to enjoy some social life. Charles records it all in his journal.

The trip up to Fez from Castel Benito was first of all over the desert white salt flats to Biskara, where we turned north west for Algiers. And now we were flying over hills and mountains. Flying over the first ridge it was strange to see the desert on one side and trees and streams on the other, though of course it was not luxuriant. In fact in one spot there was quite a large high salt flat. But as we got nearer to the coast, so the country got more interesting. More trees and steep multicoloured valleys. Our view was much spoilt by low cloud but it did not appear from the air to be as green and well wooded as the coastal strip to Tunis. The same goes for the leg to Udjah and Fez. All very hilly. In places steep valleys and some trees and verdure, in others high flat uninteresting plateau, quite dun brown. Thus it was near Fez. But I should say that earlier in the year it would all have been lovely and green, and now it is just past harvest and very hot. Therefore all the cultivated areas are yellow and brown. There are quite a few trees but hardly woods and forests.

Fez itself looks very large from the air, and is in two parts. One, I understand, the old town, or Medina, and the other the new town for European habitation and shoppers. Again the familiar white houses and flat roofs, but noticeably large and in very orderly lay out. The roads appeared very wide and all with trees and many open green spaces. All these impressions were confirmed on the trip from the aerodrome to town in the truck. A grand fresh smell came from the fully harvested fields. The surrounding hills, though bare, were not hard on the eyes, being of a very light brown, or purple and streaked and splashed with white. Just before reaching the town we passed a small native village of all rush huts. The framework was made first and then the cane fixed upright along the sides and finally bent down to the apex. Very draughty I imagine, but sufficient I suppose. Also they were built in straight rows, not at random.

In Fez itself, we found it much as we had seen it from the air. There were only one or two houses on the outskirts with red and green tiled roofs. The roads were very wide, straight and some with double rows of trees either side. All with at least one row either side. It is definitely French in every way. The hotel we were in was grand.

Food too was good. Wide comfortable bed, so much so that I could not sleep. And how like home to lean on the window sill in the evening to see the lighted streets and the lights in rooms of the houses. The buses are peculiar, being articulated, but even then the coach part being very long. A little while ago we went to visit the Medina and a look at one or two streets and came back very unimpressed.

The smell was not bad, nor noise, but the shops were something like Cairo and Jerusalem – little holes in the wall – a single room, open at the front about six feet wide and nine to ten feet deep, and sometimes about two feet above street level. Flies and dirt as usual, but not over bad. Streets were narrow and with carts and cars using them. Other streets though were wide with pavements and large shops. The two minarets we saw were square with the tricky small inlaid stone effect or carvings. The gates were Moorish. But when we got back we looked at a map and found we had hardly touched the town! French well-to-do merchants live in some parts. Palaces and forts are in others. So we shall have to go again. The old walls are interesting, although moated once and now breached to allow new roads to enter.

Fez Medina with Mosque.

Last night I went to a tennis club dance and though I did not dance it was very interesting watching the excitable French enjoying themselves with lots of camaraderie and no reticence. The French drinks, of course, are vin blanc and rouge and the light bière.

This morning we went to Casablanca. The country has little distinction. A few fields, deep cut valleys, variegated browns of the hills and higher valleys. Casablanca from the air is just another town. But the number of tall storied buildings was noticeable. All white again. The heavy Atlantic breakers along the shore and on bathing beaches looked inviting. But I did not get a chance to go in. Just land and back again. By going to Casablanca we missed all the 14th July celebrations *(Bastille Day)* and from reports they were good. But in the afternoon and evening I was able to wander round the town again and enjoy the atmosphere. All homes had bunting out and it was all over the roads. But there was no excessive celebration, just a quiet gaiety and free and easy happiness. There were any amount of Legionnaires in town with their pill box hats and variety of uniforms. Also the apparent equivalent native troops, i.e. the Riffs* etc in those brown and black robes. Bands played at intervals among the trees in the square. By evening it looked as though things were going to get more exciting. In fact I saw three patrols. One of French Legionnaires, one of Riffs and one of SPs! But I retired early to bed.

The next morning I went for a short walk round the residential parts. Mostly small detached houses, all white but very spacious and all with trees in the garden as well as along each side of all roads. In the afternoon we hired cycles and rode out into the country for a swim. It really was somewhat like Scotland in places, with the surrounding high hills and the white dusty road. The stream chattering along at the side with rushes and reeds at the banks. The ripe yellow corn, reaped or being reaped in the fields at the side, or small orchards of olive or fig groves. After half an hour's hot riding we came to where three streams join the river steeply from the hills. Here at one time was a water wheel and mill, but both have disappeared and a real dam had been built to make a lovely bathing pool, with overhanging trees on both bends way up to where the pool becomes a stream again. And along one side tables and chairs with a small refreshment stall. And the water was lovely and cool to the body.

* Riffs are a Moroccan Berber tribe.

Two days ago we went to Casablanca again. But this time we could not get away as our tail wheel burst on taxiing, and caused a night stop and 24 hour delay. Actually we expected to get one fixed and be away within half an hour, and so spent all the time on the aerodrome waiting. However, when we realised that we would have to night stop we hied us to the Yank transit camp and slept between blankets without pyjamas or a wash. But before retiring we did go for a walk down to the sea shore, south of the town and had a meal at a restaurant overlooking the sea. It was lovely sitting there, drinking the light French bière and watching the turbid green Atlantic breaking on the rocky coastline. And as the sun rolled below the sea, so land and sea got darker and breakers got whiter and more grand. Oh to be able to give a real picture of these sights that exist only in my memory. The quiet walk back under a full moon between the variety of trees thinly lining the road as it runs up and down over the small rises. Next time I hope to go into the town.

At Ras El Ma today I noticed them building huts with clay and straw, as described in the Bible. They just mix up the dry red powdery soil into a paddy and with straw leave it to dry in the mould. The resultant "bricks" about 12" x 4" x 4" are laid as usual but with a very powdery white mortar. But the corners and main parts are built with properly made bricks. This morning I went for an hour and a half horse ride on one of the Legionnaire's horses. I was not much good at the actual riding, but enjoyed it. I went up onto the hills near the old town and by an old Legion fortress, but did not get near enough to see details.

Dated 20/7/43

Now I am at Biskara. I should imagine it started as an oasis village because it is well out in the Sahara. But now it

258

Bathing Pool near Ras El Ma, Fez.

is quite a tourist centre as can be gathered from the large number of agencies and advertisements about the town, pre-war of course, and catering for those intrepid voyagers who want to be disillusioned by the romantic desert. However, the town itself has been small and quite pleasant, and absolutely overgrown with date palms. And not only in the French town, but in the native areas round about, where one sees only mud walls and palms. It is odd to see the roots starting about 2 to 3 feet up from the surface of the ground. Another thing. It is darned hot here with a particularly dry wind blowing. But in the hotel where we are – how cool! And baths! Oh boy!

Dated 25/7/43. Written while flying from Fez to Tripoli direct over Sahara, with its few high black bare peaks, its intensive plateaux – desert of a truth – a steep gorge by a river and its low sandy wastes of dunes and salt lakes.

259

I think of Fez that I have left behind. Little odd snatches of memory. As we flew high and looked down on the regular hills, all in ridges as you see when someone pours sugar into a bowl, but covered with green or gold. Or like some satin or silk hung up in a shop window. What a change that rich fertile undeveloped land was from these endless sand dunes. I think too of the cleanliness and coolness of the town compared with what I'm going to. It looks as though the service will still be going on! The crops of huge sunflowers such as I have not seen since I was very young. The Riffs and Berbers in their un-uniform uniform. Or at least the only uniformity being the thin outer blanket of black and light brown and their long rifles and bayonets. What has happened to the Moors I wonder?

Just a few days ago we went to Tunis, and I was disappointed. We landed at a nearby aerodrome and went in by car. All the surrounding land seems to be very flat and fairly rich and well cropped, but with several hills jutting up quite abruptly to as much as 3000 ft. These are mostly of flint and chalk and are being quarried, so that the roads are very dusty, and it even reaches to the town. Before actually running into the town we went through a typical village with the one storied square houses. We were making for the transit hotel and found it in a back part of the town – as was to be expected. With all the houses – hotels, pensions, business houses and flats – all crowded in together and the roads narrow and far from straight or planned. Also, plenty of locals about and a smell and noise reminiscent of Cairo, the smell even like that of dead bodies. But I found that they had been repairing the sewers, which may have accounted for it. However, I thought that perhaps we had come to the worse part of the town, and the attractive centre that could be seen from the air must be elsewhere. So we went for a shufti. I know we did not see it at its best, but I was disappointed. Trees and wide roads there were, true. But so few and dirty and disorganised. And it was not bomb damage as that was confined almost entirely to the docks area. And the Yanks as usual come making themselves unpopular. Give me French Morocco or Algeria. I'm looking forward now to the next week or so up there.

On 25 July Charles flew back to Castel Benito. His diary takes up the tale:

26/7/43 Monday. Spent the morning writing and organising things then in the afternoon I went for a swim at Tripoli. I also developed a film but not very successfully as meticulation had set in and gelatine peeled off due to heat. But hope to save a few negatives. Bed late.

27/7/43 Tuesday. Spent the morning jogging about and in the afternoon we went to Sicily for first sight of Europe. Grand to see green fields again, but I thought of what had passed there and what was going on so near. Saw Mount Etna in distance. Back late in a sand storm and had beer in mess and bed early.

Visits to Sicily were to become more frequent. The squadron Operations Record Book tells us that just two days after the first landings of Operation Husky the squadron was ferrying in supplies.

This month saw another big light in the progress of the war in the Mediterranean for which the squadron had helped to prepare. Namely the landings on Sicily, and on the 14th the first aircraft from this squadron were landed there by Group Captain W E Rankin DSO and Squadron Leader G Glen at Pachino.

In the following week the Allies made major gains in Sicily, with General Patton racing north-westwards to take Palermo on 22 July. General Montgomery made more measured progress up the east coast, but consolidated his position as he drove the Axis forces back to Catania. Patton's forces then turned east and set off towards Messina to drive the Germans into the sea. The landings had political effects too, and Italy's King Victor Emmanuel III placed Mussolini under arrest and replaced him with General Badoglio.

> 28/7/43 Wednesday. Up early and left for Cairo West as passengers. Broke journey at El Adem. Spent night at Cairo West and had beer again. Bed early.
> 29/7/43 Thursday. Set off early again for base in a DC3. Stopped at El Adem, but had a fine interesting trip. Lots of astro and loops etc. More letters waiting and spent evening writing.

The squadron were collecting more and more Dakotas to replace the Hudsons. The Operations Record Book gives details:

> By the end of the month the strength of Dakotas on the squadron was brought up to ten aircraft and as each aircraft went on inspection they were being fitted with six stretcher brackets to each side, as a great proportion of the work this month consisted of taking supplies into Sicily and bringing out casualties. ...

> 30/7/43 Friday. Did nothing all morning and in the afternoon I went down for the usual swim. On beach I

met Bill Stanton (ex 459). In evening went over to 296 Squadron to see John Stanwell and for drink. His mess is in a fine setting above grape and almond orchards and as they were ripe had some from the field.

31/7/43 Saturday. Spent the morning in room listening to gramophone and reading and writing. Then – Flap! Scramble, rush pack and lunch and off to a new forward aerodrome in Sicily via Matruh and back just before dark with casualties. Had dinner and bed early.

1/8/43 Sunday. Up late and then changed and to church and stayed for communion. Afterwards met Stanwell who said he had just seen Doc Crawford, but I missed him. Afternoon and evening writing letters and reading. Bed early.

2/8/43 Monday. Up too early and off to Malta on routine. Casualties back and then spent afternoon writing and reading. Evening went for short stroll and bed late.

3/8/43 Tuesday. Spent very idle day. Morning out on the aerodrome doing dinghy drill. Afternoon reading and a nap and had a long lecture from the CO. Bed early.

4/8/43 Wednesday. Up before dawn for dawn take off for Sicily. Brought back engines and casualties but did not arrive till late afternoon Evening to see The First of the Few at the cinema. Very good.

5/8/43 Thursday. Up late and quiet morning reading and writing. Afternoon down for usual swim. Flying tomorrow so to bed early. But Maggie came to bed and then Duffy came in and puts the light out and I had to get up and light it. Then Jimmy with more corridor gen for tomorrow. Then Maggie chased a cricket with a slipper. Then doors and windows bang and I shut them. Then George came in, went out and came back half an hour later etc etc!

6/8/43 Friday. Very tired but to Cassibile and back by 4.00 p.m. Wash etc. and quiet evening reading and bed early. Crosby brought back from Fez a barrel of beer and lots of fruit.

7/8/43 Saturday. Quiet morning reading and writing. Afternoon usual swim and evening to Yank cinema in an old Italian fort. Only mediocre film but fort very interesting and made a change.

8/8/43 Sunday. Morning writing letters and reading. Afternoon service etc. Evening reading.

9/8/43 Monday. Lazy morning and in the afternoon I could not go swimming as on standby. First book from book club arrived so got on with that in evening.

10/8/43 Tuesday. Up early and flew a monotonous Malta routine and back. Afternoon dashed down to town for shoes and bush-shirt. But did not have them, so out for a swim. Evening – agreement on leave! So I'm thinking of it now. Bed late.

In Sicily the Allies had continued to make progress. German forces had now entirely taken over the Axis defence, but were unable to withstand the steady onslaught from General Montgomery's 8th Army from the south and General Patton's 7th Army from the west. On 5 August Catania had fallen to the Allies despite fierce German resistance, and the Axis were forced inexorably towards Messina. The squadron Operations Record Book records:

As the invading forces got established in Sicily so the squadron started flights between the various aerodromes established there and the Africa mainland, taking in supplies and returning with casualties, besides the daily routine runs to Cairo, Malta, Tunis, Algiers and the Ras el Ma detachment.

11/8/43 Wednesday. Another non-flying day. Morning reading and afternoon usual swim. Evening letter writing and bed early.

12/8/43 Thursday. Up before dawn and briefed at ATC at 6.30 a.m. Then took Hudson to Heliopolis. Lots of mucking about getting receipt for it etc. Finally to Officers Club in Heliopolis. Actually wizard place – big bathrooms and showers etc. After dinner to cinema and back and bed late.

13/8/43 Friday. Did not get up too early. Spent the morning in Cairo shopping. Bought tons of little odds and ends, including silk for Marion, cream for Margaret, exposure meter and filter and spent about £10! But had jolly good day – total being £14 so I did not regret it. Afternoon I had a nap and then bath and change, and then to Hermitage to drink and dinner with Maggie, and back and bed very late.

14/8/43 Saturday. Up 5.00 a.m. and was picked up by truck and taken out to LG 224 and collected new aircraft – a DC3 – to take back to Castel Benito. Landed at Benina and got to Castel Benito at 4.30 p.m. in time to unpack and wash and change for house warming in new mess – a fine spacious place. Had about twenty sisters from surrounding hospitals. Jolly good evening. I went outside in thick trees in full moonlight and yarned about New Zealand most of the time.

15/8/43 Sunday. Spent all day between times moving to new bedroom. In the morning I went to church. Afternoon for bathe. Evening writing letters. Total eclipse of Moon.

16/8/43 Monday. Up early and on Cassibile San Francesco Routine. Did not get back till 6.00 p.m. Then after wash etc to a film, but it was not very good.

17/8/43 Tuesday. Usual tidying up in the morning then writing letters. Afternoon swim at Tripoli again and evening reading and bed early.

As Charles enjoyed his swim the campaign in Sicily was drawing to a close. General Patton finally entered Messina as the last of the German forces withdrew to the toe of Italy. Less than an hour later British forces entered the city too, but the unofficial race between Patton and Montgomery had been won by the Americans. The cost in men had been enormous on both sides. The British, Canadians and Americans had lost more than eight thousand men killed or missing and a further fourteen thousand four hundred wounded. The Axis had lost about one hundred and sixty four thousand men killed or taken prisoner. They had successfully evacuated about one hundred thousand men to Italy to continue the fight.

18/8/43 Wednesday. Up early and picked up AOV pilots from Surman for Fez. Refuelled at Biskra. Arrived Fez late afternoon. Had some ice creams and beer and changed. I shaved off my moustache in moment of aberration and laughed at myself for a long time in mirror. Do in Sergeants' mess so spent lot of evening there. Found other aircraft on detail here unserviceable so arranged to stay for a few days. Bed late.

19/8/43 Thursday. Morning up early and went for walk round old town – Medina and not very impressed etc. Very dirty and pokey as usual. But as we only touched the entrance may not have seen interesting parts. Afternoon sleep in heat of day and evening went for a stroll. Two more Hudsons arrived, so we decided to go back to base tomorrow.

20/8/43 Friday. Up early and after collecting rations set off for Castel Benito direct. Did lot of flying myself but otherwise uneventful trip. Spent evening sorting myself out and bed early.

21/8/43 Saturday. Not flying, but up early to swing compass. But the aircraft was unserviceable. Went to Accounts, Stores etc. Afternoon wrote letters then swung compass. Evening bed early as flying early tomorrow. George Ross collected a pet – a mantis which he kept with him all day. It had an unusual system of catching and consuming flies.

22/8/43 Sunday. On routine Cairo West run. Stopped at Benina on way, and arrived at 4.30 p.m. Did not bother to change, but after dinner and a few beers I went to the garrison cinema and then bed late.

23/8/43 Monday. Up very early after a very bad night and back to Castel Benito via Benina. Evening bed early as very tired and gippy tummy coming on.

24/8/43 Tuesday. Up early again for Ops Officer at 6.00 a.m. and had usual day with heaps of mail to chase. One aircraft missing and one scramble and then up half the night.

25/8/43 Wednesday. After all that I then took off early for Sicily. Fairly interesting again. Noticed old fashioned methods of threshing still employed in places. Had some lovely figs and apples in spite of gippy tum. Evening found I was flying again in the morning and as I was dog tired wrote one letter and turned in.

26/8/43 Thursday. Another early morning for a Sicily trip. Rumours there that invasion has started in France, Crete and Sardinia. Afternoon back by 2.30 p.m. for a hair cut and reading. No pictures in evening and bed early and disturbed by a bat.

27/8/43 Friday. Had lie in for a change. Then at 9.30 a.m.

started hitch hiking to Sabratha. Had interesting journey. Took three hours through colony cut in efforts of Mussolini. Spent about one and a half hours looking at 180 AD Coliseum and fifth century tower and temple. Then had topping bath and hitch hiked back. Got patches of prickly heat and had it treated in evening and bed early.

Charles devotes quite a long entry in his journal to this day out:

Just back from a hitch hike out to Sabratha. Very hot along the way, but worth it. Three new things noticed on the way. (a) The first Prie Dieu* I have seen by the road, and it was quite uninjured, looked well equipped but was soiled. (b) The usual wells and pullies, but here with a steep slope down to about ten to twelve feet below the surface of one to walk down when drawing water – (first order of pullies?) (c) The borders of Mussolini's colonisation schemes at Bianchi. At intervals along the road white walled buildings – most likely a sort of estate office, as the houses at Bianchi from the air are all this shape with a large round water reservoir, whereas these had painted in ink large letters Entre Colonizzazione Liber. The ground was very dry and sandy and was mostly planted very open with trees – olives and almonds, but there were a few crops. The irrigation is effected by a system of narrow concrete channels about four inches square and open at the top, but I don't see how as they all run down hill and are open at the bottom end.

And so to Sabratha. The Coliseum – about 180 AD – is really in a fine state of preservation, only the top of the royal boxes being overplastered and rebuilt. But mostly it

* A Prie Dieu is a piece of furniture with a kneeling pad and desk for a book.

stands as it did in its prime and is just worn. The spectators' steps and dressing rooms with inlet marble Roman numerals, and the gates are good. The marble murals round the edge of the stage or arena are mostly undamaged. And the royal boxes and main boxes with their fine tall marble and carved columns stand intact and very impressive and from them is a very commanding view. The guide that showed me all this was an Italian but we got on very well in French. At the back of the Coliseum was the old town, but only the first two or three feet of the houses' walls remain.

About quarter of a mile to the west is what is left of the fifth and sixth century forum and Byzantine temple. Here again are masses of high columns – the first thing that struck me. Then the paved approach, the thick new well worn walls, the heaps of broken pottery and tiles. But before that the marble stations mostly somewhat broken but some in very fine condition, and then the patches of mosaic flooring, some very large.

A lot of the temple had been excavated, particularly the Christian cemetery and Jove's temple etc. But it was easy to see where the excavation had finished and how they were done. The hock of the ground was about four to eight feet above the floor of the excavations. Railway lines ran up to the face of earth that was being removed. The men then followed along the sides of the walls, sifting the soil obviously for relics. These old walls could be seen just ending and disappearing into the sandy wall of earth, with other old stem walls showing through. I guess there is still a lot yet to be found. But the sea is lapping at the base of all this, in fact quite probably has already claimed large areas. As I bathed there, or walked about I thought of men and women two thousand years ago doing the same but with different ideas and purposes.

Sabratha Coliseum.

Sabratha Amphitheatre.

28/8/43 Saturday. Up early again and off to Tunis on routine and back. Took Naval type and found out that Peter was at Algiers. He took a message for me and I arranged for Peter to call at the fleet mail office for his letters. Hope it works as I sent one immediately. Pipe arrived from Arthur Turner. Bed early again.

29/8/43 Sunday. Cassibile – San Francesco. Routine but such a lot of mucking about on the other side did not get back till late. So after a wash, change and dinner wrote one letter and went to bed and read How Green is my Valley.

30/8/43 Monday. Had lie in for a change and got up at 8.00 a.m. Pottered about for a bit and then started packing for move. Afternoon off to Sicily again and this time there had been heavy rain over night and we could smell the earthy smell even in the cockpit, and the greenery was most brilliant and clean after all the dust had been washed off. Had to rush to get back before dark, and then bed.

31/8/43 Tuesday. Another lie in and potter about the morning. Then afternoon to Sicily again and got back just before dark, and so to bed early.

August drew to a close and the squadron Operations Record Book summarised an eventful month:

More Dakotas arrived for the squadron bringing the total up to twenty by the end of the month, and as they came, so the Hudsons were being withdrawn and handed over to BARU leaving only ten at the end of the month.

A detachment of three Dakotas and aircrews were established at Cassibile on 9th under Squadron Leader G Glen, doing mainly routine runs round the island, a daily service to Tunis and taking casualties to Malta. While at Cassibile the aerodrome was strafed by enemy aircraft but no damage was done to our aircraft. Later, however, in a similar attack Flight Sergeant D E Timms was injured while unloading an aircraft.

* * *

For the work done in evacuation of wounded from Sicily a letter of appreciation was addressed to 216 Group from Brigadier Graham, Headquarters 8th Army and 216 Group notified commendations for work done during the Africa campaign for Squadron Leader McLean, Flying Officer D Cole, Flying Officer R M Whitburn, Flying Officer W R Sands, Warrant Officer M G Potter, and Flight Sergeant Lusted.

On 29th an advance party with Flight Lieutenant D Grosslex in charge left for Catania in preparation for the squadron move and to arrange accommodation and supplies. It was found impossible to get suitable accommodation but an excellent site was found for a tented camp on some high ground two miles from the Aerodrome. Besides being very healthy as shown by the remarkably few malaria cases, it was picturesquely situated among almond trees and commanded a fine view of Mount Etna and the Catania plain.

CHAPTER 10

Into Europe

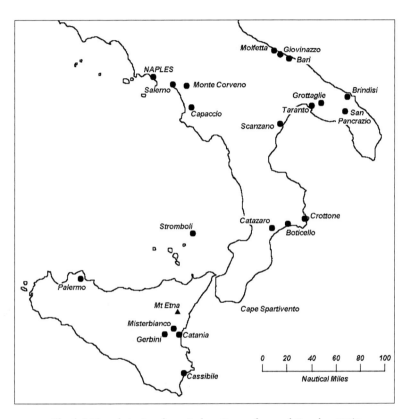

Charles's Travels in Southern Italy – September and October 1943.

Charles's diary takes up the tale again:

> 1/9/43 Wednesday. Non-flying day so had lie in and potter
> about in the morning. Afternoon was on standby so
> could not go for a swim. So read and wrote and slept.

Evening went to second house at cinema and back 10.30 p.m. for bed midnight.

2/9/43 Thursday. Got a trip to Algiers delivering Hudson. Therefore got off early. Went via Tunis and Bizerta. Arrived Blida at 4.30 p.m. and then spent an hour on the usual paperwork. Then hitch hiked into Algiers and left Maggie with all kit to find somewhere to stay, and went into docks. Spent an hour and a half going from quay to quay to get permission to go in and ended at Port Commandant who told me Vindictive had left two or three days ago! So missed Peter again. Just had the energy left to find Maggie, have dinner and drink and go to bed at transit camp.

3/9/43 Friday. Had a rather cold night and up early in the morning. After breakfast I hitched out to Maison Blanche with a Paratroop Lieutenant, who told us a bit about the Sicily effort. At Maison Blanche we got a Yank DC 3 to Tunis via Telergma and from Tunis another to Castel Benito. Arrived to find half the squadron had gone and rest to go any day now. So spent the afternoon in final packing.

No. 117 Squadron was now needed much closer to the front line, for the invasion of Italy itself was about to start. On 3 September General Montgomery and the 8th Army crossed the Straits of Messina and landed near Reggio di Calabria. They met little resistance, and established a firm foothold in Italy itself. The new base at Catania was just fifty miles from the Italian mainland, and the military situation was secure enough to allow forces to be based on Italian territory. This security was in part at least based on the fact that the Italian General Guiseppe Castellano signed a secret agreement on 3 September, taking Italy from the Axis to join the Allies. The secrecy was to protect

Cookhouse at Catania.

the projected landings at Salerno, for Italy's defection was likely to be met with German anger and reinforcements.

4/9/43 Saturday. Up early and on Cassibile routine while the rest of squadron moved to Catania. Back early and last packing and read in bed.

5/9/43 Sunday. We packed our kit and took last people over to Catania. Spent rest of day settling ourselves on top of a hill in tents overlooking Catania and Etna. Ideal place and with lots of almonds and grapes. Had shower from self propelled endless belt drawn in deep cold well. Evening sitting outside under olive trees and talking. Bed early.

6/9/43 Monday. Still flying, in fact up at 5.00 a.m. and did not finish till 6.00 p.m. Moving Yank fighter squadron from Tunisia, and we had a wizard meal there. Quiet evening and bed early.

7/9/43 Tuesday. Up late after good rest. Morning went into

Catania to try to get some laundry done! And there had good look round, but as there was a lot of damage it was not very pleasant. Got back to find Maggie had gone flying an Ismalia trip. Afternoon went for swim and found it very pleasant – the first for ages. Evening reading.

8/9/43 Wednesday. Up late again and nothing all morning. Afternoon did an air test and saw the Italian Map Section at Catania. Evening rumours that Italy has unconditionally surrendered. We were all called to ops room and told of impending invasion of Naples and we would have to assist, and warned of enemy action. Later news of surrender confirmed and so our part in the job postponed. Lots of celebration in mess, but went to bed early.

The surrender news was broadly correct, but Italy's surrender had not been the 'unconditional' surrender that many had demanded. Instead it was a negotiated surrender, and Italy would soon join the Allies in fact as well as in name, to fight their recent comrades in the Axis. On 9 September the main Allied assault began at Salerno in the Bay of Naples.

9/9/43 Thursday. Although standby all day, nothing happened. Did lots of reading, writing and then evening went for stroll round hills and orchards. At ops room in evening told we were still on standby so bed early.

10/9/43 Friday. Reported to ops room for briefing, but still on standby, and so remained all day. But late afternoon I got off, so went into town to get dhobi and take another look round. Evening mess meeting and bed late.

11/9/43 Saturday. Up 5.15 a.m. for Palermo routine. Cassibile, Catania, Palermo, Cassibile, Catania. Spent trip writing and reading, but had six hours at Palermo so had look round town and catacombs. Not a lot of damage and things very cheap. Bought silk stockings at 10/- and evening bag but had not enough cash for suit lengths. Catacombs odd and eerie with all clothed skeletons with just skin and hair. Back quietly and bed late with talking.

12/9/43 Sunday. Up late and still on standby but nothing materialised by noon and so we were stood down at 3.00 p.m, when we all went down for bathe for the rest of the afternoon. Moon full of an evening now and makes a lovely setting sitting among trees and smoking after dinner.

13/9/43 Monday. Called at 5.30 a.m. for special trip to Italy. Went to Termini to pick up fighter wing and move them. I had two fresh fried pork chops while waiting. Took the wing to Paestum near Naples via Stromboli, which has two towns on the island despite its still smoking angrily. The aerodrome we landed at was only fifteen miles from front, therefore we had fighter cover. While there there were air raids on the many ships in harbour and every time we dashed for cover and got covered in light dust. Tomatoes were growing in the fields. Lots of fighters coming back and several pranged on landing. So many we could not get off for three quarters of an hour. Eventually got back and went straight to bed after dinner.

14/9/43 Tuesday. Maggie Ops Officer, so I went for sleep in the morning, but I was woken to be told I was navigator to the CO leading a formation to Taranto. So I had early lunch – very rushed – and off with fighter escort. Uneventful trip. Overy pranged, but got away with no excitement. On way back we flew along the coast from Cape Colonne to Cape Spartivento. Very interesting but went to bed early again.

15/9/43 Wednesday. Not flying in the morning so wrote some back letters etc. Afternoon had another trip to Grottaglie and back, but uneventful. Back and dark again and so straight into dinner and then to bed.

16/9/43 Thursday. Up late again and had a good bath in the morning. Afternoon down to beach and spent rest of day there. Evening reading and bed early.

17/9/43 Friday. Up 5.30 a.m. for trip to Taranto and so got back in time to go for a swim. Spent all afternoon down on beach alone. Evening letter writing and bed early.

18/9/43 Saturday. Up early again for double shuttle from San Antonio *(Northern Sardinia)* to Capaccio near Naples. Good trip over very pretty country, and no excitement. But Capaccio area was strafed by the horrible Hun in our absence! So we got away again in a hurry. Over the clouds the light was lovely and clear and very bright as compared with the most over the sea. Saw two whales.

19/9/43 Sunday. Called early for Ops Officer but had very easy day, although not able to get down to letter writing. Evening I had to sleep in the mess, but some chaps were yarning till 2.00 a.m! So did not get much sleep and up again for early calls.

20/9/43. Monday. A non-flying day again. So in the morning I went down to Catania for hair cut and look round, even though I was very tired. Afternoon I went for swim and stayed on beach till late. Therefore missing trip to Italy again. Evening letters and reading and bed early. News came through that we could marry Italians without special permission and draw allowances.

21/9/43 Tuesday. Called early for special trip to Malta moving a squadron from there to Gerbini. Found island very quiet compared with what it used to be like. Did two shuttles and second time I was taken by car through Valetta to Sliema to mess for lunch – four courses served by pretty smiling Maltese girls and washed down with two glasses of beer. Back rather late. Bed late.

22/9/43 Wednesday. Up 6.30 a.m. for 9.00 a.m. take off to Falconara but when we got there – as usual they knew nothing about it and we had to wait three hours for a load of bombs to appear. Then took these to Boticello and flew back all along coast low. Very interesting scenery. Back in time for late lunch and spent rest of day under mosquito net reading. Maggie's Flight Lieutenant through.

23/9/43 Thursday. Nothing all morning, but in the afternoon I was dragged out for trip to Scanzano by Crotone for casualties. Took petrol to Scanzano to fighter group and when got there found ten thousand gallons had already been delivered by road. Typical! Back in time for wash down, change, dinner and usual. Spent evening sitting under trees.

24/9/43 Friday. Non-flying day but on standby even though others above us on list were not! So could not go for swim. However wrote quite a lot of letters. Evening smoking under trees again and bed late.

25/9/43 Saturday. Up early for trip to Scanzano and Cretonne again with usual amount of waiting about. On way made small detour to look at two lakes high up in La Sila and lovely and blue.

26/9/43 Sunday. Scanzano job again and called at Crotone for casualties and on way there had look round over the hills and valleys again via Catazaro. On way back had look for nudist camp but it was not very sunny and a bit bumpy so we did not bother.

27/9/43 Monday. Morning went for a stroll out in villages and orchards – aiming for Misterbianco, but stopped at farm for water and stayed talking to the mother and two lovely daughters. Had a look round wine press etc., and said we would bring some bully. Afternoon set out again and called at another farm for yarn with them. Then took the bully and collected lemons on way back – figs we ate! All the peasants here are very friendly and ask for soap, washing now being done by banging a stone.

28/9/43 Tuesday. Away early to Bari but did not stay long even though we were told town is very attractive and beer in plenty, champagne at 5/- a bottle, silk and cloth cheap etc., as due back for lunch. Called at Crotone again for casualties. Afternoon reading and writing. Bed early. Heard Oscar had been killed.

29/9/43 Wednesday. Trip to Monte Corveno but too cloudy to see Vesuvius. While there we were asked if we would take and drop some food and blankets to some paratroops behind the lines, but before we could get permission someone else went. Afternoon reading and bed early.

30/9/43 Thursday. Up early for trip from Cassibile to Brindisi, but at Casibile found load had already gone! So back and after lunch for swim. News that we were to move tomorrow, but no one knows where! We have been ready for several days and waiting for place and time. Evening writing and bed early.

Charles supplements his rather terse diary entries with much more detailed descriptions in his journal:

After about three weeks in Sicily and Italy I guess I could fill pages about things. Towns – Catania broken and wrecked, but mainly around the station and docks, with some of the main streets still fairly intact, though there is

Catania – Catania Police and Locals.

not a great deal to shout about. The streets run along the sea front and up the hill, some in the form of avenues or steps. The noticeable feature is the number of large ornate and beautiful churches. The cemetery near the Station has been considerably knocked about. This consists of mainly large family tombs, very lavishly decorated and built, and the damage looks very extensive. Outside I once saw as a contrast, by the side of the wall a small hand-made cross and a little girl placing a few drab discarded peonies there. In the town there are several statues to various popes and cardinals etc, and in the centre a strange monument of a column on an elephant's back, done in black volcanic rock. Also in the same black rock are what is left of ruins of an old amphitheatre – not a lot left of it – just recognisable. The local policemen too are gorgeous looking creatures in very elaborate uniform.

Palermo strikes me as a cleaner and larger town with bigger and better buildings and there is less damage here. There are wide main streets, but also very narrow ones – almost alleys – between tall flats and business premises. The shops (some of them) are small and generally good and cheap. And as usual lots of churches. The catacombs are a big 'draw'. Not as extensive or deep as I imagined, though

Palermo Catacombs.

perhaps only a portion was open to public. They were opened about 1600 and closed about 1800 and seem to have been used only for a show room for deceased people so that friends and relations could visit them. To this purpose they were propped in tiers along the walls or laid in open boxes, sometimes two or even three brothers in one box. Professors, clergy etc. kept separate according to profession and nobility in special passages. Apparently they were buried first, then disinterred and disembowelled and injected with some preservative. They were dressed in normal attire, even to boots and hats, and put away. Now of course, clothing is faded and dusty and skin drawn dry and brown and hairy, though bones stick out in many places. Even a child of three weeks old is there and with eyes still blue and a quaint dress and ridiculous looking hat.

A large number of small Sicilian towns are built at the top of hills, and not nearly the top of hills, but right on the peak of tall steel pinnacles, with a road winding tortuously up to the top. It looks just as if another house would push more off the top. Right in the middle – the highest point – would be a fairly large building, either a monastery or castle or perhaps both. The country round is mainly orchard and vineyards on rich lava soil. Though I suppose little is exported now, but they still stamp the grapes out in heavy stained boots and sing to a rhythm. Horse drawn seems to be the main supply of water. Almonds, lemons, oranges, tomatoes, figs, blackberries, pears (prickly and garden), and olives are plentiful. In places, mainly inland, pasture land and hay fields are more in evidence. The hay stacks being long and like a milk loaf.

Etna stands out above it all – a huge dark cone with just a faint wisp of smoke from the top. Down the lower sides are grown vineyards and orchards and scattered villages and in places, old black lava rivers. Stromboli is different rising up from the sea with more smoke billowing from the top, yellow and sulphurous (we could smell it once passing in the plane) and staining the side above the crater, and ashes and dust rolling down one side into the sea. On two of the sides are small villages with no means of communication except by sea and as far as I could see only small patches of ground to live on – and tourists. At one point about half a mile from the island a rock stuck up sheer from the sea about 50 ft and on the top there was just room for an automatic light and a tiny light house. The other islands about here do not appear volcanic and the villages are far safer.

Italy itself is greener and prettier with lovely little villages and hotels nestling in the valleys, rivers mountain railways and roads, woods and waterfalls – all a very pretty picture. Road building here must be very difficult, and though it looks attractive, the steep winding efforts I have seen must be difficult to make and travel over. Then they seem to favour the tops of hills as well! At Paestum – our first trip to Italy – I was surprised at the dusty ground. It is very fine, just like flour and difficult to run in and very clinging after lying in, as we had to do while the aerodrome was raided as the aircraft was being unloaded. Apart from that we enjoyed picking the tomatoes about here.

In the bay off Salerno were lots and lots of ships but the landings and taking of the plain and aerodrome could not have been easy. From the air I also saw a Red Cross hospital and the typical columnar ruins of some ancient Italian buildings. On the other side is Taranto, a fine, large harbour, and the usual dockland town. The immediate hinterland is widely planted with orchards, and further inland is what appears to be a sort of heathland, wooded and scrubby and with odd large houses. The houses are of the old elaborate fanciful design with odds and ends and castellated turrets and bay windows.

The trip back along the coast is full of interest. The rivers at the mouth and for quite a long way inland are very shallow indeed and very wide. At this time of year the beds are dry and gray, necessitating very long and low railway and road bridges for the coastal railways and roads.

Aircrew take a break from unloading at Catania.

117 Squadron had worked hard during September, and their role in supporting the landings at Salerno and elsewhere was rightly recognised. The squadron Operations Record Book entry for the month is unusually long:

> This was another very busy month for the squadron. In the first week the Ras El Ma detachment was recalled, the last two Hudson aircraft were delivered to Blida and from then on the new Dakotas were in constant use.
>
> On the third and fourth the squadron moved from Castel Benito to Catania (Sicily) and was so reunited with the detachment that had been in Sicily for the past few weeks. During this move the normal routine runs on operation at the time were maintained.
>
> The "Routine" varied from time to time as the war situation developed and took aircraft not only on regular runs to and from the North African airfields and Malta, but

all over the occupied areas of Italy. The most regular runs being between Catania, Cassibile and Palermo; Catania and Brindisi and calling at Crotone or Scanzano on the return; Monte Corveno and back; and Tripoli calling at Malta and San Francesco.

A more spectacular and interesting fact of the squadron's work, and that which accounted for a greater proportion of the flying time, was the moving of various units of Royal Air Force and United States Army Air Force to more forward positions, as our victorious army continued its spectacular advance, and then keeping the units supplied with fuel and ammunition. Some of the heaviest lifts were moving the American 82nd and 14th Fighter Group of Lightnings from Grombalia and St Marie Du Zit in Tunisia to Lentin, as long range escort for our amphibious landings in the Salerno area. After our forces had established themselves and prepared landing strips the 33rd Fighter Group were moved in, followed by 324 Wing, 86th Dive Bomber Group and in the critical period when the success of the venture was in the balance aircraft continued to land there with personnel and supplies.

On the 15th and for the next few days aircraft were kept busy taking petrol, oil and ammunition into the Taranto area, supplying the air forces operating from Grottaglie. On the 17th a squadron of the RAF Regiment was moved from Sicily onto this airfield and the 79th Fighter Group equipment was taken to Isola. The next day the 27th Bomber Group was moved from San Antonia to Cappacio. The next big moves were 105 Squadron and 417 Squadron from Zentini West to Givia, and 284 Squadron to Scanzano.

On nearly all of these heavy lifts, aircraft had to make two trips there and back in the one day and return to base and at

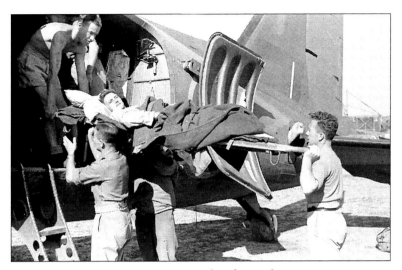

Evacuating Casualties from Italy.

no time did they interfere with the normal routine commitments. On several of these flights forward area fighter cover was provided, but a large number were completed successfully without an escort. Whenever available casualties were always brought back from these trips.

When Marshal Badoglio's representative and Staff flew from Grottaglie their aircraft was attacked by a Spitfire and engaged by ground forces en route. On the return journey the aircraft was escorted, at the request of the pilot who wished to avoid a repetition of this experience, by two aircraft from this squadron on one of their normal sorties.

An order of the day issued this month by the Air Officer Commanding in Chief, Transport Command, congratulated 216 Group on the excellent work done by the squadrons engaged in the Sicilian campaign.

The normally extensive sporting activities of the squadron had to be considerably curtailed owing to the lack of facilities in Sicily, but almost everyone took advantage of the close proximity of the sea and suitable bathing beach.

2090 hours were flown during the month, 1,793,611 lb of freight lifted and 1066 casualties moved from forward areas besides normal passenger loads.

The new month brought yet another move for 117 Squadron. The Operations Record Book summarises their view of the new location:

> The opening days of October saw the squadron on the move again, for on 2nd and 3rd we left Catania and flew to Bari, which was found to be a small grass airfield complete with modern barracks which had suffered only slight bomb damage. A number of the Officers and men of the Reggia Aeronautica were still in possession when we arrived, but most of these left shortly afterwards and so the whole squadron for the first time was accommodated in brick built quarters. Our cooks, after months of struggling with open fires, especially appreciated the well appointed kitchen.

The move to Bari was possible because of the steady Allied advance through Italy. The Germans had put up fierce and organised resistance, but by the end of the month Allied forces were at the gates of Naples. Meanwhile in a daring and spectacular raid, German paratroops had snatched Mussolini from his prison 7000 ft up in the Apennines. He was set up as leader of a new Fascist state in Northern Italy with German support.

Charles's diary again:

> 1/10/43 Friday. Up early for Bari run with Squadron Leader Glen. Went up through Straits of Messina past the pretty little bays and villages of the east Sicilian coast. Then across Italy again over Scanzano. Visibility was

good and the wooded valleys, towns and winding roads looked really lovely. Then round bay of Taranto to the fertile plateau with the large farmhouses. Did not stop long at Bari. Spent the afternoon reading and bed early. The squadron is moving to Bari tomorrow, B flight first.

2/10/43 Saturday. Some of B Flight packed and went. We did a Routine Monte Corvino. Weather bad, but earth smelled good. To Monte Corvino over sea along beside cold front – very marked – moving in towards coast. We got to Monte Corvino just before it reached coast, but the cloud rising up was beautiful. On the ground the storm burst – heavy and short downpour and wind. Then it cleared up and we flew back in the clear air watching another front move up. Arrived back in terrific storm and gale and had to shelter on the aerodrome. Vis 100 ft. Got back to camp and surprised to find tent still up, but my bed wet through. Mess running with water. So sorted things out and bed early.

3/10/43 Sunday. Up at 5.00 a.m. and on go from then till bed time with only snatched meals. Took down and packed kit and tent and mess and packed it onto the kite and off 10.00 a.m. for Bari. Arrived in rain and "herded" in a big house that 239 Wing had half vacated. Terrible mess and disorganised. All day people crowded in and put up beds. Got ourselves thoroughly hot and sweaty first, then wet in rain, then dirty. But had good wash down and complete change before bed, and turned in thoroughly whacked.

4/10/43 Monday. Up early for early breakfast. Did final organising. Can't make out what the Italians think, but they are in charge of town and aerodrome nearby, certainly the mess, and lay down all sorts of orders and laws and all walk about with firearms. In the morning went into town for shave. Clean and interesting and things very cheap. But did not buy anything. Afternoon had a nap and repacked. Evening reading and bed early.

5/10/43 Tuesday. Lay in and then mucked about in the morning. Afternoon I went into town again and found most of shops shut, so did not stay. Evening reading.

6/10/43 Wednesday. No flying as Maggie was busy getting extra messing. Morning went into town again and bought some film, album and corners and a raincoat for £3. Afternoon spent putting in all my photos and repacking kit. Bed early.

7/10/43 Thursday. Up early for flying. Went to Catania and flew through pretty bad weather. Had to return to Brindisi but could not get in due to 35 mph cross wind. Had two tries and returned to Bari. Afternoon took load on to Brindisi and got bogged there. So had to stay the night. Met Cameron from ITW Millom! There is an operational squadron there, with the usual atmosphere. They plied us with champagne and egg flip. I drunk champagne in large quantities and I was sick before I went to bed!

8/10/43 Friday. Up early and did not feel too good, so had no breakfast. Had job getting DC3s out and first few efforts to no avail. Eventually whole flight came out with two lorries. Back in time for another move. Had wash down and shave and packed all stuff and over to station (Italian) mess. Spent afternoon settling in and sorting out conflicting rumours as to what we were to wear for dinner and party with the Italians. I cleaned buttons on blue, and KDs. Eventually wore blue, and found some in KD, some in shirt and slacks! Whole evening an example of disorganised bull, so left early. Bed.

9/10/43 Saturday. Someone took the Italian Colonel's flag

in the night, so whole camp confined to camp. But it happened that I cleared off before I knew about it, but only spent short while in town looking for somewhere to repair shoes and bag and collect dhobi – but could not find shop! Afternoon I got OC's permission to go again and went in Jeep. Collected dhobi and shoes. All he wanted was cigarettes so gave him two and 1/-. Then had look all round town in jeep and back in time to wash for dinner and change! Straight to bed after dinner as we are inaugurating Cairo Routine tomorrow early.

10/10/43 Sunday. Up at 3.00 a.m. and off at first light – called at Catania, Malta, El Adem and Cairo West. Very long trip – eleven hours and I was kept pretty busy. Original plan was that we were to come back next day, but speedily decided not possible. At Cairo West sandstorms and cloud. All other airfields were unavailable. When we did pick up flare path we lost it again in circuit. At last after thirty five minutes we got down. They were very worried and had searchlights and fifty rockets up though we did not see them. The paraffin flares, they said, were six feet high. Bed straight away very tired.

11/10/43 Monday. Up just in time for breakfast then had wash shave etc and hitched into Cairo. Took things easy doing odd jobs I wanted and then did not have time to get out to Heliopolis to see Wing Commander Lyle. Met 75 OTU type at Junior Officers' Club and had lunch. Afternoon I went to the only cool place – Metro – for fairly good film and at 7.00 p.m. caught bus back to Cairo West. Had all sorts of things to do, including briefing as taking off early and so bed rather late.

12/10/43 Tuesday. Called at 3.00 a.m. local time. Had quick breakfast and crawled into aircraft and took off. I was very busy and got some good astro shots. When it

Charles takes a Sunshot.

got light we all had a shave one after the other in the aircraft. Landed El Adem, Luqa and from there to Catania and Bari. Weather very unsettled. Sometimes storms, sometimes fine. In Southern Italy much of the land was flooded, especially at Crotone and the flat dry river beds are now full and carrying an arc of brown water out to sea. Back just before dark and had wash down and change. After dinner unpacking and bed early.
13/10/43 Wednesday. Had fair lie in and then went to town in the morning with huge pile of laundry.

Pilot (Probably "Maggie") at door of Dakota.

Afternoon letter writing and reading. Evening developed films and bed early.

14/10/43 Thursday. Up early for trip to Catania with mild gippy tummy. Went into town to try to buy extra messing, but little there. Town now getting well organised and rebuilding taking place. From tinned foodstuff etc that was being still sold I imagine that there had been a lot of hoarding in Jerry's time. Did not feel too good coming back but had a navigator under training with me and I left it to him. Did some writing but had no dinner and bed very early.

15/10/43 Friday. Still feeling pretty groggy after bad night, but was Ops Officer and did not want to go sick. However, by having no meals it passed through me and I felt a lot better towards evening. Not too busy a day but lots of little things that prevented usual letter writing. Slept in ops room and had fair night.

16/10/43 Saturday. Up 3.00 a.m. for early calls and stomach pains pretty well gone. After wash, shave etc went into town for mirror and organise printing of squadron Christmas cards. Back with Squadron Leader Mac in the jeep having look at country. Afternoon played some good games of tennis on Officers' courts and then hot bath and change for evening.

17/10/43 Sunday. Foggia to Monte Corveno Routine, with binding wait of four and a half hours at Monte Corveno. But nevertheless a very interesting trip over beautiful mountains and valleys. Evening answered some of the letters I got yesterday, some nearly a year old, including income tax return. Bed late. Found that the Italian mess waiters waited till all the Italian Officers went to bed and then put on Italian BBC program. They said they always did before Italy packed up!

18/10/43 Monday. Flying – San Pancrazio.

19/10/43 Tuesday. Morning up late and did one or two personal things, and then called in a hurry for special trip and urgent. But got to Foggia and found nothing ready. Had to wait two hours and then sent to Monte Corveno only to find load was wanted at Naples. Took it

Negotiating for 'Extra Messing' near Altamura.

on there and had to come back in dark. Late dinner, wrote some letters and bed early.

20/10/43 Wednesday. Up usual time and as not flying did several small jobs in the morning and then had two fast sets of singles tennis. Afternoon went with Maggie in 15 Tonner to Giovinazzo and Molfetta to try to buy fish as the boats came in. Giovinazzo is only a small place but pretty. At Molfetta we found a large market hall, but not a lot of fish being brought in by the boats. All very interesting though. Evening tried enlarging some negatives but with little success. Bed late.

21/10/43 Thursday. Up early and shift squadron from Buruzzo to Monte Corveno but when we got there found they were not expecting to move for two days! So sat and sun bathed under the aircraft till some items were ready and then to Monte Corveno and back home via valleys. Lovely day. Evening letter writing. Bed late.

22/10/43 Friday. Up early for trip round country with Maggie in 15 Ton truck looking for extra messing. Went as far as Altamura on the old Roman Apennine Road – quite straight. Some of the towns very small and poor –

market towns. Country around is fairly fertile but is shallow and rocky and is grotty on the limestone rock. In places looks like Yorkshire Moors. Bought inter alia three sheep and then had meal with farmer in town (Altamura). Back late and after dinner did some more enlarging. Bed 11.30 p.m.

23/10/43 Saturday. Up early for trip to Catania and San Pancrazio and back all time over new and beautiful country. Late lunch and then down to town for my dhobi and some photographic material. Evening two escaped POWs came to mess with only ragged worn clothes – no money and no toilet material. So fitted them up with clean clothes, razor etc., bed, pyjamas and had dinner.

24/10/43 Sunday. No flying. Then Jimmy Craig rang me – now on 267 and here on Cairo routine. So took him to town in the morning for a look round and afternoon went for walk round about. Had good long pow wow about old times etc. But then I went to bed early as tired out. Evening went to OD service in canteen.

25/10/43 Monday. Called early with all camp and told all flying cancelled and to parade at 7.00 a.m. When we were all there CO said we (the whole squadron) were to report at Cairo with aircraft and kit by tomorrow night!! Rumours immediately rife about India, S Africa, England etc. We were to leave at 1.00 p.m, so I dashed into Bari for dhobi and then had very rushed packing and lunch and off to Malta for night. Met some more of 459 now on 267 and going to Bari to help move squadron. Bed early and realised I had left soap, shaving brush and my watch.

The stay in Bari had been brief indeed. Charles's impressions were recorded in his journal:

The mess at Bari was excellent. In fact a peace time Italian mess, but the snag was that we shared it with the Italian Officers. True they were our "allies" and made us terribly welcome, but it did not seem quite the thing to many of us and created several "fracas". However, it was set in some lovely grounds and with a goldfish pond and tennis court which was well used. The town itself was undamaged by bombs and set on the coastal plain with the low fertile plateau behind with all its fields and farmhouses all to a plan. There were many fine buildings with wide streets, the main one having a central avenue of trees and wide tree lined pavements either side. Most of the streets were paved with slabs about eighteen inches square and set diagonally. The shops were clean and well stocked surprisingly enough and the stuff on the whole cheap. On the larger buildings and Municipale and private firms offices etc, where the word "fascisti" appeared in the original title it was always removed or obliterated.

The back streets however were different. Narrow, but clean, and cobbled. The houses were small with many on top of one another, main rooms opening on to the street, probably the only room, but clean. Odd little archways over corners and between houses, and with flower pots on edges and in balconies. Unlike to Sicily there do not seem to be so many churches, but they all seem to be in those poor areas. The children, male and female, mostly seem to want cigarettes or to sell us a senorina. Their greeting is "'Allo Cigaret?" or "'Allo Senorina?"

We went back to Catania one day and found the work of rebuilding greatly advanced and going on with renewed vigour. In fact it looked a different town altogether. One very typical sight I saw though which I remember was a woman sitting on a chair in a doorway feeding her baby while another child went through her hair for nits. Nits seem to be common here, also women feeding babies and infants of all sexes standing round in short frocks and no knickers.

On the plain up round Foggia, the mathematical planning of the country was remarkable. Roads would be straight and at regular intervals would be fairly large farmhouses, all white and all identical in pattern. Identically shaped large fields surrounded them. On the plain these were rectangular, but further south where rivers and hills and slopes interfered there was a sort of radiating system of fields, also very regular, with a narrow width near the house on the high ground, and each strip widening out as it ran straight for some distance, sometimes as much as a mile, to the lower plain or river.

One day Maggie and I went down by 15 Ton truck to Giovinazzo to try and buy fish for Mess. The road was flanked by sea on one side with an intervening margin of agriculture or the usual Italian houses or villas and gardens, and agriculture on the other. Also lots of the small round stone sheds. The town itself was fairly large and with the usual large open square in the centre with surrounding trees and statue in the middle. The port itself was only small and looked just like one of our little south coast fishing villages, square in shape with houses down two sides, beach with boats one side and sea on the open side. But there were no boats coming in that afternoon so we went on to Molfetta. Here was a larger town, with the usual square, but a much larger and more ambitious harbour, in one part of which quite a large number of fishing boats were being built.

We waited round for some time for the fishing fleet to sail in. All except two of the motor boats had been taken for balloon barrage. But due to the restriction of limits they only bought in a small catch of small fish which were lost in the large hall used for the market. This was very open and airy and did not smell of fish at all. For the mess we were able to buy three lobsters and some flat fish, and then made up with some of the smaller fish which formed the majority of the haul. This town used to catch enough fish they told us to supply all Southern Italy. Now it hardly catches enough for its own use and when the boxes of fish were brought up, handfuls of the very small ones – smaller that sprats – were given to the youngsters who would eat them whole and raw, some I suppose still alive. Also in the hall were a Nun and two monks and each of these were given some of each catch which were put in a basket brought by them for the purpose. One of the little girls brought by the Nun came and gave me shyly a little St Christopher charm.

One evening when Jimmy Craig called we went for a stroll in the surrounding country. It was all very rich brown earth and mostly olive orchards with narrow white stone walled cart tracks. But the most striking thing was the absence of wild life. We did not hear a single bird or see anything in the shape of a bird or animal life. Just stony silence. We did see some crocuses (and this was October) and buttercups and daisies, though in a deep rocky valley. But the river at the bottom was very thin, and smelt which spoilt the effect.

The squadron was on the move again. The next day they moved on to Cairo.

26/10/43 Tuesday. Up early again and away at crack of dawn to Marble Arch and then on to Cairo. Parked the aircraft etc, got under a tent, and then had odd drink in mess. Rang 267 Squadron and spoke to Griff, but it was too far to walk over in dark, so went to bed early.

CHAPTER 11

India

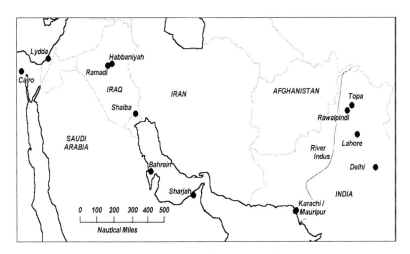

Charles's Travels – October to December 1943.

27/10/43 Wednesday. Up early and dashing around all day trying to find out what's what! But only learnt that we had to be in Delhi by 1st Nov and that not all of us were going, and kit and body had to weigh only 250 lbs – rest to go by sea. Evening went across to 267 Squadron for a drink with Griff and 459 Squadron boys, then on to party at 216 Group and bed late. Lots of chaps went to Cairo, but I was not interested.

28/10/43 Thursday. Definitely going to India and spent day packing personal kit and unpacking aircraft for weighing. In the morning Maggie told me he was to go on as a passenger in a 216 Group aircraft to prepare the route stations for our arrival and I was flying with a Warrant Officer. Bryan rang from 267 Squadron so I went across for yarn with him and Jimmy for evening, and bed early.

29/10/43 Friday. Went down and spent whole morning loading the aircraft as the Captain did not turn up. Got it all weighed and loaded before he arrived, and I was clapped. But afternoon I had to go and finish it off and go for parade where 246 Squadron chaps and Whit and Gilly were presented with DFC for the Salerno job by the AOC in C Middle East Air Chief Marshal Sir Sholto Douglas. Evening went across for brief and then had super parting from chaps who were leaving and booze party started, so bed early.

30/10/43 Saturday. Up 5.00 a.m. and took off 7.00 a.m. via Ismalia, Lydda, Jordan and along pipeline to Ramadi and down to Shaiba. Uninteresting trip over sandy waste and swamp near Shaiba. Some oil wells seen. Arrived 3.00 p.m. and had meal. Very comfortable accommodation in lighted and spacious huts. Not too hot. Evening had beer and sandwiches before going to bed early.

31/10/43 Sunday. Up at 2.00 a.m. and off after good breakfast in dark to Sharjah. Not interesting as either dark or over sea. But Sharjah very hot and humid – 97° and 95% – most uncomfortable. Only rush native huts in town and cinema and very poor. Buildings on airfield well ventilated and RAF and BOAC. After meal off along coast to Karachi. All sand desert but interest in sudden escarpments. Landed and kite disinfected and yellow fever cert examined. Then long ride out to transit camp and changed money and drew pay. Excellent quarters and mess and whisky.

1/11/43 Monday. Up at 6.30 a.m. and had good shower and shave, breakfast and long ride to airfield and away in formation to Mauripur and all up Indus with lack of any extensive agriculture, few rails or roads – many canals.

Landed at new airfield* for paratroop training! Got
sorted out, and arranged a bearer at 25 Rupees a month.
Evening invited to wing mess and opened up kegs of
beer. Went to bed somewhat bad.

No. 117 Squadron found itself starting a new month in yet
another new base. The Operations Record Book summarises the
events of October 1943:

> So ended the most outstanding month of the squadron's
> history. We had flown 2368 hours, carried 1,990,716 lbs of
> freight, transported 1425 casualties and 4150 passengers
> and moved ourselves from Sicily to Italy and from there to
> India.

The situation in India was not favourable to the British in late
1943, but it had been much worse. The Japanese had been
advancing steadily since mid-1941, when they invaded Indo-
China. In early 1942 they had started an invasion of Burma, and
by the middle of the year they had driven back the wholly
inadequate British force of two divisions and the Chinese forces of
Chiang Kai-shek under the command of the American General
'Vinegar Joe' Stillwell. By June 1942 they held all the territory that
they needed and could consolidate. Meanwhile the British and
American camps were divided by undisguised hostility between
their leaders, and within the Indian Army HQ complacency and
inactivity among the senior staff Officers were rife.

It was to this situation that General Slim was appointed to
command the two divisions of XV Corps in June 1942. He set
about training his forces in jungle warfare, learning from the
Japanese that the jungle was not necessarily 'impenetrable', and

* The "new airfield" was Qasim, two miles to the south west of the town of
Rawalpindi.

could be used effectively for concealment and surprise. Massive improvements to road and rail communications were completed. Meanwhile internal security problems came to a head as Ghandi's campaign for the British to quit India intensified. Ghandi's principles of non-violence were not shared by all Indians, and troops had to be used against internal as well as external threats.

In February 1943 Brigadier Orde Wingate took his first "Chindit" expedition into central Burma, behind Japanese lines. With three thousand men he caused severe damage to Japanese forces, and more significantly, he made them change their view of the capabilities of the British forces. He showed that with effective air support and high mobility comparatively small forces could cause major disruption in enemy held territory. The price his men paid in losses and in physical suffering was high, but their morale received an enormous boost, and the myth of Japanese invincibility was firmly squashed.

The effect on strategic thinking at home was marked too. Churchill summoned Wingate to report on his activities, and took him with him on his visit to the Americans in Canada. There Wingate's presentation on his tactics and methods impressed all parties, and helped forge the strategy that developed in the Burma theatre. By July 1943 a plan consisting of three elements had been formed. There would be a three-pronged attack in northern Burma. The Chindits would fly in to positions behind Japanese lines to repeat their work earlier in the year. And Wingate, now a General, would raise six brigades and would be inserted to cut the Japanese supply routes to the area being attacked in the north.

In August 1943 Wingate was back in India and started building up and training his force. Churchill was so dedicated to this whole operation that he told Wingate that he could, if necessary, send reports direct to him. The inertia and infighting of the headquarters in India were still apparent, and Wingate must have been sorely tempted to use this permission on several occasions.

It was in support of these operations that No. 117 Squadron now arrived in India to start training. At Rawalpindi they were still twelve hundred miles from the scene of the action, but the terrain and climate were similar.

2/11/43 Tuesday. Called by new bearer fairly early with hot water. Seems to be a fair "boy". Spent the morning on the aerodrome unloading kite and looking round. Afternoon went into Rawalpindi on a tonga to Officers' shop and for look round the place. Back early and did some reading till dinner and then went to bed early as had little sleep last night.

3/11/43 Wednesday. Lazed a bit and then had a talk with old timer about customs, changes, manners etc. in India. Then wrote some letters. Afternoon went into town again for decko and evening played bridge.

4/11/43 Thursday. Up early and to aerodrome only to potter about and then came back. Afternoon went to town for look round and to make a few purchases and then to hire a bike for a month. And then for a short coast round before changing for evening. Went to second house pictures, but found wrong place and it was tombola. Bed late. Nearly all mess now have hired bikes and looks good all going up to the aerodrome together. Truly mobile.

5/11/43 Up to aerodrome early and crewed up temporarily with Flying Officer Richardson RAAF. Had an hour and a half formation and back for lunch. Afternoon flew to Chaklala for full fuel tanks ready for tomorrow and back and start packing. Bed early.

6/11/43 Saturday. Up very early for dawn take off to

Karachi. Went direct across waste mountain tracts. Had meal and refuel at Karachi and on again to Bahrain and stayed night. Fortunately not too hot in evening, but told that it is worse than Sharjah. Wrote some letters and bed very early.

7/11/43 Sunday. Away again at crack of dawn after a good breakfast. Usual routine trip along pipeline and stopped at Lydda for refuel and lunch and saw various chaps I knew. Then on again to Cairo and got settled in at transit mess, finding that the equipment we wanted was there. Evening went over to see Griff and boys on 267 Squadron, but back early for bed as very tired.

8/11/43 Monday. Up early and hitch into Cairo. Haircut and shave and some purchases and went to Heliopolis to See Wing Commander Lyle about my eye, but he was out so fixed appointment for tomorrow. Had lunch at Heliopolis in the House Hotel and back to LG 224 and out to see Jimmy. Evening in transit mess yarning and bed early.

9/11/43 Tuesday. Into town again in the morning for my appointment with Wing Commander Lyle, but he was down examining King Peter of Yugoslavia so I had to wait till 12.30 p.m. Then he said he would have to see me again when he had his tools. So I hitched back to LG 224, had a meal and changed and back to Heliopolis where he put me through the hoop only to say he would do nothing with the eye. Spent evening in Cairo then back to camp at midnight and flopped into bed.

10/11/43 Wednesday. Spent all day on airfield loading aircraft with para-racks which we had come for, but were not able to get as many as we wanted. Also was unable to get an astro compass from anywhere. Had short doze in evening and took off at midnight.

11/11/43 Thursday. Very dark all the way but I was able to get a few fix points as the wind was not too reliable and compass deviation in doubt. However, we made Habanniya OK for breakfast and a look at gardens. Then off again for interesting trip to Bahrain. Arrived noon and had good shower, shave and change and after lunch went to Manama for look round. Usual Arab town and shops. Things very expensive. Baksheesh as usual. Back for dinner and bed early.

12/11/43 Friday. Did not get up very early and then set course direct for Karachi at 10,000 ft. Fairly cold but had good wind. Instead of going round coast it took us all over land on south of Iran and through completely desiccated hill formations. Very, very peculiar, resembling tram lines at a large junction. Arrived Mauripur early afternoon. Did all bumph and out to transit camp. After dinner direct to bed early.

13/11/43 Saturday. Up early again and off before daylight to Delhi. Flew round Taj Mahal on way to have a look but as we were at 5000 ft not very good for photography. At Delhi had meal and look at Secretariat and extensive layout planning of New Delhi. While there got touch of sore throat. Back to Rawalindi via Lahore and by time I got there felt as though I had a touch of flu. So went to bed directly after dinner.

As usual Charles wrote in his journal of his impressions of the journey:

The two shuttles I did from Cairo were uneventful but gave opportunities of landing at a few places. The journey as a whole was uninspiring. There was greenery when we left at Lydda. We flew over the painfully meandering

Jordan, from Galilee and Dead Sea, and then having crossed the hills we continued over the undulating, dark, and little changing desert till we picked up the "pipe line". The only landmark in miles and miles of desert, an almost perfect straight line of pipe and tarmac road interspersed at fairly frequent intervals by landing grounds and pumping stations. It was a monotonous run till we left it to find Habanniya, between the Euphrates and a large lake. We only had breakfast there and the town seems to consist mainly of barracks etc. But the Officers' mess has certainly been built in accommodating style and made as pleasant as possible with trees and gardens and lawns on well irrigated spots. But the smell of pitch and burning pervades the atmosphere.

From there to Shaiba it was again large desert tracts, through which the Euphrates flows with its many offshoots filled with water in the rainy season, so permitting irrigation and greenery in its immediate proximity. Shaiba itself again was plonked on an expanse of desert. But they seem to have made the best of a bad job and accommodated us really well.

The Persian Gulf looked just a hot expanse of green water fringed by desert shores and mountains, with shallow waters and sand banks visible on west side. Near the mouth of the Gulf are several large islands, and surprising enough there are perhaps two villages on some of them with one or two palms. Bahrain, where we spent one afternoon and night, was quite pleasant at this time of the year, though again it is just dark sand and some palms. The big attraction is the prolific oil supplies both on the islands and mainland, and though marked "British" on maps, actually is neutral and belongs to a local sheik. The town – and the town of Manama on the larger island – is

Double-roofed accommodation in Bahrain.

built straight on top of the sand and the streets are just the same as the desert except that they are pressed hard with traffic. Manama is quite a large town, with some large open white buildings among the many squalid mud dwellings of the natives crowding in on narrow streets. The many works of westernisation were noticeable though – large cars, sports gear, cameras etc. and clothes, all very expensive. Also a number of merchants selling set and uncut diamonds. The justice here is administered by the Sheikh and is of a very summary character, people – even Europeans – being invited to the shootings and floggings which include women as well. On the aerodrome we were accommodated in open-work rush and bamboo huts with the usual double roof.

Sharjah, where we fortunately stayed only a short time, proved very hot and humid. Again the town was built straight on the sand and is ruled by the Sheikh. The mess was of a more substantial nature and with a unique ventilating system which kept it just cool in spite of the lack of fans. Though all this country is said to abound in oil, the natives are rather hostile, though I guess this has little to do with the lack of development, transport and climate being the snag.

The peninsular which juts up into the Gulf is composed of a high 2000 – 6000 ft chain of bare black hills, yet on the several small flat plateaux, just like tables, are little apparently inaccessible villages and cabbage patches.

From here we came along the south coast of Iran, another desert coastline lapped by a green sea. In places the actual coastline was indistinguishable as it was just a large wet sandy area. In others, chains of hills formed cliffs. Some of these hills look very odd as they have been extensively eroded so that there are just lines of disclosed, almost vertical strata looking just as if someone had run their fingers through the sand. Then would come flat plateaux or sudden high escarpments sloping away and then perhaps a mud volcano, the whole presenting a very peculiar geological formation.

I was disappointed in Karachi as it appeared just a huge town on brown desert, though I found on landing that this was not the sand I was used to but ordinary dirt or earth. The only thing apparently growing was a very poor quality of stunted and shrivelled cactus. The transit camp, however, was very comfortable, even luxurious, and everything well organised, and here I had my first taste of the bearer and caste systems, though all its manifold ramifications did not unfold themselves till I got to Rawalpindi. We only passed through the town once, but several impressions linger. First I was surprised at the herds of huge cattle outside till I suddenly realised the sacred nature of the beasts. Later I found them singly in the town. The outskirts are the usual dirty Indian streets, open shops and houses and verandaed upper stories. The brothel area – Napier Street – being particularly pointed out. But in the town itself we found very wide streets, tree lined and opulent looking buildings, shops and houses, tramways, cinemas etc.

The Indian men were mostly European clad, but with shirts outside trousers and beturbanned and usually bearded. The women were in the bright flowing wraps, and the slow tenor of life was very noticeable. One thing I noticed and thought about a lot was QUIT BRITAIN chalked largely on two prominent corners.

At the Karachi aerodrome we saw two notices up side by side over two doors. Lavatory – European style, and Lavatory – Indian style. We of course went in the first and were confronted with two shelves. On one was a bowl of water and on the other one solitary enamel chamber. We investigate two doors apparently leading to WCs, but found in each just bare rooms with no water pipes laid in for cistern or outlet for drain. The obvious intention being a thunder box. Why tradition still hangs tenaciously to these as against sewerage I don't know but I am told they are still the general equipment in most houses.

The journey up from Karachi to Rawalpindi is over desert, canals and railways. Not very interesting after the first half hour. The second time we went via Taj Mahal and though we were at 5000 ft and the dome was still in scaffolding the layout and the beauty of the building could be fully appreciated. The town too is a large one on the river bank with quite a few large buildings and estates.

Delhi, at least New Delhi, from the air impressed me far more though. The ambitious and extensive scale on which the whole is based is amazing. Huge nodal points with wide tree lined avenues branching straight out and large houses set well back. Then the really unbelievable Victory Avenue leading up to the Secretariat, wide and long and straight with tree sprinkled extensive lawns either side. The

Secretariat itself is of red and greeny-white stone. It was planned and built with no limitation of space or cost apparently, and so is home for the Viceroy and the Chamber of Deputies. I should have liked to have been able to have had longer there driving about these avenues where every house is detached and in large grounds with the owners' name on the gates. Here too I saw the first pukah Indian temple dome from close up and the tall columns either side in the red and white stone that is so common.

Now established at Rawalpindi, Charles returned to the routine of squadron life:

14/11/43 Sunday. Felt fairly groggy in the morning so had breakfast in bed. Doc called but told him I only had sore throat. Got up for lunch and though back and limbs ached went down to club and had some snooker, but felt so bad when got back went straight to bed and had dinner in bed. Doc came and dosed me up. Was to have done two hours night fly.

15/11/43 Monday. Felt lots better but had to stay abed till Doc called. However, my temperature was normal so I could get up for lunch. Afternoon I went into town and back to the mess to write a few letters. Had chat with Indian tailor about India. He was not worried about full government, only a square deal from one or the other and he says that is what all want. Thrust of his stories is that they have not had it. In evening I joined Rawalindi Club and spent evening there. Bed late.

16/11/43 Tuesday. Up early and cycled to aerodrome. Not flying but had a look round and got the gen. Back in time to go into town and make a few purchases. Afternoon I went for cycle ride round the park with

Archer. Then down to club for hot bath! After dinner went to club again and wrote letters. Then to Piping Chinese restaurant for prawns ending at Cuban dance at Metropolitan Club (did not dance) and bed very late and tired.

17/11/43 Wednesday. In the morning I laid in a bit and then up to aerodrome, but nothing doing so back and early lunch for flying in the afternoon. Formation practice. But I went to sleep and when we took over the lead had hell of job finding out where we were. Then early dinner and airborne for night cross country and four drops. But too dark – no moon to map read to DZ properly. Did pretty well though. Then I got left behind on aerodrome and had to get special truck of my own back to mess and so bed very late.

The formation, the night cross country and the drops on a dropping zone were the beginning of Charles's training for the new role. The Operations Record Book explains how the training was done:

> Training continued throughout the month with day and night formation flying with and without navigation lights and making the most of moonlit nights. Practice drops and run ups on the dropping zone at Chaklala, numerous and varied cross country flights, by day and by night, flying in formation and singly to practise identifying dropping zones and timing of arrival with practice drops, dropping containers from the door and from racks at Chaklala dropping zone and finally dropping troops on this zone.
>
> Groundcrew and aircrew went over to Chaklala for a week's backers-up course in parties of about forty men. Wireless operators started jump masters courses at Chaklala

and a few crews went to the Air Landing School to drop paratroops on the dropping zone. Three of the squadron's aircraft were sent to Chaklala to help with these exercises. On all of these courses good results were obtained.

The Operations Record Book also tells of the intention to move all personnel into tented accommodation on the airfield as soon as possible. Clearly all did not go to plan:

18/11/43 Thursday. Up very early and up to the aerodrome very tired (having told bearer to pack all my kit) to move into new billets. But nothing was ready so came back and told him to unpack again. Afternoon did practice container dropping, quite interesting. Evening down to club for drink and letter writing. Bed early.

19/11/43 Friday. Did another cross country in the morning, but no flying in the afternoon. Lay on bed most of time. Then on veranda reading and yarning with the Indian tailor about India. Evening down to the club again for letter writing. Bed late.

20/11/43 Saturday. Up early and spent all day moving myself and some of the mess stuff up to the aerodrome. A lot of mess kit had been pinched, but no redress I fear. Tents terribly dusty and not well furnished. In fact nowhere near ready for habitation. By evening a lot better but in mess there is no light. Pretty well everyone went out to town so I went to bed and read till I went to sleep very early.

21/11/43 Sunday. Up early again and washed and shaved in freezing cold water. Went down to the church in the morning but it was not open till evening. So went for ride on bike and then to club for hour listening to band. Afternoon shut-eye in tent. Maggie back from convalescence. Afternoon lay on bed and slept and read till early dinner, and then away for night flying. Did two hours cross country astro trip, but soon after airborne watches stopped! Got time signal later though.

Charles had formed his general opinions of India by this time, and they went as always into his journal:

From the air the only remarkable things round Rawalpindi are the hawks, oil wells, an old walled village and several broken deserted villages on flat areas among the broken land, the winding rivers and canals and the peculiar strata jutting out of the ground again, folded up towards the Himalayas which can be seen white capped in the distance. The town itself is pleasant in the modern part, with wide streets and good shops, though everything is very expensive and there are lots of lower caste Indians about and beggars. And the roads out of town are wider still as there are earth horse rides either side. Bikes are a very popular mode of transport, and almost everyone on the squadron has hired one. At first it was useful for dashing around town and getting out to camp, but now that we are on the aerodrome, for getting into town and dashing round camp.

The caste business has taken a bit of getting used to. We could not put up our own tents and the bearers will only do some jobs, having to call in other castes for others. The bearers themselves have to be got used to as we are so used to looking after ourselves.

Just between the aerodrome and town is a small Indian village, very like the Egyptian in many ways with different smell and houses of brick but again small dirty and open. The clothes are different in that most of the women wear the white or coloured thin trousers, narrow at the bottom and turbans take the place of the fez. But just before this village is a river with a large number of Mimosa trees and the smell as we go past is a great change and very powerful.

Quite a number of the men, mostly the older ones, wear red beards to show that they have done the pilgrimage to Mecca. In town Indian ATS girls look strange when, instead of wearing the shirt, they wear the more common flowing shawls which take the place of a frock. When one of these in fine coloured material is worn at a dance etc by an Anglo Indian they really look good.

Back to the village again, the children get manure from the streets with their hands and knead it into a paddy and in pancake form stick it to the walls to dry for fuel. Very large camels are used here for transport as well as oxen. Tree rats, like little grey squirrels are very common. Another common figure is the nut seller with his two scale like trays on his shoulders as he sings along to the rhythm of his scale trays. Itinerant vendors are also very common. Barbers, tailors, jewellers etc. all coming to the camp and round the tents, some having very good wares, but mostly wanting a pretty high price.

The hair styles of the nations vary a lot. Most of them keep it cut à la European style. Some have only the small bit left with which to be pulled into heaven. The Sikhs never cut it at all. All the little girls have long pigtails which they make into a bun as they grow older. Mohammedan women of course remain completely covered from infidels.

22/11/43 Monday. Up early for Duty Officer, but had not been there long when I was told I was flying. Did cross country with Maggie – just us two so got quite a bit of second pilot hours. Afternoon I was dragged out for container dropping and not till tea time was I able to get down to work. Then after dinner just settling down to astro and censoring when the phone girl rang and we stayed talking till very late. Finally said I would see her tomorrow if I was not flying.

23/11/43 Tuesday. Up early and found I was flying so rang and said I could not come. Did cross country in the morning and lots of flying. Afternoon I was not flying, so I rang Betty but she had gone, so I wrote letters and had nap. Then into town to club for hot bath and change. After dinner took several ground astro shots and went to bed early and read.

24/11/43 Wednesday. Did another two hours cross country in the morning, starting off in freezing cold and coming back at noon very warm. Did some more formation flying. Afternoon by arrangement I met Betty in town and went for ride in Topee Park. Very nice ride, but she does not impress me favourably. Nothing to look at and nothing to talk about except small talk about herself. Back early and the rest of sea-kit arrived, so sorting it out. Then away for night flying – two hours astro cross country. Bed late.

25/11/43 Thursday. Non-flying morning so went into town with films and apart from half an hour of container dropping spent rest of day reading and writing till evening when went into town to club with gang on a "bender". Most of them got very tight and some damage was done. Back and bed very late.

26/11/43 Friday. First day of no flying. In the morning I stayed in camp as did not feel too good, but in the afternoon went into town and had game of tennis (and bought a racket) to try to get rid of rheumatism and stomach ache. On way back called in to see chaps in hospital, but by the time I got back felt too bad to go out so went straight to bed and had no dinner. In spite of which I had to get up several times in night.

27/11/43 Saturday. Did not feel a lot better in the morning so stayed in bed. Near noon Maggie came to say we were down to fly in the afternoon on a Nav test, so I said I would get up. Did not feel too good but did pretty well. Then popped into town to collect snaps and back and bed again. But got up for dinner as I needed a meal as had had no breakfast or lunch. Then bed again.

28/11/43 Sunday. Up early and getting organised and packed for week at hill rest camp. Had terrific cold in head after lunch. Had very pleasant trip right up through steep valleys and via high wooded hill to camp beautifully situated among peaks and comfortably equipped and furnished. Had evening in front of fire and reading and bed early. Had little sleep as could not breathe with nose so blocked up.

This period of leave at the Topa rest camp was a vital part of keeping the squadron at peak efficiency and ensuring that all could cope with the heavy demands of the previous months and of the new training. The Operations Record Book notes the value of the facility:

This month has been a record month for minor ailments on the squadron, due no doubt to the change of conditions and reaction after working at high pressure in the Central Mediterranean forces. A short stay in Hospital or the Station Sick Quarters and a period at the RAF rest camp at Topa proved good treatment and as most of the squadron personnel are long overdue for leave, it is to be hoped that

Officers' Mess, Topa Rest Camp.

everyone will have the chance of a week's leave of absence before the squadron moves again.

Charles certainly found it to be a most welcome break:

29/11/43 Monday. Up at 8.00 a.m. and watched sun rise over valleys. After breakfast wandered around, booked in etc., and bought tennis balls and had several good sets. Afternoon hired horses and went up into hills among typical film scenery of wooded valleys and steep hillsides and little cabins on slopes and tops. Not too good on horse, but wizard ride. Then finished off the afternoon with three sets of tennis and hot bath and change. Evening reading by fire again in lovely setting, but nose still bunged up and so bed early.

30/11/43 Tuesday. Had better night but not good and did not feel stiff till noon after I had played tennis all morning, when I stiffened up considerably. I tried to work it off by going for long walk and climbing down and up valley through magnificent country of deep wooded valley – really deep. Spent rest of day till early bed yarning in mess. So far my resolution to write lots of letters has failed miserably.

1/12/43 Wednesday. Slightly better night but not good. In

the morning I found my watch missing from room and had hue and cry after bearers. Then by car into Murree and walked back through beautiful hillside wooded lanes. Got back to find I had left a parcel of purchases by roadside when I was taken short and so after lunch walked back and found it. Then got dragged into drinking session with Other Ranks and only left after a lot to drink to play four fast sets of tennis – not a good thing. Did not feel too good in evening so after dinner wrote a letter and went to bed.

2/12/43 Thursday. Not too bad a night. But felt tired in the morning so stayed on lawn reading. Afternoon went for ramble climbing down into the valleys through almost virgin forest and worked up a huge blister on toe. Spent evening reading and writing letters and bed early. Still no news of watch and very little seems to be being done.

3/12/43 Friday. Morning resting and reading on lawn, then game of tennis. Local Indian Police came up about watch. It either meant me charging my bearer which I would not do, or giving up all hope – so that has gone. Afternoon more rest and more tennis and hot bath and change for dinner and letter writing in evening.

4/12/43 Saturday. Spent whole day either playing tennis or sitting on lawn. Very clear today and able to see snow clad peaks in distance very easily. Evening went round to Station dance where the girls seemed to come from everywhere. Japanese as well as Burmese etc! But I did not want to dance so went to bed fairly early.

Charles's journal makes only brief mention of his time in the leave centre, but he certainly welcomed the rest:

Murree – up in the hills – proved a really wonderful spot

Drinks on the Lawn at Topa.

for leave. It was 6000 – 7000 ft above sea level and the road up on the most winding I have seen, as it sorts its way along hillsides up the valleys and from one valley to the next, with a steep precipice now on the right and now on the left. Some well wooded, some bare and grassy.

Murree proved to be an average size town built near the top but on the lee-side of the hill. As a result the houses were stacked steeply on the hillside. Beyond here was upper Topa, where we stayed on the crest of a hill and with a grand view of the steep wooded hills all round. On fine days the snow could be seen in the far distance, on dull days just the valleys below in gloom. It was winter here, but the sun shone almost every day from a clear light blue sky, and was quite warm. However, a chilly breeze sometimes came down from the mountains and anyway in the shadow it was always cold. The air too naturally was thinner and at first any exercise – as walking, tennis, riding etc – made me very puffed. But I got used to it soon. Riding I found very fine as some of those mountain tracks took me to scenery I had only imagined in films. Others were too bad for horses, but scrambling up and down would be timber-laden donkeys. In those woods I saw a large number of very pretty large red birds and very small blue ones, who simply flashed from tree to tree. Jackals I heard, and opossums and monkeys I was told about.

Outside Murree Post Office I saw for the first time a native letter writer, who for a few annas would answer an unlettered native's letters for him and post it. It seemed strange, but I suppose the recipient would take it to another to have it read and get him to answer it. Coming back from Murree in a village called something like Barryalt, one could hire a bike for 4 annas and coast all the way down to Topa, followed by a chicho on another bike who would cycle back with it.

Regrettably, the leave had to come to an end. There now started a period of intensive training leading up to Christmas:

5/12/43 Sunday. Up early and on with final packing and away on 3 tonner at 11.00 a.m. down that hazardous winding road among the mountains and though fairly warm, outside post was on shady side of road and cold wind blew through the truck. Back to the dusty aerodrome and tent in time for lunch. Spent the afternoon sorting myself out and reading several letters. Then changed and ready for church at 6.30 p.m. in town, where there was quite a good congregation. Back for dinner and writing letters. Bed early.

6/12/43 Monday. Up early for a change and leave 8.00 a.m. in very cold weather for "Backers Up" course at Chaklala. First we had an hour square bashing to warm us up and then rifle and bayonet drill! Shades of ITW etc. Then lectures on Browning, rifle and sten guns and so ended the day. Back to camp. Bearer still holding out for more money and I have told him he can go if he likes. Evening night flying and formation practice so bed late.

7/12/43 Tuesday. Still colder this morning and unlike yesterday it did not get warmer as day advanced. Spent all morning on rifle and bayonet drill and unarmed combat, and afternoon on rifle range procedures and practice throwing grenades. Then into town to have bike repaired and visit various blokes in hospital and back in time to change and early dinner and two and a half hours night flying.

8/12/43 Wednesday. Away to Chaklala for course on cold morning again and out to butts, and it turned out warm sunny day. Got max possible for grouping at 100 yds. Seven bull's eyes, two inners, one middle on 200 yds application and leading on points, but only got three of twenty snap shots, so came third of course. Afternoon off, so letter writing and reading then change for new mess warming. Several guests and good dinner and lots of beer and fun. But left at midnight and away to bed.

9/12/43 Thursday. Did a spot of drill again in the morning. Rest of day on field-craft, Browning and hand grenades. Also fired sten gun. Evening back in time for briefing for night cross country. Back late dog tired.

10/12/43 Friday. Up for the last morning of tough tactics course. And live grenade throwing and verbal test on course. Afternoon spent resting and preparing for night. Fifteen aircraft in formation at night to Delhi and dropping zone one hour further. A drop to time schedule and back. Seven hours flying. Was very tired when went to bed. Had huge batch of mail arrive.

11/12/43 Saturday. Up fairly early and so was caught for Operations Officer. Had usual busy day and also had my

TAB stab and vaccination. So arm did not feel too good for rest of day. Up late too with night flying.

12/12/43 Sunday. Up on the job early getting four kites away to Calcutta. Then wash and change and spent rest of the morning and afternoon writing and reading. The first dull day we have had, but not as cold. Went into church before dinner and in again to see Five Graves to Cairo. A good film, but details bad. Bed midnight.

13/12/43 Monday. Up early and with boys to Chaklala to see the Padre about a Christmas drumhead service, but gone back to Group so left it and spent rest of the morning organising Christmas entertainment. Afternoon reading and writing. Then night flying and bed late.

14/12/43 Tuesday. Up late and then had very idle day, part getting Christmas program ready and part reading and writing. And then to bed early. Lot warmer day and popped into town in the afternoon to get bike cleaned and watch repaired etc.

15/12/43 Wednesday. Up 6.30 a.m. Started on Air Landing School in the morning. Dropped 20 Indian paratroops and then came back home. Afternoon organising concert for Christmas and evening on another night exercise. Bed 1.30 a.m.

16/12/43 Thursday. Up at 7.00 a.m. in spite of late night, and on to Chaklala for ALS course. Dropped four sticks of five troops and back to camp. Spent the morning rounding up chaps for the concert. Afternoon writing and to town shopping and to hospital to see patients. Evening had first meeting for concert and then bed early.

17/12/43 Friday. ALS again in morning and dropped sticks of ten bods. Then back again and spent rest of day writing and reading and bed early.

18/12/43 Saturday. Dropped twenty in one stick this morning and back again. Had quite an easy time all afternoon and into town for shopping, then mess meeting re-new mess changes. In the evening first concert rehearsal, and bed late.

19/12/43 Sunday. Dropped stick of twenty again. Fifteen aircraft on a remote dropping zone. Looked very good. Afternoon played some very good tennis at club till 6.00 p.m. Had hot bath and back and change. Into town for church carol service. Back for dinner and then to Sergeants' mess for house warmer, and bed late.

20/12/43 Monday. Did not get up early and then had an idle morning. Afternoon went to lecture by Brigadier on the strategy of the Italian campaign, which was mostly text book and not extra good, and spent rest of day playing tennis at the club. In evening had invite to 62 Squadron* dance. Did not dance but enjoyed it with other people and the odd drink and then back later on.

21/12/43 Tuesday. Another idle morning just pottering about. Afternoon concert rehearsal and sleep. Evening squadron dance, and it was a very good "do" for the men. I actually went so far as to have a dance in the Paul Jones. But that was all and then came back by tonga.

22/12/43 Wednesday. Spent most of morning preparing for the afternoon and evening exercise. Paratroops and supplies. Found that white ants had eaten a hole in my case and several silk clothes! Great wrath. Left for Wing at 4.00 p.m. Then to aerodrome for take off at 5.30 p.m. Twenty six aircraft all dropping at dusk. Then refuel and arm and drop supplies. Back 11.00 p.m. Fairly successful.

* 62 Squadron also flew Dakotas in the same role as 117 Squadron.

23/12/43 Thursday. Another idle morning, and in the afternoon I went to funeral party of 194 Squadron* pilot. Rather annoyed as Maggie was going to give me some dual on the Dakota. Then spent rest of day in mess reading and writing. New pipe arrived from Margaret which was timely as I had just broken my last one. Had first shower of rain in evening. Local petroleum works closed down for five days! What a war.

Despite the celebrations of the festive season, training went on as before on the squadron. However, there was also time for plenty of celebration. In a letter to his sister Margaret he described the predations of the white ants, and the various ways in which the squadron personnel enjoyed the season:

You may have heard about these white ants out here that eat nearly anything. Well, I had a large leather case in which I had kept lots of things that I had bought with an eye to the future if I got home. Grey flannels, silk pyjamas, socks and cloth. To save this I had my bearer drive four stakes into the ground and rest it on these, as they can only work in the dark and have to build their nest up to anything high. Well, one day I noticed it "down" at one corner, so I had a look underneath and found the little blighters had built a coat of earth up the stake, eaten a nice little hole in the case and the stake had gone through. Of course I whipped it off and had a decko inside and could have cried. Some of the stuff I managed to save, but I lost a lot of good stuff. Of course I roared hell out of the bearer. The poor blighter was scared, but damn it, I pay him to look after me and my stuff. If it had not been for the fact that we were

* 194 Squadron also flew Dakotas in the same role as 117 Squadron.

moving soon I would have sacked him straight off. But he has been almost a paragon ever since.

But to Christmas. As you know I was in charge of entertainments and though I say it myself I think everything went off very well, especially from what was said in letters I censored. The first event was a bit of an event for me too – the squadron dance. I had my first dance since I left England. True it was only a short one in the Paul Jones, but a dance – and I have not forgotten how, which is useful to know. Christmas Eve I decided I had done enough work and to leave the program to go itself, and so with a pal went off into the town. We did not get up till 10.30 a.m. so did not get in till lunch time. In the afternoon we went for a stroll round the native Indian bazaar. It was not as large or interesting as some I have seen, but well worth it. Then we went to the club for some drinks, dinner and join in the mass merriment, but as we found it getting very fast and very furious decided we had better leave while we had time and went to the pictures.

Christmas Day of course I spent in camp and apart from anything else, as the bars were open all day, there was lots of fun. In the morning I took a truck out to a nearby village and got three Yule logs and greenery for the messes. At noon we "waited on" the airmen at their dinner. In the afternoon all sorts of things happened, the main being a donkey race seated backwards way on, and a football match, played fifteen men a side (or thereabouts) on a round field with a rugby ball, in some odd costume, and players had to be at least half-merry (and they were not difficult to find). In the evening about 6.00 p.m. to 8.30 p.m. we had our dinner and I think I can honestly say it as about the best dinner I have ever had. I have never seen such an abundance and variety of food in one place, including a pukah Christmas

Pud and all flaming in traditional style.

Although I went to bed fairly late, I was woken again by a party wandering round the tents with gramophone and about six records and six bottles of whisky who came into each tent and played a couple of records and dispensed whisky freely, insisting, without effect, that we joined their rambles. So I lay in again Boxing morning. But as it was a Lady visitors' lunch and I had to get up and "watch". Then in the afternoon I went to the club for tennis, had a bath and tea, then went to see the chaps in hospital and to Church afterwards.

The next day I was given another job – Squadron Historian.

New Year's Eve we had a bit of a "do". Everyone went out and at 10.30 p.m. there were only two sick chaps in the mess and myself, when I went off to the Watch Night service and stayed behind for a cup of cocoa and bun. But when I got back I found the Mess an absolute shambles. I have never seen such a really good "rag". Books, broken records, torn decorations, bottles etc were all over the place. The bar broken open. In fact they had really gone to town in a big way. I was furious and went out and found four airmen, drunk nearly, so whipped them on a charge and under arrest straight away. It was impossible to do any more at that time, and as the others came home told them to leave it till morning. Fortunately, from these four and other sources we got the chief offenders. But the snag is my writing case was taken among other small personal things belonging to other people. They had just emptied out all the contents – letters, envelopes, paper etc and taken the case, stamps, address book. Of course I shall never find that.

So 1943 drew to a close. The squadron Operations Record

Book sums up the training effort:

> By the beginning of the month all personnel of the unit had accustomed themselves to their new surroundings and seemed to have made quite a good impression in Rawalpindi.
>
> Several training exercises were carried out very successfully. On the 3rd Exercise Tiger 2 was carried out, the squadron supplying only two aircraft. On the 5th Exercise Pegasus was carried out, and this time the squadron was detailed to supply twelve aircraft. On the 10th the squadron was called upon to supply fifteen aircraft for Exercise Juniper, followed on the 19th by Exercise Teal, on the 17th by Exercise Hawk and on the 22nd by Exercise Plover.
>
> Debriefing reports on these exercises showed that in addition to dropping parachutists and containers most successfully, valuable experience was gained. Apart from these exercises both the aircrew personnel and particularly the technical personnel were kept extremely busy owing to the tremendous amount of night flying carried out.

* * *

> The Christmas festivities this year were very much enjoyed by all and although the homely atmosphere and traditions were missing, it can be reported that all arrangements were entirely satisfactory, the meals being particularly well organised and enjoyed and were in fact a tremendous credit to the staff who prepared them. In keeping with RAF custom each man received his beer, and by the evening everyone on the camp appeared to be in the "Christmas mood".

A fitting conclusion to a month of hard work was witnessed on New Year's Eve when, once more the traditions of home prevailed and all personnel seemed to be in the best of spirits.

During the month 206.15 hours were flown by day and 277.55 hours were flown by night, and there have been no aircraft accidents.

The total hours flown of less than 500 makes an interesting contrast with the number of hours just two months previously in Italy. Though training hard for their new role, both aircrew and ground crew must have welcomed the cut of about 80% in their flying workload. The training was to continue into the New Year, but again the flying would be at a much more sustainable level. However, Charles was to see little of it, for his eye was playing up again.

CHAPTER 12

Hospital Again

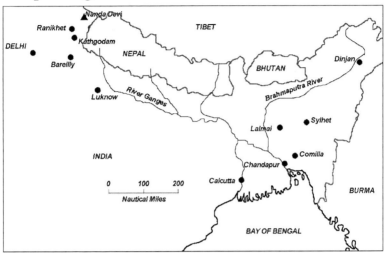

Charles's Travels in India – January to April 1944.

3/1/44 Monday. Found out from flights that I was not
flying so cycled into town for films. New razor and strop
and clothes from Officers' shop and then onto Wing for
briefing for tonight's exercise. Back at camp told I had to
report to Bareilly Hospital tomorrow or 5th. So spent
the afternoon in final things and packing. Evening rested
in mess till take off 1.00 a.m. on 4th.

4/1/44 Tuesday. Had very successful exercise with six
hundred and eighty troops with supplies all dropped
OK. Back 4.00 a.m. for breakfast and bed. Up 10.20
a.m. making final arrangements and idling. And in the
afternoon did final packing and heard at 9.00 p.m. that
final transport to Delhi would be by air and I have to
report to Bareilly on the 5th.

5/1/44 Wednesday. Up early to wait for plane from Basal

that was picking me up. Left on it at 10.20 a.m. and arrived at Delhi at 7.30 p.m. Found a smallpox plague there and had to be vaccinated again. A lot of controversy as to whether a DC3 could land at Bareilly so made enquiries about trains, but it would take nearly twenty four hours. Spent evening in transit mess at Lytton Road and bed early.

6/1/44 Thursday. Up early with rest of chaps but doubt about my going still existed till the eleventh hour when I was told of a new concrete strip north of town and so I went. They landed me there but I found only six locals there who could not speak English. However, I made one understand that I wanted a tonga and he went off on a bike. After an hour though I walked out to the road and though it was pretty deserted I stopped a Jeep and an Indian Officer who spoke English took me all the way (and through native country). At the hospital specialists had preliminary look. Said he could not do much but sent me to surgical ward. They were full so I went to medical. Then late in afternoon we were warned of convoy arriving so was told to sleep in another ward! Spent day getting bearings and bed early.

7/1/44 Friday. In morning a lot of patients went out on an ambulance train and my kit was packed on it with theirs; so if it comes back it won't be for five to seven days! At noon I saw two specialists and fate still undecided but there was talk of going up to the hills to a plastic surgeon. Meanwhile I was put in the surgical ward. In evening I went out for a beer and then bed early as very cold. Now have no clean clothes to change into.

8/1/44 Saturday. Up early and spent all day just pottering about wards, eating, reading and writing. Afternoon a Doctor came and said I was to go to hills for plastic surgeon to have a go. But I hope to delay it till my kit comes back from Poona. Evening went out to club for billiards, drink, supper and bed early.

9/1/44 Sunday. Went for a stroll in the morning and again in the afternoon. At noon was told to go to get warrants etc. from the office to go tomorrow at 8.00 a.m. Could not get my dhobi back in the afternoon either. Found some fine gardens in Bareilly. Evening stayed in writing and reading and bed early.

10/1/44 Monday. Up early and chased dhobi round but could not get my stuff before I left. So now I have only what I stand up in! Had fairly interesting journey to Kathgodam at foot of hills, where the Himalayas start, but very slow. From there by old ramshackle bus (front seat) which broke down six times up through hills on the forty miles of winding treacherous roads to Rhanikhet. But glorious country – the trip to Muree on a grander scale and finally the breathtaking sight of snow clad peaks. Found the hospital more like a rest camp on first impression. Only two other Officers and it looks as if I am going to be very comfortable.

The journey to Rhanikhet made quite an impression on Charles, for he described it in a number of letters home, but in more detail in his journal:

The train journey to Kathgodam was flat and much of the sameness. We started off among the familiar small patches of cultivation like the old patchwork quilt, passing small villages here and there. But after a while the individual areas got bigger and soon it was just acres of sugar cane or grass with an occasional pond with a few storks. We only passed one mill, where we stopped to allow one of the big cheeses to get off. There was quite a reception committee for him, from the highest to the hopeful clerk, and they all made their salaams in correct order of superiority. The mill gave the appearance of a typically old established place, where efficiency was not the key note, but penny wise, pound foolish. And the lights all along the sidings were burning even at midday.

At one of the stations en route – Lalkua – I saw monkeys wild for the first time. I could see the mountains getting nearer and nearer but yet the land did not seem to rise to meet them. The plain had now become savannah land and stretched away for miles till we came to Kathgodam, the rail head for the obvious reason that the Kathgodam foothills started here. That is just how it was – they started. From out of the flat plain rose steep wooded slopes to left and right and a line could be drawn along the ground marking the boundaries. I did not see much of Kathgodam as I got straight on one of those insecure and unsafe looking little hill buses, but it did not look a very large place.

The journey was what I had expected, a long winding precarious road running up the side of the valleys, but passing through some beautiful scenery, varied and picturesque. We climbed to 6000 ft and ran along the ridge for a bit and then cut off the engine and coasted down another winding road to the valley 3000 ft below. This I think was the finest part of the journey and to be able to catch glimpses of the river and villages way below made it the more exciting. From the bottom we again had to start climbing, and here for the first time I saw logs of timber being floated down the river. The journey up was not quite so interesting as the valleys and hills were wider and more cultivated, till we got near the top and it got wooded again.

By now I was a bit tired, when suddenly through a gap

in the trees I saw momentarily a towering peak of white and gold, and then it was gone. When I caught my breath I reasoned that I must have imagined it or that it was some peak of the clouds, but I kept my eyes open. Soon I was rewarded and my doubts were dispelled as the whole range of Nanda Devi (as it proved to be) stood revealed. The unexpectedness of it, a sight I had not imagined before and would have thought impossible, left me paralysed as I saw it for the first time, magnificent against a light blue sky and with the setting sun tingeing the snows with gold. Now, of course, it is a familiar sight, but I shall never forget the effect that it produced.

Charles's diary records his first few days in hospital waiting for the operation:

11/1/44 Tuesday. Up early and in the morning I saw the surgeon and told him history, but he was busy till Thursday so I have to wait. Then went for walk round village and bought some clothes etc. Afternoon I wandered round grounds and repaired Matron's radio and wrote letters. Evening played cards from dinner till midnight and won 2/-.

12/1/44 Wednesday. In the morning I went to the club for billiards and snooker with another patient and a Doctor. Afternoon I went for walk into the village again and ordered corduroy slacks and shorts and shirt to be made and bought several small items. Spent rest of day playing cards and writing letters. Told they were operating on me on Saturday.

13/1/44 Thursday. Had a lot of rain off and on all day with bright patches as clouds passed through valleys. Did not go out but spent some time on nurses' radio and talking with Matron in her room. Wrote several letters and read a lot. Bed very early.

14/1/44 Friday. Was to have gone riding with one of the sisters in the morning but a Brigadier came visiting and we had to stay in. Then the Doc wanted to put some florescence in my eye to see if it would come through my nose. Afternoon had good sleep, then out to the village and collected from tailor the stuff I had ordered and to pictures. Disappointed as they did not show a continuous film, but disjointed sort of efforts. Back to dinner. Bed early for tomorrow.

15/1/44 Saturday. Had my operation today (15th) and it is now 20th and the first time I have felt like writing. I had bath and shave etc and then jab of morphine at 9.00 a.m. Taken to theatre at 10.00 a.m. and put straight under ether. Returned to ward at 12.30 p.m. but did not come round till 4.00 p.m. to be sick – I was really shattered and so off again till 6.00 p.m. This time after I had been sick again and sorted myself out I felt fairly OK except that half my face was bandaged because a pipe and a great lump of bloody gauze were hanging from my right nostril. But during night I got really awful head and face ache and sister could do nothing.

16/1/44 Sunday. Awake all night and still felt very painful in the morning. Doc called over and he said it was an antrum – a bunged up sinus. So gave me inhalation which cleared a lot of it almost at once. But though I felt lot better still a lot of headache all day and nose appendage very awkward. So could only lie in bed and think. Also had temp. Again I had a sleepless night but night sister helped a lot by keeping me company.

For the rest of that week Charles made a slow but uncomfortable recovery. It seems that many of the nursing staff were posted at this time, though the Surgeon, Major Healy, and another Doctor, Captain Hirst, monitored his progress. He was pleased when his personal kit arrived back after its unintended trip to Poona and back, but he was not yet in a condition to use it at all.

22/1/44 Saturday. It started to rain at 4.00 a.m. and continued with varying intensity throughout the day but it did no stop all morning. I went to theatre and without anaesthetic they removed tape and wire effort from the nose and eye and inserted a rubber plug like a golf tee between eye corner and nose with the top in corner of eye. This is of course far from comfortable, but better than the other. Further, with a shade I can now go out, and it rains! Spent day reading, writing letters etc and bed early. Had horrid nightmare last night.

23/1/44 Sunday. Eye very bunged up in the morning but after cleaning went along to theatre again where MO took out plug and syringed and probed and seemed satisfied, so put bung back all without dope again. Afternoon went for a short stroll but headache pretty bad. Was going to church in evening but left it too late so stayed in reading and bed late.

24/1/44 Monday. Woke and breakfast in bed again. Rain and snow intermittent all day. Morning to theatre again to have plug removed, cleaned and put back. Still uncomfortable and headache bad. Spent all day in reading and writing, and bed early. Listened to all sorts of tales about the bears, panthers, tigers and snakes sometimes seen up here.

25/1/44 Tuesday. Eye cleaned and replugged in ward with

MO showing sister how to do it. Then went for short walk to Almora. Afternoon went on road all way round peak via Gunga Doeli* and Rhanikhet and back. Evening very tired and bed early. Headache not too bad today and eye more comfortable.

26/1/44 Wednesday. Wash and breakfast in bed as usual. Sister dressed and changed plug in my eye and I stayed in for the rest of the morning as very dull. Afternoon went out and right down cudd side to bottom of valley through pine forest and through the terraced fields of the next valley dotted with little houses, then up valley to Gunga Doeli past an orange orchard and back along road. Got bath, change and spent evening reading. Bed late.

27/1/44 Thursday. Up later than usual. After eye dressed by Sister I went for walk past Post Office to *(unreadable)* Lodge and back by winding road down in the valley. Stayed in reading after lunch and then popped down to Sador bazaar for one or two things and the walk. Evening reading and bed early. A scare that panthers are about, as monkeys are unsettled and orderlies heard them. Seems unlikely though.

For a week the eye remained painful, and the process of cleaning and replacing the plug got no more comfortable. To add to the problems a small abscess developed and had to be drained. When he could Charles went for walks, but a few days of snow meant that even that relief from the boredom was denied him.

---

* Gunga Doeli cannot be located, and it appears in various spelling forms in Charles' diary. It probably refers to the modern village of Gianatoli about one mile west of Rhaniket as the crow flies, across a high ridge.

4/2/44 Friday. Feeling lots better but did not go out in day. In the morning Major Healy did my eye in theatre – painful but OK. Afternoon reading and writing and then to a film which was quite good. Bed very late.

5/2/44 Saturday. Up late and across to theatre early for Major Healy to show Captain Gee how to do it. Got very busy with probe explaining it – not very nice. Then sat in sun reading. Afternoon went for long walk in woods and back for hot bath etc and writing and bed early.

6/2/44 Sunday. Night sister called at 2.30 a.m. and as we were both awake stayed yarning for some time. Up late and Capt Gee came to prod the eye but could not get the syringe in, so left it! Reading. Afternoon changed into KD and went for grand walk along cudd side and to high point overlooking several valleys. Wonderful view. Back via Chabattia about ten miles in all. Very tired and bed early in evening.

7/2/44 Monday. Went across to theatre again in morning for syringe – still very painful. Then sat in sun and read. Afternoon it turned dull and later quite chilly and I went for a short walk in valley and to Gunga Doeli and bought some oranges from the orchard. Evening reading and bed early.

8/2/44 Tuesday. Usual sort of day and rather dull so did not go out. Evening to British Other Ranks' ward to play monopoly.

9/2/44 Wednesday. Miss Gee gave the old eye a real do this morning! But I did not even grunt. Afternoon went for short walk and bed early in evening after hot bath.

10/2/44 Thursday. Spent the morning sitting on lawn reading after eye was prodded. Afternoon went for short walk round valleys and back for quiet evening. Bed early.

11/2/44 Friday. Uneventful day except that eye was a bit more difficult to probe in the morning. Afternoon I went for walk to bazaar with Capt Clark, his first walk out for two months. Evening reading.

12/2/44 Saturday. Major Healy came to probe eye and could not get passage through, but said it did not matter. Very painful. Short walk with Clark again in the afternoon. Then all my mail arrived from the squadron. Sixty letters, so busy reading it and answering it. Nurse Fairy wrote eight letters, the last saying she thought it better to close friendship. Bed late.

13/2/44 Sunday. In the morning Miss Gee tried to pass cat gut through eye but then tried with putting syringe in first and passing through the syringe. I felt it come into nose, but she could not see it to pull right down and so had to abandon attempt. So went for grand long walk again with Sister MacFarlane all up rocky river bed in a deep valley. Evening very tired and bed early.

14/2/44 Monday. Up early feeling fine but then I was told that I had to go to theatre for another dose of gas in the afternoon! Went for stroll in the morning then in the afternoon on the table and they threaded catgut through the eye and out of the nose. When I woke at 6.00 p.m. it looked and felt very odd. Later in evening began to ache a lot and so bed early, but little sleep.

15/2/44 Tuesday. Up early but felt rotten all day long mainly with eye aching and swollen and head ache. So did not go out, but found it difficult even to write letters or read.

16/2/44 Wednesday. Two more bed patients came in in the morning. Eye feeling better and with wires pulled about a bit it feels like a clear passage through OK. Afternoon changed and went to club to tea at invitation of WVS. An excellent time and games afterwards. Evening eye

*Making the most of
the snowstorm.*

swollen again. Major Healy saw it and suggested lancing it as lots of pus. Lights failed, so bed early.

17/2/44 Thursday. Up early as not too comfortable night. But "pus pocket" they examined yesterday had gone down a bit. Nevertheless Miss Gee came at noon and lanced it but nothing came out! It was just solid stuff. So I don't know what they will do now! I had a game of tennis. Bit difficult with one eye but good fun. Had several letters and parcels in the afternoon and did lots of letter writing. Bed late.

18/2/44 Friday. Up early again but day turned to rain and in afternoon had terrific thunder storm and large hail stones as big as peas. So did not go out, just read and wrote and pottered around all day. Bed late.

19/2/44 Saturday. Had very heavy fall of snow till 10.00 a.m. when it lay very thick. Then quite suddenly the sun came out warmly from a clear blue sky and started the thaw. At 2.00 p.m. it started raining and thunder again and continued for rest of day. But in evening I went to cinema to see Dumbo and bed late.

For three days Charles could do little but read, go for walks and wait for his eye to heal. Unfortunately it got little better:

23/2/44 Wednesday. Unsettled sort of day till evening when it blew a real gale and rain as well. In the morning Miss Gee told me all about the operation. It had been quite a success at first and finally Major Healy was going to connect the hole he made with the eye. But the abscess spoilt it and when the peg came out the hole was smaller than he wanted and now he is disappointed. But he still has hopes. They had looked all round inside eye for holes etc. Went for short walk to the bazaar in the afternoon.

24/2/44 Thursday. Rained steadily and heavily all morning but by evening had cleared up well and so we took two sisters to see Dangerous Moonlight with Warsaw Concerto. Spent rest of day reading again.

25/2/44 Friday. Quiet morning in while weather cleared up. Then in the afternoon went riding with orderly. After an hour his horse got frisky so we decided to change. But while getting on his it threw me over other side. Fortunately I hung on to reins and kept its head down, and also did not hurt eye, only got a nose bleed. We left horses to have a smoke and they galloped back. So we had to walk! When mail came in found my promotion to Flight Lieutenant was through so celebrate with the Captain and orderly with surplus bottles of beer. Late in evening went to station dance – did not dance – and bed late.

Still Charles had to wait to see if the operation was a success. His Doctors were becoming less optimistic:

2/3/44 Thursday. Miss Gee still seems to think nothing more can be done with my eye. In the morning I played tennis with Sister and in the afternoon I went for long walk with an orderly down to Gagas valley over 4000 ft down and eight miles away. Grand going down – almost tropical and back part way up a river bed, but climbing up the cudd side again very hard going. Bed at 6.30 p.m. very tired but satisfied. Hot bath and cold shower and reading. Bed late.

3/3/44 Friday. Very hot day but did not go out. All I did was sit outside in sun and get burnt. Reading and playing gramophone. Then in the evening went to films and then bed early.

4/3/44 Saturday. Spent day moving stuff into new day room, sitting out reading and then Major Healy came round. Said my wire could come out of eye. Afternoon went for long walk with a Brigadier who had just come in to show him paths round etc. Evening wire taken out, but cannot tell yet whether eye OK or not. Played cards and read and wrote in evening. Bed early.

5/3/44 Sunday. Spent the morning in the garden. Miss Gee came round and said operation was definitely unsuccessful and she did not know what Healy would do. Afternoon went for long walk and in evening got lost in jungle paths in wrong valleys. Did some very rapid walking to get out of them before dark, and just made the road in time. Very unpleasant while it lasted. Arrived back very late and very tired after about twenty miles. Bath and bed.

6/3/44 Monday. Stayed in gardens all day as Major Healey

Panther's Pool.

was coming to see me, but did not come till evening. Said then that he would try syringing the eye again tomorrow, but if it did not work he was not optimistic about doing another operation on it.

7/3/44 Tuesday. In the morning I went across to theatre and Major Healy gave eye a prod through and finally said it was unsuccessful and the he would do nothing more. Felt very disappointed about it all. Afternoon played tennis and lost a ball. Evening reading.

8/3/44 Wednesday. Morning sitting in garden reading etc. Afternoon went for another long walk to Panther's Pool and back. Hot bath etc, reading and bed.

9/3/44 Thursday. Got permission from Miss Gee for day off Saturday and arranged discharge for Monday.

10/3/44 Friday. Stayed in all day as I had arranged to go out for day tomorrow in car to Almora. But in evening found could not get car. In garden all day and afternoon played tennis.

11/3/44 Saturday. Still very hot. Morning reading and

View from Hospital at Rhanikhet to Himalayas and Nanda Devi.

writing. Afternoon went on another long walk to try to get to reservoir, but again got lost in so many valleys and forests and so we made our way back eventually to Chabattia and back early – 7.00 p.m. Bath and bed early. Had planned to go to Naini Tal tomorrow but called it off as doubt about getting back in time, or at all.

12/3/44 Sunday. Up early and got down to wait for bus to Naini Tal, but it was late and we thought we had missed it. The Padre's car passed us and he asked if we were going to Almora, so thinking he was we went and waited on the road for him. But he did not go. Afternoon sleeping and reading. Evening to pictures and bed very late.

So Charles's stay in hospital drew to an unsuccessful close. He was frustrated at being away from his squadron for so long to so little effect. Nonetheless, he had made the most of his enforced idleness, and as always recorded his impressions of the area in his journal:

Monkeys on Hospital Roof.

Just came back from a really wonderful walk all along the cudd side, among trees and boulders and up to a high bluff which towered above several valleys which could be seen winding away among the ridges into the distance. I must go again, though it is a long way, as it is a sight I shall not see again. But all round Rhanikhet are some grand walks as it is on one of many wooded ridges and the valleys and cudd sides are really wonderful. From the hospital too, I have a regular view of Nanda Khot and Nanda Devi ridge. It never gets stale, always a wonderful and inspiring sight.

Monkeys are common animals here, swinging among trees and onto roof tops and lawns. Very strange to see them at large, but curious animals and always good for a laugh. Just now there are lots of rumours about panthers about, possibly with some degree of truth in them. A man killing tiger is definitely at large at Kathgodam, and bears are about 30 miles north.

Rhanikhet Main Street.

Common sights here are the clouds blowing about down in the valleys, the snow blowing off Nanda Devi etc in clouds, always from the West. Little earthenware pots stuck below huge gashes in pine trees to catch resin. Men walking about with a length of rope and weight on the end which they throw over dead branches and pull them off for firewood. Also men walking about with a handful of wool which they twist into yarn and wind on a stick. Many of the men here knit it up too. The bazaar here is a typical village bazaar, two rows of small shops selling everything. And it is amazing, the variety there. One can get almost anything. Round the other side of the bluff is another small village – Gunga Doeli, about sixty percent of which is native brothels.

One thing I have noticed about the children here. They are all a begging, whining lot, miserably asking for baksheesh. Unlike their Arabic equivalent who is a cheerful and mischievous brat, almost always with a smile as he asks for baksheesh.

Rhanikhet "Street of Brothels".

The thing that I find sticks out most – apart from the mountains of course – are my numerous walks. Short and long, and the many strange and unusual sights. The terraced valleys, poorly cultivated by hand and with oxen. The houses with the back usually up the edge of a terrace and the roof on a level with it, and often broken. And the front yard, rectangular and crazy paved and with surrounding wall. And in these yards women and oxen who sleep in the next room. The haystacks were very odd – built in the trees and hanging all round the trunk, high off the ground like a straw skirt.

In the woods – mostly pine and firs, but often well mixed with deciduous trees – were a fine variety of coloured birds. Very wee chota ones, very multicoloured and some as big as a pigeon, blue and with long (twelve inches) bright

348

'Haystacks' near Gunga Doeli.

blue tail not to mention the Kite Hawks. In the green mess of the trees, the most outstanding sight was the tall rhododendron trees, as high as some of the firs and with large rich red blooms.

Panther's Pool when I found it was returning to its natural state. Two years previously the Lancashire Fusiliers had enlarged it, deepened it and lined it with cement to make a bathing pool, complete with diving board. Now it is silted up and neglected. But in obliterating man's work it is showing the superiority of nature for the achievement of the beautiful.

349

The Gagas valley is a terrifically inspiring sight from Rhanikhet, and so it is all the way down the very winding track that chooses the loveliest way down and winds in and out of all the rushing side streams. At the bottom 4000 ft below, one finds more cloud in it in spite of the width of the valley. The river is wide and fairly slow, winding in and out among the small hills, and fairly well populated with fish, particularly a hill trout. A modern bridge crossed it where we ended and surrounding it were several villages. But the heat! Gee what a difference.

Another interesting – nay delightful – walk was along the "pipe line". This carries the water supply to Rhanikhet and runs all along the valley side, through a gorge, and right down to the bottom of a valley and up the other side from an elusive reservoir. Three times I tried to find it and each time got side-tracked down the wrong valleys. But I did see it once, "way down there". It is amazingly easy to get lost in those valleys. The way they spread out and wind about, as I know to my cost when I got lost in the woods in one late afternoon and thought I would be benighted there. Around these valleys often would be a few piles of smouldering detritus of the Charcoal Burners, as done in Britain in the year dot.

But I had to leave it all at last, and as I re-travelled the road to Kathgodam in the old Ford bus, first of all winding in a leisurely way among the wide open valleys as far as Gunram Pance, then up again tortuously among the thickly wooded narrow valleys to Bhowali and Bravry, I felt thoroughly satiated with a wealth and warmth of magnificent natural beauty – more majestic that anything I have ever seen. Here I saw baboons for the first time – long tailed baboons. Then the valley widened out and round a corner I saw the flat green haze of the hot plains, way down below ahead. And slowly we wound down there to this uninteresting spectacle, while I feverishly drank in the last of all the beauty that I was so soon to leave behind perhaps for ever.

13/3/44 Monday. Spent the morning packing and seeing the CO, saying goodbyes etc. After lunch caught bus on interesting trip to Kathgodam and again admired the beauty of the valleys. Sleeping berth from there to Lucknow and slept most of the way but only fitfully.

14/3/44 Tuesday. Arrived Lucknow at 8.00 a.m. and got a berth on the 9.35 a.m. to Calcutta with a Yank and three airmen who could not get a second class seat. Uninteresting journey on the whole, over flat dry country which was just the same when I turned in.

As usual, Charles recorded his impressions of the journey in his journal. As the crow flies the distance he was to travel was more than 800 miles, and with the windings and turns of the Indian railways and other means of transport, he had probably to cover well over a thousand miles. Furthermore he had only the vaguest idea of his destination, for 117 Squadron was on the move.

The train journey from Kathgodam to Lucknow was mainly at night, but from Lucknow onwards I saw some of the real plains of India. Almost all the way across was flat plain with patches of mainly deciduous trees. The country was dry but most of the land was cultivated, the crops for the most part being poor grain crops and all looking yellow. A few areas of root crops and canes were here and there. In the east the isolated native villages became poorer and poorer, and at the stations many poor specimens were always there to ask for food.

One particular sight impressed me. We were waiting at a platform, but across the rails on the other line another train was waiting and the coaches opposite were full of schoolgirls (St Vincent's School) of all ages obviously going to the hills for the season, well-to-do and well fed. Between us were scraggy, starving women and children asking for food and about a dozen mangy dogs and several monkeys. Those girls were ignoring the human cry for food and throwing slices of bread and butter to the dogs and monkeys to watch them scrap for it while the women and children could only watch the food being thrown out of their reach.

As we got further east there were more signs of industrialisation – small coal fields, brick works, cement works etc, alongside of the line, and here as usual at least half of the coolie work was done by the women, all with the small basket on their heads. A few large ponds of stagnant water were to be seen, usually with a few attendant herons. Nearer Calcutta the ponds became swamps and the vegetation dirty, tangled and tropical in swampy areas, with bananas, bamboos and fern. One remarkable tree had nothing in the way of foliage except bright red flowers. Calcutta I found like all other towns. In the European area were fine big buildings, trams, taxis, parks and lots of natives, and rickshaw carriages and strange box looking carriages. The native bazaar was like them all – a series of stalls selling stuff – good, bad and indifferent and of a more limited variety than usual at any price that they could get. Some of the streets were narrow, crowded and with very small shops all along the pavement. Others were residential with large houses on either side and tree lined and wide.

The railway was through a flat green country, not a tropical swamp as I expected. Just wet and grassy, with the villages all in clumps of bamboo and banana trees and houses made almost entirely of bamboo and rushes. The ferry to Chandapur showed us many strange river craft from rafts to paddle steamers, with the shallow draught, high bow and stern and single sails as seen everywhere east of Cairo. The banks were either sandy waste or green grass land, and near the forest or clump of trees were the bamboo villages.

The diary again gives the bare bones of the journey onwards from Calcutta, but does not go into the details. It is clear that he had but little idea of where his squadron was now located, and he seems to have had to use considerable initiative in locating it and in planning a route to reach it. Certainly he used every conceivable means of transport to get there!

> 15/3/44 Wednesday. Woke early and found country still the same. But as we got nearer Calcutta it got more industrial and vegetation more tropical. Arrived Calcutta 3.20 p.m. and found bags of red tape, noise, heat and dirt so decided not to stay – and all hotels full. Could not get an aircraft so caught midnight train.
> 16/3/44 Thursday. Early morning had to get on a ferry steamer which left 10.30 a.m. to go down the river to Chandapur where again in the dark I got on another train and went to sleep.

The rather scruffy writing in Charles's diary appears to give the destination of his ferry trip at "Calpor" – which cannot be located – but it is likely that he in fact refers to Chandapur on the Meghna river, and that his train journey from Calcutta was to somewhere such as Faridpur, which is the closest railhead to Chandapur. The times of arrival and departure would certainly make that route a likely one.

No 117 Squadron Accommodation at Sylhet.

17/3/44 Friday. Arrived Comilla 3.00 a.m. and could not
find out where the squadron was or get any information.
So had to walk about till daylight because of mosquitoes.
Then found they had gone to Sylhet. Rang them and
Wing and finally got on an aircraft from 62 Squadron,
when I had my first wash and meal since yesterday
morning. Arrived squadron 3.00 p.m. Proceeded to get
tent, bearer and settled in, finding kit etc. The Doctor
said I should have to have a board and would probably
have to go home as not fit for operational flying.

During Charles's absence No. 117 Squadron had been
extremely busy. Indeed, he had missed the most interesting and
rewarding period in the squadron's history. Throughout January
1944 they had continued their training, and five aircraft and
crews were detached to join Special Forces operations at
Gwalior. In mid-February the squadron was on the move again.
The Operations Record Book records the details. It is probable
that the Operations Record Book entries for this period were
written by Charles himself, for as we shall see later he was given
this task while he awaited a decision on his flying career.

354

(On the 16th February) ten aircraft moved our own and No 177 Wing's advance parties to Bengal, their crews defying appalling weather conditions on the return trip in order to attend the squadron's combined messes dance. This was held at the Astoria Club and was as successful as its predecessor in December, though the watery quality of the beer evoked remarks which were far from complimentary to the contractor's pride of ancestry. Two days later (19th), with low cloud and drenching rain driving across the aerodrome and loaded well above the Plimsoll line, the squadron took off for Lalmai, our new base in Bengal. The weather across India varied from bad to unflyable, so that by nightfall the squadron was widely sprinkled over India from Ranchi to Comilla where Flight Lieutenant P G D Roberts landed in a dust storm by the light of two jeep headlamps.

Clearly the conditions required all the flying skills of the crews. However, their new home was described as being much more comfortable, with accommodation in bamboo "bashers" instead of tents. In the last week of February the squadron were employed in delivering supplies to British forces in the Akran. Then at the end of the month the aircraft were sent to be fitted with mule stalls! By 4 March all but two of the squadron aircraft were deployed forward to Tulthal to support Operation Thursday – the beginning of the campaign led by Wingate to drive the Japanese out of Burma. The Operations Record Book again tells the story:

We all knew of the brilliant exploits of Wingate's Chindit columns who in the early months of 1943 had marched from India across the Chin Hills and the River Chindwin, into North Central Burma spreading chaos and confusion far behind the Jap lines. We had read how they had been maintained by supply dropping Dakotas and how one aircraft of No 31 Squadron had executed a brilliant landing on a jungle clearing in order to evacuate the casualties of one column. We were now shown how the lessons of that expedition were to a plan whose scope and imagination was unparalleled in air history and on which the squadron would be employed for some time to come. The scheme was to tow gliders containing aerodrome construction parties complete with bulldozers and a number of shock troops east of the Irrawaddy into North Burma, land them in jungle clearings which, in less than twenty four hours, were to be made into landing strips fit to receive Dakotas carrying troops and mules together with all the paraphernalia of jungle warfare. The whole of these initial landings were to be carried out in 6 nights, and the troops so transported, whilst fanning out across the Jap Lines of Communications were to be maintained by nightly supply drops.

The first night sorties were to have been flown exclusively by the USAF, but at the eleventh hour HQ 177 Wing were asked to supply six aircraft to complete a drop of such stores and equipment as could not be carried in the gliders. We put up two machines flown by the Commanding Officer and by Squadron Leader W J McLean AFC who came back with much useful information as to the form of operations and the general lay of the land.

On the following afternoon, the 6th, fourteen of our aircraft together with others of Nos 62 and 194 Squadrons, flew over to Talikandi, which was to be our operating base for the first three nights. There with extreme coolness and efficiency, we were marshalled and loaded. As the first strings of mules came walking down the runway our crews cast anxious looks at the aircraft, remembering the days when they had carried Generals, Film Stars and other such delectable cargoes, and wondering mournfully what the condition of the cabins would be at the end of this party. This anxiety was groundless, for most of the animals took to the air nonchalantly, though they were not above expressing impatience during the period before take off by smashing the bucket slats and kicking out the odd window. Of the two hundred and sixty eight animals which the squadron flew in, only one, a mule, got out of hand during flight. In his attempts to despatch it into the eternal quietude its Muleteer put six .38 bullets into its neck. This definitely had a pacifying effect, but on arriving at Broadway the mule disemplaned under its own power and walked somewhat shakily away; some beast!

On the first night a heavy haze over Burma caused some difficulty in locating the strip (Broadway). Nevertheless an inflow was maintained at such a high rate that by the 8th we were half a night ahead of schedule and began the second phase by operating from Tulthal into Chowringhee – the Southern Strip.

The strip at Tulthal was anything but ideal for use by large numbers of aircraft since with every movement dense clouds of dust rose off its runway surface creating an atmosphere comparable to a London pea soup fog. This with aircraft taking off simultaneously from the centre towards either end. It was under such conditions and due to misunderstandings that two of our machines, B and R, each ignorant of the other's presence, opened up together and collided on the strip, B's starboard mainplane hitting R's port wing. Fortunately the situation was retrieved before further damage occurred. It speaks worlds for the efficiency and enthusiasm of our groundcrews, who throughout this detachment under extremely trying circumstances, worked superlatively well, that within forty eight hours they had B serviceable again by mating it to R's sound wing. R was handed to the RSU who were working on her when the Japs finished her career by dropping a bomb in close proximity. Despite this untoward incident we fulfilled our commitments, flying double sorties where necessary, until the night of the 11/12th when six of our crews finished the job by flying in the groundcrews, supplies and spares of the Spitfire Flight which was to be based on Broadway. During the seven nights and in 106 sorties the squadron flew 334 hours and carrying into the two strips a total of 1323 troops, 221 mules and 47 horses, together with considerable quantities of barbed wire, petrol, oil, jeeps and other items of equipment.

One of the amazing and pleasing features of this show was the slowness with which the Jap reacted. Each strip was lit up with a double flare path and extensive dispersal areas and throughout the nights fully lighted aircraft were landing at least one every three minutes. Yet the only opposition experienced was some half-hearted flak over Homalin, although Chowringhee was thoroughly bombed and strafed some two hours after it had been evacuated.

Such was the pace of events that on 11 March the squadron was on the move yet again, this time to Sylhet. Here the squadron regrouped, with the five aircraft detached to Gwalior rejoining their colleagues from Lalmai and Tulthal. The squadron was also reinforced by four new crews from the United Kingdom, replacing experienced crews who had been sent home earlier in the year. Alas, they now faced a further deterioration in the weather, as cumulonimbus clouds formed over the hills, rising to 15,000 feet or more. It was at this point that Charles rejoined the squadron. Like most aircrew, Charles wanted to get back in the air. In a letter to his sister Margaret he tells how he nearly managed it!

I am in Calcutta now waiting for a medical board, but it is a long story. After my long long trip to the squadron, the first person I saw was my Flight Commander. After the usual enquiries he said "Well Chuck, now that your pilot has gone home, you can fly with me if you like". I nodded. "And we are on a job tomorrow." Well, this suited my and I was very pleased. But when I saw the Doc, showed him the specialist's report and told him I was starting tomorrow, he just told me I was not and he would not pass me as fit till I had a medical board, and I could not persuade him any old how.

So I decided I could not wait till he made an appointment, and after a couple of days, flew down to gate crash in and get it over. So tomorrow I have to go and do some convincing talking to hard bitter medicos.

The diary tells the story:

18/3/44 Saturday. Spent the morning in the Orderly Room, Accounts, flights etc. and looking for lost kit bag which I did find. Afternoon letter writing and see Doc who definitely would not let me fly till I had had a board. Bed very early. All my mail had just been sent to hospital so I don't know when I'll see it now.

19/3/44 Sunday. Up early and spent day wandering around doing nothing in particular. In the morning completed three months back 540s. Evening drinking and bed early.

20/3/44 Monday. Arranged to go by early aircraft tomorrow for medical board and fixed up priority with them. Evening took over Duty Officer for night to see aircraft off on a "drop". But they were all recalled due to weather and so I got to bed early.

21/3/44 Tuesday. Caught the 8.00 a.m. Yank plane to Dum Dum via Comilla. Arrived Calcutta 1.30 p.m. Then to transit camp who could not book me or give me a temporary duty certificate. So on to Air Headquarters where I booked in. Saw SMO re-board. Then I found a hotel at 2.30 p.m. for bath etc. and out for stroll to do some shopping and have a look round, but was not impressed. Evening wrote letters and went to cinema second house. Back at 11.30 p.m. and bed.

22/3/44 Wednesday. In the morning I walked right down Chowringhee and about mile and half beyond looking for Central Medical Board. Found it eventually about 11.00 a.m. and made appointment for tomorrow and walked back to Hotel. Did about five miles. Afternoon went for short stroll and booked for theatre. Then letter writing till dinner. BESA concert at theatre and quite good. Very impressed with Yogi.

23/3/44 Thursday. Up early and off to Board, which with all the waiting and long explanations and deliberations with eye chappie took all morning. Finally rated unfit for flying in India. Very disappointed at first, but as day wore on got used to idea of possibility of going home. Afternoon to BHQ to book out and even met all sorts of people I knew in lounge. Dinner and to cinema.

24/3/44 Friday. Up early and out to Dum Dum via the Fort to see about an aircraft back. Could not book so back to town and shopping etc. Afternoon to cinema as the only cool place. Ditto in evening after a lot of letters and dinner. But when we came out found terrific thunderstorm with continuous lightning and streets and pavements awash. Six inches of water outside hotel. So up trousers and through it.

25/3/44 Saturday. Up late, got on with packing slowly and made way out to Dum Dum. Had to wait till 3.30 p.m. (without lunch) but I did get a plane – a meat plane to Dinjan where I spent the night at the Yank transit mess, but too late for dinner. Had pretty poor night.

26/3/44 Sunday. Got up early enough to catch 7.00 a.m. mail plane to Sylhet where I was very glad of some food and a wash. Quite a lot of mail for me including tobacco. Spent day repacking my stuff in big trunk I had bought and found grey flannels, KD, slacks, some shirts and underclothes were missing. Did usual booking and wrote letters. Bed early.

27/3/44 Monday. Spent most of day just sitting round tent and mess reading and writing. And that was about all we did.

28/3/44 Tuesday. Another idle day doing nothing in particular. Reading and writing. squadron history. Went into Sylhet town in the afternoon – not much to see except bridge. In the morning the first aircraft failed to return – Jock Lusted.

The loss of Warrant Officer A. J. Lusted and his crew was the first for about a year, and was a major blow. The aircraft had been seen starting its approach to a dropping zone, but had not completed it. Troops in the area later signalled that the aircraft had been seen to crash near the DZ, and that they had found the wreck and buried the crew.

29/3/44 Wednesday. Nothing particular all day and bed early.

30/3/44 Thursday. Up early to take over Duty Officer and

Charles uses the limited bathing facilities at Sylhet.

Ops Control for one week, and kept pretty busy running round all day and up late.

31/3/44 Friday. Duty Officer and kept busy from crack of dawn to late. Running round organising night sorties etc.

1/4/44 Saturday. As yesterday except that we had a chota monsoon and I was not able to get down to see the tent and so everything got very wet.

2/4/44 Sunday. Usual busy day and my jeep came out of MT. So had something to run round in. Evening fairly quiet, but big party in the mess. Went on all night.

3/4/44 Monday. This evening I made a boob by plotting a DZ incorrectly on the map, and the CO was going there! Neither of the aircraft found the correct one. Fortunately I was covered as I had the correct DZ on the briefing board. Bed early very tired.

Being grounded, Charles was kept employed as Operations Duty Officer until it was decided what his future was to be. The misplotting of the DZ was a serious error, for the squadron's record so far was outstanding in the reliability of its deliveries to the ground forces. However, the squadron Operations Record Book makes no mention of this failure to reach the DZ on this date, although on 5 April one of the Flight Commanders brought back his load as the DZ was not found in the given position. Perhaps either Charles or the Operations Record Book got the dates mixed up.

4/4/44 Tuesday. Heavy rain off and on all day, and I had to do a lot of running round with the Jeep, so got pretty wet! Not much action in evening so bed early. Had jab for cholera and ATT in the afternoon and that made my arm quite stiff.

5/4/44 Wednesday. As far as work went – a usual day. But in the afternoon I was told I was on my way! Evening up very late as lots of changes in program and bad weather. In fact did not get to bed till 4.00 a.m. as had to take lots of overdue action. But all the aircraft returned OK.

6/4/44 Thursday. Up 7.00 a.m. and on the job only to have another hectic day and fed up with running about and trying to get things organised. Dead tired when I went to bed at 11.30 p.m. Officially posted.

7/4/44 Friday. Another busy day till noon when I handed over and started packing and getting cleared etc. Evening had intended having a farewell party, but everyone flying and I was tired, so bed early.

CHAPTER 13

The Journey Home

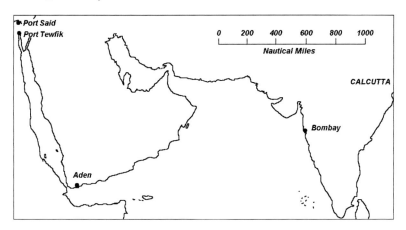

Charles's Travels – 8th April to 12 May 1944.

While Charles's trip from UK to his overseas squadron had taken a matter of a few days in 1942, the journey home was to take much longer. On 2 April 1944 he had been officially posted to GHQ Bombay, whose task it would be to arrange his repatriation. That was his destination when he left Sylhet on 8 April.

> 8/4/44 Saturday. Up very early and on plane to Calcutta. Took a nurse down and I fixed a date with her. Stayed at Grand and met her at 4.00 p.m. Spent all the afternoon with her but she had other plans for evening and as I had done a lot of running about I went to bed early. At transit camp they said I could go to Bombay when I wanted. Remembered I had left my flying clothing card on the squadron.
>
> 9/4/44 Sunday. Up early and out to Dum Dum to meet our aircraft in and ask them all about my flying clothing

card. Took all morning. Met the nurse at noon for lunch and ran around Calcutta with her in the afternoon and getting her fitted up with an aircraft back today. Got her on Mac's aircraft in the evening, but the other aircraft was unserviceable so I brought crew in again and showed them where to go etc. Evening drinking in lounge and bed late.

10/4/44 Monday. Up very early. Down for photograph but not ready. Then out to Dum Dum waiting for plane all morning, for my clothing card, but it did not turn up! Afternoon lots of shopping till nearly dinner time and then did not get all I wanted. Evening stayed in reading and bed early.

11/4/44 Tuesday. Another futile wait on Dum Dum aerodrome till noon, and no clothing card. Afternoon round bazaars again looking for things and realized what a poor sort of chap I was at buying things. Evening to film and bed late.

12/4/44 Wednesday. Up early and round doing last minute shopping. Then at noon found that tailor had not finished the sports coat and flannels he promised. Terrific rush at noon to be ready for transport, but got to station in plenty of time. Sharing a carriage with a civvy going to see his wife off to England. Turned in very early.

13/4/44 Thursday. Not too good a night and early start rolling up my bed etc. While stropping my razor and talking cut top of my finger very badly and only stopped bleeding by tight bandage till next stop where found a Doctor to clean it and bandage properly. Day spent reading and looking out of window at monotonous plains and hard working natives. Bed early.

14/4/44 Friday. Arrived Bombay 11.00 a.m. after very

interesting run down West Ghats*. Change made me sing and laugh. At the station everything was well organised. RTO rang for truck which took me first to SSQ, SHQ and billet in flats on South Point. After lunch to town for look and shopping and meet Bea for tea and dinner at Chinese restaurant. And while in town two terrific explosions occurred in docks – ammo ship went up. Many killed and lots of damage. Panic in town amazing, broken glass etc and rushing transport. Came back in bus full of babbling Indians.

The explosions that Charles heard were indeed terrific. An ammunition ship, the *Fort Stikine*, had blown up while in dock. The damage was immense, and the docks were not back in full use until November 1944. An inquiry into the causes and the lessons to be learned was commissioned under Sir Leonard Stone, the Chief Justice of the High Court of Judicature at Bombay. His preliminary report into the causes of the explosion was published in September 1944, and it demonstrates how a series of errors and small events, each minor when taken in isolation, can lead to a catastrophe.

The *Fort Stikine* had been taken over by the Ministry of War under the Lend Lease agreement. It had left Birkenhead on 24 February 1944 with a cargo of aircraft, general stores, explosives and ammunition. It also carried one hundred and twenty-four gold bars to the value of about £2,000,000, sent by the bank of England to help to stabilise the Indian Rupee. Part of this cargo had been discharged at Karachi at the end of March, and the empty space had been filled with other cargo. This consisted mainly of cotton, but also included resin, lubricating oil, sulphur and other commodities. The commission described the method of taking on cargo as "haphazard", and noted that there

* The West Ghats are the mountains running down the coast near Bombay.

had been no protest about the cargo, although there was evidence that the Chief Officer, who was killed in the explosion, had expressed concern about the cotton stowage.

Under normal circumstances a ship with such a hazardous cargo would have been barred from entering the docks, but Defence Rules of India allowed this rule to be suspended if a high ranking military Officer signed a "Certificate of Great Urgency". Such a certificate had indeed been signed. During the lunch period on 14 April, when no watch was on duty, a fire broke out in No. 2 hold of the vessel. Its seriousness was not at first realised, and when it was realised that there was a major risk, several senior Officers came aboard. These included the Docks General Manager, the head of the Fire Brigade, the Chief Salvage Officer of the Royal Indian Navy and an Officer attached to the Indian Army Ordnance Corps. The report dryly describes the results of their discussions:

> These Officers all expressed divergent opinions as to the course of action to be taken and the Master could not make up his mind.

By this time thirty-two hoses were fighting the fire, and there had been an unsuccessful attempt to get at the seat of the fire by cutting a hole in the ship's side. Again, the report sums up the events:

> There is little doubt that the water projected into the lower hold floated some of the burning cotton upward, thereby bringing it towards the underside of the magazine and increasing the heat there until ignition took place. At about 3.45 p.m. some of the explosive must have ignited, as smoke and fierce flames appeared. At 3.50 p.m. the firemen were ordered to withdraw. No steps had been taken

to batten down no 4 hatch, which contained explosives more dangerous and in greater quantity than No 2. No effective warning was given to any other ship in the docks and the Fort Stikine was not flying the red flag indicating that she had explosives on board. At 4.06 p.m. when the firemen were still quite near the Fort Stikine, there was a terrific explosion. Government House, the Bombay Municipality, Police Headquarters, the Chairman of the Port Trust and Naval headquarters thereby received their first intimation that something unusual had happened. .... At 4.33 p.m. a second explosion occurred with the detonation of No 4 hold. The total casualties in the disaster include at least nine hundred killed and missing.

The first explosion scattered blazing bales of cotton around the harbour area and set hundreds of acres of the city on fire. Also blown into the air were the one hundred and twenty-four gold bars. Most were apparently soon recovered, but others were found some thirty years later during harbour dredging operations. The report into the incident found a number of causes of the disaster. The state of war meant that there was no alternative to the ship being in dock. It criticised the stowage of the cotton in the hold, the failure to realise how serious the fire was, and, most tellingly, the absence of any centralised executive control of the fire-fighting.

A series of telegrams from the military authorities in Bombay to the Secretary of State for India summarised the damage. The *Fort Stikine* is described as "blown to atoms". A 4000 ton freighter was lifted bodily twenty feet onto the quayside. The Prince's and the Victoria Docks were rendered unusable. Some sixteen ships had been sunk or damaged, about half of which could be moved out of the area under tow. Most important, however, although about half the Bombay dock capacity was out of action, it was believed that there would not be a serious effect on operations in Burma.

Perhaps unsurprisingly, movement of British forces around Bombay was much curtailed. Charles could only wait for a ship home:

15/4/44 Saturday. Up early and spent the morning pottering round getting what gen I could – not much. Afternoon set off to go for a swim, but found all confined to camp. So wandered round native stalls and made a few purchases. Evening went to camp cinema.

16/4/44 Sunday. Laid in a bit and then repacked a lot of my kit. Afternoon went to Willingdon Club for swim and spent the afternoon there. Very nice, cool and clean. Evening pictures again.

17/4/44 Monday. Confined to camp again and I wanted to go and see Bea, arrange for card to be sent home, and collect photos! In the morning I went to SSQ, Adjutant, Moochi with shoes and shopping. Afternoon got more gen about kit so repacked it all and listed it. Difficulty about diary, notes, photos etc. that I wanted to take. Hid it where possible – also silk etc. Evening reading. Bed early.

18/4/44 Tuesday. Up early and as still confined to camp, down to Adjutant to get permission to go to town. Told them that on boat tomorrow. So rushed in to get films and travellers cheques, but no time to see Bea. Got involved with bus and trams coming out and wasted an hour. Afternoon finished packing, to SHQ for insurance of kit, booking out etc and to bazaar for final purchases. Also down again in evening. Lots of final packing and marking of baggage – wanted – hold – cabin – invalid's baggage. Red crosses all over it. Bed late.

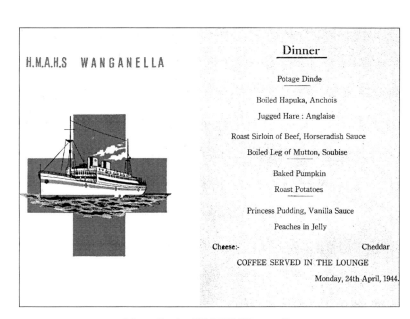

H.M.A.H.S   WANGANELLA

Dinner

Potage Dinde

Boiled Hapuka, Anchois

Jugged Hare : Anglaise

Roast Sirloin of Beef, Horseradish Sauce

Boiled Leg of Mutton, Soubise

Baked Pumpkin

Roast Potatoes

Princess Pudding, Vanilla Sauce

Peaches in Jelly

Cheese:-   Cheddar

COFFEE SERVED IN THE LOUNGE

Monday, 24th April, 1944.

Menu Card – HMAHS Wanganella.

19/4/44 Wednesday. Up at crack of dawn and final packing, hasty breakfast and lashings of coolies to load all kit in lorries and so away to docks. Here all kit, regardless, was taken into hold leaving us only one small case each and most of us had not packed on this scale so we all wore dirty clothes with no choice of a change. Changed all our cash to English and got on board with no chance of getting off again. Assigned to a ward and proceeded to look round. Found all very acceptable. Staff very good and ship spacious. Food excellent. Left all my cleaning materials at camp! Bed early.

Once more Charles was with the Australians, for he was embarked on the Australian Hospital ship HMAHS *Wanganella* for the first part of his journey back to UK. It seems to have been a comfortable ship, and the menus certainly showed no signs of wartime austerity!

20/4/44 Thursday. Up early. Spent the morning getting more gen, reading on deck and trying to get into the hold to get my kit, but no luck. More troops (casualties walking and lying) came on board and their kit was loaded. At 3.00 p.m. we cast off from India. Spent a long time going round and round in harbour swinging compass and degaussing. Finally, dropped pilot and steamed full speed out of sight of land. Do not feel sea sick! Strange at night to see a ship all lighted up from the ship itself. The MO came round and now for first time I have four hourly washing of eye.

21/4/44 Friday. A long day over a fairly calm sea with nothing to see but sea. But a cool breeze to allay the hot sun. Had spot of sunbathing in area at stern. Afternoon I saw the MO and had eye bathe. But spent whole day reading and grand idle life of luxury. Rumours, of course, still flying found ship. Saw plenty of flying fish. Had five excellent meals and evening to bed well contented at 9.00 p.m. Clock going back nightly.

22/4/44 Saturday. In the morning we had a thing arranged with Army, but they did not turn up. Played deck quoits and had sun bathe in stern, but not so much wind and so very hot. In fact sea almost calm as we ploughed through it at about 15 kts. Afternoon I got into hold at last for some clean clothes and then did some washing. Had beer issue, evening community singing and a film show and then some good music on grand piano. Bed early. So far have broken one glass.

23/4/44 Sunday. Quieter day (yesterday we saw a convoy and a destroyer signalled "Good luck"). Several services all day. Went in the morning and did not know till then that it was St George's day. Spent most of day reading and did not get a lot of sun bathing in.

Also sorted my photos and found I had lost one whole roll of film. Sea still calmer than yesterday and a few more clouds in the sky.

24/4/44 Monday. A very quiet day, sea calmer, less or no wind and getting humid near Aden I guess. Did some sun bathing and heard lots of rumours. Spent most of day reading and bed early. Saw porpoise.

25/4/44 Tuesday. Woke up in the morning to find Aden in sight. Moored outside for a bit. Then after a while pilot came out and took us in to refuelling point and took on oil and water. A good wind blowing, so not too hot. Seemed funny to be looking at Aden again from this angle. Could not get ashore. Afternoon spent in sticking in the rest of my snaps and now complete. Pulled out about 3.30 p.m. and set off for Perim with a following wind.

26/4/44 Wednesday. Passed through Dead Man's Straights first thing in the morning then later passed the *(unreadable)* and throughout day passed odd ships. On the whole a quiet day. Very hot in evening. Went to pictures.

27/4/44 Thursday. In the morning did some more washing. Saw the MO and had a hair cut. Then a spot of sun bathing before lunch. Lazy afternoon with a little bit of sun bathing. Saw whole school of dolphins having a real jumping session. Evening went down to the stern and had several glasses of beer with some of the Australian crew. Swapped yarns and had a go on a *(unreadable)*. Good types.

28/4/44 Friday. Up late! All sorts of gen about Britain being a closed fortress from last midnight and all wondering how it will affect us. Saw the CO in the morning and played deck quoits and had spelling bee with Army. Won 21 – 18. Afternoon some sun bathing and then watched deck cricket Aussie v England. Then a Sergeant took three of us to his cabin for some beer (eight bottles between us). After dinner yarning and to film show. In day all orders for disembarking given out. Had a boat drill. Passed Three Brothers in the afternoon and a lighthouse in the evening.

29/4/44 Saturday. Got up early to see ship pulling into Port Tewfik and, joy of joys, saw another hospital ship waiting. We had berthed by 9.00 a.m. and then we heard that the hospital ship was to go to Durban and back. So all sorts of rumours were rife. The Aussies had disembarkation all planned, but in the afternoon the British wanted things done differently and absolute shambles resulted as usual. Some sent to a hospital and a lot to a transit reception (Army). I left at 1.00 p.m. and we stood in the back of a 3 ton truck and trailer like cattle. At the camp there was no lunch, no beds and no blankets. No one knew we were coming and no one worried. Saw liaison Officer who could not help. We could not get to our kit for beds or washing etc. Evening beer in the mess, so had a session. Then I went round to see all the RAF people, and most of ORs fairly comfortable. Bed with three blankets on the sand late.

30/4/44 Sunday. Had very bad night and up early. Had poor breakfast and spent the morning trying to find things out and advising ORs. Seems we are to go to 21 PTF soon. No decent washing facilities on camp, so at 10.00 a.m. went for a shower and shave to club. Afternoon went to Tewfik docks to see about kit then look round Suez. Back early and spent evening in mess till all kit arrived and then sorted it out and bed on my camp kit.

There followed several days of intense frustration. The RAF contingent seems to have been regarded as nobody's problem, and was often left ill-informed. Charles tried to find more information, but had little to pass on to the Other Ranks of the RAF. He spent much of his time swimming, reading or just sitting at the club. On 1 May they had been told that they would be departing from Port Tewfik on 7 May, but that date came and went. On 8 May there were signs of activity:

> 8/5/44 Monday. Had a lie in and after shower and shave spent the morning reading. At noon orders came out for Army to move in the morning. They would not include us and the RAF liaison Officer said we come under the Army and not him. Lots and lots of argument. Squadron Leader Ridley went and saw Embarkation Officer (a Wing Commander) and told him all. He chivvied up liaison Officer, sorted it all out for us and said we would move with the Army. Afternoon swim. Evening Club Anniversary Ball. Really good band and company, good dancing and fun with hats, pom poms etc. Did not dance, but lots of beer, though could not get drunk on it. Bed at 12.45 a.m.

> 9/5/44 Tuesday. In the morning the whole move was cancelled, so went to Suez to cash another £10 travellers' cheque, buy some rope etc. Then to Tewfik for final look-see and sit on beach until back for lunch. Afternoon bathing, and when we got back told to have all heavy kit by 11.20 a.m. tomorrow. Spent evening reading and bed early, but at the last moment the move cancelled again.

> 10/5/44 Wednesday. No gen at all in morning except to keep looking and waiting. Rest of RAF – not invalids – packed and kit went in the afternoon. We gave up waiting

and went swimming again in the afternoon, but it was not very sunny and so we came back early. Found everyone packing to go, made lots of enquiries but no gen for us. And still arguing as to whether we come under RAF or Army. Evening spent reading. To bed early.

11/5/44 Thursday. Rumours very rife and we were told to stand by from 11.00 a.m. But no news by noon and so we went for swim. Best afternoon so far and stayed till 6.00 p.m. No news when we got back but at 8.00 p.m. told to have kit and everything needed to move off at 6.30 a.m. in morning. Had to go and do a lot of organising with the troops, then at 10.00 p.m. they told us that two men were to go with the kit and the rest were going by train to Port Said. Noisy night but got some sleep.

12/5/44 Friday. Up before dawn. Packed all and shave etc and had breakfast and all ready to go at 6.30 a.m. Got away at 7.00 a.m. leaving kit to follow with two Senior NCOs by road. Train left Haka as soon as we were on board and went right through to Port Said along canal, arriving 2.30 p.m. We found that they did not know about us or where we were to go. But the Embarkation Officer was clued up and got us on the Reina de Pacifico by invasion barges. A large, seemingly good ship. Kit arrived on quay later. Settled in and then found bar open for beer whisky etc. tonight only. So spent evening playing cards and drinking.

13/5/44 Saturday. Air raid in night. Ill omen. Up early in the morning and started wandering round to get my bearings, but several times got lost. Squadron Leader Ridley went sick so I am now in charge of the detachment. Arranged for airmen's cabin to be changed and got details for exchange of piastres to sterling.

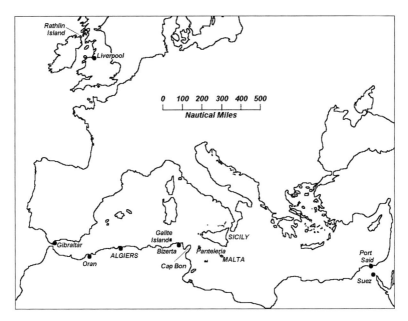

Charles's Travels – 13 May to 1 June 1944.

Thousands of sailors came in the morning and in the afternoon tons and tons of kit and more airmen. Evening reading and to bed very late.

14/5/44 Sunday. Very idle day – mainly reading. Sun bathing and watching people and kit come on board – mainly women and children, to spoil everything. People already running round after them and screaming babies spoiling meals. More ships came in from Suez, quite a big convoy ready now. Evening cards in lounge then later given all the gen for abandon ship, air attack etc.

15/5/44 Monday. At 8.00 a.m. left quay. Passed De Lesseps statue at 9.00 a.m. and set out on voyage. Had practice firing at drogue towed by an aircraft and then practice action stations and emergency stations. Then left alone for rest of day reading and sun bathing. Women and children a bigger nuisance than ever. Fortunately children are not at second sitting at meals. Convoy consists of seven troopers, one merchant vessel and two destroyers but might increase to five destroyers and one aircraft carrier. Evening tombola in lounge – no peace at any time as full of women and children in day. Blew up rough in evening so enjoyed spray on deck. (Had action stations for one and a half hrs at 7.00 p.m.) 18,000 tons, convoy speed 12 Kts approximately.

16/5/44 Tuesday. Up early to find storm had cleared and promise of fine day. Convoy now ten merchant vessels, five destroyers, two aircraft carriers. Not bad. Had emergency boat stations in the morning which meant nothing. Spent most of day on boat deck reading and sun bathing. Evening had a band and some music as sun went down on calm sea and with other passenger ships around. A grand setting. During day just missed a floating mine. Evening reading in lounge and finished last book. Must borrow some more. Bed late and clocks back.

17/5/44 Wednesday. Awoke to find sea just like a mill pond – in fact like a bowl of water with just slight wide undulation caused by swell. But most of day very dull till late afternoon when sun came out grand. Spent most of day again on deck reading. Evening concert, and a good one in the lounge. Order came out that from tomorrow blue to be worn. Great outcry.

18/5/44 Thursday. Bright hot day. At crack of dawn I went to first voluntary PT class on boat deck. Then had to change into blue. But soon the order was changed and blue had to be worn till after practice emergency stations and at meals. Hot day and lot of sun bathing and deck tennis. Convoy passed between Sicily and Malta and joined by other ships from Malta. Now thirteen merchant vessels, six destroyers and four aircraft carriers. Evening tombola but no luck. Then reading till bed.

19/5/44 Friday. In night passed Pantaleria and at dawn could see Cape Bon. Bizerta at 9.00 a.m. and Galite Island at 6.00 p.m. Off Bizerta convoy joined by more making total of nineteen troopers, nine destroyers and one cruiser. PT in the morning again but very dull all morning. Turned brighter in the afternoon and was able to get into sports and do some sun bathing. Evening yarning on deck and cards after blackout. At bed time great flashes of lightning lit all of convoy and gave it quite a sinister appearance.

20/5/44 Saturday. Awoke to see depth charges being dropped on starboard, but false alarm. Warm sunny day again and Algerian coast looked grand. At 3.00 p.m. passed Algiers and several troopers left us and more joined us. Wind sprung up to about 30 mph and got a bit of a swell on sea. Four balloons broke loose and burst high up. Evening tombola – not a successful night yet!

21/5/44 Sunday. In the morning off Oran some ships left and others joined us. As it was Sunday, no PT, no boat drill. Services all day. Sunny OK, but bit too windy for sun bathing. Lots of reading. At 4.00 p.m. we could see Spain and for all the evening could see the snow on top of Sierra Nevadas. Evening concert in lounge, and quite good. A WAAF singing a song forgot the words and there was dead silence. She exclaimed "For Christ's sake, won't someone help me?!" And later a Wing Commander Admin Staff Officer (Flt Sgt at 1939) said he would report her. The Padre had used the expression several times in the day. I did not like the expression, but I don't like the action taken.

22/5/44 Monday. Woke up to find us heading west south

west approx somewhere out in Atlantic having passed Gibraltar in night. Changed escort and lost some more ships and collected some more. Very little wind all day and sea calm except for heavy long swell which made several people sick. Did quite a lot of sunbathing and reading. Evening got into discussion on evolution and final stage of life in universe and enemy religion etc. Rumours that not going home for some time, others that we will be home on the first of June. Turning west north west at bed time.

23/5/44 Tuesday. A fairly uneventful day and weather dull mostly. Still held west north west course but during night steered due north. Clocks now one hour forward of Greenwich so must be some way out. Food getting a little "off" and not too good. Brain contests and deck tennis championship in the afternoon. Evening reading and bed very early.

24/5/44 Wednesday. Kept west north west till evening when got on 339°. Just as dusk fell everyone started flashing lights, almost stopped dead and DR firing small arms. Appeared to be a mine or so ahead. Spent all evening playing tombola and cards. Sunny day and probably last day of sun.

25/5/44 Thursday. Did not wake till too late for PT. Getting on a more northerly course now. During the afternoon the sea blew up a lot and had quite a storm and swell. Lot of pitching and rolling and a number of people went down sick. Dining hall fairly empty and was able to get a seat in lounge early in evening.

26/5/44 Friday. Very heavy sea all day and plenty of roll on the ship. Lots of people sick but I was still OK. Bit of sun in the morning out now and again but mostly overcast and cold. Once a sea actually came over the boat deck! Evening tombola.

27/5/44 Saturday. In the morning burial at sea of a young wife – twenty three – going home with her husband. Died of pneumonia. Seems hard luck. Sea now lighter but still heavy roll. From the destroyers, it appears that we arrive on Tuesday morning. But can tell from lowering cloud and greyer clearer light that we are getting near and in evening was surprised by length of sun set and bright light. But somehow I still do not feel that I am getting home and it seems that I am just as far away as ever, and I can feel no excitement on going home. It seems vague and impossible. Clocks go on one hour.

28/5/44 Sunday. Sea a lot smoother today but still roll and pitch a lot. Spent all morning in the cabin but afternoon on boat deck as sunnier. Sea darker green now. Evening a steady drizzle set in. Another sign of England.

29/5/44 Monday. Saw lots of basking sharks. Woke to find ourselves surrounded with fog and could not see the ships. But after breakfast when I looked out of porthole saw land (Northern Ireland) on starboard. The Mull of Kintyre on Port and Rathlin Island on Starboard. Fog cleared and convoy went into line astern. Some went to Glasgow and we sailed off down Irish Channel in lovely weather with land on either side. Our first sight of Britain and yet it still feels a hell of a long way from home. Gave in emergency lights and passed in surplus baggage and got gen and what to do for disembarking. Lazy day and evening cards and watch sunset – lovely.

30/5/44 Tuesday. This morning I found the ship stationary in the Roads surrounded by mists and other ships at anchor. In the morning a pilot came aboard and everyone got excited. But we still did not move. Depression set in and rumours rang high. Tides, the

Second Front, no trains etc. given as the reasons, and Thursday morning seems to be the estimate. Real hot day, so got into shorts and shirt and sunbathed in the afternoon. Tombola in evening. Well out of sight of land and light till 11.00 p.m.

31/5/44 Wednesday. This morning we upped anchor and sailed into Liverpool docks and anchored again just off the dock, and spent all day there just so that we get used to England slowly and can see what it is like when we do get off. EMOs and Embarkation Officers came aboard though in the afternoon and got some things. We were assured we are to go tomorrow direct to London with medical papers which we all unsealed and looked at. But what's going to happen to baggage I don't know. Evening tombola again and still I did not win.

1/6/44 Thursday. In the morning ship pulled in to shore to music of brass band which gave a more cheerful air to wet morning. But everyone was happy. Cheers went up when the first rope was thrown, hisses when three SPs appeared etc. But a lot of hopes were dashed when it was learnt that many would have to stay on board till tomorrow, us included. But they unloaded our baggage and Squadron Leader Ridley went along with it to Customs and got the lot through without a search! Then in the evening I got a pass off ship and had some real English Bass. So much that felt woozy. Then we met three girls and went to their flat till midnight for swinging evening and fun and games and back on ship somehow at 1.00 a.m.

CHAPTER 14

Non-Effective, Sick

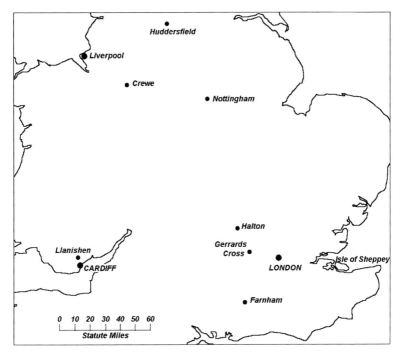

Charles's Travels – June to September 1944.

The Britain to which Charles returned on the *Reina de Pacifico* in June 1944 was much changed from the one he had left in July 1942. The Allies were not yet assured of victory, but they were very much further from defeat. The successes of German U-boats in 1942 had threatened Britain's ability to feed and supply herself. But new technology in radar, breaking of the Enigma codes used by the German navy and the introduction of long range maritime patrol aircraft had reduced, if not completely neutralised this threat. Furthermore Britain had adopted the "Dig for Victory" policy that meant that much more food was produced at home rather than having to be imported at great cost in the lives of merchant seamen.

Elsewhere in the world the Allies had achieved other successes. Charles had played his own small part in the victories in Africa, southern Europe and in India. Hitler's ill-advised foray into Russia, having started well in 1942, ground to a halt in the Russian winter, and was steadily reversed throughout 1943 and 1944.

Back at home, air raids still occurred on occasions, but on nothing like the scale that Britain had suffered in the Blitz. Intelligence had found Hitler's preparations of his "Vengeance" weapons, the V1 and V2, but they had not yet arrived on British shores. Indeed, it was the people of Germany who were now suffering the nightmares of strategic bombing. As far back as mid-1943 Hamburg had suffered terrible damage in a huge firestorm caused by the bombing. By the end of that year Berlin was being bombed regularly. The relative effects of the bombing efforts are illustrated by the figures. In April 1944 German bombs dropped on Britain caused 146 deaths and 226 injuries. In a single allied bombing raid on Frankfurt the previous month, there were 948 deaths and one hundred and twenty thousand people were made homeless. But the next big step was just a few days away as Charles prepared to disembark at Liverpool. Preparations for the invasion of Europe had been going on for months. Since April there had effectively been an exclusion zone around the whole of the south coast in order to preserve security.

> 2/6/44 Friday. Called at 5.00 a.m. For breakfast at 6.00 a.m. But I did not feel like any! Got our evening cases wangled past customs, picked up rest of our kit and got transport to the station. Caught 10.00 a.m. train – reserved accommodation to London. What a pleasure to see real green fields and woods, and a big surprise to see so much in the shops and plenty of food where we had

imagined shortages. And food and beer! Made me wonder if I have brought unnecessary stuff home. Arrived at 3.40 p.m. and found transport and accommodation waiting for us, and a meal – everything beautifully organised. Then transport to the Air Ministry and fixed board for tomorrow. Went and saw Vi till 7.00 p.m. and phoned Soli and Auntie Marie. Got Margaret's and Peter's addresses and sent telegrams. Drink at Piccadilly and food at Haymarket Brasserie. To Bed 11.00 p.m.

3/6/44 Saturday. Called early after a good night between sheets. Hurried off round to Central Medical Board but although we were very early on the list, we were among last to leave as all had to see specialists. Eye bloke said I was to see a consultant on Monday. Had lunch at Euston Hotel and collected small baggage from Emsley Hotel and off to Vi's place in Edgware. Spent the afternoon sitting on the lawn. Just before tea started digging and continued after tea while she mowed, and we did not finish till dark. Bath and to bed almost immediately as very tired and slept well.

4/6/44 Sunday. Up early – before Vi – and we both got away at 8.00 a.m. In town I caught very quick connection to Farnham and then taxi to New Moon Garage. Found the place bedecked with flags and "welcome home" posters. They were very annoyed when I said I was not able to stay night. Grandpa very low and looks bad, but pleased to see me. Peter could not come but was ringing at 7.00 p.m. As I had to leave, I asked Auntie to tell him to meet me at Waterloo. Left 6.00 p.m. and wait for Peter till 8.30 then on to Edgware. Spent evening yarning. Vi might have been in musical mood, but I went to bed.

5/6/44 Monday. Up early again, said goodbye to Vi at 8.30 a.m. and got to Medical Board at 9.00 a.m. Waited till nearly noon before consultant saw me and then he said I was not his case and referred me to someone else. We were told to come back at 2.00 p.m. so another fellow and I went out and had four pts of beer and when I got back the Air Commodore seemed to take a poor view. Sent on three weeks leave and then to Hospital again! Got Ration Cards, Warrants etc, but could not wait for identity card or permits. Taxi picked up kit and caught 5.11 p.m. from Charing Cross. Changed at Chatham and Sittingbourne and arrived home with kit at 9.45 p.m. Did a lot of nattering and bed late.

6/6/44 Tuesday. Spent most of morning trying to sort things out and pack my stuff. Have not got half enough presents. Went to get Peter's bike and found he had a puncture, and a fast one. So walked to Auntie Nellie's. Afternoon I did several odd jobs and wrote lots of letters. Then down to see Dil from 4.00 p.m. till 6.00 p.m. Evening spent back and indoors.

7/6/44 Wednesday. Up early and spent the morning on the garden and Peter's bike. Then in evening got down to packing some of my kit away for storage. Oh how I hate this packing and unpacking. Evening along to Auntie Nellie's with photographs etc. and then down to Dil's. She just looked at them, and we sat and talked. Left 12.30 a.m. but Dad still awake when I got home.

8/6/44 Thursday. Up late and pottered about in garden in the morning. Then went for walk over hills. Afternoon went down to Reed and had a yarn and then on down to Dil's to tea and stay till 7.00 p.m. yarning about this and that. Back and did a bit in the garden with Dad and when it started to rain I looked at snaps with him.

This routine continued for another week, with regular walks with Dil, and tea and evenings spent at her flat. Charles did a lot of work in his father's field and garden, and prepared the bees to go of to the orchards for pollinating. Through all this time he was waiting to be seen by a medical board who would decide on his future employment. His diary made no mention of the progress of the war, despite that fact that the D-Day landings had started on 6 June. Nor did he mention the first of the V1 flying bombs falling on London on 13 June. However, he was soon to see them for himself.

16/6/44 Friday. Up early and finished off packing away trunks. Left about 10.30 a.m. with heavy case. Good train to London and arrived at King George Club in time for wash and lunch. Then to Nuffield house and saw Jack Hepworth. On to Air Ministry for Warrants etc and then Vi to cancel tonight's date at Hatchett's. Then met Peter from School. Had lots to yarn about and wandered round London having the odd drink. Felt queer when went to bed. Air raid alerts on and off all day and night. Strange new aircraft worrying them – Radio controlled?

17/6/44 Saturday. Very restless night with raids of pilotless aircraft. Up late but in time for food. Then called to see Jack. Had a yarn with him and then strolled out shopping and telephoning etc. At Simpson's Club met Ridler and had few drinks. Then dashed out to Peter and we came to town again and I wandered about looking for theatre, hotel etc for next week. Then I left him and went to Moorgate for identity card, but too late. So rushed back to club for wash and shave etc and to meet Vi and take to Hatchett's for party till 11.00 p.m. with Ridler and his popsie. Raids all day and all night off and on.

18/6/44 Sunday. Warnings and "planes" all night again. But slept well. Up in time for breakfast and walk to Buckingham Palace to see changing of Guard and meet Peter. While there one of those pilotless planes dropped in Wellington Barracks only about a hundred and fifty yards from us. We dived for cover, but explosion very small, though for rest of day it was pretty unnerving when they came over. Morning in the park. Lunch with Soli and Marian. In park till tea then news theatre, so Soli on bus and then out to Marian's flat with Peter and photos. Back at 11.00 p.m. still to the accompaniment of planes. But slept OK.

The V1 that fell on Wellington Barracks caused a large number of casualties, despite Charles' description of the explosion as "very small". It fell on the Guards Chapel killing one hundred and nineteen members of the congregation assembled for the Sunday morning service. Charles was doubtless pleased to get out of London.

19/6/44 Monday. Up early, bath etc and bus to Euston and then St Pancras. Got a good seat to Nottingham and arrived 1.10 p.m. Parked my case, Fairy met me and we went for lunch and a row on River Trent. I had arranged to go to Huddersfield the same evening or early tomorrow morning but she persuaded me to stay night. So collected some things from case and went to her house for tea. Then to film Sahara of all things. Spent rest of evening looking at snaps and then to bed late. Had good night and lay in.

20/6/44 Tuesday. Fairy persuaded me to stay till lunch time, so stayed in bed till 11.00 a.m. She came up and we sat talking till I got up. Then wash etc. Breakfast and down to catch 1.00 p.m. train to Huddersfield. Missed connection at Leeds and went on by bus, and at Queens Hotel at 5.45 p.m. Wash and up to St Luke's, changed into civvies and to see Matron and Wilkins. Then down to Rovers till midnight. Pleased to see they still keep vigil going even if only one present. Walk back to Hotel and bed 1.00 a.m.

21/6/44 Wednesday. Up at 8.00 a.m. Bath etc and up to hospital by 9.00 a.m. Saw everybody by 11.00 a.m. and down to see Lillian and daughter and at noon on to see Phyllis. Stayed to lunch and then for walk with her to Deanhouse to see Audrey and for stroll over moors. Back by 7.00 p.m. to meet lads for drinking session and then to my old rooms to finish off. But saw Phyllis home and then stayed till morning bus 6.00 a.m. Funny how she is determined to be a good girl against all comers.

22/6/44 Thursday. Went to bed at 6.00 a.m. and up again at 8.00 a.m.! Did a bit of running about town and then went to see Sylvia. Then up to St Luke's and went round wards etc. Had lunch with Matron and then to Lillian's with snaps and camera to take photos of baby. Down to see Phyllis and the up to see Sister Pachter for half an hour. Back to Phyllis for tea, then up to see Audrey. Stayed till 9.00 p.m. and got into trouble for only sparing short time after two years! Joined Bayldon and Phyllis at Commercial just in time for drinks and back to Bayldon for supper. Then saw Phyllis home and stayed till 4.00 a.m.

23/6/44 Friday. Walked to Queens and straight to bed and off like a rock. Wake at 8.30 a.m. and up at 9.00 a.m. Did packing, paid up and took case to Station. Up to St Luke's and said farewells, changed to uniform and down to lunch with Phyllis, who came with me to station, and Wilkie and Nevin came there too. Arrived Leeds 2.10 p.m. went to Connie's flat but she was out and on to Tommie's and stayed yarning and arguing till 9.30 p.m. when I caught tram to station for Crewe train on which I could not get a seat and did not arrive Crewe till 1.30 a.m.

24/6/44 Saturday. Went to Officers' room at YMCA and had nap on sofa and then got ready to meet Joyce at Station at 8.30 a.m. and took her to London. Good to see her again and we had some grand yarns. Peter met us and took charge of Joyce. But he told me Grandpa had died, so that will curtail the weekend. Went to Bonnington, then went off to Air Ministry etc. on business and back at 4.00 p.m. to find Dil waiting. Went to Strand for good meal and on to see Lisbon Story. Very good. Then for stroll round town before back to bed. Spent all night with Dil but air raids very close and kept us disturbed.

25/6/44 Sunday. Up early in spite of all and dodging about clearing things up, sending telegrams and phoning. Saw Dil off at midday, said goodbye to Peter and Joyce, and then caught train to Farnham and taxi to New Moon Garage. Everything was a bit upset, but they were taking it well. Evening for drink with Uncle Albany and then across to sleep at Rutter's for night.

26/6/44 Monday. Did not get up till 8.00 a.m. After washing etc cycled into Farnham for wreaths and several odd jobs for them. Rain all day. Met Uncle Nigel there who had just arrived, so had drink together. After lunch had nap and sat talking. Uncle Gordon arrived at 2.00 p.m. and after I dashed to Rowledge for more shopping and to the Doctor's. In evening Uncles and I went to forest and then I went to bed early.

27/6/44 Tuesday. Up at 8.00 a.m. after unfortunate

experience of waking in night to find myself peeing bed! In the morning I did all sorts of odd jobs then with all Uncles and Peter who had just arrived went for a walk to Wrecclesham and call in for drink on way back. Peter tells me he is going to get wed in October! 3.00 p.m. off to funeral. Weather very unsettled, rain and sun. Plenty of flowers. Left Grandmother at home. Then sat round fire yarning till Peter and I left for town and I went straight to King George's Club and bed early. When we got off train at Waterloo, an aircraft was overhead and we took shelter as it whizzed overhead.

28/6/44 Wednesday. When I went to bed several of the planes flew near and went in quite close, but I was asleep by 10.00 p.m. and slept until 8.30 p.m. Got up in a hurry and caught 10.00 a.m. train from Baker Street and on way there had to lie down – on a girl in a bus – as a bomb went over. Gather one fell near the rail line ten minutes before we got there. So I was not sorry to get clear and out into the country. It was raining continuously but it looked good and green. Arrived at Halton Hospital in time for lunch. Afternoon reading and writing etc, and seen by specialist who was undecided and not very optimistic. Now have to await a conference. Evening reading and bed early.

29/6/44 Thursday. In the morning Squadron Leader Cross came to see me. He said he recognised my face but would give no decision till someone else had seen me. As that someone did not materialise I languished all day reading and writing and sleeping in chairs quite a lot. When I came to shave in the morning I found the current was DC, so could not use my electric razor. Sad blow. At dinner had half a pint of beer. I don't know if it is a permanent drink or a kind hearted Sister.

30/6/44 Friday. I have been trying to get a hair cut since I have been here but barber still has not come. Did not feel so tired today so only slept a bit in the morning and spent the rest of the time reading etc. Afternoon I went down to see ENT specialist who examined me with a periscope affair with light on the end but could not see where old opening had been made into nose. Had beer again for dinner. Hope they keep it up. Bed early.

1/7/44 Saturday. A very unsatisfactory day when I saw nobody and nobody seems to have done anything about me. No mail which I was hoping for, and bad weather all day. Spent all day reading and sleeping and bed early.

2/7/44 Sunday. Today I did lots and lots of sleeping. In fact I slept nearly all day except in morning when Squadron Leader Cross spent lot of time prodding and probing and trying to syringe eye. They of course found no passage and were even pessimistic about operation. Did fair amount of reading between sleeps. Then did not get to sleep till late.

3/7/44 Monday. At first it looked as though I was going to be left alone again all day. But at 5.00 p.m. Sister came and told me I was for the table tomorrow at 9.30 a.m. But I did not know what they proposed to do so went and saw specialist to get gen. Apparently they funk the real thing and are really going to reduce gland that makes tears. Not very keen but no option if I want to fly again and go abroad. Went for stroll down to Wendover and back. Bed early.

4/7/44 Tuesday. Woken at 5.30 a.m. for toast and Bovril. Then everything went to plan till they gave me jab. I spent the morning in theatre and I went off like a shot. Came to at 4.30 p.m. and felt OK and clean and had not been sick. One eye bandaged only. Had short doze but otherwise after that spent rest of time reading loads of mail that had arrived. In the evening I got up and walked to the sink to clean my teeth, and was very much told off!

5/7/44 Wednesday. Tried to get up today as I was feeling OK, but Sister would not let me as CO's rounds were due. One of the Sisters said I would not be able to get up today, so told her I would take her for a drink in the evening. Eye Specialist came at 4.00 p.m. and redressed eye. Asked if I could get up and he said OK for a short time. I surprised Sister by getting dressed. Then when the one I had spoken to earlier came off duty I met her and went for drink! She should not have gone out with patient and I should not have gone out at all as patients are not allowed in pubs. Several comic bombs have landed near here recently.

6/7/44 Thursday. In morning I had bandage off the eye and a shade put on. Everything very comfortable. Spent the morning reading and in the afternoon went for long, grand walk on the Downs and in woods. Got back to find MO had been looking for me! Evening went out again with two of the Sisters to pub for odd drink and back 10.30p.m! Then in night terrific thunder and more rain.

7/7/44 Friday. Had arranged for Vi to come down in the afternoon but it turned to rain all day, so I phoned and told her she had better leave it. Spent the day indoors reading and sleeping. In the evening after tea I went to pictures at Aylesbury and then met three Sisters for dinner and few drinks. Walked through town with Sisters and to last train back. Jolly good evening, except that we arrived back at 11.45 p.m. But nothing was said.

8/7/44 Saturday. Very wet morning but the afternoon turned out fine. In the morning I had three stitches out, which was a bit awkward but I soon settled down comfortably. Stayed in afternoon but after tea went to Amersham with two Sisters for walk and then to Mill Stream for dinner-dance and drink. Quite a good evening on whole, but not as lively as last night. Crept in at 11.45 p.m. again. But although a new Sister was on she said nothing.

9/7/44 Sunday. Rained all day so spent it in reading and writing. Had arranged to take some girls out in evening, but cancelled it due to rain. Then it turned fine. But they had gone, so Bill and I went down for drink and back to bed early.

10/7/44 Monday. Alternate rain and sun all day, so did not go out at all, even though others went out and had a jolly good time. Then as I was not tired I went to bed late.

11/7/44 Tuesday. Up early to find the commotion last night was Bill, who was not obviously drunk, shitting in other people's lockers. He remembers nothing of it and of course was pretty cut up about it. We had a good laugh. Afternoon I went down to theatre to have corns cut out. Local anaesthetic made me feel bit sick but did not mind bloody mess. Wet all day again, so did not go out.

12/7/44 Wednesday. Spent the morning reading. Then in the afternoon I was told I was for discharge tomorrow for three weeks leave before next operation. Darned annoying as I hoped to be off with Dil. Did lot of running about getting forms etc and writing letters. Then in evening went out with Collins and four Sisters for drink and frolic in fields on way back. Bed late.

13/7/44 Thursday. Up early and packed and all ready to go well before time, but by time I had done other little things just caught train. In London went round to Moss Bros to see if could get sports coat made from tweed, but they said there was not enough stuff. Had lunch with Vi then to bank and caught 3.45 p.m. train home. Slept all way. Left case in station and along to see Dil for an hour. Then collected case and on way home met Daphne. Had long yarn and she asked me up one evening. At home spent most of evening helping Dad painting.

Charles's service records show his parent unit as being No. 3 Personnel Holding Unit at Morecombe. As he was currently classed as "non-effective, sick", there was little the PHU could do for him and even less he could do for the PHU. Leave was therefore the only practical option. The next few days were spent in the usual round of visiting friends, especially Dil, in helping his Father in the field and garden and in other social activities.

17/7/44 Monday. Up early again and down to Sheerness to get dance ticket and take in material for sports coat. Sun well warm before I got back so could not work in field because of bees. Spent all day in garden and painting. Evening tea with Dil and to pictures to see Madame Curie which was not at all bad. Then back with her and in our talks it was as good as decided that we would get wed. Stayed late again.

With that somewhat laconic entry, Charles records his proposal of marriage to Dilys. Perhaps his actual words were more romantic than his diary would indicate!

18/7/44 Tuesday. Another lovely day and spent all of it in garden and got a lot done. Digging, weeding and planting out etc. Evening I popped down to see Dil and we were working out when best to get married, but no decision. Before Peter? What a shock for everybody when they know. Then round to pick up Edna and took her to a dance at Wheatsheaf, which was quite good, and straight back for early bed – 11.30p.m.

19/7/44 Wednesday. Felt somewhat tired in the morning so I spent half the time in the garden and half writing letters. Afternoon I did bit more in garden then had a bath and change and to went out to see Onslow. After tea down to see Dil again and spent the time yarning and planning for future. Back early.

20/7/44 Thursday. Eventful day. Up early and caught 8.00 a.m. train to London to meet Olive and Billie. But waited all morning at the club and rang all afternoon but they did not come. When I got home in evening found note to say my wire not delivered. I had sent it to them at Reading instead of Oxford. However, I went to Book Club and Remington and spent a lot of time waiting about deliberating about two rings for Dil. In fact I decided and bought the better one and did all the necessary. Then out to see Peter and had the evening and a few drinks with him and told him news. His exams on at the moment. Home at 10.30 p.m. and told Dad and Florrie. No one seems surprised. Can't make it out! Then down to tell Dil news and fix up about collecting the ring. Bed late.

Once more Charles got into the routine of helping his father. He and Dilys visited a number of friends, few of whom showed any surprise at their engagement. The couple themselves seem to have been the only ones who had not been expecting it.

In the wider world the war was going well for the Allies. The invading forces that had landed in France had now established solid beach heads and were joining up. The giant Mulberry harbours were in place, allowing secure resupply of the armies. In Belorussia, Russian forces were advancing rapidly and driving out the invading German army. In the Pacific the US Navy had won a solid victory over the Japanese fleet in the battle of the Philippine Sea. And in Burma, which Charles had left just seven weeks earlier, the Indian Allied divisions had inflicted a serious defeat on the Japanese forces besieging Imphal.

At the end of the next week Charles went down to visit his aunt at Farnham, and Dilys came to join him for the weekend.

> 29/7/44 Saturday. Up early and cycled down to station with Auntie's bike as well and left them there. Met Dil in London in pouring rain, and she had not brought a rain coat! We had a walk round and did a bit of shopping before early lunch and out to Regent's Park for open air play of Twelfth Night. We got a little rain but they did not stop play, which was excellent. At the beginning several flying bombs burst near. Then one came down very close. I threw Dil on ground and lay on her but it did not come near enough, though I thought it was our last. After a big and quick dinner, saw Sylphides, Prospect, and Dante Sonata by Sadlers Wells Ballet and had no more bomb scares. Caught train to Farnham and arrived in a cloud burst, so Dil had to wear my coat and I got sodden cycling up. Arrived to find Jack.

> 30/7/44 Sunday. I got up and made tea for everyone and then walked with Jack to station and saw him off, picked up bike and cycled back. Then had walk with Dil in woods. The first time I had seen her alone since I put the ring on her finger yesterday morning. She and everyone were pleased with it anyway, even if it is a bit big. After lunch caught 3.00 p.m. train to London and straight to Victoria and on to Sheerness. Arrived 7.00 p.m. Home to tea and show off the ring and then down to No 2 for evening and long talk about life. Bed late very tired.

31/7/44 Monday. The wretched cat woke me up several times in the night and I slept late. Very tired all day but kept going all day on putting in bulbs and going to town to see about sports coat. To Robertson's to meet Dil's male pals for a drink. What a drink! Late lunch and back again in the afternoon. Evening all through bees with Dad till 7.30 p.m. and then down to see Dil till late.

1/8/44 Tuesday. Up early and again felt tired all day. Spent day tying up tomatoes and putting out more crocuses. Then down to town and back in time to meet Dil and bring her up to tea. Played piano till Dad came home and then after tea for long walk over hill and call into to Auntie Nellie's. Took her home at 9.30 p.m. and back by 10.30 p.m. So bed early.

2/8/44 Wednesday. Spent the morning packing and putting some of my things away. Florrie had been upset by something I said yesterday and I had to do a lot of persuading and soft soap. In the afternoon I had a nap and then down to No 2 to wait for Dil. Had tea and then developed film. Left it in fix while I went back to say goodbye to Dad. He then told me that he was thinking of selling Chalet! Florrie's influence. If I have to buy that as well as the boat I want I'm sunk. Back to Dil and when I left at midnight found film had not hardened. So had to mix more fix and leave it soaking for her to wash and dry.

The "boat" to which Charles refers was a vague plan that was forming in his mind of buying a small boat after the war and perhaps using it as a home and for transporting goods.

3/8/44 Thursday. Up 6.30 a.m. and off to catch 8.20 a.m. train. Dil met me at the station and came as far as

Queenborough with me. There is no doubt about it; she had considerable affection for me and this last two weeks has been a wonderful experience for her to really know love for the first time and give expression to it. Taken years off her life and made her so happy. I must do nothing to hurt or disappoint her, if I ever could. Arrived Halton Hospital 12.30 p.m. The MO on the ward said it was to be a simple operation but may not be able to do it till Tuesday – did I want leave? Not worth it for few days! Reading and writing and bed early.

4/8/44 Friday. Squadron Leader Cross saw me in the morning and after seeing Squadron Leader Matthews it was decided that to make a passage was impossible. Strikes me Squadron Leader Cross is not interested in trying something. Anyway, no operation tomorrow! Spent day reading, writing and sun bathing and then bed early.

5/8/44 Saturday. Had rotten nightmare in night and woke all the ward. In the morning the MO said they could not operate to get a passage and would have to leave it for a few days. Spent day reading and letters and sun bathing. Realizing more and more that in last three weeks have been surprised with three large possible expenses. Marriage, buying the Chalet and starting boat project. Don't know how I'll cope! Bath and bed early.

6/8/44 Sunday. Up early and spent a bit of time reading in the morning and had a nap. And then rang Ifor Jones *(Dilys' Older brother)*. In the afternoon I went down to see them at Gerrards Cross. They have a nice house and made me quite welcome, though obviously summing me up to see what sort of chap I was. And there were not many subjects we could discuss and we did not seem to have many in common. I left soon after tea and got back for dinner. Spent evening writing.

7/8/44 Monday. Idle morning reading and writing and sleeping. Had first batch of letters – good. Afternoon went sunbathing. Then after tea shaved arm for skin graft. Had bath and then had arm prepared. Spent evening reading and yarning but had good meal, as my last for some hours.

8/8/44 Tuesday. Did not get up as early this morning, then had a walk and shave etc and tidied things up. Prepared arm and was jabbed at 10.00 a.m. and at 11.00 a.m. I went down. Came to at about 4.00 p.m. They say I was down two hours. My feet had been done as well, but I could not open my eye without it watering. Spent the afternoon and evening sleeping and talking but did not have too good a night as the eye was painful. Anyway, did what I said and got up to go to toilets.

Charles spent the next few days recovering from yet another operation. The pain in his eye wore off quickly and within a day he was up and was allowed out for the evening to see his brother Peter. On occasions he was late back, but seems to have talked his way out of trouble. A week later he was discharged from hospital.

15/8/44 Tuesday. Up early to get all ready in time. Packing done by nine and I did a lot of heavy work on Sister to get me through parade quickly, and eventually she rang. I was called across to Registrar by 10.00 a.m. and clear at 10.45 a.m. Rang for taxi at 11.05 a.m. to catch 11.23 a.m. train but I dawdled saying good bye to chaps etc and missed train. On the next (12.23 p.m.) I could just catch 1.55 p.m. from Paddington, so I rang Baker Street to order a taxi. Got there early. Good time across and Cardiff train late so plenty of time. Good trip down, but had big job getting across to Dil's Aunt's in Llanishen lugging huge case. Three sisters and an Aunt there and great excitement. Sat on lawn and talked till very late.

The three sisters were Dilys and her older sisters Nana and Fanny. Nana was considerably older than Dilys, and had two daughters of her own, Gwyneth and Mona, who were almost contemporaries of Dilys. The Aunt was a rather formidable lady called Edith Morgan. Charles was in Cardiff for approval!

16/8/44 Wednesday. Did not get up very early. Then after breakfast Dil and I went to town for some shopping (bought some books) and then met Gwyn and all went home. After dinner sat on lawn and some more relations arrived. Had early tea – a birthday tea for Aunt and for our engagement. Then just sat around and waited for taxis to pick us up for the station. Met Mona at the station and all crowded in taxis to Nana's. Once home all had lots of fun and bed late.

17/8/44 Thursday. Up early, before most others about. Had work done in kitchen and early breakfast and then listened to Dil on piano while others got done. Seem to settle down here very quickly, very pleasant people. Afternoon Gwyn, Mona, Dil and I went for a walk up hills and look at valleys, and then back for 3.00 p.m. to see Mona on train home. Evening played Map the Hearts and reading till bed very tired.

For another week Charles and Dilys did the round of her many relatives. They spent the rest of their time walking, and in the evening played cards, played the piano and generally had a quiet, domestic lifestyle. By the following Thursday Charles in particular was ready to leave.

24/8/44 Thursday. Decided to go home tomorrow night. So did bit of packing in the morning and sending of parcels and shopping. In the afternoon, as it was a very fine day, all of us went for long walk on hills and back for late tea. Evening yarning and bits of packing and reading. And bed late again. We are rather glad to be going home I think. It has been grand here and I would like to stay another day. But I must stay at home to dodge flying bombs and travel at weekends is too crowded.

25/8/44 Friday. Of course being the day we decided to leave it was a lovely day all day. But the morning was taken up with packing etc. Then in the afternoon we rested ready for night. Dil and I had short walk and then she made some sweets for journey. Evening played piano and yarned till we left at 9.15 p.m. for Cardiff. Dodging about there with all the luggage just missed a whole empty first class compartment on "Extra", then could not get in first class on normal. But were lucky enough to get seats in third class. Did not have too good a journey.

26/8/44 Saturday. Though with only snatches of sleep, arrived London 6.30 a.m. Took luggage across to Victoria. Had wash and brush up and then some breakfast before going off on shopping expedition. Caught 11.40 a.m. from Victoria which was packed out, and as it was a hot day, sardines were lucky in a tin. But we did have seats. Taxi from Sheerness to No 2. I stayed there till 4.30 p.m. resting, then left. I got down to a bit of work in field with Dad. Then packed up some clothes and down to Aunt Lottie's and Dil's for hot bath and first real evening together for long time. Home and bed 11.00 p.m.

29/8/44 Tuesday. Went up to London on "Jews" express. Arrived at 9.30 a.m. but by the time I had found CME I was forty fourth on the list. So had lots of waiting and got thoroughly cheesed. Finally got out with A3h Bh. Not Ops flying, UK only, so fairly satisfactory. But they sent me to Air Ministry and I wanted to get 4.30 p.m. to Huddersfield. Got to Air Ministry at 1.00 p.m. to be told they had gone to lunch! So decided to get my case from Victoria to Euston ready for dash! On way "Alert" stopped me at Charing X and they closed the tubes. Too heavy to go by bus so waited and so by time I got back to the Air Ministry it was 3.00 p.m. and there was a long queue. Eventually it was too late to get to Huddersfield by 10.00 p.m. They gave me fourteen days more leave. Decided to come back home. But too late to warn Florrie so stayed at No 2. Lot better and Dil pleased to see me.

30/8/44 Wednesday. Got home late morning and Florrie was out so I left a note and went back to No 2. Did a bit of shopping in the afternoon then otherwise stayed in. Matters seem to be pushing on even more now that I have got a flying category. Dil obviously wants to get married soon and we talked round the subject. The snag is Peter, so wrote to ask him if he minded us getting in first. Got home early to find Uncle Bert at Coronation road, so went to see him. In bed tried to plan for wedding next Thursday or Friday.

31/8/44 Thursday. Up late. Did several jobs about field and garden including drive out marauding cows. Then down to Dil's. Spent the morning writing letters again and the afternoon trying to organise the wedding for Thursday. Went up to see Olga about it. But her information not very good. Dil very disappointed in evening. Will try again. Also learnt that Hendy and Nana had particularly wanted a church wedding. So much planning wanted. Gee what a lot of mucking about! Bed late.

1/9/44 Friday. In the morning I went to see Olga at Copland's where she had definite information. But still did not seem easy. However, in the afternoon wrote to Superintendent Registrar at Chelsea and Registrar General for special Licence and will see what happens.

2/9/44 Saturday. In the morning I did lot of shopping and also got several preserving jars. Then got down to it and at Dil's bottled twenty four jars of apples and pears – a good day's work. Made more plans for wedding if it comes off. Afternoon I came up home to tea and early evening and told Dad. He was tired and not too well but he said little.

3/9/44 Sunday. Spent the morning with bees and in garden. Dil came up to lunch and stayed for bit in the afternoon and then we went along to Auntie Nellie's. Down to No 2 for tea and evening.

4/9/44 Monday. Up early. Popped down to see Dil before school. Then final packing and off to Queenborough for London train. Took luggage to Euston. Had lunch and then to Chelsea to see Registrar to try to fix wedding then. But he would not as we had no residence. Wired Dil. Then met Peter and we went out for yarn about things and to fix things up. Caught 8.20 p.m. train and had seat and sleep to Crewe. But next train to Huddersfield packed out and I had to stand.

5/9/44 Tuesday. Arrived Huddersfield 2.00 a.m. and too tired to walk with case to hospital, so had to sleep in waiting room till woken by a Bobby asking what I was doing there! Trolley to St Luke's and to see the Night Sister. Then bath, shave etc at my flat and up to nurses' home for breakfast. Everyone very excited about engagement. Afternoon to see Lillian and Miss Berry. To Bayldon to tea and to Rovers – more excitement. Then back to Bayldon for night. Wire from Dil to say she had fixed it for Saturday morning

6/9/44 Wednesday. Up early to hospital for bath and saw Sister Wilkie. Got a lot of my stuff out to bring back. Afternoon with Wilkie and saying goodbye to others as decided to go on 11.20 p.m. train. Took cases down to station luggage office and then bike to send in advance. Then met Phyllis and Bayldon for bachelor drinks and later they persuaded me to stay and go round to their house for supper. Took Phyllis home and stayed for little before going to sleep in nursing ward.

7/9/44 Thursday. Up betimes and bath and shave to catch 8.20 a.m. to Stockport and change to London. Not bad train and seat most of way. Arrived 2.15 p.m. Thousands of people on tubes and telephone engaged. So took chance and went to Charing X and got good quick train home. Took luggage in taxi to Dil's and found her in terrific state of flap. Florrie had taken all plans out of her hands and organised terrific food and guests. Both very annoyed and worried. Went home, but could not say anything to Florrie to hurt her.

8/9/44 Friday. Hinted to Florrie that it was not what we wanted, but let her carry on. Spent day running around and seeing people and organising things. Never knew there was so much fuss about getting wed. Poor Dil very worried, but had quiet evening together trying to sort things out.

9/9/44 Saturday. The great day. Spent the morning running about on bike getting things for Florrie and seeing Dil etc. The Hoopers had been asking her silly questions again

Charles and Dilys shortly after their wedding.

and her brother Ifor had not turned up and she was worried. Anyway in the afternoon Ifor turned up with his daughters Morna and Julia, and Peter arrived. All met at No 2 then to Registry Office where Dil got locked out! It was all over in a few moments and then by bus to Chalet where Florrie had marvellous spread for us. Great! But we had to leave early to see Jim off. Peter came round to No 2 then and later Barrie called.

10/9/44 Sunday. Peter called in the morning. Up late and spent the morning at home. Then in the afternoon up to the Chalet and Aunt Nellie's and then to Lutfoot's for tea. Then saw Peter off and spent rest of evening together.

11/9/44 Monday. Up early in the morning and after house work and letters went out changing Dil's name at Registry Office, Food Office, ARP, bank etc. and shopping. Then I went off home to bring down things to take back with me. In the afternoon Dil worried with all she had to do etc. and how to get through it. So after a bit I got her to lie on the bed and then went to let her have a good cry. After that we sat and wrote or read. In the evening Ted Friday came up and we yarned and played cards and bed early as very tired.

12/9/44 Tuesday. Up at 7.00 a.m. with Dil and went with her on way to school house. Then had to do lots of running about for Florrie. Town and back. Collected clothes etc and brought them back to the flat and then met Dil for lunch at the British Queen. Did some shopping. Home again for more stuff then letter writing. Wrote to the RAF as I should have been returned from leave, but had no posting through. Dad and Florrie came to tea and then down to unite two hives, but did not stay long and came back and read. But bed early as both tired.

For the next two weeks Charles and Dilys settled down to domestic life. Dilys continued her teaching in Queenborough. Charles presumably heard from the RAF in reply to his letter of 12 September, but he makes no mention of it. He continued to help his father with the field and particularly with the bees. They continued to visit many friends in their newly wedded state and were warmly received everywhere. They had planned to visit London one weekend, but in his diary for 15 September Charles notes:

Heard that shells and flying bombs had landed in London again. So with them and my cold decided not to go to London tomorrow in spite of good shows.

The threat from the "Flying Bombs" – the V1s – was reducing as the allies advanced through Europe at this time, though a few were being launched from Luftwaffe aircraft over the North Sea.

The "shells" to which he refers, however, were a new menace. They were not shells, but were the V2 rockets, launched from mobile launchers in Europe. Their arrival was entirely unpredictable, so the authorities could not even give the population of London the benefit of air raid warnings. Indeed, the threat from air raids had reduced so much that some of the blackout restrictions that had been in place since the beginning of the war could now be lifted. Ordinary curtains could now replace the heavy blackout material, street lighting was increased and diffused car headlights could be used.

Not everything, however, was going the way of the Allies. The gamble of Operation Market Garden, with the paratroop landings at Arnhem, ground to a halt at the end of September, and the plan was a costly failure. Nonetheless, almost all of France and Belgium were now once again under Allied control, and the Russians continued to advance through the Balkans.

Eventually Charles's leave came to an end, and he was posted to the Aircrew Allocation Centre at RAF Brackla near Nairn on the Moray Firth in Scotland. He could hardly have been much further away from his new bride.

CHAPTER 15

Grounded

As its name implies, the role of the Aircrew Allocation Centre at RAF Brackla was to redeploy aircrew who, for various reasons, had some restrictions on their flying. Some perversity in the military mind had located this unit, at which aircrew could normally expect to remain for only a few weeks, in the far North

Charles's Travels – September 1944 to March 1945.

of Scotland. The RAF surgeons had now done all they could for Charles's eye and his medical category had been confirmed as A3h Bh, which meant that although he could continue to fly, it was to be in UK only, and on non-operational duties. He might get some flying in a training role, and he had highly optimistic aspirations to join BOAC, to which some service aircrew were being seconded at this time with a view to the opening up of overseas routes after the war. Clearly he hoped that some improvement in his medical category might be considered.

> 28/9/44 Wednesday. Up early and regretfully. Had good bath and breakfast and Dil saw me off on the 7.22 a.m. train. Poor girl looked so lonely standing on platform waving goodbye. Arrived in London in time to change to

409

King's Cross and catch 10.00 a.m. to Edinburgh. Good journey, in a corner seat. Reading and sleeping. Got considerably colder as went north. Immediate change at Edinburgh, arrive Perth 9.15 p.m. and had to wait till 11.15 p.m. for train which left at 1.25 a.m. So had good sleep. Met chap going up who had all the gen on the place. Changed at Aviemore and Forres and arrived Nairn 7.15 a.m.

29/9/44 Friday. Somewhat tired and weary phoned for transport and arrived in camp 8.30 a.m. Booked into guardroom. Had breakfast. Got billet in cold Nissen hut and bath and shave. Orderly room, Adjutant, Accounts etc. Usual walking about. But found would not be here long with them on base. Just allocating us to jobs and they give us a choice. Considered everything and decided to try for BOAC and after that anything with promotion. Afternoon slept and read and then bed early in evening.

30/9/44 Saturday. Went on parade in the morning. Then down to SSQ for medical board. Waited two hours before got it, and then cursory glance and out. No time to do anything else. Afternoon wrote letters then at 3.00 p.m. walked into Nairn. Made few purchases. Last look round and to a film. Collected case from the station and then back in RAF truck. To bed early.

1/10/44 Sunday. Up late, breakfast, bathe etc., and down to billet writing. After lunch reading and summarising diaries till weather cleared at 4.30 p.m. when I donned coat and went for a stroll in typical Scottish woods – grand. Back for dinner and evening writing and reading again. Bed early. Place walked to was Cawdor.

2/10/44 Monday. In the morning had intake lecture – apparently they assess one here for one's whole service career. So I must look out. Took intelligence test at which I think I did fairly well. Afternoon I dodged parade and had short walk and back to spend rest of day reading and writing and bed early – perishing cold.

3/10/44 Tuesday. Had nothing to do all day. Spent time walking round (and to library) reading writing etc in mess and billet and in evening went to ENSA show – usual sort of thing, mostly very second rate. Bed early, getting too much sleep.

4/10/44 Wednesday. In the morning I had my first interview. Prospects of staying in RAF seem good and of getting to BOAC. So as preferences decided BOAC, RAF – transport or admin, as seems best thing for promotion and comfort for my little Dil. Afternoon writing reading; same in the evening and bed early.

5/10/44 Thursday. Frantic appeals for navigators in Transport Command. Wanted immediately. Did a power of thinking. Would like to keep flying and travelling but demand for navigators after the war seems likely to fall and disappear and I go back straight on ground floor again in admin. Dil does not want me to fly I think and wants me with her all the time. Therefore decided at next interview to alter to admin, BOAC, transport, though I think BOAC would be better for promotion.

6/10/44 Friday. Nothing on all day and in evening went to Nairn and saw Alf's Button. Browned off. Saw dentist.

7/10/44 Saturday. In the morning we had a second lecture and I amended my order of preference to admin, BOAC and transport. Wire from Dil – she could not get days off from school for next week and wants me to come straight home. So goodbye all my plans for holiday at Crieff. Afternoon had long walk in wood as weather fine.

8/10/44 Sunday. Another idle day. Played cards in the

morning. Afternoon dentist for two fillings and letters, and evening reading and bed early.

9/10/44 Monday. Second board. Nothing to do. In the morning I went and had another filling done. Afternoon wrote letters and then went for a lovely walk before dinner. Telegram from Dil now to say that she can get off for Crieff! Oh dear.

10/10/44 Tuesday. Wrote letters in the morning and went to dentist for final filling. Afternoon board. Really nothing I could do as I did not want to fly because of Dil. So put admin first, then Provost Marshall, then transport. They said they would suggest work on the International Commission. Also they would hold my papers back so that I got a chance of week's leave with Dil. Spent the afternoon getting clearances. Then reading in evening. Wire from Peter; he had passed his exams and come top.

11/10/44 Wednesday. Up late and did final clearing and packing. Caught 2.30 p.m. train and arrived at Perth in rain at 7.30 p.m. and could not get a hotel. Eventually fixed at Royal George and bed late very weary.

At last Charles and Dilys were to take a belated honeymoon. Charles had yet more leave until the last week of October, and they had decided that a holiday walking in the Scottish hills would be ideal. After that Charles was to start a new job, the location and nature of which were still to be decided.

12/10/44 Thursday. Up late and after breakfast shopping in Perth. Afternoon I went for walk along the Tay. Then to the pictures. Another walk along Tay and then to pictures again in evening till end and then waited all night in station waiting room for Dil.

13/10/44 Friday. Train very late but arrived in time for me to rush her across station for Crieff train on other side. Arrived 8.05 a.m. and had wash and breakfast. Made us very much at home. After unpacking etc. went for walk round village and to river. Afternoon we went for a long walk in rain but it was good. After tea played cravat and after dinner to bed early both very tired.

14/10/44 Saturday. In the morning we went for a walk up river and back for lunch. Afternoon it rained but we went for walk along roads. Had Dil's shoes nailed. Evening letters and cravat.

15/10/44 Sunday. The morning was fine and so we took a long walk to Strowan and back another way. Dil a bit stiff but doing well. Afternoon Dil had a cold so she stayed in and I went for walk. Evening reading and cravat.

16/10/44 Monday. Up early. Dil's cold a little better, but bought some stuff at a chemist. Then caught bus to St Fillans. Climbed onto the hillside and along paths above Loch Earn to Derry and then down onto road and back to St Fillans, picking lots and lots of hazel nuts on the way. Views spoilt by low clouds but it did not rain. Back tired in time for tea, but went to bed soon after dinner. Dil doing well.

17/10/44 Tuesday. Up early and Dil a bit better, so though it was dull we set out walking and went up to Barwick Falls and Turret Falls. Two glorious sights, but a long way off and on the way back rained hard and got in 1.00 p.m. wet through. Rained rest of day and Dil had a cold. So apart from some shopping we stayed in and bed early.

18/10/44 Wednesday. Dil's cold lot worse. Decided to go home Friday. In the morning in rain walked up Knock and over past Monzie Castle to Gilmerton and back.

Afternoon we did some shopping and then spent the evening indoors and packed my big case. Dil very bad in evening and all night.

19/10/44 Thursday. In the morning we sent off my case. Dil was feeling better in the morning so we took a bus to Muthill and walked back via Dummond Castle and Loch Balloch. Afternoon we did final shopping of things we could not get in Sheerness and packed Dil's case and sent it off in the evening then walked to the park to see trout jumping again. Evening bed early again and hope that Dil's cold goes.

20/10/44 Friday. Up early and final shopping in the pouring rain. Then we sat in lounge till noon when the taxi called. Caught 12.30 p.m. train to Edinburgh but when we arrived it was still pouring with rain which rather spoilt Dil's impressions. Had a lousy meal, a look round and another meal before taking a bus out to Forth Bridge and back in time to catch 7.50 p.m. to London. Had good carriage and plenty of room to sleep.

21/10/44 Saturday. Arrived London early and still raining. Crossed to Victoria and had breakfast and arrived Sheerness 11.00 a.m. very weary. Shopped on way home and then bath and clearing up. Lunch and unpacking and then rest at home till evening. Dil had an attack of migraine. So I put her to bed after tea and she went to sleep. I read and wrote till she woke at 9.00 p.m. when I gave her supper in bed and went myself.

22/10/44 Sunday. Up late and both got on with tidying up and lots of washing of clothes we dirtied in Scotland. Then while Dil cooked I cycled home on her bike. Did few things at home and saw Dad. Collected my bike. Afternoon I sat and read and wrote till we went to Lutt's for tea. Then at home for evening and bed early.

23/10/44 Monday. Up early and saw Dil to school. Then home and picked fruit and puttied windows. Afternoon was spent at No 2 working and shopping. But it came on to pour when Dil came home at 4.00 p.m. with a temperature. I put her to bed after tea and to home for thermometer and she had temp of 102°. So I rang the doctor and went round for medicines then home, work etc till bed time and slept on floor by the side of the bed.

24/10/44 Tuesday. Dil lot better but kept her in bed till Doc called and said she had to stay in till Thursday. Did all housework and felt tired and got all meals. Afternoon a wire came to post me to Peplow for compass swinging. Very browned off. Evening reading and bed early.

25/10/44 Wednesday. Dil not so good and I had a very busy day with all the home work, cooking and shopping etc and so by the evening was very weary, but worried about Dil.

26/10/44 Thursday. Up early and got cracking so that Dil could get up when I had done front rooms etc. Then while she sat in front of fire I did the bedroom. The doctor came in the afternoon and said she had dry pleurisy and was to stay home for week. So sent request for leave extension. Then popped home and back but Dil was very tired and she to bed early and me swotting.

27/10/44 Friday. Dil bit better but still a lot of pain. In the morning I received a wire extending leave. Up late and all behind. After I had washed up Mrs B came up and cleared up while I went shopping. Dil got up for lunch but I was late getting it. Afternoon I dashed home and did shopping and took in the radio, which had packed up. Evening reading and letters and bed early. Another wire came cancelling the leave extension – I am to report on 30th now!

28/10/44 Saturday. Dil up in the morning. Spent all day pottering about. Afternoon I packed one case and sent luggage in advance. Met Peter in town in Officer's uniform! He came round to tea and stayed part of evening. Bed late after listening to play.

29/10/44 Sunday. Up late and it was a rushed morning to get finished before the Doctor came, but he did not arrive till the afternoon. In the morning I popped up home to say goodbye to Dad and other things. Back for lunch. Afternoon I changed and was quiet for rest of day. The Doctor said Dil was a bit better and to go for X-ray on Wednesday and so she is worried. Evening had last of chocolate, pears from home and wedding cake. To bed early.

Charles must have been desperately worried about Dilys, but his extended leave had been cancelled, and after four months in UK, mostly on leave, he probably felt that he should really be getting down to a job once more. The progress of the war had continued to favour the Allies. The Russian army had now established itself in Poland, Hungary, Romania and Bulgaria. British troops had landed in Greece and had liberated Athens itself. In the north, the Russians had advanced to the coast of the Baltic. The German U-boat force, however, after suffering terrible losses to air attack, gained a new lease of life with the introduction of the "Snorkel", which allowed the submarines to charge their batteries while remaining submerged. They started to sink merchant ships again, and tied up large numbers of naval escorts.

RAF Peplow in Shropshire was the home of No. 83 OTU of Bomber Command, but that unit was due to move as Charles arrived. All he knew was that his posting was for "compass swinging duties".

30/10/44 Monday. Up early, packed and left Dil at home at 10.00 a.m. Train to London. Bought Peter wedding present (spoons) and train to Peplow via Wellington. Arrived 8.00 p.m. Four and a half miles to camp in moonlight! The station is changing to Training Command and no definite gen on what I am to do. Dinner and temporary billet for night. Wrote to Dil before bed.

31/10/44 Tuesday. Spent part of the morning going round signing in etc. Found that I was i/c nav section and spent rest of day clearing out section of mess left by previous occupants and looking round all I am in charge of. Evening writing and reading.

1/11/44 Wednesday. Fairly busy in office, but only sorting things out; that was all. Afternoon I moved from my temporary billet to two bedded bunk and got unpacked and organised. Bed late.

2/11/44 Thursday. Quite busy today getting maps sorted and plans ready for night flying. Evening study. Sent for books and registered for exam (DPA). First letters from Dil.

3/11/44 Friday. Slack day in the office. Evening study and getting ready for tomorrow.

4/11/44 Saturday. Up at 6.30 a.m. and spent from 7.00 a.m. to 8.00 a.m. cycling all round Salop in the dark trying to find way to station, arriving just in time covered in mud to catch train to Crewe for Peter's wedding. Met him at hotel for breakfast with Barbara, Eric etc. Then to Joyce's to get briefed and on to church to look after Peter till she arrived. Terrific ceremony and then good feed, speeches etc and back to Rathram before catching 5.30 p.m. back to camp. Arrive in time for dinner and bed early. Not much reading.

Peter's wedding. On the left of the picture are Charles's and Peter's Father and their Stepmother, Florrie.

5/11/44 Sunday. Quite busy in the morning in various ways. Afternoon transport to Seighford to take maps and see what else was wanted in nav line. Good pleasant run out. Evening reading and study.

6/11/44 Monday. Another busy day again with plenty of dashing about fixing things. No time for reading or for letters. Evening it poured in torrents. Had bath and nap after tea then good long swot after dinner and bed late. Second day running with no letter from Dil.

7/11/44 Tuesday. Busy day with nothing special. Evening

discussion on economics with another chap which showed I did not know a lot. Bed late. Letter from Dil!

8/11/44 Wednesday. Had conference in the morning on training programme and nothing else special. Evening lots of reading. Bed late.

9/11/44 Thursday. Lazy day in office and study in evening.

10/11/44 Friday. Felt very browned off today with nothing to do either. Letter from Dil said she was too, but weary with too much work. Evening study again.

11/11/44 Saturday. Usual day. Chief Instructor is binding about rooms etc.

12/11/44 Sunday. Usual day.

13/11/44 Monday. Easy sort of day till ten to five when I was told I could go to Seighford if I liked! Said yes, and had to get away by 11.00 a.m. tomorrow so rest of day spent in rush getting cleared and packing in evening and sending parcel off to Dil. Bed midnight!

Charles's brief stay at Peplow had clearly not impressed him, and he was pleased to move to RAF Seighford, which was a satellite of RAF Peplow. It was home to the Heavy Glider Conversion Unit, among others.

14/11/44 Tuesday. Up early for final packing and dashing about getting cleared by 11.00 a.m. when on transport to Seighford. Found everything unsettled and all billets (one and two bedders) taken. But I got a small room at the end of a big communal hut as I want to be alone for studying. Afternoon spent having look round and at nav section. Seems a lot more free and easy, clean comfortable office so should be OK to work here. When went to bed in the evening I found no light!

419

15/11/44 Wednesday. Spent all day pottering about nav section and organising. But not a lot to do so spent the time making ourselves comfortable. Evening, still no light so spent evening in office studying. But running short of books.

16/11/44 Thursday. (*No entry*).

17/11/44 Friday. Slack morning, but I left at 11.40 a.m. to catch bus to Station. Nobody saw me! Caught 12.09 p.m. to London but arrived one hour late. However, by taking taxi caught 4.32 p.m. from Canon Street just, and arrived home 7.00 p.m. Dil very pleased of course. Had quiet evening and discussed all sorts, including children and decided not to wait.

18/11/44 Saturday. Not much sleep. Did clearing up then shopping while Dil cooked. Afternoon we sat and talked and gramophone etc till 8.00 p.m. when I had to leave on 8.20 p.m. train. Very slow and arrived London 11.30 p.m. Caught 11.55 p.m. to Stafford. Slept part of way, but not sound, and arrived 5.00 a.m.

19/11/44 Sunday. Found no trains, buses or taxis ran on Sunday. So only thing was to walk – five miles dark, strange, raining and heavy case. However, arrived in good time, change, bath and office. Very tired all day and did not do much. Evening bed early. Thought a lot about Dil. Why she should not want me to fly when I am just yearning to inwardly. I should love to if it was not for her and am terribly torn, but just can't hurt her or give her days of worry even if not necessary. And why should she want babies so. But she does.

20/11/44 Monday. Quiet day. Saw all navs and told them I expected some work done. Rang The Eagles re-putting us up for Christmas and all OK. Evening reading and bed early.

21/11/44 Tuesday. Bloke wandered into office in the morning and told me he had booked up at Eagles and was living there etc. Talked of this and that and work here for long while before I realised he was new Chief Ground Instructor! But he was good scout – in ops, and ran me out to The Eagles in his car for look found and to fix it with Mrs Morris. Normal day and swotting in evening.

22/11/44 Wednesday. Gave first day swings to some navs and told them all they had to do one by next Wednesday. Idle day. Evening swotting and packing.

23/11/44 Thursday. Fairly busy morning and caught noon train to London. Arrived home 7.00 p.m. and surprised Dil again, though she was half expecting me. Quiet evening in – probable conception of first born.

24/11/44 Friday. Up 6.00 a.m. and caught 7.35 a.m. train. Arrived at Central Medical Board at 9.30 a.m. and waited all morning and saw no one. At lunchtime I went to the Crown Agents for Colonies about job abroad but not optimistic. Back to CMB and waited till 3.30 p.m. before saw specialist. Got full flying category and arrived home 7.00 p.m. Both went round to see Doc MacNamara and he said Dil fully OK. Back and bed late.

Charles's "Full Category" was something of a surprise. His eye still gave some trouble and was always prone to watering, and remained so for the rest of his life. However, the President of the board seems to have taken a practical view that there was little point in downgrading a navigator who was otherwise physically fit, and who, at this stage of the war, would almost certainly not be posted to an overseas operational squadron. Charles told me much later in his life that he effectively promised the board that he would not actively seek to return to operational flying.

25/11/44 Saturday. Up late, late breakfast, tidy up etc and shopping. Afternoon spent sitting talking. Evening up home to see Dad and Florrie and to tea. Back and packing for tomorrow and played cravat till late.

26/11/44 Sunday. Up at 6.10 a.m. having overslept half hour. Terrific rush and caught 7.45 a.m. to London and 10.15 a.m. to Stafford. Arrived 2.45 p.m. and rang for transport and rest of the afternoon in the office. Evening study.

27/11/44 Monday. Uneventful day – fog stopped flying. Wrote five letters and did bit of reading, but tired in evening and bed early.

28/11/44 Tuesday. All day in office thinking about my plans. First it was running a boat with Dil still at school: cancelled. Then overseas – squashed. Then RAF – cancelled. Now willy nilly local government. Now this evening had long conversation with MacLaren who I found also interested in boats. To bed late.

At this time Charles, like so many others who had spent the last few years at war, was having to make long term plans for his future. Dilys was much opposed to his remaining in flying, and he was not enthusiastic about remaining in the RAF as an administrator. His ideas about making a living by owning a boat were only partly formed. He was hedging his bets therefore by getting a qualification in local government, in the hope that he could use that and his previous experience as a hospital superintendent to ensure that he could make a living when the war ended.

For the next three weeks Charles went about his rather limited duties at RAF Seighford, but there is hardly any mention of his work in his diaries. He managed one weekend at home with Dilys, and notes that his brother Peter got a ship and so would soon have to go to sea and leave his new wife, Joyce. He was not impressed with his accommodation, and notes on 13 December:

> Evening no fire, no wood, no coal. So stayed in mess and read.

He was clearly still considering his options for post-war employment, for on 17 December he wrote:

> Considering pinnace now instead of Thames barge. Did lot of planning.

He also made plans for Dilys to come up to Seighford for Christmas and New Year, and to stay with her in the local hotel.

> 22/12/44 Friday. Very unsettled day and in the afternoon I packed cases and gave them to Watts to take to Eagles. Evening hung about in mess reading till I caught the last bus to Stafford and waited on station for Dil. Lost library book.
>
> 23/12/44 Saturday. Dil arrived 4.00 a.m. after bad journey, and sat in waiting room till the morning and caught 8.00 a.m. bus to Eccleshall. Dil had been ill previous week, had rotten journey and no sleep and now arrived at cold room. Very nice place but very cold, and had spent day reading and talking with MacLaren. But by evening after heavy meal Dil very ill. Migraine in evening.
>
> 24/12/44 Sunday. In the morning I left Dil in bed (cold bath) and went in to camp with Mac. Did one or two things. Back as Dil got up. Good lunch and she felt much better. So went for walk in the afternoon. Decided now after talking to Mac to cancel barge idea and definitely have motor yacht. Early to bed tonight.

25/12/44 Monday. Christmas day, but it did not seem like it. Quiet morning and excellent meals. Afternoon, short sharp stroll in thick fog and late dinner. But fun. Then sitting round telling tales till late and bed very tired.

26/12/44 Tuesday. Dil had a touch of bronchitis and coughed rather badly. Popped into camp in the afternoon and found a session had been in mess and it was a bit of a shambles. Dil somewhat disgusted. Rest of day quiet and yarning. To bed early.

27/12/44 Wednesday. Went into camp in morning. Had lot of dodging about to do and bathed as overslept and too late to bath at Eagles. Then caught a bus to town. Met Peter and Joyce from train, taxi to Eagles and spent lunch and afternoon there. He off tomorrow for warmer climes. Dil and I went to Stafford with them to see them off and then straight back and another early bed.

28/12/44 Thursday. Mrs Mac left in the morning. Nothing much doing in the morning and so came home with Watts in the afternoon and for walk. Some more talk re-boats and seem to have decided on motor cruiser. Bed late in Mac's room as double bed.

29/12/44 Friday. Gill back in office from leave so still less to do. Stayed in all day and had rotten cold. Wrote to agents for details of boats.

30/12/44 Saturday. Cold worse. In afternoon went to Stafford with Mac for one or two things for Dil and back early.

31/12/44 Sunday. Up late and in to offices. Cold lousy. Got browned off and so cycled back to Eagles for lunch and afternoon and spent rest of day talking about boats.

1/1/45 Monday. Woke up at 2.10 a.m. with Dil – New Year – our first. Then packed up early in the afternoon to get home. But she still had a rotten cold.

2/1/45 Tuesday. Fog cleared and heavy frost made country look grand. Packed up at lunch time and cycled home for rest of day and short walk with Dil. Her cold a bit better.

3/1/45 Wednesday. Usual sort of day, but did not go home at lunch time. More talk in evening about boats but mainly on wild life. Decided to go to see "Tina" at Littlehampton, but I think she will be too small.

4/1/45 Thursday. Up late. Nothing in the morning. Afternoon I went to Stafford with Mac to send luggage in advance and get ticket and then went to The Eagles early for last night there together as Dil leaves tomorrow and I start day off!

5/1/45 Friday. Up very early and rush round saying goodbye etc and caught bus to station for 9.10 a.m. Arrived London 1.15 p.m. and straight off down to Littlehampton after parking luggage. Rotten journey but country and weather fine. Dil had very bad head. But went and looked at boat which really was lovely but alas accommodation too little. Good run back to London and finally arrived home 10.45 p.m. very tired – too much to read letters properly even.

6/1/45 Saturday. Up very late and by time we had bathed and eaten too, only just time to go to bank etc and building society. But they could not advance money on a boat. Lunch out and had a quiet afternoon till 4.00 p.m. when we went up home to see Dad and for evening. But did not stay late. Have decided that at bigger boat is necessary. I'm anxiously waiting to see if we are going to have a baby.

7/1/45 Sunday. Up rather late after a good night and spent all day in together. But I popped out to Lutt's and for bread. Afternoon we just sat and talked and bemoaned our fate that we had to part. Can't make up our minds about boat. Left at 8.00 p.m. and said goodbye on station for trip to London for midnight train to Stafford. 8/1/45 Monday. Arrived Stafford 4.45 a.m. and slept in waiting room till 6.45 a.m. to Great Bridgeford, and walked from there in snow to arrive at camp from my day off in time for bath and breakfast. Spent the morning sorting out and getting organised. The afternoon was spent preparing for a court of enquiry and evening writing and reading. To bed early very tired.

The court of enquiry did not take long to complete, and Charles then found himself with little to do. His Commanding Officer sent him off on leave again on 16 January, and he arrived at Sheerness to find winter truly set in. He planned to go to Plymouth on 18 January to buy a boat called *Goblin*, but at the last minute the visit had to be cancelled. It became increasingly likely that Dilys was pregnant, but the doctor would not commit himself for another two weeks. Clearly they were both excited by the idea and mention of "a baby" features almost every day in the diary.

The weather worsened, and there was heavy snow for several days. The bath froze and Charles spent several hours thawing out the outlet pipe. Then his leave was extended, apparently indefinitely, while he waited for yet another posting. Finally he was told to report to the School of Administration at RAF Hereford on 7 February.

7/2/45 Wednesday. Up very early to start getting ready. Dil had the day off so we jogged along taking it easy and then I caught 11.05 a.m. from Sheerness. Had rush at London and arrived at Hereford after reading all the way down at 7.30 p.m. A truck met the train and took six of us out five and a half miles in the rain. Had dinner, booked in and got bed in a twenty roomed hut, and slept cold!

8/2/45 Thursday. Up 7.00 a.m. bathed etc and lectures start at 8.45 a.m. Air Force law etc all day, a boring monotonous intricate subject, but made pretty interesting by a good instructor. Evening reading and writing and bed early. Don't know yet whether I am posted here or only attached.

9/2/45 Friday. Lectures all day and mess reading and writing in evening.

10/2/45 Saturday. Easy lectures all morning. Transport called at station for my case and was told it was not there. So instead of going to Abegevenny with hockey team for the run I had to queue for an hour and a half for a bus into town and tell them off at the station and collect my great coat for tomorrow's parade and back at 4.00 p.m. and the afternoon was wasted. Rest of time in mess reading. Dance late in evening but I did not stay.

11/2/45 Sunday. Up late and to compulsory church parade. It was a rotten afternoon and rained, so spent rest of day reading and writing.

12/2/45 Monday. Usual day – bind. Waited patiently all day for news of baby from Dil, but not in her letter this evening. Reading.

13/2/45 Tuesday. News from Dil did not come till evening when she said Doc had confirmed it! Good show, big excitement. Wrote letters.

14/2/45 Wednesday. More lectures and more bind to learn. Evening no letter from Dil. Did NALGO exercise and read letter from Mashford. I go on the 18th to look at "Goblin".

15/2/45 Thursday. Two letters from Dil and a Valentine –

my first. Lovely day but we had to stay in for lectures. Evening read and yarned with chaps. To bed early.

16/2/45 Friday. Very interesting lecturer all day. Evening two or three letters and then looking over notes for tomorrow. Bed early.

17/2/45 Saturday. First exam in the morning and very fair questions. Should have done about average I should say. Afternoon wrote eight letters, had a nap and read. Evening wash shave and change and to station and on the 11.30 p.m. train to Plymouth.

18/2/45 Sunday. Not very good sleep. Change at Bristol and arrived in fog at Plymouth 6.00 a.m. and sleep on station till 8.00 a.m. Walked to Admiral Hard and got ferry to Cremyll and spent the morning poking about on the boat. Accommodation looked satisfactory but wanted well doing up. Was getting optimistic till I saw engine shaft corroded to bearings and corrosion on parts of hull. Very rotten! Left at noon very disappointed and arrived from changing at Bristol at 8.00 p.m. too late for dinner at camp so stayed in town.

19/2/45 Monday. Up early even though tired. Had two letters from Dil saying how tired she felt and lonely with baby coming. Made me want all the more to go home. Not too good a day on whole and could not concentrate. Evening washed some socks and bed late.

20/2/45 to 22/2/45 Tuesday, Wednesday, Thursday. Just lectures and reading in evening. Lovely weather and lots of hope for weekend.

23/2/45 Friday. Spent most of spare time today busy revising. Evening went to Hereford to buy a ticket to London and spent rest of time swotting and reading.

24/2/45 Saturday. Fairly straightforward exam papers in the morning and then when finished I shot off to Hereford to catch 12.45 p.m. to London. Very late and only just made connection to Sheerness and arrived home 8.30 p.m. for food and quiet evening. Doc says Dil's tummy muscles very taut and strong from PT and she must leave school.

25/2/45 Sunday. Not much sleep – too pleased to be with Dil. But got up very late. She slept a bit more than me. Had short stroll in the morning but most of time in doors as she very sore from Doc's manhandling yesterday. But I had to leave at 6.00 p.m. for London train and 9.40 p.m. from Euston to Crewe. Lousy wind in London.

26/2/45 Monday. Arrive Crewe 1.30 a.m. and shocking train to Hereford arrived 5.00 a.m. Got taxi 5.30 a.m. to camp and went to bed and sleep till 7.30 a.m. for ablutions. Surprisingly enough did not feel tired during day, but went to bed early. All my hope now is on getting to RAF Eastchurch, though to avoid disappointment I've told Dil it was impossible. Have tried every way to get in to teaching but must wait till demobbed. If I can't get to teach will stay in RAF. No letter from Dil.

27/2/45 Tuesday. Sunday's letter from Dil, and of course she misses me. Exam results out – four "A"s for me – good. More lectures and bed early.

28/2/45 Wednesday. Letter from Dil that she had definitely packed up school, which is a good thing. Very easy day and tent pitching!

1/3/45 to 2/3/45 Thursday, Friday. Medical lectures all day and reading in evening. Friday lots of study as felt bad on exam.

3/3/45 Saturday. Exam all morning and really shocking papers. Gave me a headache to look at and left me down in dumps. Worse still when came out found no letter from Dil. Caught train to Cardiff and bus to Tonypandy where Gwyn met me and took me home at 4.00 p.m. Talk mainly baby talk rest of day and late bed. Wrote to Dil all about it and grand situation if not surroundings.

4/3/45 Sunday. Up early and stayed in all morning with Nana talking etc as she did not go out, but it was a lovely day and I would have liked to go up the Valley. Caught 1.00 p.m. bus to Cardiff and out to Auntie's by 3.00 p.m. for talk about things and then left at 5.00 p.m. to catch 6.00 p.m. train to Hereford with a family of six, and they were grand. Early bed.

5/3/45 Monday. Exam results – more "A"s. Odd lectures and an exam! Saw the Adjutant and he said I would have to go on leave again pending posting. Great joy. Wrote to Dil but did not tell her in case it fell through. Reading and bed early.

6/3/45 Tuesday. Final lectures. At noon the Adjutant called me and said I was posted to Gloucester and had to go direct tomorrow – and I had planned to go home tonight. Properly down in dumps but glad I did not tell Dil and so disappoint her. Packed up early in the afternoon but stayed in and read all time and to bed early, but could not sleep.

7/3/45 Wednesday. Up 5.15 a.m. after a lousy night for breakfast at 6.00 a.m. Transport to station 6.30 a.m. Train to Gloucester 7.30 a.m. Arrived at No 1 Personnel Holding Unit and reported. The Adjutant said I could have leave and live out! Filled in all forms etc and was out again at 10.30 a.m. Caught 11.50 a.m. train and arrived home 7.30 p.m. to Dil's huge delight, as she had had no letter for two days and was not feeling at all well. Bed late.

Once more Charles was on leave awaiting a posting. His course at Hereford had qualified him as an RAF Administrator, though despite his diary recording that he passed with As, his RAF service records show that he passed "Below Average". He hoped for a posting to RAF Eastchurch, just six miles from Sheerness, but did not hold out much hope. Dilys was not having an easy pregnancy, and suffered from sickness, leg cramps and high blood pressure. On the advice of her doctor she had given up teaching, and was told to rest as much as possible. Charles spent much of his time, as he had always done, helping his Father in his field and garden. Finally he received a telegram instructing him to report to RAF Sunningdale.

25/3/45 Sunday. Up early and loads of preparation for departure and at last had to say goodbye. Good journey all way to Sunningdale. But on arrival 1.30 p.m. found it was 54 Group HQ and no one was about as all the Officers were rehearsing a play. No one could do anything. They wanted me to go home and come again on Monday! Then they found there was no bed for me and eventually found one after waiting two hours. Someone dressed as Henry VIII came and told me I could be posted to Eastchurch! Got warrant and hurried home to Dil!

26/3/45 Monday. Up early and odd jobs shopping. Up home and along to see Uncle Albany just out of hospital. Heard of house and Dil came up with me to Minster to see about it, and I on to Eastchurch. Saw everybody and was put in charge of P & D section. Left early and home late. Dil not too good and no luck with house.

27/3/45 Tuesday. First long day. Missed bus in the morning so I cycled. Found it quite convenient, so decided to do so always. Going to take a long time to pick up the work. Called at Chalet on way home and moved hives.

28/3/45 and 29/3/45 Wednesday and Thursday. Busy at

getting used to work. Cycled via house and found it quicker. Called in at Chalet each day. Possible news about a house. Dil busy at home buying all sorts of things.

30/3/45 Friday. Good Friday. Usual busy day at office and terrific winds to cycle against. Called in at home on way back.

31/3/45 Saturday. Only spent the morning in the office, where I found lots of visitors so decided not to stay. All the afternoon in, as it was very wet.

As Charles settled into his new job at the end of March, the German Third Reich was in its death throes. For months Allied bombers had roamed almost freely over Germany, and had brought terrible devastation to many of its cities. In desperation Hitler had sent to the front line old men and teenagers, but to no avail. The question now was not whether Germany would be defeated, but how far the Western and the Russian armies would each advance before that defeat. Resistance in the Japanese theatre of war was more stubborn, but again the Allies were slowly winning, albeit at terrible cost as the Japanese fought, literally, to the death.

CHAPTER 16

Administrator

Charles was now a fully qualified administrator, and had the posting to RAF Eastchurch that he wanted.

Eastchurch had been associated with aviation since the earliest days of flying in Britain and it was this location that Short Brothers chose to build their first aircraft manufacturing site. The grass airfield had a varied military career, being run initially by the Fleet Air Arm, then passing through a phase of being in Fighter Command, then in Coastal Command before coming into use as a Technical Training Command airfield in 1941. From time to time it was used as a forward operating base, and was visited by various aircraft in distress or with emergencies. In 1943 the station had become home to the Miles Magisters of an Armament Practice Camp, and had frequent detachments of target towing squadrons to provide the necessary training. Although the APC had moved from Eastchurch by the time Charles arrived there, detachments from that unit continued to use the facilities of the airfield. A Combined Aircrew Reselection Centre was also established at RAF Eastchurch in 1943, and this was the main resident unit when Charles arrived.

The daily cycle ride from Sheerness to Eastchurch must have kept him fit, and with the start of spring would have been quite pleasant. He did not have any real job yet, and appears to have been shifted to various tasks as the need arose.

1/4/45 Sunday. (*No entry*).

2/4/45 Monday. Up early and lots of cooking. Then rest in the afternoon till 3.30 p.m. and then up to Halfway to

Chalet, Onslow, Watkins and Auntie Nellie and had a quiet evening. Second day off. Yesterday stayed in all day as weather lousy.

3/4/45 Tuesday. Flight Lieutenant Knight back to take over. Then there was a flap to decide where I should go. Got away early in evening with NAAFI Stores. Found Dil had had lots of work and was not feeling too well. Afternoon spent reading and bed early.

4/4/45 Wednesday. No news as to where I was to go. Afternoon there was a job to be done at the dockyard so I left at midday. Found Dil with rotten head and stomach. She lay down while I went to dockyard. When I got back found Mrs Emmerson there. Evening Dil to bed very early. Then Dick Pellett came up to see me and stopped talking till late.

5/4/45 Thursday. In the morning I was told I was to take place of an Adjutant on one of the squadrons. Went over and saw him to get all the gen and see OC. Just settling down nicely when Station Adjutant rang to say I should be on a course at Brize Norton today. So I got warrants etc. and buzzed off at 4.30 p.m. Got home and found Dil had been in bed all day and not at all well. It did not help when I told her either. I went and phoned the Doctor in spite of her and he came and saw her in evening. Was very nice but seemed concerned and gave her a pill and said he would come again tomorrow. I did all clearing up and packed a small case for two weeks, and bed late. Dil feeling a bit better.

6/4/45 Friday. Up early, got breakfast etc, finished packing, left Dil comfortably in bed and caught 10.30 a.m. train to London. 1.45 p.m. to Oxford and 5.05 p.m. to Brize Norton and arrived at 6.00 p.m. Was told I was two days late for course, but not the only one. Had tea, unpacked and dinner then to flicks (Carman Miranda) with a bloke I knew. Bed late.

7/4/45 Saturday. Up very early to see the Chief Instructor then the Adjutant etc. and to first lecture. Course on admin etc, organisation and lecture procedures. Finished at 12.20 p.m. Had photo taken and caught 1.10 p.m. to London. Arrived home 7.45 p.m. Dil in bed but not really bad. She was as pleased as Punch to see me and full of news about 17 Marine Parade which she had just taken, also ordered a whole lot of furniture. Very excited and wondering if I approved! She got up and cooked meal. We talked about lots and went to bed early.

8/4/45 Sunday. Spent the morning indoors on house work and talking etc. I had to leave at 2.30 p.m. to catch 3.00 p.m. train. All trains all way were packed. Had three hour wait in London. Went to news theatre and then wandered to Paddington. Seat to Oxford OK and on Brize Norton line, though packed. Got half way and the train packed up. Could not go further and we had to wait for another. Arrived 12.45 a.m. very weary and only time to write one letter to Dil.

9/4/45 Monday. Up early. Lectures all day and till 7.00 p.m. Dinner and then notes and lecture prep.

10/4/45 Tuesday. Very binding day all day. Gave ten minute lecture on bees. Comment – voice husky and too loud and quick. Wire from Dil about flat. Evening prepared lecture for tomorrow. Notes and bed early.

11/4/45 Wednesday. Usual busy day and gave second talk which seemed OK. Evening very browned off with nothing to do and bed early.

12/4/45 Thursday. Wing Commander Coles from 117 Squadron came to give lectures and I had long yarn about chaps who had left and died etc. Evening writing and bed early.

13/4/45 Friday. Usual day. Saw CO for interview in the morning. Evening reading and notes and letters.

14/4/45 Saturday. Gave second lecture. Told I was to be prosecutor at mock court martial. Noon sorely tempted to go home to Dil but put it aside and so spent the afternoon in almost deserted mess feeling very lost with nothing to do. Played billiards, wrote letters, notes, read and prepared prosecution and bed late.

15/4/45 Sunday. Up late and as fairly fine went for pretty walk to Shilton and back. The afternoon was still finer, sunnier and hotter so for another pretty walk to Bampton – six miles and got back very hot. Evening studying for tomorrow, reading and getting prosecution ready. Bed early full of sun.

16/4/45 Monday. Up early and fairly interesting day, but aching to get posted. Afternoon was the court martial and I won my case. Evening all course went down to local pub but I stayed behind and read. Could not study. Bed early.

17/4/45 Tuesday. Up early and had two lectures before exams. Very easy before and after lunch. Then fixed clearances and off on 4.40 p.m. train. We made good time to London and just caught connection to Sheerness. Arrived 10.45 p.m. and Dil very pleased to see me and full of news. Did not get to sleep till very late with lots of talking.

18/4/45 Wednesday. Got down to moving furniture across to No 17. Did lots and rather rushed Dil. But went up to see Florrie in the afternoon while she slept. Carried on till 8.00 p.m. Then rest for little while and bed early very tired.

19/4/45 Thursday. Up early again and carried on with good work till 9.00 p.m. but we were then able to sit back and sleep at No 17 for the night.

20/4/45 Friday. Again all day moving and putting things away and shopping, and by evening had only a few odds and ends left. Bed early.

21/4/45 Saturday. Up very early and cycled to Eastchurch. Found I had nothing to do at all. Filled movements book etc and to NAAFI and left again at 11.00 a.m. Went home for flowers etc. Dil surprised. Early lunch. In the afternoon we did the final clearing up at No 2 and said goodbye to it, and had long quiet evening in our new home.

22/4/45 Sunday. Morning, Dil cooking, I washing and tidying stuff, putting up shades etc. Afternoon lots of rest as very weary. Got some coal on tick and had fire as it turned very cold. Had first lazy day for a week and bed early.

23/4/45 Monday. To Eastchurch again. Still at B Squadron with nothing to do. Afternoon went to workshop for look round. Would like to be posted there and so saw the Adjutant to see what he could do. Accounts queries and records queries. Evening odd jobs and reading.

24/4/45 Tuesday. Off to Eastchurch and to B Squadron. Had lazy day. But in the afternoon went and had look workshops. Very well equipped and I thought it would be a good thing if I could get there. Made tentative enquiries. Evening more work in house – shelves etc.

25/4/45 Wednesday. Bit more to do today. CO asked why I had not been on parades. So I will have to in future. Asked the Adjutant about going to workshops. But they are adjusting establishment. Evening more work. Dil not so well.

26/4/45 Thursday. Up early and to Eastchurch by 8.30
a.m. for parade. Slack day. No news of workshops. Had
second of two fillings done by the dentist. Evening very
cold and had lots of coal and big fire.

Charles established himself back into the daily routine at
Eastchurch, though now he had to attend the morning parades.
There seems to have been no real progress in getting him a
permanent post, and he spent much of his time on small,
though essential, administrative tasks around the station. With
an establishment review coming up, he must have worried
whether there would still be a post for him at Eastchurch.

7/5/45 Monday. To camp late and got on with inventory.
Nearly finished it in the morning. At 3.00 p.m. the radio
announced that Germany had finished and Churchill
would broadcast later. Tension high all day so I left early.
In the evening they announced on the radio that VE day
would be tomorrow and Churchill broadcast at 3.00
p.m. I rang the camp and had to go in tomorrow to a
victory parade! Quiet evening. Bed early.

8/5/45 Tuesday. Up early and got puncture on way to
camp. But by many pumps got thereby 9.00 a.m. to find
the parade now not till 11.00 a.m. I was i/c one flight
and lead parade. Really an excellent turn out and a good
show. Home immediately. Afternoon short walk after
Dil had tooth out. Then Churchill's victory speech.
Mended puncture. Lazy afternoon and evening.

The war in Europe thus stuttered to a halt. Defeat had been
inevitable for Germany for several weeks, and the arrival of
peace was a welcome relief to Allied and German forces alike.
Some areas of token resistance faltered on, but generally with

acts of defiance rather than hostility. In the Channel Islands the German Vice Admiral in command gave orders for his troops to salute British Officers only with the Nazi salute; he was largely ignored. Some U-boats were scuttled by their crews rather than being surrendered. In Prague the war lasted an extra day, as the German SS troops defiantly continued to hold out, only to be crushed by the advancing Russian Red army.

In the Far East the war with Japan still had some way to go. This war, however, did not directly affect Charles at Eastchurch. It was vanishingly unlikely that he would be called to go to that theatre of operations, and once the euphoria of VE day had worn off, work had to continue as before. The transition to peace brought its own changes to the administrative workload. Victory prompted many to apply for leave, and Charles spent much of his time processing those requests. He seems to have had another Officer working with him, but was clearly not over-impressed with his enthusiasm or efficiency.

> 25/5/45 Friday. Again very busy, mainly with letters, naughty boys and boys wanting leave. Bill not very helpful and only keeps me getting away early. Called at Nellie's for gooseberries. Stayed in in evening pottering about and listening to Tempest on radio and bed early. Both tired.
>
> 26/5/45 Saturday. To camp early and very hectic morning. Bill again unhelpful. Some Warrant Officers reported him to the Chief Instructor for swearing! Got away eventually and straight home. Plenty of odd jobs in the afternoon and I went shopping. Evening to Doctor's, when he said baby's heart was beating and gave us quite a thrill and Dil was all OK. Then to Rebel Maid by Co-op operatic choir in Pavilion. Quite good and bed early very tired. Saw Kemp there.

27/5/45 Sunday. Up late and did cleaning while Dil did cooking. Afternoon we had a rest and then up to Aunt Nellie's and got some gooseberries, flowers and cabbage as she said we could till she came back. Uncle not so well now and she very worried. Evening just sat and listened to radio and gramophone and bed early.

28/5/45 Monday. Up early and had very wearying day with so much to do, and had to put two NCOs on a charge as well. There is a terrific lot to do and not a lot of help and short staffed. Home via Chalet and very tired. So was Dil after working and shopping. So just sat and read and played mandolin and bed early.

29/5/45 Tuesday. Hear from Eve that Reggie is missing from Ops on 5th May. Wrote to her from office. Had quiet day in spite of the fact that Bill went off in the afternoon. Dil rang through for yarn in the afternoon too! Called home on way home and quiet evening doing nothing.

30/5/45 Wednesday. Bailey again conspicuous by his absence. But got on OK. The afternoon was a non-working day but I was busy all time till 5.00 p.m. clearing up and getting ready for tomorrow off. Left 5.15 p.m. and called at Chalet and Auntie Nellie's for flowers. Then had quiet evening in at home reading etc. and bed late.

The month of June continued in the same sort of routine, though Charles comments that the workload began to ease. He stood in for the station Adjutant for a week or so, but found little of interest to record from his service life. At home he and Dil continued to make No. 17 more like home, and again his diary is mostly a record of domestic chores. July was much the same, and his diary records a period of lovely weather, during which he took some leave. Then at the end of the month his job changed again.

> 30/7/45 Monday. Up early to start work. Had very busy day getting ends sorted, then heard I was to take over as station Adjutant tomorrow. So cleared up as much as possible. Home and found Dil much worse and with touch of bronchitis. Got tea then Bourne came up. Bed early.

> 31/7/45 Tuesday. Group Captain did not turn up. So I did not take over station Adjutant. Had fairly easy day and left at 4.00 p.m. to hurry home to meet 4.25 p.m. train with Nana and Ifor and on way got puncture. For all rush had to wait for train. Spent evening showing them round, yarning and repairing puncture.

> 1/8/45 Wednesday. Still not wanted at SHQ. Had slack morning till noon when it got very busy. Left 12.45 p.m. called home and then had late lunch. Nana had been busy in the morning finding her way about. Before I left I had cleared her room and the decorator spent all day there and I cleared mess in evening and put stuff back. Afternoon I went with radio to be repaired and did odd jobs and read. Then bed early.

> 2/8/45 Thursday. Fairly quiet morning till SHQ rang and I had to go and take over from station Adjutant. Getting gen in the morning and carried on into the afternoon. He has left me with half yearly reports, four courts martial, two reductions among other things. Hard at it till 5.30 p.m. He goes on leave tomorrow and comes back to take over as Senior Admin Officer. Evening very tired. Played shove halfpenny and read and bed early.

> 3/8/45 Friday. Officially took over station Adjutant and had hectic day with umpteen things including rushing

things for Group Captain who was going away at 3.00 p.m. till Wednesday. However, got over it and coped OK. Called at Chalet on way home and evening all three of us went to see Blyth Spirit at Rio and enjoyed it. Back late and bed late.

4/8/45 Saturday. Dil had a bad night so took a pill and was still asleep when I left. At office all camp had packed up by 11.00 a.m. for a long weekend but I stayed till 12.45 p.m. to try and get cleared. But no success! Afternoon was spent on shopping, some work at home and reading. Nana doing well. Evening, a swim and then spent quietly and bed late.

5/8/45 Sunday. Up late and had lazy day. In the morning I pottered about on odd jobs. Afternoon spent reading and sleeping. Evening thunder storm so went to bed early.

6/8/45 Monday. August bank holiday. Surprisingly few crowds here. Up late and chopped firewood and repaired stool and washed windows. Afternoon up to camp to clear arrears of work – notably send off two courts martial. Back late with flowers. While having dinner Joyce came but did not stay long. Good thing as Dil not at all well all day. Evening reading and bed early.

7/8/45 Tuesday. Arrived late and had terrific day. Only half hour for lunch and did not leave till 6.15 p.m. The Group Captain rang to say he would not be in. Called at Chalet on way home. Evening did nothing except go to bed early.

8/8/45 Wednesday. Boss not in all day again and I had another hectic day but coped. Dil not at all well in evening and we went to bed early. Doctor had been and said X-ray tomorrow. Baby may be large and advanced. She half expected it all night.

9/8/45 Thursday. Another terrific day, but worst seems over now Groupie is signing letters. Evening quiet and bed early. Dil X-rayed and seemed to think OK, but no definite results yet.

10/8/45 Friday. Terrific day with loads of work, courts martial, enquiries, summaries etc. Got home early though, via flowers and home and quiet evening and bed early.

11/8/45 Saturday. Worst morning so far and had to bring some work home late. Afternoon shopping with Nana, swim and bed late after work in the evening and listening to radio.

12/8/45 Sunday. Up early and had quiet day pottering about and quiet afternoon and evening. Dil still not too well. Lots and lots of anticipation about coming or alleged coming of answer to our ultimatum to Japan.

The ultimatum to Japan had followed devastating air raids across the whole country. The atomic bombs on Hiroshima and Nagasaki on 6 and 9 August were the most spectacular demonstration of the force ranged against the Japanese, but conventional bombers had flown almost freely over the country for months. On 13 and 14 August, for example, sixteen hundred USAF bombers attacked Tokyo. The end was inevitable.

13/8/45 Monday. Had very busy day again sorting ends of Bailey case and came home late somewhat weary and bed early. Dil a bit better.

14/8/45 Tuesday. Lots of hanging about for Bailey's trial, but not very busy all day which was a change. Dil felt better in evening so played cards with her etc. Still lots of rumours about victory, so sent out tannoy message with instructions if victory occurs.

15/8/45 Wednesday. Victory announced at midnight last

night. Dil told me in the morning that there were sirens, hooters, rockets, searchlights etc and fun and games on the sea wall but I slept through the lot. Went in in the morning to do what was necessary and essential, but only routine stuff. Announced rest of day as day of rest and working day tomorrow and came home via Chalet with fruit. Afternoon odd jobs and rest. Then the Doctor came and said Dil was OK but could go to hospital on Sunday. Evening reading in spite of noises, fireworks, music and shouting outside till late at night.

16/8/45 Thursday. VJ day. A slackness hung over the camp after a night of celebration and no one felt like work. The Group Captain rang but did not come in and camp packed up at noon. So there was not much work done. Had quiet afternoon home but got some odd jobs done. Doctor came and said Dil could go to hospital on Sunday.

So the World War ended, and the foundations of the Cold War were laid. Charles remained as Adjutant at Eastchurch for some time after the end of hostilities, and like all his contemporaries had to make decisions about his future employment. A son was born to Dilys and Charles a month after the end of the war, and they soon moved to a house in the countryside just a few miles from Eastchurch aerodrome. There they all settled into a post-war world. Charles continued to keep a daily diary, and all this and much more was faithfully recorded almost till the day he died.

Index

(Page numbers in italics refer to illustrations or maps).

1 METS 222, 223
1 Operational Training Unit (OTU)
    84, 85, 97
1 Personnel Holding Unit 430
2 Air Observers' School 55
2 Initial Training Wing 35
2nd Armoured Division 117
3 Personnel Holding Unit, Morecombe
    395
5th German Army 221
6th Australian Division 116
7th Armoured Division (Desert Rats)
    116
7th US Army 253, 264
8 Squadron RAF 195
8th Army 117, 160, 237, 253, 264,
    271, 274
9th Australian Division 117, 146
10 Casualty Clearing Station 214, 215,
    216
14th American Fighter Group 286
15 Group RAF 93
22 PTC 205
27th Bomber Group 286
31 Squadron RAF 356
33rd Fighter Group 286
54 Group RAF 431
62 Squadron RAF 325, 354, 356
75 Operational Training Unit (OTU)
    218, 222, 225, 231, 233, 291
79th Fighter Group 286
80 Squadron RAF 215
82nd American Fighter Group 286
83 Operational Training Unit (OTU)
    416
86th Dive Bomber Group 286
88 mm Anti-aircraft guns 117

105 Squadron RAF 286
117 Squadron RAF 230, 237, 238,
    274, 285, 288, 303, 305, 326, 351,
    354, *354*, 435
177 Wing RAF 355, 356
194 Squadron RAF 356
201 Group Headquqarters RAF 225
203 Squadron RAF 175, 176
216 Group RAF 230, 271, 287, 301
235 Wing 203
239 Wing 289
246 Squadron RAF 302
267 Squadron RAF 296, 299, 301, 306
279 Squadron RAF 98
284 Squadron RAF 286
296 Squadron RAF 263
324 Wing 286
417 Squadron RAF 286
454 Squadron RAAF 224
459 Squadron RAAF 85, 89, 90, 126,
    127, 145, 193, 196, 200, 201, 207,
    219, 223, 224, 233, 263, 296, 301;
    Formation Strike *147*, 147
500 Squadron RAF 90, 91
1444 Ferry Training Flight 104

Aboukir 229
Abraham's Dome, Jerusalem 167
Abu Hamed 198
Abu Suweir 127, *131*, 133, 157, 158,
    175, 179
Aden 176, 177, *179*, 182, 183, 186 –
    189, 194, 196, 201, 214, 373; Gulf
    of Aden 183; Little Aden 186
Afrika Corps 201
Air Landing School, India 314, 324
Air Raid 15, 29, 30, 46, 78, 150, 202,

216, 218, 376, 387, 390: at
  Gibraltar 114; at Malta 122
Aircraft Delivery Unit 227, 228
Aircrew Allocation Centre 408, 409
Alan Brooke, General 160
Albany, Uncle 390, 431
Alexander, General 160
Alexandria 143, 144, 151, 172, 203,
  214, 226, 227, 229, 231 – 232
Alfrey, Lieutenant General 221
Algeria 202, 221, 250, 254, 261
Algiers 246, 247, 250, 254, 270, 274,
  379
Ali 192, 193, 194
Almaza 205, 206
Almora 338, 344, 345
Altamura 295, 295 – 296
Amanyer 206
Amersham 394
Anson 58, 59, 62, 196, 197, 225, 229,
  234
Armament Practice Camp 433
Arnhem 408
Arnim, General 221
Asmara 196
ASV 88, 105, 125
Aswan 198
Atbara 197
Atomic Bomb 443
Auchinleck, General 117, 118, 119,
  146, 160
Australian Club, Jerusalem 164
Avro Anson See Anson
Axis 30, 116, 117, 146, 201, 202, 221,
  235, 249, 253, 262, 264, 266, 274,
  276
Aylesbury 393
Azzaz See Cape Azzaz

Backers Up Course 322
Badoglio, Marshal 262, 287

Bahrain 306, 307, 308, 309
Bailey, Bill 439, 440
Balloch 414
Baltimore 225, 228, 234
Barasoli 196
Bareilly 331, 332, 333
Barge See Boat, Plan to Buy
Bari 280, 288, 289, 290. 292, 296
Barrett, Lee See Lee Barratt
Barwick Falls 413
Basal 331
Basutos 172
Bathford 18
Bathurst (Gambia) 119
Batmen 187, 193, 305, 310, 314, 315,
  320, 323, 326
Battle of Britain 16, 30
Bay of Gabes 239
Bay of Sollum See Sollum
Bazaar, Cairo 156
Beagling 26
Bearers See Batmen
Beaton, Dave DFC 195
Beaufighter 147, 147, 228, 234
Beaufort 234
Bedouins 185
Bedwell, Eric 84, 90, 127, 229
Ben Gardane 253
Bengal 355
Benghazi 202
Benina 265, 267
Berbers 260
Bethlehem 166
Bhowali 350
Bianchi 268
Bircham Newton, RAF 94, 96, 97, 98,
  100
Bilbeis 238, 252
Bilbera 188
Biskara 254, 258, 266
Bisley 222, 225

Bizerta 274, 379

Blackpool 58, 59, 60, 70, 81, 82, 83, 84, 88

Blenheim 186, 223, 228, 234

Blida 274, 285

Blue Mosque, Cairo 152, 156

BOAC 302, 409, 410, 411

Boat, Plan to Buy 398, 399, 422, 423, 424, 426, 428

Bombay 365, 366, 367, 369

Borden Grammar School 99, 148, 150

Boticello 279

Bradbury, Tom 59, 65, 66, 70

Brakla, RAF 408, 409

Bravry 350

Brindisi 280, 286, 290

Bristol Bombay 237

British V Corps 221

British XV Corps 303

Brize Norton, RAF 434, 435

Broadway 357, 358

Bryan Rostron 85, 102, 104, 107, 121, 136, 143, 147, 150, 162, 170, 174, 177, 183, 186, 189, 190, 203, 209, 210, 216, 217, 220, 221, 222, 230, 301

Burma 303, 304, 355, 357, 370, 397

Buruzzo 295

Cabaret Birat, Cairo 152

Cadiz 108

Cairo 115, 119, 126, 136 – 140, 149, 152, 153, 156, 160, 174, 200, 203, 204, 206, 220, 224, 230, 238, 243, 252, 255, 260, 262, 264, 265, 267, 291, 296, 299, 306, 307, 353

Calcutta 324, 351, 352, 353, 359, 360, 365, 366

Cambridge 33, 35, 46, 50, 53

Camels 153 – 154, 316

Canals (Egypt) 137, 138

Cap Bon 247, 250, 379

Capaccio 278

Cape Azzaz 147, 157, 216

Cape Colonne 277

Cape Spartivento 277

Cape St Vincent 108

Cardiff 400, 401, 402, 429, 430

Carter, Flying Officer H M See Maggie Carter

Casablanca 228, 256, 258

Cassibile 264, 265, 270, 271, 275, 276, 280, 286

Caste System 310, 315

Castel Benito 240, 241, 242, 244, 247, 252, 254, 261, 265, 267, 274, 285

Castellano, General Guiseppe 274

Catania 262, 264, 271, 272, 274, 275, 275, 276, 278, 280, 281, 285, 285, 286, 288, 290, 291, 292, 293, 296, 297

Catazaro 279

Cecil Bar, Alexandria 227

Central Medical Board 385, 386, 421

Chabattia 339, 345

Chaklala 305, 313, 314, 322, 323, 324

Chandapur 353

Chiang Kai-shek 303

Chin Hills, Burma 355

Chindits 304, 355

Chindwin River 355

Chowringhee 357, 358, 360

Church of All Nations 166, 167

Church of the Holy Sepulchre, Jerusalem 165

Church of the Nativity, Bethlehem 166

Churchill 30, 117, 160, 304, 437

Citadel, Cairo 204

Coastal Command, RAF 59, 88, 90, 433

Coles, Wing Commander W 435

Combined Aircrew Reselection Centre

433

Comilla 354, 355, 360

Commissioning 70, 75, 77, 78

Coniston 61, 62, 65

Conscription 12

Constantine 246

Craig, Jimmy   *See Jimmy Craig*

Crater 187, 188, 193

Cremyll 428

Crete 125

Crieff 411, 413

Cross, Squadron Leader 103, 391, 392, 399

Crotone 279, 280, 292, 286

Cunningham, General 117, 118

Cyrenaica 143

D-Day 387

Dad 29, 45, 51, 66, 78, 98, 231, 386, 395, 396, 398, 402, 404, 407, 414, 416, *418*, 422, 425

Dakota 237, 251, 262, 265, 271, 285, 290, *293*, 326, 332, 356

Dalton Computer 102

DC 2 237

DC 3 *See Dakota*

Dead Man's Straights 373

Dead Sea 166, 168, 308

Delhi 126, 301, 307, 311, 323, 332

Delta (Nile) 125, 144, 228, 238, 248

Derna 117, 143

Derry 413

Desert Rats 116

DH 8 237

Dhow 137

Dilys (Dil) Jones / Collins 13, 45, 51, 65, 66, 78, 98, 99, 100, 103, 107, 202, 386, 387, 390, 394 – 444 passim; Sisters and Aunt 401; Cousins Gwyneth and Mona 401

Dinjan 361

Djebel Bou-Aoukaz 235

Djem   *see El Djem*

Docking, RAF 96, 97, 100, 101

Douglas, Air Chief Marshal Sir Sholto 302

Driffield, RAF 102

Drummond Castle 414

Duce, *see Mussolini*

Dum Dum Airfield 360, 361, 365, 366

Dunkirk Evacuation 12

Eastchurch, RAF 429, 430, 433, 437, 438, 444

Edfu Temple *199*

Edku 147, 172, 225

Egypt 19, 30, 125, 188, 201, 237

Eisenhower, General 201

El Adem 207, 262, 291, 292

El Agheila 117, 118

El Alamein 119, 143, 144, 146, 161

El Djem 239, 240, *241*, 247

Enfidaville 249

ENSA 228, 411

Etna, Mount 253, 261, 272, 275, 283

Euphrates River 308

Excelsior Hotel, Alexandria 226

Eye injury and treatment 37 – 39, 41 – 44, 49, 51 – 53, 70, 103, 217 – 218, 243, 306, 330, 335 – 344, 360, 372, 385, 392 – 394, 400, 409, 421

F540   *See Operations Record Book*

Fairy, Nurse Vera 25, 202, 340, 388

Falconara 279

Farnham 21, 81, 87, 96, 385, 390, 397

Fez 253, 254, 255, *256, 259,* 259, 260, 264, 266

FFI (Free From Infection) 14, 33, 35, 43, 54, 57

Fighter Command 433

Florrie Wilburn/Collins 10, 24, 396,

398, 403, 405, 406, 407, *418*, 422, 436

Foggia 294, 298

Fort Stikine Ammunition Ship 367 – 369

Fredenhall, Major General Lloyd 221

French Club, Ismalia 142, 152, 159

Gagas Valley 343, 349

Galilee 308

Galite Island 379

Gambut 200, 201, 202; Gambut Cup 218, *219*

Garden of Gethsemane 166 – 167

Gazala 118

Gee, Captain 339, 341 – 344

Gerbini 278

Ghandi 304

Gianacles *141, 142*, 142, 150, 156, 157, 158, 160, 200, 220, 224, 231, 235

Gibraltar 109, 110 – 114, 120, 124, 182, 380

Gilmerton 413

Giovinazzo 295, 298

Givia 286

Gladiator 122

Glen, Squadron Leader G 262, 270, 288

Gloucester, RAF 430

Gold Mohur Bathing Beach 197

Good Samaritan 168

Gott, Lieutenant General 160

Gozo 247, 250, 251

Grand Hotel, Cairo 152, 174

Graziani, General 116

Gremlins 172

Great Bitter Lake 125

Grombalia 286

Grottaglie 278, 286, 287

Gulf, "The" *See Persian Gulf*

Gulf of Gabes 250

Gunga Doeli 338, 347, *348*

Gunram Pance 350

Gwalior 354, 358

Habanniya 307, 308

Haifa 169

Haka 376

Halton, RAF Hospital 51, 103, 391, 399

Healy, Major (Surgeon) 337, 339 – 344

Heavy Glider Conversion Unit 419

Heliopolis 160, 174, 175, 200, 203, 205, 252, 265, 291, 306

Hennock, Wing Commander 126

Hepworth, Jack 12, 43, 101, 103, 387

Hereford, RAF 426, 428, 429

Hill of Blood, Palestine 168

Himalayas 315, 333, *345*

Hitler 117, 235, 384

Holby, Squadron Leader George 127, 135, 158, 175 – 176, *176*, 200, 202, 229

Homalin 358

Home Guard 30

Homs 244

Horsham St Faith, RAF 98, 101, 126

Hotel de la Poste, Port Said 158

House Hotel, Heliopolis 306

Howson, Wing Commander 175, *219*

HQ Middle East 126

Huddersfield 10, 13, 17, 24, 31, 39, 50, 63, 65, 67, 72, 73, 81, 83, 90, 91, 100, 388, 389, 403, 404

Hudson 59, 85, 88, 90, *105*, 114, 115, 195, 223, 225, 234, 237, 251, 262, 265, 266, 271, 274, 285

Hullavington, RAF 18, 21

Hurricane, Hawker 215

Identity Card 129, *130*
India 126, 127, 296, 301, 303, 304,
    305, 312, 313, 314, 355
Indo-China 303
Indus 302
Invasion (of Europe) 267, 396
Iran 307, 310
Irrawaddy River 356
Isle of Sheppey 10, 24, 81, 91, 98
Ismalia 136, 142, 148, 152, 158 -- 159,
    177, 238, 276, 302
Isola 286

Jaundice 161, 190, 192
Java 188
Jedarbia 239
Jericho 166, 168
Jerusalem 163, *165*, 166, 167, 168,
    192, 195, 255
Jimmy Craig 85, 86, 107, 162, 163,
    170, 183, 184, 186, 220, *221*, 230,
    296, 299, 301, 306
Joan Acton 16, 20, 24, 25, 26, 28, 29,
    31, 32, 39, 40, 41, 47, 50, 52, 68,
    71, 72, 81, 83, 85, 87
Jones, Ifor (Dilys's Brother) 399, 406
Jordan 168, 302, 308
Joyce Collins 33, 50, 58, 59, 60, 82,
    83, 95, 390, 417, *418*, 423, 424
Junior Officers' Club, Cairo 203, 204,
    230, 291

Karachi 302
Kasfareet 125, 131, 200
Kassala 197
Kasserine Pass 221, 222
Karachi 306, 307, 310, 311, 367
Kathgodam 333, 334, 346, 350, 351
Kesselring, Field Marshall 253
Khartoum 237
Khormakser 190, 194, 195, 197

King George VI 33, 244, 245
King, Marian 66, 388
King, Nurse 17, 45
King Peter of Yugoslavia 306
King, Squadron Leader 197
King Victor Emmanuel III of Italy 262
Knock 413
Koeltz, General Louis-Marie 221
Korba 247

La Sila 279
Lahore 307
Lakej 182
Lalkua 334
Lalmai 355, 358
Landing Ground 15 (LG 15) 115
Landing Ground 204 (LG204) 200
Landing Ground 224 (LG224) 265,
    306
Landing Ground 226 (LG226) 144,
    145
Landing Ground Z (LG Z) 126
Le Kef 246
Lee Barrett 85, 107, 162, 170,183,
    186, *221*, 230
Lend Lease 30, 46, 367
Lentin 286
Libya 30, 201, 237, 254
Licota 253
Linosa 120
Lion, General *See King George VI*
Littlehampton 425
Liverpool 382
Loch Earn 413
Lockheed Hudson *See Hudson*
Lodestar, Lockheed 237
London Gazette 208
Lucknow 351
Luqa 121 – 124, 241, 247, 292
Lusted, Warrant Officer A J 271, 361
Luxor 199, 200, 203

Lydda 302, 306, 307
Lyle, Wing Commander 291, 306
Lyneham (RAF) 104, 126

Madsen, Freddie 97, 127, *219*
Maggie Carter 245, 251, 263, 265,
  274, 276, 277, 279, 290, *293,* 295,
  298, 301, 314, 318, 326
Maintenance Unit 174
Maison Blanche 253, 274
Malta 119 – 125, 241, 246, 247, 251,
  263, 264, 271, 278, 285, 286, 291,
  296, 378; George Cross 123
Manama 307, 308, 309
Marble Arch 239, *239*
Mareth 210, 222, 235
Margaret (Charles's Sister) 11, 17, 19,
  29, 45, 51, 52, 65, 78, 87, 95, 99,
  100, 202, 252, 265, 326, 385
Margaret Birnie 86, 88
Marie (Aunt) 21, 22, 81, 95, 96, 101,
  202, 385
Marriot 220
Martin, Tony 210, *219*
Maryut 145
Master (Hospital) 12, 25, 31, 32, 39,
  40, 68
Mauripur 302, 307
McHale, Jimmy 176
Mecca 205
Mersa Matruh 115, 143, 146, 158, 263
Messina 262, 264, 266; Straits of
  Messina 274, 288
Metro Cafe, Cairo 152, 252, 291
Metropolitan Club, Rawalpindi 313
Millom, RAF 54, 55, 57 – 72, 77
Minster 29, 45, 51
Misterbianco 279
Molfetta 295, 298
Monastir 248
Monkeys 334, 338, *346,* 346

Monte Corveno 280, 286, 289, 294,
  295
Montgomery, General 160, 201, 210,
  235, 253, 262, 264, 266, 274
Monzie Castle 413
Morocco 202, 254, 261
Mosquitoes 134, 135, 157, 181
Mount Carmel 169
Mount of Olives 166
Moustache 191, *191,* 266
Muala 188
Mull of Kintyre 381
Murree 320, 321, 322, 333
Mussolini 116, 214, 235, 239, *244,*
  262, 268, 288
Muthill 414

Naini Tal 345
Nairn 410, 411
Nana (Dilys's Sister) 401, 404, 441,
  443
Nanda Devi 335, *345,* 346, 347
Nanda Khot 346
Napier Street, Karachi 310
Naples 276, 277, 278, 288, 294
National Hotel, Cairo 203
Nellie (Aunt) 29, 45, 51, 65, 66, 100,
  386, 398, 406, 434, 439, 440
New Delhi 307, 311
New Zealand Club, Cairo 140, 152
Nile 197, 198
Noah's Ark 198
North Africa 19, 46, 79, 115, *116,*
  117, 117, *118,* 118, 215, 220, 235,
  237, 244, 285

O'Connor, General 116, 117
Officers' Club, Cairo 152
Officers' Club, Heliopolis 265
Olive 61, 64, 65, 71, 72, 73, 74, 75,
  76, 77, 78, 83, 84, 85, 91, 92, 202

Operation Husky 253, 261
Operation Lightfoot 201
Operation Market Garden 408
Operation Supercharge 201
Operation Thursday 355
Operation Torch 201
Operation Vulcan 235
Operational Training Unit (OTU) 129
Operations Record Book (F540) 135,
  183, 210, 222, 223, 224, 228, 229,
  233 – 234, 237, 248, 261, 262, 264,
  270, 285, 288, 303, 313, 314, 318,
  328, 354, 355, 363
Oran 379
Oscar 66, 67, 70, 74, 77, 280
Oxen 316

Pachter, Nursing Sister 39, 40, 389
Padgate, RAF 13, 14
Paestum 277, 284
Palermo 262, 275, 281, 286; Palermo
  Catacombs 276, 281 – 283, 283
Palestine 161, 161, 188, 193, 203
Pantelleria 120, 379
Panther's Pool 344, 344, 349
Panzers 235, 253
Patton, General 235, 253, 262, 264,
  266
Peplow, RAF 415, 416, 417, 419
Perim 182, 196, 373
Persian Gulf 308, 310
Peter Collins 10, 12, 22, 33, 50, 51,
  53, 65, 66, 78, 86, 87, 89, 242, 246,
  270, 274, 385, 386, 387, 388, 390,
  391, 395, 400, 403, 404, 406, 412,
  416, 417, 418, 422, 424
Piaggio 108 115
Poona 333, 337
Port Said 144, 145, 158, 159, 376
Port Sudan 189, 182
Port Tewfik 374, 375

Portreath, RAF 104, 105, 107
Potter, Norman 194
Prince's Dock, Bombay 369
Pyramids 152, 153, 153 – 156, 230

Quasim 303
Queen of Sheba 187

RAF Regiment 245, 286
Ramadi 302
Ranchi 355
Ras El Mar 253, 258, 259, 264, 285
Rathlin Island 381
Rawalpindi 303, 305, 307, 310, 311,
  312, 315, 329; Rawalpindi Club
  312
Red Sea 179, 180, 183
Reggia Aeronautica 288
Reggio di Calabria 274
Reina de Pacifico 376, 383
Rhanikhet 333, 338, 345, 346, 347,
  348, 350
Richardson, Flying Officer RAAF 305
Richie, General 118, 160
Ridley, Squadron Leader 375, 376, 382
Riffs 257
Robinson, Squadron Leader 228
Rommell, General Irwin 117, 118,
  119, 126, 135, 146, 160, 161, 201,
  202, 210, 221, 222, 235
Rostron, Bryan See Bryan Rostron
Rovers 9, 11, 12, 13, 19, 24, 25, 31,
  40, 107, 389, 405

Sabratha 268, 270
Sador 338
Sahara 258
Salerno 275, 276, 284, 285, 286, 302
San Antonio 278, 286
San Francisco 265, 270, 286
San Marino Cabaret, Tel Aviv 170

San Pancrazio 294, 296
Sand Fly 190, 192
Savoia Marchetti 79s 237
Scanzano 279, 286, 288
School of Administration 426
School of General Reconnaissance 77, 81, 88
Seighford, RAF 418, 419, 422, 423
Setif 246, 248 – 249
Sfax 239, 246, 249, 250
Shaiba 302, 308
Sharjah 302, 306, 309
Sheerness 28, 51, 65, 99, 397, 402, 414, 426, 430, 433, 436
Sheikh Othman; Airport 182, 186; Artesian Wells 187
Sicily 121, 251, 253, 261, 262, 263, 264, 266, 267, 270, 271, 274, 280, 285, 286, 287, 303, 378
Sidi Barrani 116, 157
Sidi Bou Zid 221
Sikhs 316
Silecroft 57
Silloth, RAF 84, 97
Sirocco 252
Sittingbourne 99, 386
Skinburness 84, 88
Sliema 279
Slim, General William 303
Socotra 183, 184, *184*, 194
Solomon's Caves, Jerusalem 166
Solomon's Temple, Jerusalem 164
Solum 151, 201, 209
Sousse 246, 248
South Point, Bombay 367
Special Licence 404
Spendules 172
Sphinx *154*, 154 – 155
Spilsby 204
Spitfire 286, 358; Collision 246
Sporting Club, Alexandria 226, 227

Squires Gate, RAF 77, 81, 83
St Anne's 82, 83
St Fillans 413
St Jeans 193
St Luke's Hospital Huddersfield 10, 13, 25, 28, 31, 39, 40, 41, 50, 81, 389, 404
St Marie Du Zit 286
Stanwell, John 247, 263
Steamer Point 186, 187, 188
Stillwell, General "Vinegar Joe" 303
Stornoway, RAF 90, 91, 93, 94
Stratford 20, 22, 27, 33
Stromboli 277
Strowan 413
Sudan Railway 197
Suez 179, 374, 375, 377; Suez Road 200
Suez Canal 116, 144, 145, 159, 160, 183
Sunningdale, RAF 431
Surman 266
Sweetwater Canal 126
Sylhet 354, *354*, 358, 361, *362*
Synthetic Trainer 88

Tactical Floor 83
Taifa Rocks 157
Taj Mahal 307, 311
Talikandi 356
Taranto 30, 277, 278, 284, 286, 289
Tebessa 221
Technical Training Command, RAF 433
Tel Aviv 161, 169, 170
Telergma 274
Termini 277
Thebes 199
Tobruk 116, 117, 119, 135, 143, 146, 201, 202, 207, 210, 211, *212, 213*, 239, 243

Toc H 47, 216, 218
Topa Rest Camp 318, *319*, *321*, 322
Training Command, RAF 417
Trans-Jordan 168
Tripoli 210, 239, 243, 246, 259, 261, 266, 286
Tulthal 355, 357, 358
Tunis 235, 237, 246, 247, 249, 254, 260, 264, 270, 271, 274
Tunisia 202, 210, 221, 240, 275, 286
Turner, Arthur 12, 31, 246, 247, 270
Turret Falls 413

Udjah 254
United Services Club, Ismalia 142, 148, 158 – 159, 177
United States of America 29, 30, 46, 79
Unites States V Corps 221

V1 384, 387, 388, 407
V2 384, 408
Valetta 120, 279
Variation 102, 144
VE Day 438, 439
Vesuvius 280
Vichy French 202
Victoria Dock, Bombay 369
Victory Avenue, New Delhi 311
Vindictive, HMS 274
VJ Day 444

Wadi Akarit 235
Wadi Haifa 198
Wailing Wall, Jerusalem 164
Waganella, HMAHS 371, *371*
Wavell, General 117
Wellington *141*; Crash at Gibraltar 113, 114
Wellington Barracks, V1 bomb 388
Wendover 392

West Ghats Mountains 367
West Kirby, RAF 14
Wilkie, Nursing Sister 67, 389, 405
Willingdon Club, Bombay 370
Wingate, General Orde 304, 355
Worsdale, Jack 20, 21, 22, 23, 25, 26, 27, 32, 33, 41, 42, 43

Yemen 186

Zentini West 286